NOW

The six essays comprising this volume explore the nature and purpose of human life—and how it can be lived creatively, joyfully, and wisely. They were originally published as separate pamphlets during 1976 and distributed as part of an ongoing subscription series. Since then, they have been collected and issued as a single book. This is the first paperback edition.

The significance of these essays is best attested to by those who have already read them:

"When people ask me to recommend books on the higher self to them, *The Art of Living* is first on my list!"

—Dr. Steven Patascher, Arizona

"*The Art of Living* has done more to change my attitudes and outlook on life than any of the religious institutions I was educated in. Already you have opened six doors to a new way of thinking, and I hope you can help me open many more in the essays to come."

—Michael P. Wilson, New Zealand

"Your teachings present and convey the ancient wisdom in techniques and methods that are practical and most effective. This work reflects tremendous effort and great dedication."

—Johanna Manning, Maryland

"*The Art of Living* is an excellent source of inspiration, very useful both personally and professionally. It's the best guidepost that I'm aware of for cultivating the good qualities of life."

—Dr. James L. Kwako, Wisconsin

Other essays written by Dr. Robert R. Leichtman and Carl Japikse in The Art of Living *series:*

Living Responsibly
The Nature and Purpose of the Emotions
Cultivating Tolerance and Forgiveness
Seeking Intelligent Guidance
The Bridge of Faith
Discerning Reality
Cooperating With Life
The Mind and Its Uses: Part I
The Mind and Its Uses: Part II
Coping With Stress
Enlightened Self-Discipline
Inspired Humility
The Act of Human Creation: Part I
The Act of Human Creation: Part II
The Work of Patience
The Pursuit of Integrity
The Way To Health: Part I
The Way To Health: Part II
The Process of Self-Renewal
Filling Life With Beauty
Becoming Graceful

Each of these essays is available in individual pamphlet form for $1.95 apiece. A subscription to the twenty-one essays listed above plus the remaining three yet to be published in the series costs $28. If ordering the whole series, please specify that the order does not include this book (Volume I). Subscriptions and individual essays can be ordered by writing the publisher: Ariel Press, 2557 Wickliffe Road, Columbus, Ohio 43221. For foreign delivery, please add $5 for a full subscription. In Ohio, please add 4% sales tax.

The Art of Living

VOLUME ONE

A COLLECTION OF ESSAYS
BY ROBERT R. LEICHTMAN, M.D.
& CARL JAPIKSE

with a foreword
by C. Norman Shealy, M.D.

ARIEL PRESS
The Publishing House of Light
An Ohio Corporation Not For Profit

No royalties are paid on this book.

Copyright © Ariel Press
1975, 1976, 1977, 1979
All Rights Reserved

11-85

ISBN 0-89804-032-9

Second Printing

ARIEL PRESS
2557 Wickliffe Road, Columbus, Ohio 43221

TABLE OF CONTENTS

Foreword by C. Norman Shealy, M.D. vii

ENRICHING THE PERSONALITY 1
   Transcending Limits 3
   Paying Attention 10
   Refining the Raw Materials 21
   Ensuring Permanence 26
   A Masterpiece of Humanity 31
   Becoming Universal 36

THE PRACTICE OF DETACHMENT 39
   Who We Are 41
   Quiet Confidence 48
   The Discipline of Detachment 53
   Loosening Attachments 59
   Expressing Poise 68
   The Universe Responds 75

FINDING MEANING IN LIFE 79
   A Hidden Message 81
   Duty and Discipline 88
   The Roots of Destiny 94
   The Fate Within 101
   Sowing Goodwill 115

BUILDING RIGHT HUMAN RELATIONSHIPS.. 125
- A Living Art 127
- Crucibles of Growth 132
- The Inner Reality 138
- Stumbling Blocks 140
- The Seed of Beauty 152
- The Door of Brotherhood 162

THE SPIRIT OF GENEROSITY 167
- Giving a Hand 169
- An Investment in Life 172
- The Value of the Investment 174
- Activating the Universe 192
- Being Generous 197
- Sharing in the One Life 201

JOY 205
- Something Extra 207
- Delightenment 217
- The Ways Joy Works 223
- Becoming Joyful 232
- Worthy of Immortality 238

FOREWORD

by C. Norman Shealy, M.D.

During the last three years I have had the continuing pleasure of reading *The Art of Living* essays as they have arrived. These essays are erudite, intelligent, and common sense guidelines for a healthy and sane approach to life. The thinking individual will find them provocative and, above all, useful. Even good artists need sustenance, and the intellectual food presented in *The Art of Living* series will provide a boost to personal growth for anyone willing to read with an open and questioning mind.

Dr. Robert Leichtman is the best clairvoyant I have personally investigated. His forte is reading the personality of individuals he has never seen; knowing only their names and addresses, he delivers more incisive and accurate information than that usually obtained with extensive personal testing. I have found him to be ninety-six percent accurate in the work he has done for me. Mr. Japikse is also an excellent clairvoyant who works closely with Dr. Leichtman and teaches the same principles. The ability of these two gentlemen to intuitively perceive the psychological natures of people makes their insights into the art of living even more worthy of careful study.

The messages in these essays are clearly outlined

and discussed. The basic theme set forth in the following pages is that human life is an art form and that we, as individual human beings, should strive to become inspired and accomplished artists of living. A premise adopted right from the start is that human life is rich in creative potential, a potential that can be tapped by any man or woman. Then, from the raw materials of our lives—the daily events, our interpersonal relationships, and our emotions, thoughts, acts, and attitudes—we can create works of meaning, beauty, and purpose.

To some, it may seem that human life is far from artistic. But just as a rough block of granite does not appear to be very artistic until an accomplished sculptor has taken it and transformed it into something quite different, so also our lives will not seem very artistic until we deliberately and with dedication impose order where there has been chaos, meaning where there has been nihilism, control where there has been immaturity, talent where there has been mediocrity, poise where there has been doubt and worry, goodwill where there has been animosity, and purpose where there has been confusion.

This book sets forth the basic principles of becoming an artist of life—and in addition gives a number of simple and easily understood methods of working more creatively and effectively with the energies of our livingness. It is not a book that can be skimmed through lightly; it requires careful reading, thoughtful reflection, and then application. But if it is used in this way, it will open up a new world of inner richness and achievement. Thus, the reader is invited to unlock his or her mind so that it may be challenged by provocative new ideas.

If the great leaders of the world will read and take advantage of the expert philosophy provided by Dr. Leichtman and Mr. Japikse, our world will indeed be revitalized. The golden age of humanity is yet before us. Material in *The Art of Living* series is as appropriate to us as great writings of the past were in their respective time periods. Anyone interested in creating a more harmonious, successful, and rewarding life will benefit from reading and using the material in this guide to successful living.

C. Norman Shealy, M.D., Ph.D., is president of the American Holistic Medical Association, founder of The Pain and Health Rehabilitation Center in LaCrosse, Wisconsin, and author of The Pain Game, Occult Medicine Can Save Your Life, *and* 90 Days to Self-Health.

ABOUT THE AUTHORS

In the late 1960's, Dr. Robert R. Leichtman's interest in intuition and spiritual growth caused him to close his medical practice and devote his energies to personal psychic work, lecturing, teaching, and writing. His pioneer work as a psychic consultant to psychiatrists, psychologists, and medical doctors has helped him become recognized as one of the best psychics in America today. Dr. Leichtman is also the developer of "Active Meditation," a comprehensive course in personal growth and meditative techniques. This teaching is aimed at helping people better understand their lives and develop intuitive skills. He is the author of the paperback series, *From Heaven to Earth,* also published by Ariel Press. Dr. Leichtman currently resides in Baltimore, where part of his time is spent working with Olga Worrall and the New Life Clinic.

Carl Japikse grew up in Ohio, where he still resides. A graduate of Dartmouth College, he began his work career as a newspaper reporter and freelance writer. He has worked for several newspapers, including *The Wall Street Journal.* In the early 1970's, he left the field of journalism and began pursuing his current interests: teaching personal and creative growth, lecturing, and consulting psychically with businesses and individuals. Mr. Japikse is the developer of "The Enlightened Management Seminar," an educational program for executives and managers, and various courses in spiritual growth.

DEDICATED
TO OUR INVISIBLE FRIENDS
WHO HAVE INSPIRED MANY
OF THE IDEAS IN THESE ESSAYS

The Art of Living

ENRICHING
THE PERSONALITY

TRANSCENDING LIMITS

In the world of art, the highest praise is won by the artist who infuses his creations with universal and timeless perspectives. A provincial artist may work with a great degree of technical proficiency, yet his success will be limited, for he does not have the universal breadth to appeal to a large sampling of people. He may build up a devoted clique of admirers, to be sure, but he does not tap into the real essence of human experience; he does not capture the vital flame. Just so, the artist who is a "man of his times" may enjoy great popularity during his lifetime, but if he does not transcend his age and epoch and draw his inspiration from the timeless streams of human experience, his work will not endure. It is not the provincial and the timebound that we admire in art or any form of creative expression; it is the universal and timeless. And so, the artist who seeks to be a master of his craft must expand the scope of his perception from that of his immediate circle to include the vast panorama of all human endeavor, all possible experience, all conceivable worlds. In short, he must try to encompass the universe.

If we wish to enrich the personality and our life, we must do likewise. We do not enrich the personality merely by growing older—or by reaching a higher level of status, by following passing fads, or by accumulating a larger store of wealth. Rather, we add richness to our life by seeking to *universalize* our perspectives, our attitudes, our moods, our habits, our principles, our skills, our traits, and our convictions—by passing beyond the tiny sphere of our limited interests and our self centeredness and finding that which is universal and timeless. And we achieve this universalization in much the same way that the artist becomes a master of his art, by approaching all of life as an art form that can be understood, improved, and enriched in scope and vision.

Throughout human history, people have recognized the need for this universalization of the personality. But, as in any area of human endeavor, some of the attempts to achieve the recognized goal have been misdirected and have not produced fruit. In most cases, the problem has lain in misunderstanding what universalization really is. Many people think it can be gained by traveling extensively throughout the world. Others try to achieve it through the study of astronomy. Some seek it by risking their lives to climb the lofty Himalayas in Tibet in search of gurus who would teach them what they choose not to learn by themselves. And there are always those who try to achieve it by creating a Hollywoodish utopia of love and passion. There are undoubtedly virtues in all of these enterprises, but none of them is likely to produce the true universalization of the personality.

Instead, what we must understand is that we dwell in a multi-dimensional universe and live in a multi-dimensional personality. The universe consists of more than physical substance alone. It is also composed of psychic substance, mental substance, and many levels of spiritual energy. Similarly, each human being is more than a physical body alone. We also have emotions, a mind, and a vast spiritual existence. As long as we live in just the one dimension of the physical, our life is flat, mechanical, and uninspired. It lacks *perspective,* in the artistic sense of the word. It lacks the breadth and timelessness of true art. But as we expand our perception of the many dimensions of the universe, we become truly universal.

An analogy from physical life may be helpful in understanding this concept. Here on earth, we are bathed in a universal atmosphere of oxygen, nitrogen, carbon dioxide, and other gases. It surrounds us, and we breathe it in to sustain our physical life. In much the same way, we are also bathed in a universal atmosphere of thought and feeling. This atmosphere of collective consciousness is not wholly accepted by science, but a growing number of intelligent people are aware of it and are working with it. It is an environment of moods, emotions, thoughtforms, ideas, desires, and attitudes that surrounds us at all times. Some of the currents in this atmosphere are clean, others are polluted. But wherever we might be, we are constantly "inhaling" this atmosphere into our heart and our mind. Just as breathing oxygen is indispensable to physical life, so also the inbreathing of this collective consciousness is necessary for the life of our emotions and thoughts—the life of the personality.

In addition to this collective consciousness, however, there are even more refined and subtle realms of formless life essence in which we constantly live.

Unknown to most people, these regions contain intangible qualities that also bathe and support our life expression in the same way that oxygen bathes the body and collective consciousness bathes our emotions and mind. These qualities form a universal pool of living electricity and vitality that inspires, vivifies, and directs all thought, feeling, and activity.

The person who seeks to enrich his life on just the physical level is the most provincial of all artists. Those who seek enrichment also in the collective consciousness of thought and feeling have added a second dimension and at least have an inkling of what a universal perspective can be. But only those hardy individuals who have opened themselves to the universe of subtle and refined qualities—the universe of joy and nobility, of courage and grace, of wisdom and maturity—can be truly considered masters in the art of living. Thus, the process of becoming aware of these greater realms and searching in them for the qualities that can indeed enrich the personality is the real key that unlocks the door of the universe to humanity. It is a process that can aptly be called the *universalization of the personality*.

In this innermost atmosphere can be found such riches as love, beauty, dignity, harmony, reverence, and wisdom. While many people consider such qualities as mere psychological abstractions, nonetheless they are quite real. And we depend upon them greatly, for they are the "art supplies" that we must use in enriching our life. Just as the artist needs his paints and brushes and thinners to create his art, so too do we need the analogous materials of these most subtle realms of the universe to create our art form—our livingness.

It would be a mistake, however, to think that we can obtain these particular art supplies as simply as today's amateur artist can obtain his—by walking into an art supply store and selecting from the shelf the paints, brushes, canvases, thinners, and pigments he needs. For the right price, excellent materials are readily available to today's artist. But alas! we human beings cannot walk into a "psychological supermarket" and buy ready-made goodwill, polite habits, wisdom, generosity, compassion, affection, and joy. These qualities of life do not come packaged in pint cans, neatly labeled and listing ingredients. Nor do dedication, perseverance, and idealism come in shiny plastic tubes with varying shades to choose among, ready for instant squeezing into the circumstances of our life. We cannot even buy a bottle of forgiveness or tolerance to thin and temper our attitudes with patience and understanding; we cannot beg, borrow, steal, or purchase the brushes of courage, vision, and commitment that must be used in applying our pigments to the canvas that is our life.

Enriching the personality is not that easy. We have to search for and manufacture our art supplies, just as the great masters of the Renaissance had to search for and manufacture theirs. These great artists spent an extraordinary amount of their time not behind the canvas, creating, but out in the world, searching for the right pigments with which to mix their oils. And they had to use their imagination to help them in this quest. There were no bushes or shrubs with signs nailed to them identifying them as "red pigment bushes." They had to have the scope of vision to realize that the ideal shade of red they were seeking lay hid within this berry or that rock.

Indeed, it has been recorded that at times precious jewels were ground up into fine dust to provide some of the pigment for the paints. These pigments, from whatever source, were then blended with very carefully refined oils and emulsifiers. Thus, the truly great masters always sought out the very best of materials and expended enormous effort in preparing and blending them.

If we are ever going to "paint" upon the canvas of our life with the qualities of love and joy, dedication and courage, and serenity and affection, we will have to become a Renaissance master ourself. We must learn to seek for the raw materials of universality in the midst of nature and our environment, and likewise learn to extract the essence that will help us, blend it into our own being, and apply the result actively in our life. We will need a discerning eye to search out the finest and most precious resources, and wisdom and skill to ensure their careful refining and blending.

This responsibility of creating our own "art supplies" in the art of living is one that each of us must assume for ourself, if we are going to create anything worthwhile or meaningful—anything *universal*—in life. True, it would be nice to have a psychological supermarket with rows and rows of bottled and tubed humanistic virtues, skills, and strengths, all on sale at discount prices. But such a store will never be established.

This revelation may come as a disappointment to the dilettante artist in human psychology, the seeker of pseudo-enlightenment who struggles in angry frustration (because he believes that is the proper style for the aspiring artist) to create sloppy forms of the living art. He may be disheartened that he cannot buy the materials with which to work for a single payment of $250. Yet if he continues to believe that he can, he will end up working toward his noble goal with materials that are wholly inadequate for the task.

The dilettante makes the error—and this *is* the major error—of "provincialism." He may see the need for acquiring an abundance of love, wisdom, goodwill, and humanistic skill, but he does not understand that he must *look for these qualities in the universe*. This mistake greatly limits his creative efforts. He remains cramped within the confining boxes of his physical body, emotions, and thoughts. He gains a certain limited degree of proficiency in working with these materials, but the artistic effort is roughly on a par with the "art" of stringing popcorn. No matter how skillful he may become, he is grossly restricted by a very narrow medium.

Therefore, it should be obvious that the mature artist does not limit himself in this fashion, but like the ancient masters who left home to search in nature for plants and minerals with which to work, he journeys forth into the finer realms of life to find those raw materials that will do justice to his creative efforts. He seeks these in the great abundance of life all around him. He is helped, moreover, by understanding that he does not need to search only in the abstract and intangible realms of consciousness, where the pure qualities exist. He can seek his raw materials also in the more familiar physical and emotional levels of life, for these are but manifestations of the invisible, finer realms. But he must never forget what he is really searching for—the qualities that will help him enrich his personality and his daily life.

PAYING ATTENTION

The failure to appreciate that the world is teeming with the raw materials that we need to live a rich life is an all too common mistake. Unfortunately, it inevitably impoverishes our existence. And the poignancy of the tragedy is magnified by the fact that we are choosing poverty while literally existing within the midst of great psychological riches! We do not have to travel to some fabled Eldorado to find the riches of grace, harmony, beauty, love, and compassion; they are in the "air" around us all the time, no matter where we are, no matter who we are. It is only our ignorance and perversity that cause us to languish spiritually, like the eccentric misers who die of starvation while lying upon a mattress stuffed with thousands of dollars in cash and stock certificates.

The treasures of the earth are virtually handed to us, but we seem not to have the eyes to see. There are many stories that illustrate this point; perhaps the best is an old Persian fable, one version of which was made famous by Russell Conwell in his essay, *Acres of Diamonds*. As well known as this story is, nonetheless it is worthwhile retelling it.

There once was a wealthy farmer who owned vast acres of land. But he was not content with what he had; he wanted what he didn't have. One day he heard from a visiting priest a report that somewhere in the world there was a whole acre of land covered with diamonds as big as marbles, all lying loose in the soil, just waiting to be picked up. Tantalized by this prospect, he sold his farm and struck out on the road to search for the acre of diamonds. His quest carried him to every land, to every corner of the world. But he did not find what he was seeking. Finally, in his old age, having spent all of his riches in his search and too broken and exhausted to enjoy the diamonds even if he found them, he returned to the farm he had sold in his youth. And there he found a great change. New buildings had been erected, and the farm was filled with many people scurrying to and fro. He inquired to find out the purpose of all the activity. "Why, where have you been that you haven't heard what has happened?" came the answer. "They discovered an acre of diamonds here. It's the richest mine in the world!"

Why do we so often fail to recognize the riches at hand? The answer is a simple one: we hypnotize ourself into not perceiving them. Over the years, we let our attention be entranced by the day-to-day mundane events of life and our negative reactions to them. The repetition of the unpleasant becomes hypnotic in effect, and soon our senses are dulled and jaded, unable to perceive the finer realities of goodness which surround us at every moment, like a veritable acre of diamonds. We develop a consciousness of negativity, until all we can see is darkness, selfishness, and cruelty. By not using our eyes to see the goodness and light in others and in the world, we begin to lose our sight. Our perception becomes dim and feeble, until we become totally blinded in our effort to *escape ugliness*. The great mistake, of course, is in the basic attempt: escaping ugliness. The whole framework of such an attempt is geared toward and measured by ugliness. Whenever we try to escape anything, we only succeed in being sucked in further, because we are devoting our complete attention to what we are trying to escape. In effect we *magnify* it.

But we can magnify the enriching elements of life just as easily as the unpleasant and mundane ones. It's all a matter of learning to *pay attention* to the qualities of life that ennoble us and help us grow, instead of being hypnotized by the illusion of negativity. The manner in which we focus our attention will determine the quality of our life.

Therefore, if we find ourself in a sea of ugliness, we must realize that it is just a hypnotic effect—and more importantly, a hypnotic effect that we can break. It is broken by paying attention to the beauty in our life, not the ugliness. At first, we may think this impossible, since we have paid so much attention to the ugliness. But the beauty is there— we've merely lost sight of it temporarily. Just as it takes a few moments for the physical eyes to adjust to bright sunshine after being in a darkened building for several hours, it may take our "spiritual eyes" a little while to readjust to the impulse of beauty after having been focussed on the ugly so long. But it can be done. After all, even the ability to endure ugliness is in itself a form of beauty—the quality of endurance.

It takes discipline to learn to pay attention to the enriching qualities of life. For most of us, *inattention* has been the usual state of mind and feeling. We rise occasionally to brief moments of attention, to be sure, but the constant watchfulness and vigilance which are required for *control* are usually missing—except in those few of us who have practiced self discipline and self awareness for some time. More often than not, we exercise no control at all over our focus of attention; we let it wander to anything that magnetically attracts it—often something morbidly fascinating or pleasurable. It seems to make little difference: the sensation itself is usually of greater interest than the *quality* of that sensation.

In other words, we tend to be distracted from paying attention to the rich cornucopia of the qualities of consciousness that make up our world. Hypnotized by sensation, our subconscious becomes progressively blinded and incapable of perceiving the finer elements of life. By allowing ourself to be distracted in this way, we surrender to mere habit our capacity to generate a better quality of thought and emotion. We indiscriminately give up a valuable portion of our humanity—our capacity to think and act for ourself. This, in turn, erodes our ability to be truly self determining. If unchecked, we slump into a stupor of discouragement and passivity.

Distraction, of course, is a kind of reverse or negative state of attention—an attention to the dulling and anesthetizing opiates of our life. It is really an attention to the shell of form rather than to the animating qualities in that form. It is attention to a single dimension of the visible rather than to the many dimensions of our multi-layered universe. And as we condition ourself in this way, our personal world begins to contract in size; we psychologically wall ourself into a tiny closet of shortsightedness and perhaps despair. In the process we become "numb, dumb, and unaware" of the potential for renewing ourself. Our hope in better things is stilled; our faith in ourself and in life is extinguished. Our lack of understanding prevents us from taking the very simple steps which would improve our condition.

The subconscious, being the willing servant of the conscious mind, is quite ready to accept years of persistent instruction that life is *not* abundant, that it is not possible to find true enrichment, and that we are caught in a web of grief and sorrow from which it is impossible to extricate ourself. But of course such conditioning of the subconscious is most unhealthy. It produces a distorted and unreal conceptualization of reality. It induces a mood of pessimism that eventually begins rejecting all opportunities for improvement, undercutting any efforts that might be made to partake in the richness which is our birthright. Thus, we learn to discount, discredit, scoff at, and ignore the evidence of the real wealth of consciousness everywhere around us. Our blindness becomes a habit which is as persistent as a con artist pursuing his mark, until *something* happens to force us to break out of this hypnotic sleep.

It is not easy, however, for a hypnotized person to awake from his or her trance, arise from the ranks of the walking dead, and rejoin the living. It is not enough, for example, merely to substitute one hypnosis for another, although it is often tried: the pessimist sees through his pessimism, and in the effort to change, fiercely proclaims a feverish optimism and a frenzied enthusiasm. Such efforts, however, do not result in much change, even though they may be sincere. They just add a new layer of habit on top of an older layer, as if laminating the subconscious. Unfortunately, the mechanism of the subconscious at the bottom layer is still attuned to the same old pessimism. The loud affirmative proclamations of optimism do not get relayed to the core of the subconscious; the "motor of the mind" has been switched off.

What is needed, of course, is the proper use of the

technique of "paying attention." Rather than just proclaiming optimism, we must search for and find the *quality of optimism* somewhere in the world around us and focus our attention on that quality. Instead of letting ourself be hypnotized by the shell of form (the physical universe), we must begin to see the animating qualities which use those forms for the purpose of manifestation. We must begin to realize that our physical body is more than just a mechanism for stubbing our toes on rocks. It is a "receiving station" through which we can register input from other physical forms—but also from the other dimensions of the universe. As a result, we can use the perceiving mechanism of our physical body and brain to look at other forms of life and see not only the physical width, height, depth, and color, but also the inner qualities that animate them. For just as we have inner qualities which animate and motivate us, so do all other forms as well.

Hence the need for becoming like the Renaissance artist. If we are to find the raw materials we will need for developing these qualities of consciousness, we will have to make the search ourself. We will have to go out into the universe and look for them.

Thus, the reforming pessimist should seek an outstanding example of optimism—perhaps a friend, perhaps someone he sees on television. By paying attention, he can observe this optimism in action and contemplate its inner quality. He should not, if he's sincerely looking for enrichment, respond with envy or jealousy that this other fellow can be optimistic when he himself is so pessimistic. That's the kind of response which hypnotized him into spiritual blindness in the first place! Rather, he should savor and delight in such a wonderful expression of optimism and try to identify with the spirit behind the form. He should *admire* the optimism and be inspired by the quality of confidence which is radiating so fully from this other person.

Or, this pessimistic fellow might take a walk on a warm, sunny day just after a spring rain, when the sun pours through the clouds once more. As he strolls along, he should observe and admire the eternal presence of optimism in nature, causing his heart to leap up in response and thus learn anew what the quality of optimism really is.

Of course, this process of paying attention can be used for building an awareness of the existence of *any* raw material in the art of living—not just optimism. That is only one example. The person seeking the pigment of joy can look for it tucked away in the corners of a bemused smile; the person in search of love may perhaps find it in the tenderness of a mother caring for her infant child. The man seeking awe and reverence may get his first clue in the radiant effulgence of a sinking sun; the woman who wishes to increase her patience may find a great resonance in the ceaseless cascading of a majestic waterfall.

This search for the raw materials with which to enrich our personality must be conducted in the midst of our daily life and among the circumstances that surround us. As indicated in the fable of the diamonds, it's just another distraction to think that these raw materials can only be found somewhere other than where we happen to be, in some "holy place" or Mecca. Instead, they are gathered in ordinary haunts: in an afternoon's visit to a playground filled with happy children and small animals; in a drive through the local countryside; or perhaps in visits to art galleries and concert halls. They can be collected by reading great works of fiction or by tuning in to the many cultural events brought to us on television.

We need not look for our pigments and art supplies solely on the physical plane, either. The Renaissance master was restricted to physical sources, but we are not. We can seek our raw materials on all of the psychic planes as well as the physical. To do this, we must simply remember that the physical plane is only one of many octaves in a multi-dimensional reality: the universe. And so, while a rural brook may inspire serenity, is it not likely that the psychic perception of Isaiah's "peace like a river" in a moment of quiet contemplation will also inspire great serenity—and quite likely a good deal more?

Actually, any event in which we seek inspiration is apt to occur on more than one level. Thus, we may be listening to a recording of a great symphony on our phonograph, and that is a physical event. But if we have any depth at all, we will be responding emotionally and mentally—and perhaps even spiritually—to the physical sounds being produced by this machine.

Even small and trivial happenings provide fertile ground for our search. We might very well find more joy and enthusiasm in the dancing of a friend's eyes than by attending some contrived, spectacular extravaganza with a cast of thousands.

Nor should we overlook the role that can be played by total strangers and distant events—distant both in terms of time and space. That which is universal is also timeless, and so it only makes sense to include all of history in the domain of our quest. It is quite productive, for example, to read biographies of great people. Perhaps we are seeking the qualities of logical thought and philosophical comprehension. We would therefore read the life stories of great philosophers. We do not personally know these people nor live in their epochs, but nonetheless we can be inspired by their thoughts and ideas—and the qualities they manifested.

Thus, it matters little *where* we focus our attention. It is more important that we pay attention with intelligence and discernment, so that we will see the shadow or reflection of the qualities of good living in whatever we are observing. We must essentially *identify* ourself with the spirit of whatever is happening before our eyes. It is not enough just to see; we must also comprehend. We must admire this example of grace or wisdom or honesty or whatever it may be; we must want to express this same quality ourself. When a gold medalist at the Olympics stands to receive his or her recognition, for example, do we merely see a person standing on a platform and hear a national anthem being played? Or do we perceive the pride of achievement that is overwhelming this youth at this moment? Do we then participate in this event by deciding that achievement is a noble thing and that we should aspire to it, too? If we can admire and identify with this radiant sense of accomplishment, then we are capturing the essence of *paying attention*.

Admiration and identification are important to this process. We are not just collecting memories and images of memorable moments to be stored away and forgotten. When we want to enrich our optimism, it is not enough just to go outside and stand in the sun. When we want to learn about innocence, it is not enough just to take a stroll through a playground of children. The sunshine does not contain optimism. The playground does not contain innocence. The physical events are really just physical events, after all—*unless* we recognize their value as focal points for our attention; *unless* we pierce through the physical events and make contact with the quality behind them.

And yet, we are not just looking for the quality, either. We cannot arbitrarily appropriate the inner qualities of other people and make them our own. There may be a deep sense of serenity and peace in the eyes of a person we are talking with, for example, but we cannot absorb that tranquility just by staring at him. Instead, as we pay attention to the world around us, we must seek the *seed* of enriching qualities: the seed of faith, love, patience, courage, hope, honesty, tolerance, purity, logic, abstract thinking or whatever it might be.

This requires imagination and patience, just as the Renaissance artist needed imagination and patience as he sought out the ideal pigment. Perhaps he needed the color purple for painting the rich robes of a king. He could find it in a stone such as amethyst, but obtaining it was not as simple as picking up the stone and carrying it back to his easel. True, he had found the evidence—the "seed"—of his purple pigment, but he then had to remove the trace of purple from the stone, pulverize it, and blend it with oils and other pigments before he produced his paint.

It requires even more imagination for us, although the effort is really no more difficult. We cannot pick up a stone which inspires us with endurance and extract the vein of endurance from that rock, grind it up, blend it with oils, and then spread it on our face like a beauty cream, so that it will soak in! Rather, we must understand that the reason why a rock inspires us with endurance is because it is a physical *reflection* of the invisible, more subtle quality of endurance. And so we leave the rock where it is, and we make contact instead with the seed of endurance which exists in the finer realms of the universe. We focus our attention on that seed, and as we do, we begin to realize that this same quality of endurance also exists *as a seed within ourself!* In fact, the seeds of all of the great and noble qualities of humanity exist within each one of us — at the innermost levels of our being. We use the perception of outer events only as a means to refocus our attention upon these seeds within ourself. We make contact with an example of a desired quality in the outer world, and we keep on making this contact (or similar ones), *until we begin to sense a response to the outside stimulus from the seed of this quality within us.* Then we can turn our attention within and proceed with the business of nourishing and nurturing this seed, which is beginning to spring to life.

In simplest terms, the process of paying attention is primarily a matter of realizing that the Life of the Universe speaks through all of its forms. Thus, when we see a child laugh or the sun set or the rain fall, we understand that in this fashion the universe is speaking to us. And so we listen!

REFINING THE RAW MATERIALS

Once the Renaissance master had gathered the various physical substances containing the pigments he sought, he then needed to extract from those substances the essence which would form the base of his paints. So, he would crush the berries to distill the vivid red or blue. He would grind the stones to free from them the tiny grains of purple. He would work laboriously at this task, much like his medieval counterpart, the alchemist, until he had refined out of these raw materials enough concentrated essence to prepare his paints.

In building our character, we must do the equivalent. Having learned how to pay attention to outstanding examples of humanistic qualities and identify with their essence, we must also learn how to separate that essence from the outer impurities that may accompany it, and increase our response to it. This is achieved through *concentration*.

Concentration is a good deal more than just paying attention. It is an intensification and magnification of the richness and purity of our perceptions. It may be nice, for example, to discern the quality of humility in the way a certain person beholds a flower he has never seen before, but that observation will come to nought if we then dismiss the whole impression from our mind five minutes later. To make this observation meaningful to us, we must refine it through concentration. We must dwell repeatedly upon it until we have magnified this seed of the quality of humility to the point where it is strong enough to have an impact upon our subconscious. Repeating the memory is very important. In addition, it is also helpful to associate this memory with similar examples of humility that we have extracted from the world around us. Seeing the similarities in our imagination and thinking repeatedly upon the entire sequence is a powerful way of applying concentration.

Most people, of course, are already quite "proficient" in the art of concentration—except that they use this tool to harm themselves rather than gain enrichment. Instead of refining out the noble qualities of a situation and discarding the dross, they unthinkingly refine out the negativity and dispose of the goodness. They concentrate large doses of distress, agony, pain, grief, self pity, or fear and then complain that there is no joy in their lives! They distill a mood of ugliness in spite of all the beauty everywhere and blend it into their character. Is it any wonder that they quickly become ugly themselves, at every level of their being?

Few people do this deliberately. Most of us aspire to something better—but fall victim to our own laziness. It requires a certain amount of work and dedication to collect the appropriate seeds of consciousness and then integrate them into our own attitudes and habits. Even in the Renaissance, not that many artists took the trouble to search out the absolutely best materials. Many settled for second or third best rather than put a premium on perfection. And so they produced less magnificient results. That is why there are so few truly great masters in any field. Many people find it easier to concentrate on ugliness and distress than on beauty, love, and wisdom. Of course, that does not produce intelligent and desirable lives; it does not lead to greater enrichment of the personality or to an increasingly universal outlook. It leads to impoverishment of thought and feeling, and provincialism in our attitudes.

In this process of refining, we are dealing with our *responses* to the initial observation. An excellent illustration of both intelligent and thoughtless responses can be found in the way people have reacted to the movie *The Exorcist,* a motion picture about the possession of a rather impressionable teenage girl by crude and malevolent demonic forces. The film is filled with scenes of great obscenity, violence, and literal stench and filth. Several people are killed by the possessed girl, including the priests who are called in to exorcise the demon. But the exorcism is successful, due to the dedication of the priests and their willingness to sacrifice even their lives to cleanse the girl.

In addition to the obvious obscenity, profanity, and repulsive ugliness in this movie, however, there is also a most inspiring presence of rich and noble human qualities—almost exclusively in the character of the two priests. There may never have been a more graphic presentation on the silver screen of human courage, hope, faith, nobility, strength, and dedication than in this picture. Much of the credit must, of course, go to the two very fine actors who portrayed the priests and who were able to distill the nature of these qualities in their performances. The visual picture of the exorcist reading the rites of exorcism without hesitating and without flinching, while the whole room is shaking, while vomit is being thrown at him, and while the holy symbols of the church are being desecrated, is a powerful demonstration of nobility and strength. The image of his vigorous use of holy water as a force of exorcism—not just sprinkling it in the hope that something might happen, but commanding with all the power of the heavens that this demonic entity obey the will of God—lingers in the mind as an unsurpassed example of faith and correct cooperation with the forces of the universe.

But how many people who saw the movie were impressed by the dignity and the nobility of the priests? Judging from the typical comments of the moviegoers, not many. Most were impressed by the obscenity, the crudeness, the violence, the terror, and the fear. That is what they talked about after the movie. That is what they repeatedly talked about and thought about for days and days afterward, for the movie made a powerful impression on most. And that is what they were paying attention to and refining into their consciousnesses—the ugliness and depravity! With both nobility and obscenity to choose from, most people who saw the movie chose to concentrate on the obscenity. With both dignity and fear to choose from, most chose fear. They extracted the dross and left the precious jewels behind, all but untouched. And then they wonder why they have fears, obscene thoughts, and strange urges!

The movie contains many diverse elements, as does life; if we are intent upon enriching our life rather than impoverishing it, then we must be careful to extract from the movie, and from life, only the ennobling and uplifting elements. We must leave the trash behind in the theater; *we must not take it along with us!*

This is not a question of being naive or simplistic; it does not mean that we go through life in Pollyanna fashion. It's merely a question of correct perspective. We have the right and the option to choose what kind of raw materials to use in refining our moods, emotions, thoughts, skills, habits, and traits. If we are sensible and intelligent, we will select our "art supplies" from the examples of nobility, courage, faith, dignity, joy, compassion, wisdom, and tenderness that are presented to us, and *not* from the examples of stupidity, grossness, greed, profanity, lust, hate, or malevolence.

So, we respond—hopefully to the humanistic and the enduring. But to be most effective, our response must be made with admiration, respect, and perhaps even a sense of awe. In this way we concentrate the quality we are focussing on.

Some people, unfortunately, confuse the response of awe with the reaction of fear; they speak, for example, of "fearing the Lord." This is a terrible misunderstanding of awe, for fear is really an aspect of hate. Awe is just the opposite: it is an aspect of love. Thus, as we respond to a happening with admiration and awe for its inner quality, we are building love. We marvel at its glory and goodness, and we begin to love that quality.

Having seen *The Exorcist,* for example, we replay in our mind's eye the scenes in which the priests display the courage, the strength, and the faith we want to acquire. We concentrate on the particular moments when these qualities are most pronounced, and respond to them with as much awe, admiration, and respect as possible. We reject the profane elements of the movie and love the strength, courage, and faith. In this way, we magnetize our awareness to be responsive to these seeds of consciousness. And as we do, something quite remarkable occurs: the love and awe we are silently expressing magnetically draws a response from the living streams of courage, strength, and faith in universal consciousness. Our personal expression of admiration is thus magnified and enriched.

Here again we can see the need for intelligently choosing the kind of raw material that we will be working with. After all, we can as easily draw in a pure stream of iniquity from universal consciousness, if our response is an admiration of wickedness, as we can draw in a pure stream of nobility when we are responding to nobleness. This is the reason why concentration upon such negative qualities as fear, obscenity, and depravity can quickly lead to nightmarish circumstances in life. But it must be understood that such conditions are always of the individual's own making and choosing.

We make our own heavens and hells in life. The process is the same in each case. Only the blueprints and the focus differ—and the results.

ENSURING PERMANENCE

His concentrates refined, the Renaissance master would then proceed to the third step of mixing the various pigments together and blending them with delicate oils and emulsifiers to produce the shades and textures of paint he needed. This stage required a cultivated sense of proportion, a fine eye for color, and some understanding of which oils would be long lasting and which would quickly fade and lose their luster. Being a master artist, he sought to create works of permanence that would not fade after a few years' time.

Just so, we must work at creating masterpieces of permanence in our life. It may be nice to have a few years of good feelings and happiness, but it is immeasurably more valuable to create *permanent* qualities, such as joy, serenity, and wisdom, and *permanent* skills in living. Such qualities and skills can be built—qualities that endure not just for the rest of this life but throughout all our future life experiences. That is permanent!

As might be expected, the permanent enrichment of the personality is not achieved just by wishful thinking. It is achieved by skillfully and patiently mixing these newly refined qualities into the existing streams of thought and emotion in the subconscious. Nor can this integration be accomplished by any short and easy trick; it is not possible to go to the store and buy a "mixmaster of the mind" into which we can dump the various ingredients and qualities, give it a whirl, and pour out a parfait of joyfulness, an ice cream soda of wisdom, or a frappe of humility. Rather, it requires the same personal effort that the Renaissance artist used in mixing and blending his paints.

The key word to this third stage is *blending*. The concentrated quality—be it optimism, dignity, serenity, or something else—must now be introduced into the appropriate pools of memory in the subconscious and blended in. It must be integrated into the very fiber of our being and made a part of us. Otherwise the richness and nourishment of this quality will pass through us and be lost.

This blending cannot occur if the content of the subconscious is radically different from the seed of quality we are trying to promote. Oil and water do not mix. Neither do conceit and humility, love and hatred, and so on. So we may very well have to perform some selective "tuning" in the subconscious before we will be able to adequately blend in these new ingredients We tune the subconscious by *thinking*—by considering how this insight or mood which we have now concentrated can be related to our life.

After seeing *The Exorcist,* for example, and being impressed by the qualities of nobility, dignity, courage, and faith demonstrated by the priests, we can begin to relate the seeds of these qualities to our own life. Of course, we probably are not priests, and even if we are, it is not too likely that we are often called upon to perform exorcisms. But that does not matter. Remember, it is not our objective to incorporate the actual quality that we have seen into our consciousness—just the seed of the quality. Then that seed can be nurtured so that it will grow within us in whatever ways will be appropriate for us. And so, even though we will never perform an exorcism or have a face-to-face confrontation with a demon, we might nonetheless decide after some thought that we do need courage, nobility, dignity, and the other qualities that the priests so skillfully expressed. Perhaps we need courage to help us deal with the prospect of a beloved friend's imminent death. We may need nobility to better meet and control certain sordid memories tucked away in our subconscious—memories that from time to time leer at us from the depths. In such reflection we think about these human qualities and relate them to our life. Indeed, we will probably conclude that the situations we must face are less strenuous and less demanding than the challenge the exorcists met. If they could maintain courage and nobility in such trying conditions, then why can't we do likewise in the face of less difficulty?

The intelligent person thus relates the inspiring

elements of the movie to his own life and blends the seeds of the qualities he seeks into his subconscious. He enriches himself. The unintelligent person, on the other hand, goes out gushing about the obscenity, the depravity, and the terror. He relates the fear of the mother with his own fear. He relates the obscenity of the possessed girl with his own obscenity. And in this way he succeeds only in integrating himself with the gross elements of the movie. It is about as intelligent as taking a swim in a cesspool or eating garbage.

As suggested, this process of integration depends upon being able to harmonize the subconscious with the seed of the quality we seek. There is one very good way of achieving this. As we think about the quality of courage, for example, we can think of a number of times in the past when we have not expressed sufficient courage. We can then mentally re-enact each of these memories and imagine how we could have acted and behaved, if we had possessed the degree of courage manifested by the priests in the movie. In this way, we modify the associations connected with this memory in the subconscious. Until now, the subconscious has associated this memory with cowardice. Cowardice, however, does not blend with courage. But if we alter the associations the subconscious has made with this memory, we will be able to blend the seed of courage into our subconscious. In doing this, it is important to understand that we are *not* changing the facts of the memory or pretending that the past happened in an untrue way; we are just changing the associations we make with this memory. We are preparing ourself so that we can associate this memory in the future with the *possibility of courage!* We can then confidently proceed with blending in the new pigment—the seed of courage which can be nurtured and grown into a manifestation of our own.

Or, if we have just witnessed the sight of an eagle soaring majestically through the air and have drawn from that experience the seed of the quality of grace, we would then need to blend this seed into our own livingness. We do not do this by pretending to be an eagle and leaping off a cliff! Nor should we rush out and sign up for a hang-gliding course. Rather, we recall moments of our life when we have been less than graceful—perhaps in social settings, perhaps in the way we have spoken to our children, or perhaps in the way we have faced difficulties. We then imagine how that same situation could have been dealt with gracefully. We do *not* imagine the absurdity of how the eagle might have handled it!

As mentioned earlier, this mental activity of blending noble qualities into our own subconscious will draw forth a magnetic response from universal consciousness, complementing our efforts and helping us nourish the growth of this new seed. The qualities which flow to us from the universal consciousness in response to our work are literally living, brilliant lights. They are seen by the clairvoyant as streams of intensely colored light, each color being associated with a different quality such as love, joy, grace, peace, or wisdom. As we proceed with the work of blending and achieve some success, we draw in these brilliant rays of light and mix them with the patterns of light that form our emotions and mind. Then, as these inflowing rays of light circulate throughout our being (which happens automatically as the result of effective integration), they seem to actually bleach out the darkness, impurities, and ugliness which have hitherto discolored our stored memories and habit patterns. Naturally, this bleaching does not occur all at once—it takes repeated effort over a period of time to achieve complete success. But the enrichment of the personality is not a metaphorical process which has no basis in reality. It is a very real and necessary procedure which can be easily observed by those with eyes to see.

Nothing much happens, however, until we cause it to. It is not enough just to have wonderful and uplifting experiences—not if we want to truly enrich our personality and our life. It is important to be able to appreciate the hidden essences in the smile of a child or in the way in which an Olympics medalist takes pride in his achievement, but these experiences, no matter how moving, remain worthless to us unless we integrate them into useful expressions in our own life.

What does not exist in the very fabric of our being does not really exist at all—for us.

A MASTERPIECE OF HUMANITY

The rocks and berries of the forest and streams have now been transformed into oils; at last the master artist is ready to paint. He is ready to apply his refined and blended pigment to the canvas. But preparing these supplies in no way guarantees the creation of a masterpiece. If the artist never uses them, or if he uses them without creative inspiration, he fails to complete the creative cycle.

Just so, in order to enrich our personality, we must be willing to work hard and use inspiration to make manifest in our life suitable expressions of these newly-refined and blended seeds of quality. If we are not, then all of the magnificent sunsets of history cannot help us. Our aim is to create a masterpiece of humanity, a full and inspiring example of the humanistic qualities of love, joy, nobility, and wisdom—and that requires more than wishful thinking. Indeed, to achieve this goal, we must begin acting in a new and more humanistic fashion. We must dedicate ourself to the *application* of our refined and blended seeds of quality to the canvas of our life.

In making this application, we must let our imagination and our inspiration guide us as we confront the challenges of life. When we face crudity, we must try to act with the nobility of the exorcist—but in these different circumstances. When confronted with our own clumsiness, we must try to somehow express the gracefulness of the eagle. When presented with a difficult decision, we must try to capture for ourself the essence of wisdom in nature, which always seems capable of evolving a new species of plant or animal that is better able to cope with the demands of its environment—and simultaneously is better able to express the purpose of evolution. When met with a mood of despair, we must put into expression that same effervescent quality that we caught years ago in someone's gentle laugh.

Unfortunately, no easy formula can be set down for obtaining the imagination and inspiration that is needed for successful application. But the right attitude certainly helps. If a budding artist picks up a "paint by numbers" kit at his local hobby store, that's a good sign that he's not especially interested in developing his creative inspiration. Nor is there much hope for him if he is content to reproduce copies of great masters, although he may develop a certain technical skill. But the artist who picks up his brush with the intention to create an expression of beauty, and a determination to increase his personal talent, has an excellent chance of stimulating an inflow of inspiration. Just so, the artist in human life who approaches each day as a canvas upon which a mural of enlightenment can be drawn, and regards each experience as a wonderful experiment in inspiration, will have an excellent chance to apply his accumulated insights in creative ways. Moreover, his attitude will invoke many opportunities for just that kind of expression. Thus, the activity of application presupposes a certain enthusiasm for living; just as it is hard to imagine a good artist who does not like painting, it is difficult to envision a human being creating much out of his life in the way of beauty, grace, and wisdom if he does not basically like himself and enjoy expressing his highest qualities and ideals. It also presupposes a person who wants to express himself fully on *all* levels of his being—in his physical activities, in his emotional responses, in his moods, in his thoughts, and in his spiritual pursuits.

Perhaps the best way to stimulate the inspiration we need is to ask introspectively: what have we done today which might inspire someone else to be more humanistic? Have we managed to express these inner qualities that we've worked so hard to cultivate? Have we acted with the gracefulness of the eagle? If not, what can we do to express that quality through the way we relate to others, the way we behave at work, or even the way we walk or smile? Have we acted with the courage of the exorcist? Has our adaptability reflected the same wisdom found in nature?

The purpose of such introspection is not to be critical of ourself but rather to invoke inspiration. Our daily life is filled with countless opportunities, big and small, for expressing the richness of life—for creating a masterpiece of humanity. Every relationship provides opportunities to apply the seeds of nobility, love, and generosity; every assignment at work gives us a chance to apply our skills and competence; every difficult decision that must be made provides a chance for acting with wisdom. Nonetheless, if we have not taken the time to recognize these opportunities and consider how we wish to respond to them, we will surely miss them. Our life will remain unenriched. A daily introspective review of how we want to act in specific situations, therefore, is of great importance. By establishing the useful habit of *expecting* to be inspired in everything we say and do, we strengthen the psychological momentum for applying just that kind of inspiration.

It is crucial not to let the seeds of goodness, nobility, honor, love and wisdom die stillborn within us. Yet if we do not insufflate them with the breath of inspiration and apply them in our daily life, then die they surely shall. Thus, whenever we gather within us even the smallest grain of grace or nobility or wisdom—and many of us have gathered much more than just a grain—we are *honor-bound* to express it some way, somehow, some time. Such expression is as much a part of being human as breathing, smiling, or laughing. It is a bare requirement. And the consequence of not expressing these qualities creatively is serious: it leads inevitably to a constipation of consciousness which is every bit as serious as physical constipation—and cannot be relieved medicinally. It constitutes a "damming up" of our humanity; the unexpressed seeds of enrichment build up as though contained by a barrier, growing in pressure until the dam bursts.

The alternative—the ideal application of our human qualities in creative expression—is much more promising. Nothing is constipated; indeed, our personality life becomes a most beautiful and awesome display of our higher humanity. It was stated earlier that these qualities appear as colored lights. As we begin to express them creatively in our life, we quite literally begin *radiating* these streams of intensely vivid light into the world around us. This radiation can be seen clairvoyantly. Our joy streams forth and touches the emotions of those around us, shimmering with brilliance and pure life. Our wisdom pours forth and illuminates the dark corners in which others dwell.

Having drawn these qualities from the universe, we therefore return the favor by sending them back into the universe. With practice, this reciprocal activity of application becomes as natural as the evaporation of water after a rainfall, the formation of new clouds, and the commencement of a new cycle. In this way, we call forth more of the same seeds of quality, but with expanded possibilities. We have sown a new crop, which will spring to life in the near future; we have increased the scope of the universe in which we can operate. We are less restricted than before, because we have pushed back the barriers of restriction through our efforts. We are less provincial; we come closer to the true universalization that will make us a master artist in human living in our own right.

And there is one other very practical benefit: as we begin to express these qualities that we have refined and blended through our own experiences, we evoke a similar expression in other people. The potential in human beings to respond to a good example is remarkably great. Our own creative efforts draw forth magnetically the seeds of enrichment in others, to one degree or another. That, in turn, makes it easier to find inspiration ourself.

BECOMING UNIVERSAL

The process, then, of enriching our personality and universalizing our perspectives consists of four stages: attention, concentration, blending, and application. These four steps are not, of course, entirely separate and distinct: they overlap to some extent and lead quite naturally from the one to the next. But all four are *dynamic* activities of human expression which tend to accelerate and build their own momentum as we engage in them and develop our proficiency. In the beginning, each step may have to be worked on quite deliberately, until skill is gained. Such deliberation is important and should not be a cause for discouragement; it is always wisest to take the time to learn new ideas thoroughly, until they are truly mastered. Casual and careless efforts usually end up producing more mistakes than positive results. And the undoing of such mistakes is often itself a distraction.

But there has been much more set forth in this essay than just a mechanical process of four stages. The whole key to enriching the personality lies in becoming more universal: that is, in becoming more universal in its true sense. We must apprehend that we live in the midst of enormous wealth—a wealth of consciousness, humanity, and wisdom that exists on many different levels of perception in the universe. Our physical perception reveals only a tiny fragment of that wealth. Our emotions and mind reveal a good deal more of it, and it has been primarily with these levels of perception that we have been dealing. The remaining realms—the greatest glories of all—are revealed to us by our innermost, spiritual perceptions as they are developed and nurtured. Of course, it is in the unfoldment of these innermost perceptions that the greatest enrichment of life occurs. But so very much enrichment can occur at the emotional and mental levels—especially when compared with the usual state of impoverishment of most people—that the average person will find ample room for immediate growth there.

It is the universal implication of this process—the implication that we can slough the chrysalis of our limited, constricted, self-centered worlds and gain the freedom of the unlimited and infinite universe of *values and consciousness*—that should give us each a great sense of hope and a genuine, deep appreciation for the intelligence and benevolence of the forces that created this universe and continue to sustain it. And this prospect should stir in us a deep commitment to act boldly to *aspire* to nobility, dignity, beauty, and all the other rich qualities of humanity. It is *not* enough just to be intellectually aware that these humanistic qualities exist and that it is theoretically possible to develop them within ourself. Rather, we must actively involve ourself. To enrich our life, we must connect ourself to the life force that animates all life forms. We must first of all let the universe speak to us by listening to what it has to say; we must seek the inspiration of the inner dimensions. Then, we must respond to that inspiration with aspiration—the aspiration to express what we have glimpsed. Such aspiration will surely lead to further inspiration, and that in turn will stimulate greater aspiration. In this fashion we make our growth.

The moment we stop being hypnotized by the baseness of our thoughts, feelings, and sensations, that moment we begin to realize that the word "universe" no longer describes some abstract astronomical model of perplexing infinity. That moment the universe ceases to be populated by stars and planets, although they are still there, and it starts to be populated with the qualities of joy, wisdom, courage, dignity, nobility, optimism, serenity, benevolence, and goodwill.

In such an environment, we *can* live and move and have our being. Furthermore, we can grow in consciousness and attain the freedom of understanding what it truly means to be *infinite*.

THE PRACTICE
OF DETACHMENT

WHO WE ARE

Throughout life, we form attachments. In our infancy, we form attachments to virtually everyone and everything in our immediate environment. We reach out and pull to ourself our toys, our blankets, our nourishment, our parents. At first, these attachments are largely automatic responses of physical need, and not the results of either emotional or mental needs. Later, we begin to develop tastes, and our attachments become subdivided into "likes" and "dislikes." In addition to pulling desired objects to us, we learn to repel. We decide we like chocolate ice cream and dislike vanilla. But in each case, we have formed an attachment: we desire to avoid vanilla as much as we wish to obtain chocolate. As we grow older, we continue building attachments: we choose friends and foes, we accept and reject ideas, we decide what's right and what's wrong.

By the time we reach adulthood, we have defined our identity in terms of our attachments—in terms of the car we own, where we live, whom we are married to, how many kids we have, the problems and temptations we face, the political and religious beliefs we hold, and a number of unvoiced prejudices, insecurities, and fears.

In short, we have become enslaved by our attachments. Our identity hinges on a superstructure of what we do, what we have, and what we like or dislike, believe or disbelieve. We retain little if any control of our life: if our spouse is unkind, we become depressed; if loving, then we are happy. When the boss barks, we fidget with insecurity; when the boss praises us, we're on top of the world. When someone supports our cherished ideas, we are charitable and gracious; when criticized, we angrily react with defensiveness. Most of our life is thus spent *reacting* to what others do and say—and to the ups and downs of daily life. Seldom, if ever, do we initiate action of our own. Instead, all of our "buttons" are pushed for us, and we simply stumble through the results as best we can. We have abandoned our free will by entangling ourself in countless attachments; we have bartered away a real sense of identity for the convenience of not having to think much about our life.

But it need not be thus. The birthright of our identity can be reclaimed. It's a slow and delicate process that requires both intelligence and determination. It is, however, worth the trouble involved. Our efforts are rewarded with freedom: freedom from physical infirmity, from emotional stress, and from mental isolation and confusion. With freedom also comes greater maturity—the ability to make increasingly positive and significant changes in our attitudes, habits, beliefs, and actions. *We achieve the capacity to fulfill our potential as a human being.*

Gradually, as we examine the core of our identity, we begin to realize that there is an important difference between appearance and awareness: between what we do and who we are, between what we have and who we are, between what we like or dislike and who we are, and between what we believe or disbelieve and who we are. We begin to comprehend that there is a part of us—the personality—that does things, that possesses things, that likes things and people, and that believes in certain ideas. In short, the personality forms attachments. But we also come to see that there is another part of us that remains constant and unaffected while the personality forms these attachments. It is this part of us that contains the key to our identity—to *who we are*.

And what is this part of us? Quite simply, it is that part of ourself which is permanent, which existed before the birth of the personality and will continue to exist after its death. It is that deeper part of ourself which is the essence of our humanity—the part which is divine. It has been called many names by many different people; the religious call it the soul or spirit, esotericists label it the causal body, psychologists refer to it as the superconscious. In simplest terms, it can be called the center of our being, the deepest level of our consciousness, the inner self.

The principal quality of this inner self is consciousness: the ability to know. By contrast, the hallmark of the personality is "not knowing." Indeed, human life begins in a fog of unknowing; the infant personality has virtually no awareness whatsoever, be it self awareness, awareness of others, or even awareness of knowledge. But, because it is the reflection of the inner being, the personality wishes to know, it wishes to grow in awareness. The resulting problem should be obvious. Born into a state of unknowing, the personality nonetheless dimly senses the value of knowing (the value of being conscious as the inner self is conscious) and desires it. But being unknowing, the personality can't possibly know how to reach that exalted state. It is forced to pursue its quest of awareness in blindness. And so it takes the only course open to it: it begins to experiment.

As we have seen, this experimenting is usually conducted by forming attachments. The personality forms attachments in order to gain greater knowledge and cope with its environment. Through trial and error, it gradually determines what it must seek and what it must avoid in order to stay alive. It also learns what kind of attachments will produce, at least temporarily, a degree of satisfaction, happiness, and accomplishment. From the point of view of the personality alone, this is quite right and correct.

The personality, however, is *not* alone. On the contrary: it is the creation of the soul, the inner self. And from the point of view of the inner self, there comes a time when the habit of the personality to form attachments must be stopped and redirected, and for a very good reason. The unknowing personality quickly becomes a slave to its attachments, as it succumbs to the enchantments of the external world. Every time we forge a bond of attachment, we submerge our awareness in the mere appearance of things. We let our attachment—instead of our inner self—define our identity. We lose sight of who we truly are. We dim our understanding. We fall into the all too common trap of believing that the physical world is the only level of being. We deny the existence of all motivating causes in our life. We lose effectiveness in living by reacting to randomly chosen attachments rather than acting under the intelligent, ordered guidance of the inner self. As a result, we waste time and miss opportunities; in darkness, we loudly proclaim that there is no such thing as light. We move farther and farther from the ultimate basis of our identity—the soul, which is pure consciousness.

The personality is not alone. Until this great truth is realized, we labor under the restrictiveness of a mighty self deception. But just recognizing this truth is not enough; it must be made an active part of our daily life. There are many people who acknowledge the existence of the inner being in addition to the personality, but in how many of them does the inner self shine forth unimpeded? How many have successfully emancipated themselves from their attachments? How many stand free of all doubts, all fears, all worries, all feelings of guilt, all misconceptions, all compulsions, all negativities—not only within the sphere of their own individuality, but also within the collective consciousness of the human race? How many perfectly express benevolence and compassion in their dealings with other people? How many personify the wisdom of a fully illumined mind? Very, very few. But it can be done.

This process of gradually emerging into the consciousness of the inner self (as opposed to further submerging consciousness into the personality) is called *detachment*. It is the process of learning to control—rather than being controlled by—our physical vitality, our emotions, our desires, and our mind. It is a technique for disengaging ourself from the *need* to form attachments. Detachment is the rediscovery of the true center of our humanity, the innermost self, and a gradual realignment of our priorities. Slowly the value we place on the superficialities of the external world lessens, and we emphasize more and more the eternal realities of our inner existence.

The end result of detachment is a well-balanced personality which effortlessly and fully expresses the qualities of the inner self in daily life—the holistic qualities of love, joy, wisdom, strength, courage, and steadfastness. And because detachment leads to greater maturity, it likewise enables us to correct the weaknesses of our personality with intelligence and compassion. It frees us from the fears, worries, doubts, and frustrations that subvert most attempts at personal growth. Hence, the great importance of detachment is that it enables us to work in a state of relative objectivity and thereby create changes which are truly *improvements*.

Most simply, therefore, detachment is the process of gaining perspective—first in particular situations, and eventually in every aspect of life. As such, it is a completely natural part of life. After all, whenever we lose perspective, we must detach ourself from the problem before we can regain the clear-headedness needed to resolve our difficulties. We learn this lesson from the earliest age: when two children begin fighting, their parents separate them and admonish them to "calm down." In most cases, the children quickly forget their differences and are soon playing peacefully together again. This is an elementary kind of detachment through physical separation—but the principle is the same.

Adults often seek some kind of artificial detachment to help them gain perspective at difficult moments. A couple with severe marital problems, for example, may opt for a legal separation to give them a chance to clear their heads, define what it is they are seeking from marriage, and decide if they should reunite or terminate the bond.

In its fullest sense, however, detachment is not something that is resorted to when all else fails. The intelligent person who is seeking to increase his identification with his inner self uses detachment as an approach to life in general—to gain the broadest perspective of every circumstance in his life. Thus, he practices detachment by diligently learning to control all of the energies of his life—his physical energy, his emotional energy, and his mental energy. He learns the science of detachment just as a child learns to read and write—through long years of application and intelligent practice.

It should be emphasized, however, that detachment is in no way an escape from the activities and pressures of daily life, nor in any way a withdrawal into isolation. Neither is it in any sense a repression of the personality or a benumbing of the emotions, the desires, or the mind. The use of the word "detachment" should not suggest that we "detach" from our personality. That would be counterproductive and unhealthy. Rather, we seek to detach from our long standing habit of forming physical, emotional, and mental attachments—attachments which have diverted our sense of identity away from the inner self.

It is necessary to make such a clarification because many people, unfortunately, have mistaken ideas about detachment. This confusion is the legacy of medieval monks who retired from secular life because they could not cope with it and who popularized such aberrations as mortification of the body. It can also be traced to the influence in the West of Zen, which attempts to annihilate (quite wrongly) the mind, as well as to certain corrupt schools of yoga, which advocate destruction of the emotions and desires. All of these are distortions of the basic principle of detachment.

Suffice it to say, achieving detachment has nothing to do with damaging or destroying the body, the emotions, the mind, the desires, or anything of value. Detachment does not destroy—it leads to greater awareness and maturity. It honors the mind, the emotions, and the body, and helps us see that they are the channels through which love, joy, wisdom, strength, courage, and steadfastness flow. By learning detachment, we learn the proper use of the personality and increase our effectiveness in active and dynamic living.

Thus, there need be no fear that the practice of detachment might sacrifice the personality upon the cross of the soul. In actual fact, the achievement of detachment raises the personality to its highest expression within the loving aura of the inner self.

QUIET CONFIDENCE

An attachment is not a static bond; it is not a rope which can be tied or untied but which itself never changes. Quite the contrary, an attachment is a stream of energies, constantly in motion, living, and ever flowing. This idea can perhaps be best understood by visualizing an attachment as a beam of light always connecting—like an emotional or mental umbilical cord—the individual with the object of his attachment. The object of attachment might be another person, as in the case of attachments such as emotional love, hatred, friendship, lust, and jealousy. Or, it could be a physical object, as in the case of greed; or an obsession, as in the case of fanatical adherence to a religious or political philosophy.

Along this corridor of light, energy flows to and fro, just as traffic moves on a two-way avenue. On the one hand, the object of attachment draws the attention of the person and drains his energy. Greed is an excellent example of this: the lure of material gain captivates the whole imagination of the individual, until it becomes a compulsion. But energy flows the other way as well: the undetached person tends to generate the energies used in his day-to-day activities by drawing them from his favorite objects of attachment. And so, if he feels depressed, he seeks a kind word from a friend to "give him a lift"—to help him generate energy for his own use.

Regardless of which way the energy is flowing, it is the attachment which governs the undetached individual's use of that energy; it is the attachment which either depletes or replenishes his energy reserve. And, of course, the implication is the same in both instances: he is a slave to his attachments.

The proper source for the energy we use in our daily life, however, is not our attachments. It is the inner self. This inner being has contact with infinite resources of energy. The sum of all emotional, mental, and spiritual energy in the world can be thought of as forming a vast reservoir of energy, a veritable ocean of life. The inner being does not store up energy, but does have direct contact with this ocean of life; as a result, it has instantaneous access at all times to unlimited quantities of courage, strength, steadfastness, love, joy—whatever might be needed.

The detached person, being in rapport with his inner being, can therefore make contact with this ocean of life at any time and use its energies for his own self expression. Consequently, he has no need for the energies of attachments. He has a much better source at hand to call on—a source which will not entrap and enchant him or cause him to forget the nature of his identity.

Thus, detachment is much more than just a liberation from attachments. That is merely a necessary step toward the real goal: the unfettered expression of the energies of the inner self through the personality. Far from being a withdrawal from life, detachment is an *active affirmation of life itself*. It is the capacity to act with *poise*.

Poise is one of the most fundamental ingredients in mental health. A person who lacks poise swings back and forth between extremes—from "up" to "down," from pain to pleasure, from positive to negative, from depression to happiness. Such a person has no sense of consistency, of permanence, of self knowledge. It is only when we halt the swing of the pendulum and seek to balance the extremes—to find the transcendent value of *both* the positive and the negative—that we begin to discover the capacity to *act* in life.

Being poised means truly knowing who we are: knowing that our fundamental identity is pure consciousness. (*Consciousness*, a quality of the soul, should not be confused with *sensation*, the means of perception used by the personality. Consciousness is the knowledge of our identity; sensation is the knowledge of attachment.) With this understanding comes the further realization that our life and efforts have genuine significance, that we are immortal, and that the daily activities of life have purpose and meaning. With it also comes an awareness of the unlimited strength and love of the ocean of life which supports our efforts and gives us the steadfastness, courage, and stamina to face without fear any situation in life.

A person without poise is constantly at the mercy of the people and the situations of his life. As they go, so he goes. Such a person is always in danger of complete and absolute collapse. If the bottom falls out of his own personal world he will be utterly destroyed, because his personal strength has been built on gossamer illusions. When the last of his crutches is kicked out from under him, he falls down in utter despair. At worst, he is a candidate for suicide or a mental institution; at best, he bitterly concludes that the earth is a hell indeed.

The person who has poise, however, needs no crutches to prop him up. He is aware that he exists simultaneously on several different levels—the physical, the emotional, the mental, and the realm of the soul. If he encounters difficulty on one level, say the emotional, he can compensate by contacting and expressing energy from a higher part of himself. He knows he can instantly tap into the unlimited strength and power of the ocean of life, and so nothing can sweep him into despair. He is, in truth, a pillar of strength, capable of acting with quiet confidence.

When a person has achieved this state of poise,

not even the pressure of his own expectations can interfere with his understanding of who he is. One of the most common problems the earnest student of life faces is disenchantment with his progress. He sets a goal, makes a certain amount of initial progress, and then begins to think he is slipping back, not accomplishing anything. He becomes depressed, because he does not have poise—he lacks the quiet confidence that is the stamp of the more seasoned individual. *Straining* for success does not bring success any sooner—it only creates a barrier of static between the personality and the soul and postpones the likelihood of success. The person who is truly poised is able to relax, laugh gently at his shortcomings, and focus the energy of the ocean of life through himself in skilled and creative ways.

This last idea is an important one: harnessing the energies of love, wisdom, joy, and courage for meaningful expression. The energies of the ocean of life need not be forced into expression, but they do have to be directed purposefully. It is impossible to focus them through a personality in turmoil, or one that is not properly prepared.

The full expression of our individuality depends upon the ability to control the channels of self expression—our emotions, our thoughts, and our physical vitality. Without the quiet confidence that comes from the practice of detachment, our self expression becomes mired in unimportant matters, wasting our time and squandering our resources. But when we begin acting with poise and self knowledge, we are able to marshal our energies into productive achievement. We reach the goals we have set. We find joy and fulfillment.

Much *can* be accomplished in our lives. While

many of us never see it, every situation in life has within it the seeds of perfect beauty. In many cases these seeds lie dormant, having been neither planted nor tended. Indeed, some aspects of life may be so unpleasant to us that it is difficult to envision anything of perfect beauty springing forth from such soil. But the seeds are there—the problems of life *can* be transformed into expressions of beauty through correct action. This transformation does, however, require commitment, deliberate activity, love, and hard work. These are the ingredients of quiet confidence—and of detachment.

Detachment is an integral part of intelligent evolutionary unfoldment. It is the process of bringing order out of chaos, of finding beauty where only difficulty once reigned. It makes whole that which has been imperfect—the human personality—so that we may radiate forth purity, benevolence, and illumination, touching all mankind.

THE DISCIPLINE OF DETACHMENT

There are a number of ways the discipline of detachment can be learned. It can be part of a regular program of meditative growth, in which we use mental techniques to break the bonds of our attachments and purify the personality. Or, it can be integrated into the lessons of day-to-day living, as we work to overcome physical attachments by observing a sensible regimen of diet and health, emotional attachments by curbing desires and harmful feelings such as anger, jealousy, or fear, and mental attachments by increasing our service to our fellow man. Athletics, for example, often teach a youngster the practical rudiments of detachment, through emphasis on training rules, good sportsmanship, and teamwork. (On the other hand, the fanaticism often associated with sports can negate these positive accomplishments.) Detachment can also be approached as an object of philosophic contemplation; in so doing, we reflect upon the idea that our life expression consists of both a personality and an inner essence. The personality is imperfect, transient, and prone to error; the soul is perfect, immortal, and acts intelligently. As a result, we come to recognize the desirability of shifting the focus of our life from the personality to the soul. And, as we become more and more convinced of the substantiality of our contemplations, the conclusions we draw gradually seep into active expression in our daily life. Finally, there is also the mystical approach to detachment, in which we transform the attachments of the personality into attachments to God.

The fastest way to reach the state of detachment, however, is to combine the best features of each of these approaches. Any genuine attempt at detachment should be structured around a daily practice of meditation, should be expressed in the discipline of an active life, and should include periodic times for contemplation and reassessment. The meditative work should be primarily devoted to making contact with the inner being and to learning to express the inner qualities of love, wisdom, strength, and courage in every facet of daily life. Then, this work should be reinforced by changing our behavior, attitudes, and habits as necessary to make detachment and self discipline actual realities in our life. Finally, periods of contemplation and review are important, for they permit us to take stock of what we have accomplished and what the next step should be. This review keeps the process of detachment forward moving and vitalized. It also helps keep us focussed upon the *constant influence* of the inner self, which insures that the changes in the personality made during the practice of detachment are made wisely.

The best way to pursue detachment is quietly, with common sense. Zealousness and fanaticism are out of place, for they lead to self abuse and establish attachments of their own that are hard to break. It is also important not to pursue detachment with false motives—for example, to impress others of our holiness or spiritual accomplishment. Since quiet confidence is one of the characteristics of detachment, we must strive always to work at learning detachment in a quiet way, rationally and sensibly.

The discipline of detachment also requires a certain degree of flexibility, for as we mature and gain freedom from our attachments, the methods of detachment must be adapted to keep pace with our progress. In the earlier stages of the work, we are most naturally concerned with detaching from the objects and situations of our immediate sphere of life. Later, we must broaden our horizons and likewise detach ourself from group thought-forms—national fears, religious prejudices, and the mass mind.

Whether we are striving to detach from a single person, an object, a doctrine, or a worldwide thought-form such as fear, there are five stages to the process. These stages overlap—we usually work on all five simultaneously—and should not be thought of so much as sequential steps as goals to be reached. Only three of the five stages involve withdrawal from personality-formed attachments. The other two deal with the progressive development of the expression of the qualities of the inner self. The five stages are:

1. Detachment from negativity, both emotional and mental. This is usually the first step of detachment for everybody, as we try to rise above and dominate whatever hurts us, causes us pain, and produces suffering in our life. In this stage we break the bond of emotional attachments such as fears, worries, hatreds, jealousies, and lusts, and mental attachments such as prejudices, crystallized ideas, and false premises. Anyone with a smattering of self knowledge can recognize the major negative attachments in his life, and thus these become (and rightly so) the primary target for the practice of detachment. The goal of this stage is increased efficiency in daily life and relief from stress.

2. Development of the ability to love the person or the situation which is expressing the negativity described in stage one. Often, that includes ourself—many of us do not love ourself and are quite masochistic in our attempts at detachment. This is not desirable. Nor is it necessary or desirable to become indifferent to another person while we're detaching from the negativity of our attachment to him. However, it is the common mistake most of us make in our initial attempts at detachment—and we pay the price of emotional suffering as the result. In cases of marital difficulties, for example, it is often sadly true that when one person finally manages to separate himself or herself from the negativity in the relationship, he finds that his original

love for his partner has evaporated into indifference. He no longer cares whether the marriage succeeds or fails, whether his mate has an affair or not. This is not true detachment; it is just withdrawal into a zombie-like state devoid of emotion. The remedy is to practice this second stage of detachment—the ability to love—while proceeding with the first stage. This lets us express our essential humanity more fully.

3. Detachment from *positive* attachments, both emotional and mental. Many attachments are basically good and useful to us, but we have indulged them to excess and have lost our sense of balance. Examples would include possessiveness (there is nothing wrong with owning material goods, but hoarding them is carrying a good thing too far), ultradependency upon friends and family, the need for always "being up" and "feeling good," and elitism. Detachment from these so-called positive attachments does not involve giving them up. Instead, it means restoring balance to our life by not letting the attachments control and dominate us. It is not necessary, for example, to abandon reading altogether in order to cure a compulsion to read twenty-four hours a day. It is merely necessary to adopt a reasonable habit pattern and stop being a slave to the compulsion. Thus, the goal of this third stage is to learn to use the energies of life correctly and wisely.

4. Development of the ability to use *all* instruments of the personality—the physical body, the emotions, and the mind—at their peak capacities and for the expression of the purposes and qualities of the inner self. The attachments we make tend to block the free expression of these qualities in the

personality. Thus, as we make progress in our practice of detachment, we open channels through which they can flow more freely. These energies must then be used by the personality in active expression, or they will cause severe cases of psychic constipation, which can lead to serious physical problems as well as emotional and mental disturbances (due to the built-up pressure). Hence, the physical body must be used in the work of serving others. The emotions must be used to express goodwill and compassion to all people. The mind must be used to express the illumination of the inner self in the understanding of our purpose in life. As we master this stage, the personality as a whole becomes active in the world, large or small, in which we find ourself. And we begin to act and think as the inner being acts and thinks.

5. Detachment from glamorous expectations. The subtlest kind of attachment formed by the personality—and the hardest to discern—is the attachment of naive aspiration. It is certainly worthwhile to set for ourself the goal of full contact with the inner being, but when that goal is defined by the personality (rather than the inner being), then our perspective becomes distorted. In this condition, the personality invents various erroneous ideas of what the soul is like: visions of heaven, hints of miraculous powers, and other glamorous notions. These fantasies spur us on, but in the wrong direction; they must be discarded before the practice of detachment is complete and reality fully comprehended. An active "wish life" is not what produces genuine personal growth. Personal growth is achieved as we learn progressively to express the qualities of the inner being *as they are,* not as we

fantasize them to be. Learning to identify with the soul in this way is the primary purpose of detachment. Detachment, therefore, does not put us to sleep, as some people apparently believe (those who confuse it with indifference); it wakes us up! It awakens us to our full heritage of consciousness—the consciousness of the soul. It calls us to greater activity: to the inspired expression of the soul through the responsive personality.

It is interesting to note that the goals of detachment are implicit in the steps required to reach an accomplished level of detachment. This is because the practice of detachment is a natural process, one which each of us must undertake sooner or later in order to grow and mature. The ultimate goal of anything worthwhile always lies implicit in the very first step taken—even if it cannot be clearly seen at the time.

LOOSENING ATTACHMENTS

The actual work of detachment begins with the untying of our bonds of attachment. But before rushing headlong into this activity, it is wise to take some time to separate our various attachments into two groups: positive attachments and negative attachments. Positive attachments are those ties that we like and find useful to us: they link us to people and objects and ideas that we find attractive. From the perspective of the personality, they do no harm and indeed are quite beneficial. A positive attachment might be a feeling of personal love, a sense of security, a comforting belief in a certain philosophy, a value we learned in school, pride in achievement, or many other very positive things.

By contrast, our negative attachments are those strong pulls and tugs that we have been trying to resist. In some cases, the attraction has been too great, and we have given in to temptation. In other instances, we have indeed managed to resist, but with great stress and no guarantee of continuing success. At some earlier time we probably considered this negative attachment to be desirable, but as the years have passed we have begun to realize that it is detrimental to our greater goals. A strong inhibition about sex, for example, might be useful to an unmarried, immature teenager, but if the inhibition were to remain after marriage, it would soon cause serious problems in the relationship. Thus, a once-useful attachment becomes a negative one. Fear, hatred, jealousy, lust, greed, prejudice, paranoia, and pride are other examples of negative attachments.

There is a very good reason why it is necessary to detach from positive attachments as well as negative ones: any attachment tends to control our life! The extent of this control depends only upon the strength—not the quality—of the attachment. An attachment controls the flow of our emotional and mental energies, and this means that the inner self is not in control. The attachment, positive or negative, blocks off the downflow of energy from the inner self into the personality. Thus, we operate at less than maximum efficiency in our life—often far, far less.

Let's suppose, for example, that we adhere to a certain dogmatic philosophy. It may be that this philosophy is all good and all wise, but the fact remains that we are letting its dogma dictate the manner of our thinking. Consequently, we have lost control of our mental energy—we are letting our chosen dogma do our thinking for us. We have abandoned the free will of our mind and have accepted a substitute for the higher intelligence of our inner self. Thus, we have formed a positive attachment.

We can also consider the example of being in love with another person, in the sentimental, heart-throbbing sense of the word (there is an important difference between the romantic passion we call "love" and the enduring quality of love which links all mankind at the level of the inner self). "Being in love" (a phenomenon of the personality) makes us happy, so we would definitely classify it as a positive sensation. But it nonetheless attaches us to the person we love. We surrender control of our emotional reactions to this person. As it has often been expressed in the literature of romance, we become like a marionette, with the strings of our heart manipulated by our lover. If this other person treats us well, we react happily. If not, we react with irritation, depression, or anger. In either event, the fact remains that we have abandoned control of our emotions. The attachment of passion prevents us from thinking rationally about the relationship and makes it impossible for the inner self to use our personality as a viable channel for the expression of its holistic qualities.

It is not especially hard to detach ourself from these positive attachments. As stated before, *we do not give up our association with or use of the objects of these attachments!* We do not withdraw from our relationships or abandon our beliefs or sell our cherished possessions. That would be something akin to throwing the baby out with the bath water, and contrary to common sense. After all, these attachments serve useful purposes to us. That is why they are included on the "positive" list.

Instead, we take each positive attachment and realize that it has a higher correspondence—a higher correspondence that can be found at the level of the inner being. We can safely assume that such a correspondence exists, because everything that is good and beneficial to us has its origins at the inner levels of the soul.

And so, for example, if our positive attachment is our passionate love for another person, we would simply realize that this "love" is a somewhat imperfect reflection on the personality level of the perfect love that connects all of our inner beings with one another. Or, if the positive attachment is to a certain religious doctrine, we would realize that our own inner being has an innate ability to perceive and interpret religious truths. We do not need, therefore, to trust in the questionable dogma of unenlightened theologians. We can use the dogma as a guide, but we should always let the light of our soul lead us and show us the truths we accept and believe in. This understanding is the higher correspondence to the need to believe in a specific dogma.

Having discovered (through simple reflection) the higher correspondence to our positive attachments, we can then resolve to operate more with the understanding of that higher correspondence and less with the obsession of the attachment. In this way, we loosen the bond of this positive attachment.

Thus, to deal with our romantic attachment, we would seek to become familiar with the love of the inner being and use that in place of the sentimental love of the personality. We would seek to act with love in unselfish ways—in ways that would help us express the principles of brotherhood. We would try to touch all of our loved ones and friends with this higher quality of love, in practical ways in our daily life.

Or, in our quest for truth, we would stop and question the dogmatic religious statements that we have accepted without thinking over the years. We would not proceed in a spirit of rejection, for that is unintelligent, but rather in a spirit of thoughtfulness: what does this statement really mean? What does it tell me about the nature of reality and about my role in the universe? Is this dogmatic statement an expression of truth, or a distortion of it? Throughout this questioning, thinking process, we would appeal to our own inner wisdom for guidance.

In this way, then, we can work to loosen the ties of our positive attachments: by seeing the higher correspondences to them, and by working gradually to *replace* the attachments with these higher realities—realities which are founded on universal patterns. In no instance is the object of the positive attachment destroyed—or even purged from our life. *Rather, it is being seen as a part of a larger and greater whole, and we are merely adjusting our allegiance to the whole, rather than the part.*

Such is the method for disentangling ourself from positive attachments. By contrast, the procedure for freeing ourself from our negative attachments is considerably different, as might be expected. After all, these attachments clearly work against our best interests and harm us in some way—emotionally, physically, or mentally. And so we must defuse the power of their attraction to us. While it is often not necessary or desirable to get rid of the objects of negative attachments, it certainly is necessary and desirable to neutralize their control and domination over us. A powerful tool that we can use to get started in this work is our own *creative imagination*. We can best see why this is so by briefly reviewing the way attachments are formed.

All attachments are made of either emotional or mental energy. When we first formed these attachments, we used our creative imagination to bring the energy together and form a bond from it. This use of the imagination gave the energy cohesion and pattern, and thus the bond was formed. As long as we continue to nourish the bond through repeated use of our imagination, the bond will continue. When we stop "energizing" the bond, the attachment will gradually dissolve.

An example would be a man obsessed with a fear of night. Some experience early in his life caused him to associate nighttime with unpleasantness, perhaps with terror. He then allowed his creative imagination to conjure up images of many different horrible things that could happen to him at night. In reality, it was not the night that had harmed him—nighttime is neither good nor bad, it just is. But that distinction was soon overlooked, and the man created an attachment of fear with the night. Whenever he is alone at night, his imagination recalls the memory of his fear and strengthens both the emotional and mental energy he has already invested in his fearful bond. Thus, the bond becomes quite strong over a period of years.

Since all negative attachments are constructed through the use of creative imagination, it should be obvious that this is also the ideal tool for dismantling these bonds. The key to success is twofold: having control of that creative imagination, and using it with common sense. We must therefore select images and symbols which are appropriate for the work we wish to accomplish, not images which are complicated, exotic, or strange. For safety's sake, we must shun the unusual in using our imagination.

A good symbol to represent the attachment we are seeking to dissolve is the image of a cable or thread. After all, it is a strand of energy which connects us with the object of our attachment—a living strand of emotional or mental energy. So it is a convenient image, and not the least unusual. If the attachment is emotional in nature, the cable can be visualized extruding from the area of the stomach or solar plexus; if the attachment is primarily mental, it will extrude from the throat. This strand snakes out through space and hooks around the object of our attachment—be it a person, a habit, an ideology, a material object, or a prejudice—thus linking it with us.

As these strands were originally constructed by our own creative imagination from our own emotional and mental energies, we are therefore wholly responsible for their existence. They are *not* the responsibility of the object of our attachment. (The night is not to be blamed for our fear of it!) By acknowledging our responsibility, however, we also affirm our full control over these bonds of energy. What we have attached we can now detach. We can disconnect each strand from the object or person it is hooked around. This detachment is achieved by using our creative imagination and visualizing the strand being untied at the other end. Theatrics are unnecessary: there is no need to cut or burn or bite or yank. It is best to remain completely objective throughout this process, working as much as possible from the point of view of our inner being. The inner being loves and cares for the personality and views the practice of detachment as a healing process. The more we can work with this attitude, the more successful we will be.

Thus, we envision (with focussed attention) the connection of our attachment being dissolved. Then, once the strand has been loosened in this manner, we must further imagine drawing the disconnected strand back into our aura. We are responsible for this energy and must reclaim it. This step is as easy as winding in a loose rope, but it must be done with care: as the energy is being reclaimed, it must be purified. It has been extended into the outside world for a period of time in a negative way. It would not be wholesome to draw in the negativity with the energy.

The perfect way to purify this energy is to imagine it being cleansed by the great power of the inner being. In fact, it is a good idea to think of the inner self participating actively in this whole process of loosening the negative bond—almost as if it were lovingly looking over our shoulder, guiding us and giving us inspiration.

In this way, the creative imagination can be effectively used to loosen the bonds of negative attachment that it originally created. But it must be forcefully added that loosening our attachments is just the beginning of a long process. It must be followed by strict discipline in our daily attitudes and habits, lest the attachment be quickly formed again. It would be pointless, for example, for a man with a compulsion to gamble to loosen his attachment to speculation as described, then take a trip to Las Vegas! Thus, an attitude of close surveillance must be adopted—and this surveillance must be accompanied by consistent enforcement of the ideal modes of behavior we are striving to establish. It often takes years before the force of a negative attachment can be completely neutralized—years requiring constancy of effort, commitment to our new values, and discipline. During this time we may have to repeatedly reaffirm to ourself that our identity exists independently of our attachments; we may have to repeatedly call in the power of the inner being to give us the strength and the courage to overcome the force of the negative attachment. We may have to repeatedly engage our creative imagination in loosening a bond that has once more drawn taut in spite of our best efforts, and to recall the energy back to ourself again.

Actually, the use of the creative imagination as described is symbolic of the real changes that must take place within us to achieve detachment—the change of heart, the change of attitudes, the change of approach to life. With our imaginations we can *create* new trends and new patterns of behavior, but only through dedicated hard work can we *nourish* these new patterns and cause them to grow into permanent habits of maturity.

But regardless of the effort required, it is well worthwhile, for it places us in control of the energies of our life. It gives us new insight into our true identity and the nature of our inner strength and fortitude. It gives us poise.

EXPRESSING POISE

We have learned that attachments can be loosened and eventually neutralized. But it is not enough merely to cleanse the vessel and leave it spotless. The vessel must then be used for the fulfillment of the purpose for which it was constructed. This, too, is an integral part of detachment.

In other words, the personality must become a useful channel for the expression of the qualities of the inner self. These qualities are many, but the three most closely related to the practice of detachment are love, wisdom, and courage. When we have learned to use our emotions with detachment, we express love. When we have mastered the use of the mind with detachment, the result is wisdom. And when we can regard our physical life with detachment, the expression is courage—not recklessness, but courage.

By nature, these are universal energies. They are not the property or privilege of any one individual. It is not possible, for example, to be truly wise unless that wisdom enables us to comprehend our relationship to all humanity, civilization, and the universe as a whole. Nor is there any love unless that love links us with all other members of the human race and is expressed in caring, helping, and healing. And the only genuine courage is the strength that is drawn from the universal ocean of life, knowing it to be an infinite reservoir of all we need.

Detachment is a state in which these universal energies can flow through us without being distorted into negative emotional or mental behavior, or without being diverted to selfish ends for the sole purpose of satisfying our vanity. It is *not* a state of indifference to the needs, wants, and suffering of the people around us. Quite the contrary, it is a state of active involvement in meeting the needs, wants, and suffering of these people. But because it is a state of poise, the detached person is never pulled down by these difficulties. Rather, he meets them constructively: with understanding, compassion, goodwill, and competent aid. With wisdom, love, and courage.

In practicing true detachment, we do not cleanse the vessel of our personality merely for the purpose of making us, as individuals, feel better. That is a side effect, to be sure, but not the primary purpose. Instead, the principal purpose for the practice of detachment is to learn to transmit and reflect the energies of love, wisdom, and courage into the world around us, for the improvement and benefit of all. Thus, it may be helpful to examine each of these qualities in greater detail.

Love is the energy which links all mankind at the level of the inner self. At this inner level, its expression is perfect, but this is not true on the personality level, where it is often colored and distorted by our attachments of jealousy, possessiveness, malice and selfishness. Thus, an important part of the practice of detachment is learning to express love perfectly in our daily life.

Many people are confused about the meaning of love, because it is so often thought of as an emotion, rather than a universal energy. Love is commonly believed, for example, to be a personal possession that we can either express or withhold, depending upon our mood and whim at the time. This is an illusion based on popular myths. In reality, love belongs to the universe, not to any one individual. Therefore, it is a quality we express because we are citizens of the universe, not because we like someone.

Some people confuse love with their attachments; they think that love enslaves them to other people. This, too, is an illusion. Love is an energy freely used by the poised, detached person to reach others, to teach others, to help others, and to heal others. Love liberates us from the prisons of selfishness and pettiness that we have erected in our life.

Being an energy, love can only be known by us if we make the effort to express it. It must be used. This requires more than mere intellectual reflection. It demands active work. Love is living, flowing, moving. It must be woven into every moment of our daily life—every act we perform, every sentence we speak, every plan we formulate. It must be cultivated in our attitudes and behavior. It must become a constant expression of our humanity—without conditions or reservations attached.

Because love is a universal energy, it must be used by us to bring ourself into closer ties with *all people,* not just a chosen few. This is not an easy requirement for most of us to fulfill, for we still have our enemies, our prejudices, and our dislikes. But a universal energy cannot be known in part—it must be known in full.

One of the best descriptions of how love is expressed perfectly through the vessel of the human personality was given us by Paul in 1 Corinthians 13. "Love is patient and kind; love is not jealous or boastful; it is not arrogant or rude. Love does not insist on its own way; it is not irritable or resentful;

it does not rejoice at wrong, but rejoices in the right. Love bears all things, believes all things, hopes all things, endures all things." Thus, to learn detachment, we must become patient and kind ourself; we must express gentleness and respect to all others. We must become humble and generous, affectionate and tolerant. We must be steadfast and inspired by the ideal of love itself. Nothing less will suffice.

Wisdom, too, must be expressed by us if we are to practice detachment. Wisdom is not the same as knowledge; many people have acquired a vast amount of knowledge without any real measure of wisdom. Like love, wisdom is a quality of the inner being. It is the ability to perceive accurately and fully the meaning of events, the purpose of our life, and our relationship with the rest of the universe.

Above all, the undetached person lacks wisdom. He has not learned to use his mind effectively to gain clear insights into what happens in his life. Instead, he worries and frets. When he has a specific problem, he turns it over and over in his mind until he reaches the point where it is frustrating just to think about it. He broods over every detail, and yet none of this so-called "thinking" helps solve the problem. He understands *how* the problem affects him but has no inkling of *why* it is a problem. Nor does he have any concept of what purpose this difficulty is serving in his life—what lessons he is learning, what character strengths he is building, and what changes in behavior and attitude would solve it. He does not comprehend the inner meanings.

To express wisdom, we must stop thinking as the personality thinks (with its multiple fears, doubts, and frustrations) and start thinking as the inner self thinks. We must let the aggravating details fade into the background and concentrate instead on getting insight into the total picture—the total picture as seen and understood by the soul.

How does the inner self think? *It thinks with total comprehension.* As strange as it may seem to those of us who are only accustomed to thinking as the personality thinks, the inner self can concentrate on an aspect of life and gain complete insight into it. This process is much like examining an object in brilliant sunlight. Nothing is hidden in obscurity. Everything is revealed.

Of course, very few of us have mastered the ability to think in this way. But we can all dedicate ourselves to learning to think with this kind of wisdom—with this kind of poise. Learning to express wisdom is a process that takes a long time to develop, but with patience and application, it can be achieved.

First, we must learn to spot the times when our thinking becomes confused. Confusion is like a shadow cast upon the object we are trying to examine, blocking off the sunlight. As long as the shadow remains, we cannot see clearly. But in truth, this shadow is most often our own: our own emotional prejudices and preconceived notions, our own faulty habits, our own shortsightedness. Many people are blind to the fact that they create their own confusion. So, the first step is to overcome our blindness and recognize confusion, worrying, and doubting when they arise.

Of course, recognizing blind spots in our thinking is just a preliminary step. The next one is to learn to think carefully about these areas of confusion. We may not be able yet to think with wisdom, but we certainly can learn to think carefully—it just requires practice. This means not letting our emotions or desires creep in; it means thinking objectively. Moreover, it means thinking patiently. Whenever an idea does pop into our mind, we must carefully examine it to discern its meaning, purpose, and relevance to us. First, we must try to understand the idea as an entity unto itself—its origin, its quality, its potency, and its basic meaning. Next, we must evaluate whether or not this idea can help *us*. Does it shed fresh light on the problem at hand, or does it merely rehash old details that we've churned over and over hundreds of times? Has it added to our wisdom and our ability to act skillfully in this situation? What is the purpose of this situation? What is the real self trying to achieve?

If the new idea does not meet these criteria, then it must be set aside, and we must seek out a more relevant one. Then, when yet another idea comes, we must once again patiently examine it to determine if it gives us the insight we are seeking.

This is careful thinking. It may seem laborious, but we must understand that there are no short cuts to enlightenment. If this formula for careful thinking is patiently applied, it will gradually clean out the cobwebs of thought that have accumulated in the subconscious during many years of careless thinking. As this cleansing occurs, it then lets the wisdom of the soul pour through, just as sunshine can pour through unimpeded if there is no object blocking it, causing shadows.

Courage is another important expression of detachment. It, too, is a quality of the inner self—and the natural result of understanding that the universe is an orderly place and supplies all our needs. This may seem like a trivial statement, but nonetheless it contains the clue to the significance of courage.

We are often afraid to face the situations of our life. We become attached to a need for comfort and security and place these above the values of the inner self. We fear the loss of possessions, we fear the loss of friends, we fear embarrassment and the loss of social standing, we fear the loss of life. But fear is one of the most insidious of all attachments; it thwarts the ability of the inner being to use the personality as a channel for expression. As is true of all attachments, such fear is an illusion. The personality was created by the inner being and will be preserved and protected by the inner being so that it can be used to fulfill its purposes. It will be nourished and sustained by the universal forces of the ocean of life. Thus, fear is groundless. But as long as we trouble ourself with fear, we will actually *attract* the very conditions we fear. And we will strengthen our attachment to our misplaced notions of comfort and security.

Obviously, such conditions do not lead to the development of poise. Consequently, part of the practice of detachment must include the expression of courage—a courage that is infused into every part of our life. We must use this courage to face difficult problems with steadfastness and optimism; we must use it to hold fast to our convictions and deeper purposes in the face of opposition; we must use it to retain perspective during moments of seeming failure or defeat.

The expression of courage is not difficult—*if* we comprehend the statement made earlier that it is "the natural result of understanding that the universe is an orderly place and supplies all our needs."

Comprehending this statement means *relying* on the ocean of life for all our needs—not just glibly saying that we rely on it, but truly opening ourself up to the vast energies and strengths within it and using them. Relying on the ocean of life is nothing like leaning on a crutch; it is more like feasting at a banquet. But courage comes only from practical experience in using these energies and seeing how they do indeed support all life—including ours.

These, then, are the expressions of love, wisdom, and courage. They are an important, indispensable part of the practice of detachment, for as our use of them grows, so does our ability to operate in life as the inner being operates. Combined, these energies manifest as poise, the stability which comes only when we fuse the universal qualities of the soul with the activities of the personality.

THE UNIVERSE RESPONDS

So far, we have been considering what steps must be taken by the personality to achieve detachment. This process is twofold: the personality must disengage itself from the positive and negative attachments that have enslaved it, and it must actively express the energies of love, wisdom, and courage in its daily life. Then, as this work progresses, it produces a redefinition of who we are: whereas once we thought of ourself in terms of our attachments, we come to consider ourself in terms of the inner being. Whereas once we sought out sensation and valued it, we come to understand the nature and meaning of consciousness. This redefinition, then, sets the stage for the inner being to respond to the work and the accomplishments of the personality.

As stated earlier, the personality is not alone. It is the creation of an inner self, and is designed to fulfill the purposes of the inner self. It therefore follows that the personality does not do the work of detachment alone. It must *initiate* the effort and remain constant in its aspiration, but once the practice of detachment has begun, the inner being participates actively in every phase of it. In the earlier stages it works "behind the scenes," unperceived by the personality. Later, its constant presence and inspiration become noticed.

The work of the personality is to raise the level of its awareness. The response of the inner being to that effort is to raise the *quality of substance* of the personality: the physical, emotional, and mental substance of which the personality is composed. In undeveloped and undetached personalities, this substance is quite coarse; in more advanced and spiritual people, it is refined and of high quality.

The implications of this idea are worth reflecting on. As the quality of the energy of our personality is raised, so is the quality of our life. Good health, serene emotions, poise, and clear thinking become natural expressions. And there are other rewards for the personality, too: freedom from stress and adverse sensation, a greater sense of maturity, and the capacity to face difficult situations calmly.

But the inner being responds in other ways as well. For example, as the personality masters the practice of detachment, it commands an increasing degree of attention from the inner being. The inner self sees that the personality is becoming a useful channel for expression, and thus it starts to use its personality in a more active way. The personality begins to share in the work of the universe—participating, creating, and healing. Like a house that has stood vacant for many years but is at last occupied by its owner, the personality steadily becomes more useful. The mind is illumined; the emotions become radiant with love and compassion. Purpose is fulfilled, and that brings with it a tremendous reward of satisfaction and joy.

The soul can finally be assured of the cooperation of the personality. It can therefore work with a much freer hand through this channel. In earlier times it had to be careful, lest it burn out the personality by overloading the circuit. Now, it can greatly increase the potency of the personality and thus achieve a much fuller expression. It can operate without restraint, *but on the personality level as well as on its own*.

Not all responses to the achievement of detachment come from the inner being, however. There is also a response from the universe itself, and it is a great help in our daily life. As we gain expertise in relying on the ocean of life, for example, and truly open ourself to its goodness, we steadily gain more access to the universal stockpiles of support and sustenance. We become the beneficiary of more good fortune in our life, the recipient of more kindnesses and help from other people. Good opportunities flow forth from the sustaining heart of life itself. Nothing is handed to us on a silver platter; we must still work to convert these good opportunities into meaningful achievements. But the obstacles to success have been removed; the right things happen with right timing.

These are benefactions of the universe—and the natural consequences of the practice of detachment. And as we become aware of this universal response to our efforts, we gain a new perspective on the importance of detachment. Whereas once detachment was a means of avoiding distress and confusion, it now becomes a means for transforming our life so it becomes *a working alliance with the universe!* Whereas once we dedicated ourself to our own personal unfoldment, we now re-dedicate ourself—to universal evolution.

This, then, is the freedom of detachment. No longer a slave to our attachments, we become a citizen of the universe: the true scientist, the true participant in life, the true servant of God.

FINDING
MEANING IN LIFE

A HIDDEN MESSAGE

Every one of us who attempts to find meaning and relevance in the vast number of events in life faces the same problem: the individual events, by themselves, are like tiny pieces in a complicated puzzle. They make sense only when we realize that each piece is part of an extensive panorama that must be viewed from a more distant perspective. Then we can readily see how the pieces fit together, and why, and the beauty of the total picture. We discover that there *is* a pattern to human events which, when discerned, gives insight and direction to our experiences.

Finding this pattern of purpose is not as difficult as it may seem. We must simply learn where to look and how to evaluate the data. We will fail only if we refuse to look—or if we look without seeing. If we let that happen, then we may perchance stumble into the trap of believing that there is no meaning to life. There are, after all, people who have been victimized by this devastating illusion of chaos. But the belief in the meaninglessness of life is just that: an *illusion*. It is the product of thinking without understanding—or not thinking at all. And it can only be perpetuated by an incredible intellectual myopia that militantly ignores the constant signals of meaning that arise from the circumstances of life.

We need not be blinded by this illusion. As we move through our life, we are constantly "handed" messages which contain the hidden insight we seek. Not knowing how to decode these messages, we often overlook their significance; we do not put them together, and so we miss the unfolding story. We can, however, learn to recognize these messages and read them.

To do this, it's necessary to start with fundamentals. After all, it is ever the general which gives significance to the specifics, just as the tree gives meaning to the leaves attached to it. Thus, we must seek those insights that will provide a proper context for our understanding. We must not be distracted by looking for meaning in the wrong places.

The fundamental premise of learning to read the hidden messages of meaning in life is that we must first look for this significance in the nature of our relationship with the universe. It is in our connections with each other, with humanity and civilization as a whole, and with a deeper, invisible dimension of life that we discover the vital purpose and meaning that makes our experiences worthwhile. Just as the whole landscape gives significance and relevance to the tree and the tree to the leaves, so, too, does the basic order of the universe give meaning to our personal existence.

This *universal connection* is as real and as relevant as the sun in the sky. The sun shines for all of us whether we like it or not, whether we see it or not, whether we understand it or not, and whether we accept it or not. In the same way, the pervasive order of the universe powerfully influences each individual life form in that universe—whether or not it is recognized, accepted, or understood. The collective life purpose in the whole universe sustains and regulates the individual parts within it. And so, to comprehend the significance of our individual life expression, we will have to understand something of the nature of this universal connection.

Only part of a tree's significance, however, is derived from its relationship to its surrounding environment. Its own individual unfoldment of the characteristics of its species is important as well. Just so, each of us has another vital connection with life that adds to our meaning. This is the *transcendent connection*—our individual relationship with our innermost self. This innermost self is a center of consciousness formed of our deepest humanitarian impulses and qualities. It constantly seeks to overshadow the peripheral and ephemeral activities of our personality, and thus sends us many messages in an attempt to apprise us of the fullest meaning of our life. It is the seat of our conscience, the home of that "still small voice" which speaks to us in silence. It is the core of our humanity and the springboard for our dynamic will to exist.

These two dimensions, the universal and transcendent connections, may seem unduly mysterious and perhaps unimportant to many. But this is only because most of us are unaccustomed to looking beyond the superficial joys and sorrows that fill our lives. The clutter of day-to-day events in their seemingly endless succession tends to hypnotize us into paying excessive attention to them. The glamour or pain of these experiences blinds us to their significance. Their apparent urgency prevents us from pausing long enough to perceive the real but invisible thread of destiny which connects them in meaningful patterns.

Our obsessive reactions to these events and our self-centered, petty concerns can easily become hindrances to the accurate understanding of meaning in life. The more we become engulfed by them, the less we pay attention to everything else that is happening in the universe.

Indeed, whenever we become trapped in hindrances, they end up seeming more real than the messages they hide—just as the leaves on a tree seem more real to a nearsighted ant than the landscape surrounding it. We fall prey to perceiving confusion and disorder in life, when with clearer vision we could see the underlying orderliness—as well as the principles that govern orderly change, in our life and in the universe. However, this distressful situation need not prevail if we recognize the illusion of these hindrances. Fortunately, proving that we do not live in a capricious universe is not difficult. After all, if we stand still, life quickly passes us by, for it has a momentum of its own. Or, if we strain with a mighty effort to resist the invisible order of life's phenomena, our personal will and resolve are eventually broken by the far greater power of the universe. Life, therefore, has a reality, purpose, and order independent of our own personal existence.

Fate is not fickle; our destiny is not clouded in chaos. If we sometimes think it is, then this is just the result of not paying attention to the hidden message of our life. To correct this situation, all that we need to do is rediscover the missing elements: our link with the universal connection (which gives meaning to the events in our life) and our link with the transcendent connection (which gives meaning to our reactions to those events).

Our hidden message is one of wisdom and love. To comprehend it, we must read it with insight and reverence. It is not possible to see it or understand it as long as we are blinded by defensiveness, anger, or ignorance. We must read it, therefore, with self honesty, an aspiration to honor the nobility within life, a willingness to sacrifice, and a resolve to confront opportunity and responsibility with compassion and integrity.

The underlying theme of this message is the same for all of us, as it is written by the Creative Intelligence of the universe. Furthermore, it is a theme which is relevant for all of us, as it is rooted in the ultimate purpose of the collective human races and their accumulated culture. Thus, it is known by our own innermost essence, and it has been interpreted by this inner self so that it can be understood and read by our own conscious mind.

Of course, the specific message read by each of us varies somewhat, for it originates in the events and happenings—the basic script—of our individual life. But when we read with understanding, the message reveals to us the hidden purpose that is the superstructure for all that we do and all that happens to us. And, by grasping this inner purpose, we then come to understand the significance of these events.

Even though this inner purpose is intangible, invisible, and abstract, there are many clues that we can use in deciphering it. Just as we can estimate the shape of an object by studying the shadow it casts, so we can discern much about this hidden message by studying our personal experiences and seeing them as symbolic "shadows" cast by the intangible principles of life. Thus, for example, we can look to the relationship between our *superficial reactions* and our *dominant tendencies*. Our personalities react to circumstances; they are torn by whim and are often confused by our emotions. They are intimidated by people and events. Our character, on the other hand, is the invisible pattern that molds the personality in the first place and determines the nature of its actions and reactions, its impulses and responses. If the character is weak, the personality will be afflicted by difficulties and strife. If the character is strong, the personality will express competence and achievement, and will register satisfaction. Consequently, much can be deduced about the nature of the inner character by a study of the events and reactions of the personality, and this is an important clue to finding meaning in life.

But to fully comprehend this hidden message, we must do more than just study the implications of our own life. We must study the implications of *all of life* as well. Since the theme of the message is originally written by the Creative Intelligence of the universe, we must recognize and consider the principles with which it operates.

This is the Intelligence that dominates the whole human race and all other life forms, impelling us to respond to Its principles and laws. It is known by many names but is of one quality. Whether or not It is recognized, accepted, or understood, Its very heartbeat is the life force which courses through all things manifest. Strong men may fear It, the weak may grovel before It, and the devious inevitably try to deny Its existence. But without some understanding of It, our hidden message cannot be interpreted. Not only would we be missing some vital pieces to the puzzle, we would actually be missing the entire picture! For this impersonal Creative Intelligence is the inherent will to exist within all created things.

The intelligent person knows this truth instinctively and seeks to cooperate with this dominant force in life. The ignorant person will insist that It does not exist at all, since he or she has not found it. But the price that is paid for such ignorance is the inability to comprehend the meaning of life. To blind people, fate will always seem blind. Every unpleasantness, disappointment, and sacrifice will seem purposeless and cruel. And so these blind people will react adversely to such events, because they seem to be punishments for unknown crimes—or meaningless events that interfere with their blind desires and expectations. As negative reaction is thus piled on top of negative reaction, the blindness increases. More and more attention is directed at avoiding adversity and seeking escape, and less and less is spent in searching for meaning in life and in enduring the struggle to resolve that adversity.

Obviously, the intelligent approach to life is to discern and then cooperate with the invisible order of the universe. When we do, we avoid the devastating consequences of opposing irresistible forces. And we begin to see that fate is something that dwells in our innermost self—not in the apparent caprice of external events. Far from being a punishment, it serves our best interests.

This realization gives us new direction. With *wisdom* we learn to discern what the life within us wants to do. With *love* we harness our innermost humanitarian impulses and qualities. With *patience* we adapt our character and personality to harmonize with our inner purposes. And more and more we learn to read the clues of the hidden message—and understand them.

While the consequences of ignorance are confusion and despair, the consequences of cooperating with Life Itself are greater success and fulfillment, and more meaningful responses to our past and present. For as we intelligently clean out the clutter of our self-imposed hindrances, we unleash new powers from the innermost spirit—powers that can be used to accelerate the development of our character and personal expression.

DUTY AND DISCIPLINE

One of the most important principles which governs life is the Law of Consequences. Briefly, this law states that our actions of today will produce logical consequences in the future, and that the events which unfold in the present are the natural consequences of our actions in the past. Thus, this law correlates our present with both the past and the future; correctly understood, it reveals a consistent thread running throughout all episodes of our life.

The Law of Consequences applies to all levels of our activity: mental and emotional as well as physical. It produces two kinds of phenomena in our life: rewards and discipline. When we live up to our duty and purpose by expressing our humanity in successful achievement, then we receive rewards: opportunities for greater accomplishment, deeper friendships, new talents, and a strengthened character. But when we ignore or fail in our duty to be responsible, helpful, and mature, then the consequence is a repetition of the difficulty, so that our weaknesses can be more clearly defined and we can once more work on overcoming them. In other words, such failure triggers events and individual reactions which make discipline possible.

This is, however, self discipline. The standards of skill and humanity used in measuring success and failure are inherent in the Creative Intelligence of the universe, but the judgment of our individual performance is made by our own innermost self (*not* the conscious mind with its manifold imperfections). Thus, through the use of the Law of Consequences, our own inner being maintains balance and order in our life—much as the Creative Intelligence uses its basic principles to maintain a constant state of order and balance in the universe.

The fullness of this law as the hidden regulator of our life cannot be seen within the span of just a few years, however. Some types of actions do lead to immediate or prompt compensation, of course: competent work often leads to rapid promotion, for example, just as chronic neglect of business responsibilities usually leads to hasty demotion or dismissal. But it is not uncommon that achievements and acts of goodwill go seemingly unrewarded and that acts of deceit, malice, and incompetence go seemingly unexposed. Similarly, many events of our life seem to come to us without prior antecedent—strokes of good fortune or episodes of great trauma, embarrassment, or danger.

Such conditions are not inconsistent with the Law of Consequences, which operates smoothly and efficiently regardless of the inability of the conscious mind to keep track of the details, the pluses and the minuses. The working out of appropriate rewards and disciplines is a complicated affair, often taking many years. But the universe is not in a hurry, even though we sometimes are.

Quite simply, the short span of a single personality is often insufficient for the full working out of just compensation. There are always loose threads left untied, and these must wait for future existences. Just so, no one lifetime starts from scratch in terms of its experiences: it builds on the events, the skills, and the livingness of earlier existences. These form the basis for the rewards and disciplines which seem to evolve without obvious antecedent during any given life.

While unknown to the conscious mind, which is limited by a memory veil to the affairs of the current personality, the record of our past accomplishment and our future consequences *is* known to our unconscious mind. It includes the good, the bad, and the indifferent, plus our reactions to them and to life in general. Every facet of our humanity is recorded: our skills, achievements, and maturity, as well as our imperfections and failures. This unconscious memory, however, is more than a dusty record that makes interesting reading—it is a major influence on the quality of our life and personality. It is the source of our strengths and weaknesses, our wisdom and our incompetence. At its higher levels, this unconscious record is filled with our accumulated nobility, wisdom, and compassion. The lower regions, conversely, are filled with the accumulated toxins of indiscretions, resentments, fears, ignorant habits, and the like.

In short, the unconscious mind retains the essence of our previous experiences—in other lives and also in other dimensions unknown to us consciously. At the end of our current lifetime, it will retain a record of unresolved conflict and unrewarded achievement, so that they may be justly compensated in the future. In this way, the long arm of Universal Order reaches into successive lives and times when our conscious mind has no recollection of the original experiences. This permits the inner self to create conditions that are more appropriate for inducing correct behavior—or for rewarding past merit.

Thus, although a strong person may *seem* to escape his or her fate on occasion, it is only a temporary reprieve until a more refined compensation can be arranged. The universe cannot be mocked.

Of course, this understanding of the Law of Consequences is founded on a recognition of the principle of rebirth. While some people react with hysteria to this principle, it is nonetheless true that rebirth is just as common and as inevitable as death. It is unfortunate that it is death that receives the greater emphasis in our culture, just as it is unfortunate that disappointment and frustration in daily life receive more attention than joy and achievement.

Rebirth is a process that affects not just the body but the whole personality—not just once a lifetime but daily, if we persevere. Whenever we purify and enlighten our mind and emotions to some degree, the personality is reborn. Indeed, any expansion of consciousness is a form of rebirth.

Thus, rebirth is meant to be a continuous occurrence—and to some degree, it usually is. And the fact that this continuous process includes physical rebirth is only a logical result of the evolutionary principles of consciousness. To fully understand this concept, therefore, we must consider more than just the limited space of one lifetime. The phenomenon of rebirth is a matter that dates from uncountable millenia in our planet's past and will stretch into a very distant future.

It may seem unfair to some that the conscious mind is denied full knowledge of the past events that have set the stage for a current lifetime. But this "limitation" is a part of rebirth—and a great advantage. Rather than being unfair, it lets the personality start anew with fresh vigor and hope, instead of the same restrictive frustrations and resentments. Moreover, it must be understood that the personality is the growing tip of our evolving character. It is not able to be an adequate vehicle for the totality of our undivided consciousness, except in the rarest of circumstances.

It must also be understood that successive lifetimes are not just repetitions of an unchanging, static script. Each life has its own purpose and flavor, its own degree of specialization. Thus, many remembrances from earlier lives would be irrelevant and interfere with the purposes of the present.

Therefore, prior to each lifetime, the inner essence reviews the past records and the current opportunities for progress. Then, in accordance with applicable universal laws, it chooses the major work to be attempted. The bulk of this projected work is carefully designed to complement the resources of our character. In other words, our inner being uses the wisdom and skills that we have nurtured in prior lives to shape the opportunities and responsibilities of the coming one. Likewise, it makes plans to correct the imperfections of character left over from earlier times.

Sometimes the inner being bargains for more than the personality is willing to bear. Yet, the challenge is set down in the hope that significant progress will be made. The inner being invests itself in life in order to fulfill definite purposes. It repeatedly reappears in physical forms, working in accordance with the Law of Consequences, until it reaches its full potential for manifesting the ideal of Creative Intelligence.

Fullness of purpose, however, can only be understood within the context of the evolution of all humanity—and the universe itself. Yet these are dimensions so vast that they are difficult to comprehend. Indeed, it is this *vastness* which inhibits our recollections of earlier existences and creates a memory veil. And so, the personality is often confused about the meaning of life's events. It is apparently blocked from the direct knowledge of its purpose in life—as well as its capacity to fulfill it.

Fortunately, this barrier is only a partial one—it never blocks out complete knowledge of purpose. Because the sustaining life force which vivifies the body and personality is conditioned by our inner essence, automatic guidance steadily flows into the personality. The conscious mind, of course, is unaware of this automatic guidance—but this lack of awareness merely keeps it from interfering in matters it does not comprehend.

There is great wisdom in this form of "handicap." Just as the athlete lifts weights to build strong muscles, so must the average person struggle in partial ignorance to find the way as best he can. The process of trial and error is *designed to help us* acquire perceptive senses, make accurate observations, deduce appropriate principles of action and patterns of conduct, separate worthwhile insights from trivial details, and accumulate skill and wisdom. One seed may reproduce itself into thousands of its kind eventually, but it is only the sturdiest of the seed that will survive and flourish. Human growth occurs in similar fashion. While an automaton might be more efficient, real growth would not be possible—there would be no new input. But the human being who stumbles through error and hardship eventually learns—and grows.

Thus, whenever we find life perplexing we should pause to wonder about the hidden consequences of our actions and to inquire what distant purpose is being served at the moment. Much of this can be learned by studying the consequences of duty and discipline in our life—and in the universe. While complete knowledge of these inner purposes is rarely achieved, we can nonetheless develop a partial, intuitive perception. We can logically speculate about the nature of these purposes and draw conclusions based on the events in our life and our responses to them. To do less is to waste much experience and to wander about in eternal confusion.

THE ROOTS OF DESTINY

When the inner being chooses the basic conditions of a lifetime prior to creating a new personality, it assembles a package of circumstances, attitudes, opportunities, and problems that can be labeled the "fate" or "destiny" of the coming life. As we have seen, these choices fall into two categories: duty and discipline. The duty—sometimes known as "dharma"—is designed to cause us to make use of our human resources and qualities through constructive work. The discipline—sometimes known as "karma"—is structured to force us to build our character through the struggle of overcoming carefully selected adversities. The soul makes its choices for both duty and discipline after surveying the events of earlier lives—the trends of dharma and karma. Thus, our "destiny" is not an arbitrary fiat imposed on our individual will; quite the contrary, it is a decision we make for ourself, and it is an integral part of our continuous evolution and life expression.

These choices are made in accordance with universal law, which is known to the inner being through the Universal Connection. Thus, the principles of growth, expression, and discipline are applied equally to all. However, within this uniform structure, each of us *is* an individual. We have each reacted to opportunity, limitation, stress, and success throughout the eons in individual ways. Consequently, there has evolved enormous diversity within the human family, and this diversity accounts for the inequality of life circumstances which is so easily observed. This factor must be kept in mind in understanding the roots of destiny. Because each of us varies in our experiences, skills, wisdom, mistakes, and indiscretions, each inner being naturally selects different opportunities and problems to manage.

These differences can be seen in the conditions of birth, the type of parents, the quality of social and economic circumstances, religion, and other factors. All of these conditions are carefully picked by the inner being to fit most suitably its overall needs for growth and expression—for duty and discipline. The major events of a coming lifetime are also designed in like fashion—marriage, school, important friendships, occupational opportunities, and even "lucky breaks" and "accidents."

This, then, is the general mechanism used by the inner being in creating a personality. The more we appreciate and comprehend the value of this process, the more we prepare ourself for the task of intelligently analyzing the nature of our birth conditions and the major events in our life. That evaluation, in turn, will enable us to determine for ourself the general trends of duty and discipline influencing us. Armed with that knowledge, we will then be able to act with maturity and wisdom in the future. We will be more "at one" with the purpose of our unfolding fate.

If we pursue these insights with sufficient wisdom and patience, we will eventually develop the skill of being able to anticipate the consequences of our actions—a most useful tool in the art of living. To achieve this ability, however, we must thoroughly understand the Law of Consequences—that every mental, emotional, verbal, or physical act is followed by a reaction which *compensates* for the original act. Harmful acts cause reactions that are destructive to the victim—and self-destructive to the person performing them. Benevolent and generous acts, performed in a responsible manner, cause responses of reward and good fortune.

Of course, the nature of the compensation will vary depending on the intensity of the action and the state of our indebtedness to life. An act of generosity performed by a usually miserly or hostile person will draw a different compensation than the same act performed by a habitually generous individual. The miser would receive a cancellation of part of his accumulated debt of selfishness, rather than an overt reward. The generous person, on the other hand, would be abundantly rewarded — although not necessarily in kind. The giver of money might, for example, receive good luck, many fine friends, and always enough material supply to sustain life comfortably. The giver of compassion and affection might receive greater opportunity and good fortune, as well as kindness.

The exact accounting under the Law of Consequences may seem obscure and puzzling, unless we realize two points. First, reward and discipline must often be deferred until subsequent lives. After all, if someone is on a mission to learn humility, faith, and perseverance, he may well encounter repeated unfairness and unkindness. But until the lesson is completely learned, it may not be possible to reward him for the gains achieved, lest it interfere with the overall purpose. And so the compensation for acquiring these qualities may have to wait for a future life, when he will indeed receive better treatment. Similarly, the cunning person who artfully avoids his just deserts would hardly be receptive to discipline without changing his attitude. Thus, he may have to wait until a subsequent life, when reduced circumstances and the constant threat of being deceived by others *can* change his thinking.

Second, proper conduct and achievement are less important than the *need to learn to do the right thing*. In other words, the evolution of consciousness is more important than the events which stimulate that growth. Goodwill and honest effort are more valuable than "putting on a good front" or conventional "niceness." But because of this factor, strange circumstances often come to us as *training maneuvers* designed to develop our skills in living. Although these events, being somewhat unpleasant as a rule, may well seem unjustified to us when they occur, they nonetheless serve the hidden purpose of forcing us to develop some special talent, quality, or type of knowledge—which, once we have developed it, we are very glad to possess. (By fully understanding this idea, we can get a glimpse into the truth that mercy is inherent in the universe.)

Typically, these training maneuvers relate to some tendency in our past. If we are a hypochondriac in one life, we will develop genuine sickness and disability in a future one. If irresponsible, we end up trapped in circumstances which compel the pursuit of duty and prevent us from leaning on others. We are therefore forced to become more self sufficient. In like fashion, the malicious gossip eventually falls victim to slander; the boor is offended by someone even more rude than he. The bigot becomes the victim of someone else's wrath and prejudice.

And so it goes until the lesson is learned: until we recognize our inadequacy and correct it. The hypochondriac must realize that sickness is truly unpleasant and that feigning it is an error. The rude person continues suffering rudeness until he finds it unreasonable and unpardonable—and desists in his own rudeness. The bigot is discriminated against until he discovers that bigotry is a source of great suffering—and becomes tolerant. In this way, these training maneuvers instruct us that it is wrong to engage in such acts of omission or commission. We acquire heartfelt understanding through direct experience—a much better teaching device than mere platitudes and moral precepts.

Recognizing the error of certain attitudes is only one half of the purpose of these training maneuvers, however. They are also designed to develop positive qualities of consciousness, such as a strong aspiration for physical health, considerate and compassionate treatment of others, honesty, diligence, good manners, and open-mindedness. Indeed, the unfoldment of humanistic qualities is the underlying purpose for such adverse circumstances and is a process that can be traced over many lives.

Of course, the severity of our training maneuvers will always depend upon the nature of the indiscretion or wrong that prompted them. The overt criminal, for example, will be robbed of material goods, family, health, and contentment. The mother who abandons her children for grossly selfish reasons will perhaps find herself orphaned in a future life and neglected in times of crisis. But minor indiscretions will merit far less severe compensation for most people.

In spite of all these considerations, there still remain some puzzling paradoxes which defy explanation, unless we also realize that the inner selves of well experienced (and therefore advanced) individuals will eventually choose to develop competence and strength of character far beyond the norm. In such cases, the inner being will arrange training maneuvers that will be more difficult and complicated than is customary. And, the adversity and struggle may be far worse as well. In fact, if we were to judge on an evaluation of adversity alone, we might not be able to distinguish between the hardened criminal and the nearly enlightened individual.

These two types of people do differ, however. When great crisis engulfs the advanced person, he will have certain advantages to fall back on and use to meet the challenge—a strong character and innate competence, plus perhaps good parents, wealth, and special training. Friends will come to his aid. By contrast, the chronic criminal will be devastated and bereft of such advantages—poorly educated, lacking in sympathetic friends, weak in character, and unable to defend himself. He will be unable to recoup his losses.

Once we understand these applications of the Law of Consequences, we can then use this principle to review the events of life and discern our own roots of destiny. In doing this, we must keep in mind that *all* events and circumstances in our life, major and minor, reflect the hidden order of the universe and the purpose of our inner being. Likewise, it will be helpful to appreciate that in most cases our destiny will not include the spectacular elements cited in some of the preceding examples. In fact, it is usually the most mundane events—*and our defeatist reactions to them*—that are the most significant clues to our hidden message.

Too often people claim to search for meaning in their lives but actually seek only glamorous and exciting sensations, ending up sidetracked in their quest. The act of fulfilling our destined purpose and pursuing competence in humanistic skills is rarely as thrilling as it would be if concocted by a professional storyteller. Yet life *is* full of adventure and satisfaction when we do our duty *and learn to like it*. Doing whatever we please may be momentarily appealing—but often it is something other than what needs to be done.

THE FATE WITHIN

As we begin our review of the specific events and training maneuvers of our own life, however, we must bear in mind that we are looking for clues that may not be entirely obvious. The significance of any situation of life depends on two factors: the quality of the people or circumstances our inner being has selected, and our reactions to them. The quality of people can be assessed by evaluating if they are friendly, helpful, and intelligent on the one hand, or selfish, cruel, or incompetent on the other; the quality of circumstances can be discerned by judging whether they provide new opportunities for achievement, growth, and fulfillment—or are limited, unsatisfying, and restrictive. These conditions indicate the quality of life we have merited by earlier behavior. By contrast, our reactions to them indicate to us how well we are handling our destiny at this time. If we have squandered favorable opportunities, then this reaction has diminished their significance. Conversely, if we have found ways to overcome unsatisfying work conditions and increase our competence, then this action has added to the original meaning of those events.

A good place to begin our review of our life, obviously, would be at the beginning—with an examination of our birth conditions. The type of parents chosen by the inner being, for example, reveals a great deal about what we deserve and how we have responded to it. If for example, we have been born of friendly and helpful parents, this good fortune suggests that in previous lives we were benevolent to our children and respectful to our parents. Furthermore, if we have responded in our current life in loving and appreciative ways to these compassionate parents, then we can be sure that the selection of our parents was indeed a reward merited by our earlier behavior—and that we have been automatically capitalizing on the significance of this part of our life.

The more we pursue this type of review, the more we begin to realize that the second factor—our reactions to our conditions of life—is really the more important. It is our key to comprehending the value of what is happening at present in our life. Moreover, it reminds us that ultimately we are the final determiner of how significant our life is or will be. If we react with dignity, compassion, and intelligence to the circumstances of life, our life will have great meaning. If we react with anger, impatience, and stupidity, we will be puzzled, bereft, and frustrated.

Thus, our conditions of birth indicate primarily the point we have started from. We are not the products of our childhood circumstances—we are the products of our *reactions* to them! The selection of simple and gentle parents, for example, might indicate good fortune for us, if we have learned to respect the goodwill and sacrifice with which they have raised us. But if we have chosen to resent excessively our parents' ignorance and lack of gracefulness, then such a reaction points to an obvious weakness in our basic character.

Intolerance of a trait or deficiency in others, or

rejection of some situation, usually indicates a need on our part to acquire greater understanding, compassion, and skill in the area scorned. Increased *understanding* would help us comprehend that imperfection in others is not a personal attack against us; therefore, we should not react with so much distress. By learning *compassion,* we would discover that we can discern not only imperfections but also actual or potential good in others and in circumstances. Greater *skillful use* of our humanity would help us develop immunity from possible harm or loss that might be caused by such people or situations. But most importantly, the mastered qualities of skill, compassion, and wisdom all give us the *strength* needed to correct our imperfections. Herein lies the real potential for healing any character flaw.

Many purposes are thus served by placing us in a family situation in which one or more family members is seen as flawed from our personal view. If, as in the earlier example, we are embarrassed by the crude manners and lack of education of our parents, this reaction may indicate the need to acquire the type of tolerance which stems from greater compassion for all such people. It may further indicate that we have been intolerant of such people in earlier lives and have failed to comprehend that simple people also are competent in many ways and serve valuable roles in society. Consequently, growing up with such people as parents may help us respect the humanity in uneducated and simple people. It will also encourage, by default, greater self reliance on our own resources and wisdom. In this way, it aids in stimulating our skillfulness in coping with life's problems.

Similarly, when one or both parents are hostile and selfish, this type of condition helps us develop an awareness of the devastating wrongness of such traits. A lifelong *object lesson* of this nature often teaches us with such poignancy that it may well overcome the moral blindness and insensitivity of several previous lives.

The irritating qualities of others will inevitably clash with similar tendencies in ourself. Thus, a bigoted parent will clash with the bigot in us; a lazy parent will clash with our own indolence. An alcoholic parent will clash with our tendency to self indulgence and will tend to build in us the resolution to be disciplined. All of these adverse situations teach us valuable lessons that indelibly imprint our consciousness with grains of wisdom. To some degree we are forced to confront our weaknesses and bad habits and overcome them.

The purpose of our existence is far more often fulfilled in these mundane struggles than in openly recognized acts of heroism. The quiet, daily effort to cope with difficulty is never meant to defeat or punish us. Rather, it is meant to serve—and does automatically serve—to build a more noble and competent character. Through a lifetime of struggling to cultivate steadfastness, courage, resolution, compassion, and wisdom, we can create a *permanent heritage* of "treasures of heaven": various humanistic skills, wisdom, joy, and grace. These earned qualities then become the nucleus of our destiny in future lives, leading to better relationships, personal success, material rewards, and greater opportunities—the secondary results of evolutionary changes in our character. But it is these changes in character that are most important;

they are the accomplishment! Physical achievements are often far less significant.

These achievements of competence in human living are never acquired magically, however; they are accumulated through the quiet effort to endure and achieve—through responsible action and nothing else. They do not come as the result of wishful thinking, or from good intentions not applied; these can only achieve imaginary results. Nor do they come as part of a visionary existence in some fabled summerland or paradise awaiting us after our physical death. They come little by little in the here and now as we achieve greater skill and power in the art of living.

These are the reasons why a close analysis of our birth conditions is important; these seeming "accidents of birth" are often carefully arranged circumstances that will help induce desired developments in character. But, of course, there is more to consider than just the irritating and adverse traits in our parents or childhood events. Sometimes these conditions set the stage for later growth, when we have become adults. For example, if our parents were indulgent and permissive, we would probably grow up spoiled, ill-mannered, and lazy. Prepared in this way for adulthood, we would begin to discover that our bad habits create irritation in others and embarrassment in ourself. Eventually, however, they would stimulate their own correction, once we had resolved to overcome them and become more mature. We would practice—and learn—self discipline and motivation.

It is precisely this kind of family setting that is provided for individuals who have had paranoid tendencies in earlier lives, blaming others excessively for holding them back—when in fact they were merely seeking to cover up their own incompetence.

Indeed, the inner being will often give us *exactly what we have craved before,* in order to teach us the mistake of undisciplined desires. The purpose of such a lesson is not to teach us that the desired object is bad, but rather that our motives for wanting it—and our plans for using it—fall far short of wisdom. Many people, for instance, lust for money and the conspicuous goods it can purchase. Some seek it to indulge their sloth, vanity, and scorn for "lesser people"; others seek it largely for the security it seems to offer. There are also those who desire money in order to wield power over others and to augment their feelings of authority. In each of these cases, the motive is a wrong one. And so life might well arrange for such people to come into great wealth for a short while, so that they can learn that self esteem, security, and authority cannot be bought—that in fact, they are often substantially threatened by great possessions. Other valuable lessons can be learned in such circumstances as well. With money come various subtle forces that can create great stress; learning to work intelligently and responsibly with these forces often requires a dramatic object lesson to drive home the point. The idleness of independent wealth, for example, might lead to destructive indulgences otherwise impossible: gambling, drink, and other forms of mischief. Similarly, greed can be a habit that becomes an insatiable lust, as the acquisition of material wealth leads its owner to an ever greater need to exceed past achievements—a need that brings with it frustration, anxiety, and often despair. Many people—

having expected that material wealth would bring them a life of ease and comfort—are chagrined to learn that a life of wealth can be filled with incredibly hard work, the strain of supervising great obligations, and the fear of loss.

Abundance and success, therefore, can teach even more deadly lessons than impoverishment and hardship. As ever, the lesson of a balanced and wise use of material wealth is learned most efficiently through actual experience of its limitations and possibilities. Through multiple experiences in managing money, we eventually come to recognize the simple but profound fact that increased benefits must go hand in hand with increased responsibility. Also thoroughly learned is the simple precept that *every benefit desired or gained must be earned*—a rule that applies to any desired goal, be it material wealth, a personal quality, a talent, the respect and friendship of a person, a position of authority, or anything else. By repeated demonstrations in the laboratory of life, we come to understand that when anything is acquired dishonestly by cunning, deceit, or the aggressive abuse of others, it can only be kept by engaging in ever increasing criminal and defensive activities. Furthermore, such gain will be temporary and will end in inevitable loss. Permanent gain can only be won through honest effort.

Of course, not every financial loss implies that the original gain was achieved by some sort of wrongdoing—even in an earlier lifetime—or that it was unmerited for other reasons. The universe never operates exclusively for one person's benefit, either to make him wealthy or to teach him a lesson. There are cycles of achievement and progress that affect us all. They eventually come to an end because *a purpose has been fulfilled*. Our own financial, social, and occupational fortunes can be decidedly influenced by the end of such a cycle (or the beginning of one as well). We must keep this notion in mind, lest we judge apparent failure on superficial and purely materialistic grounds. If instead we learn to measure success in terms of ability developed, wisdom gained, and productive service rendered, we will come to understand that few seeming failures are real ones.

Obviously, an awareness of the vast nature of cyclic patterns and phenomena is an important part of understanding the full meaning of life. Large cycles of "success" and "failure" influence nations, religious groups, businesses, and civilization as a whole, just as smaller cycles affect us individually. Often, our own destiny makes sense only within the context of a number of these cycles. Once again, it is not the cycle itself that gives our life significance—it is our reaction to it. Thus, if our personal fortune is washed away in the tide of a national depression and we are unable to recover from it, then that tends to indicate that our erstwhile wealth had been gained more to teach us a lesson than because we had earned it through competent activity. Conversely, if we react to this personal tragedy by finding new psychological sources of strength and endurance, and launch ourself on a new program of achievement, then this more favorable reaction reveals that while we can be affected by larger cycles of destiny, we cannot be victimized by them.

Sometimes the inner essence chooses types of abundance other than physical wealth to teach the profound lessons of life. Beauty, great talent, cleverness, physical strength, and steadfastness can all be used to stimulate growth; often they cause even greater disappointment than wealth until the dangers of imbalance, excess, and indulgence are seen, and the lesson of responsibility is mastered. Of course, to some it may seem impossible that such attributes could lead to any sort of hardship. But such disbelief is precisely the reason why these lessons must be learned in the context of *direct personal experience*. Only immediate involvement can reveal the full potential of the danger of misusing such attributes and the shortsightedness of our disbelief.

Great physical beauty, for example, exposes us to all the pitfalls of vanity. Similarly, outstanding genius can create terrible imbalances in the personality, leading to the starvation of our essential humanity as we devote too much of our time and energy to just a few successful activities. The difficulties attending steadfastness and patience are perhaps less obvious. These strengths enable us to accomplish a tremendous amount of work when others might well be overwhelmed with despair and frustration. Yet these wonderful traits can also inhibit necessary changes in attitude, behavior, and conviction. In other words, they can cause a rigidity and a stubborness that stifle progress.

Abundances of popularity, skill, prestige, beauty, and genius can also subject us to the "embarrassment of riches." A beautiful lady, for example, may be unable to handle the attention her beauty attracts. Unsolicited advances and propositions may annoy and distress her. The genius, too, may be pestered by unwanted attention: his noble intention may be jeopardized by people who would exploit his talent, his humility may be weakened by flattery, and his self discipline may be undermined by greater opportunity for indulgence. In much the same way, the person with great power may find his subordinates usurping his authority, causing him embarrassment, and perhaps entrapping him within the protocol of his position.

By being placed in such circumstances of success, we expose our basic weaknesses to the pressure and strain that will cause them to be magnified. In this way, the problem areas can be more easily identified and repaired.

To be sure, abundance and skills are not given to us only to help us learn from them. Success, talent, and position usually come to *those who have earned them* through many prior (and often forgotten) experiences and accomplishments. These advantages are well deserved rewards and also fresh opportunities for even greater expression. Yet, even in these cases, some growth of character can be expected, as we face the challenges of life. Only personal examination and evaluation can reveal just how much of a lesson, versus how much productivity and expression, is intended. Usually, it's a strong dose of both.

In these ways, circumstances of both adversity and success can be deftly used by our inner essence to set the stage for meaningful growth in any one lifetime. Other conditions inherited at birth or developed during the life are rich with significance as well. Our racial heritage, for instance, is often quite important. Due to the Law of Consequences, a person who commits an injustice will often suffer as a victim of the same injustice. This is not punishment, but rather a fair discipline—an exquisitely appropriate teaching device. Thus, a persecutor of minorities in one life may subsequently play the role of the oppressed, to learn the inhumanity of his persecution. Of course, these people are often the ones who suffer discrimination and oppression most poorly: habits of insensitivity and prejudice change very slowly. The trait of bigotry will characterize such a person no matter what race he is born into — white, black, yellow, or red. But gradually, through repeated experiences of being persecuted, he will learn to respect the needs and attitudes of minority groups. He will develop tolerance and even sympathy.

Religion frequently provides a learning opportunity as well. The malicious and rude atheist of one life may well be born into a narrow and strictly religious family in the next. As unconscious attitudes from the past clash with the principles of his upbringing, he will have to struggle to reconcile the opposites in his life. In this way, he learns the need for compassion and humane treatment of others, regardless of their beliefs. At times the lesson is even more poignant: he might, for example, develop a problem or illness that could only be relieved through religious faith or healing. In desperation, he would be forced to revise his thinking.

Our physical health is another clue revealing a great deal about our duty and need for discipline. Chronic disease and disability are often signs of character weaknesses and the need for character development. If in one life, for example, we repeatedly feign or exaggerate illness in order to avoid work and responsibility, we may well inherit a sickly body afflicted with genuine illnesses in some later lifetime. It would thus become our destiny to learn to place a high premium on physical health.

A fussy and excessively critical individual will often draw a body riddled with allergies, skin rashes, and chronic indigestion as a natural consequence of his or her psychological irritation. Similarly, the sadist who inflicts physical pain and causes damage to others may likely end up with a physical body that must endure great pain and discomfort. The same type of body may also be selected by people who have been grossly insensitive to the physical anguish of others.

For a woman, the inability to have children may possibly be the consequence of neglecting children in an earlier life. But it could also be the result of complaining too much about the problems children cause, and not properly appreciating the joy and fulfillment they can bring. In such life circumstances the woman, regretting her loss, might decide to adopt—often a long and complicated procedure. When she finally did acquire children, they would be much more precious and dear to her, and she would be far more inclined than before to treat them properly.

A person prone to mental-emotional illnesses such as schizophrenia or uncontrollable fits of temper is likely to have been highly irresponsible in earlier lives. A willful lack of emotional self restraint, for example, can lead to a terrible accumulation of harmful acts of thought, speech, and deed. As a direct consequence, the physical mechanism for self control is often missing or seriously impaired in the next lifetime. By having to suffer through a life of constant embarrassment and compromise, the person learns the value of voluntarily exercising greater self control.

Many of the more deadly conditions of life are

prompted by the active expression of hatred in earlier lives. Hate and its derivatives—contempt, fear, and envy—destroy life; they are regressive to character growth and damage the mind and brain of both the hateful person and his victim. But the impact of hate will more seriously affect the sender of it than his victim, as the intensity of any emotion is greatest at the source. The consequences of such hating upon future lives can be mental retardation, premature senility, and degenerative diseases of the brain and spinal cord.

Some of the worst fates are reserved for people who have been consciously evil in their conduct—people who have deliberately sought to harm others, even when they knew it was wrong. Having literally destroyed their minds with malice and evil, such people usually must join those individuals who have destroyed their minds with alcohol or drugs and endure lifetimes of severe mental retardation, hopeless psychoses, and marked congenital malformations—bodies defective from birth. These experiences are not punishments—they are simply the unavoidable consequences of earlier action, just as losing an arm is the unavoidable consequence of holding it in a fire until it burns.

It is helpful to be able to view life with these perspectives as we try to understand the meaning of our own health problems, big or small. The healing of the whole individual cannot be completed until these deeper aspects are considered—and balanced.

Of course, there are many, many other circumstances of birth and later life that give us important clues to our hidden message of destiny and purpose, and what it means to us. The loss of one or both parents, for example, would produce a tremendous pressure for developing greater self sufficiency and courage. Marriage to a person with precisely the same faults that we have would force us to face those faults more directly. Similarly, marriage to a person who abuses and torments us might indicate that we have been entirely too passive in earlier times; we have not stood up to evil and defeated it, but rather have meekly tried to co-exist with it. Our working conditions, our friendships, "accidents" and "coincidences," the circumstances of our education, our rapport with our children, the nature of our weaknesses and temptations—all of these key events and conditions have meaning to us, if we take the time to examine each one carefully and see what *it has encouraged us to achieve*.

We must remember that these key circumstances have been carefully planned by our inner essence to help us more rapidly fulfill our purposes in life. Combined, they are our destiny and fate for this life. They point out to us the areas of duty and character growth that we should be most energetically concentrating on. In other words, they are invaluable signposts to self understanding.

Life is full of dangers, problems, and difficulties which teach us strength, ability, compassion, and courage, by forcing us to cope with them. But life is also rich with opportunities which can teach us prudence and caution if we do not handle them wisely. The purpose behind all of these experiences of life is to aid us in nurturing the seeds of our humanity— our love, our competence, our wisdom. This purpose, hidden and yet obvious, can be discerned by anyone honest and courageous enough to seek it.

Our destiny is based on a principle of causation

that is neither capricious nor without mercy. It is, however, impersonal and operates in predictable ways. Therefore, we can accurately interpret our destiny by studying the nature of the experiences we encounter and the quality of our reactions to these events. When we make a diligent effort to live our life in harmony with this principle of causation—by sowing goodwill in our current activities so we may reap goodwill in our future—then there will be a generous return indeed on the investment we make in life. In fact, we will have discovered the secret of intelligently creating our own destiny, our own fate.

But for those who persist in wailing and cursing about their hardships and for those who cultivate a cavalier indifference to life, there awaits a worse set of problems in the future. Our problems do not go away just because we dislike them or try to cleverly ignore them, any more than hunger and malnutrition vanish through some clever self-hypnotic trick. *Our fate lies within. It goes with us wherever we go. If our fate is based on problems and indiscretions, then those problems and woes will follow us wherever we go. If, however, it is based on the nobility of human achievement, then we will encounter achievement wherever we go!*

SOWING GOODWILL

The whole process of finding meaning in life must involve more than just intellectual speculation about lessons hidden in the external events of life. It must include the development of wisdom, courage, steadfastness, and greater competence.

To some degree, just staying with a problem and coping with it will lead to substantial increases in insight, capacity, and ability. Having to live with a sick body, for example, eventually teaches some degree of patience, courage, and respect for a well-functioning body. But if we must struggle with such conditions, it will help us immensely to comprehend how much we gain as human beings *even when outer circumstances do not seem to change.* Even when adversity is not entirely overcome, it can nonetheless serve the purpose of helping us conquer fear, insensitivity, and contempt, while also stimulating the cultivation of patience, forgiveness, and the compassion to tolerate what cannot be changed. Furthermore, a strong desire and respect for whatever we may be lacking eventually invokes its appearance, even if another lifetime is required. Success in fulfilling our destiny, therefore, is something which must be measured by our growth of character and evolution of consciousness, rather than by the seeming importance of concrete events.

If we fail to recognize this truth, we will inevitably end up searching for accomplishment in the avenues of life least likely to produce reward and satisfaction. Growth of character and evolution of consciousness tend to occur automatically if we are patient enough—or are forced by destiny—to stick with our life situations. But those who greet every problem with resentment, intolerance, and impatience are the ones who gain the least; those who act with irresponsibility, insensitivity, and selfishness are the ones who actually lose ground just to gain some temporary and superficial advantage.

Indeed, many people make a bad thing worse by

their adverse reactions to it. They expend tremendous energy in scheming to avoid problems and commitments when a lesser amount of honest effort would actually solve the difficulty. In some cases, they do put forth the required effort, but with so much resentment or fear that the benefit is all but cancelled out. The quality of consciousness does not improve, and so a similar situation has to be faced again in the future, until the challenges of life can be met with serenity, good cheer, and optimism.

But even in mistake and error, a grain of truth can often be found. Thus, although some people do indeed make a bad thing worse by their ill-conceived reactions to it, there is nothing to prevent us from learning a lesson from their mistake. And if we do, we will then be better prepared to improve upon the good aspects of life, by reacting to them in mature, inspired, and benevolent ways. Our destiny for this lifetime is out of the control of the conscious mind, since it has already been cast by the inner being. But our *reactions* to the events of this destiny have not been cast, for they are even now emerging and evolving, as we proceed through life. We therefore always have the opportunity to purify our reactions, to cease from reacting in harmful and negative ways, and to transmute our reactions into positive expressions of our humanity—sympathy, courage, poise, acceptance, goodwill, and intelligence.

We can be poorly treated, abused, and even denied our rights and freedoms, but *no one* can ever deny us the opportunity to grow and become more mature. This is because the mechanism of human growth *works through our reactiveness*. Our future, therefore, lies not so much in our fate as in *what we do with it!* Only through the purification and improvement of our reactions can we permanently reduce our weaknesses and vulnerabilities—the vulnerabilities that magnetically draw problem situations into our destined path.

It is extremely important, however, to realize that it is not just the conscious mind and feelings that react, but rather *the whole of our consciousness*. It is the whole being—the conscious mind, the subconscious, and the unconscious—that is responsible for attracting problems or repelling opportunities. If we are to purify and change our reactions, we must be sure to work carefully on all levels of our being, with all our resources. The person who tries to discipline his reactiveness by turning off his conscience with boorish or sophisticated indifference will succeed only in changing the conscious mind and a small part of the subconscious. In the untouched realms of his unconsciousness, the seeds of recurrent conflict will continue to lurk.

The conscious mind can work only with the tip of our adverse reactions, as the bulk of them live in the unconscious. But not realizing this, we often overestimate the effectiveness of our resolves and efforts at self improvement. What seems to be total forgiveness and unqualified compassion, for example, is frequently just *that moment's worth* of forgiveness and compassion. It is no more enduring than the neat appearance of a lawn that's just been mown, clipped, and raked. In a few days the grass grows back. Similarly, an occasional effort at improving our reactions has no real permanence. Fresh shoots of anger, fear, depression, guilt, and bitterness quickly spring from the "soil" of the unconscious to clutter our conscious thoughts and feelings. Little is gained without periodic maintenance.

Of course, some shortsighted people would rip up their lawns and replace them with green concrete rather than maintain them. In dealing with our reactions, that would be like walling off our conscience with indifference, refusing to face the fresh issues of unresolved conflict rising up from it. But that kind of reaction would actually require more effort than maturely allowing the conscience to work within us. It would also mean opposing the purpose and force of the inner being—a force which inevitably can exhaust, and if necessary outlive, the personal will.

A much better alternative is to harness the purpose and power of this inner being and use it to add new life to the personality. We have already seen how to get in touch with the purpose of the inner being, by using the mind to ponder the nature of our universal and transcendent connections with life and to understand the meaning of our experiences. But getting in touch with the power of the inner essence is equally important, for without it we cannot succeed in our efforts to purify our reactions. This part of the work is not as difficult as it might seem. Much can be accomplished on a very simple level: just listening to and heeding the voice of our conscience can help place us in touch with the power of the inner being. And every time we *use* the inspiration of our conscience to make a practical change in our daily life, we are employing this power. When, for example, we make the disciplined effort to extend goodwill to people we have previously disliked, we are harnessing the power of the inner being. When we conquer our temptation to harshly criticize, when we face up to our problems of health with courage, or when we overcome our self pity and more actively work to express our destined purpose, again we are touching this inner power.

Unfortunately, many people cannot be bothered to really get in touch with their inner essence. Instead, they hypnotize themselves into a mood of bland peacefulness and turn over control of their lives to their subconscious. A few years later they are surprised to discover the same old problems returning—only more strongly. Of course, their "mood of peacefulness" was only counterfeit bliss, simply reflecting a temporary absence of distressful events rather than the signs of genuine contact with the inner essence: positive growth in character, resolution of conflict, and healthy integration of new wisdom, skill, and courage into the personality expression. These changes require hard work: to succeed, we have to root out *all* unresolved conflicts lurking in the subconscious and unconscious. This is why it is so important to review the events of life in the broadest possible scope. Until the deeper level of conflict is uncovered and neutralized, it will linger to poison a fuller enjoyment of current opportunities.

Just realizing that all the events of our life have had meaning and have helped us grow will do much to resolve old conflicts, erase resentment, and bring us a more permanent peace of mind. But in addition, there is a practical method for neutralizing conflict that can be easily learned. When used, it greatly expands our capacity for growing.

This method is the process of learning to react to all the events of life with compassion and goodwill. It is based on the idea that the attitude of goodwill can go where words and hands cannot reach in the physical plane. Hands can build, but only goodwill can fulfill purpose. Words can soothe, but only love can heal. Just so, compassion and goodwill can move into dimensions of consciousness that cannot be reached by mere "positive thinking" or the superficial rearrangement of beliefs. The activity of love can indeed transcend the limitations of conscious thought and theory. It can penetrate into the full recesses of the subconscious and unconscious—even into blocked and repressed memories—to neutralize much negativity. Moreover, the use of compassion and goodwill and their sister qualities of affection, forgiveness, pity, benevolence, and reverence is the key to linking ourself with the inner essence in the higher unconscious mind, as well as for focussing healing energies into our personality.

Thus, by acting with goodwill in our search for meaning in life, we harmonize ourself with the best elements within us. This is the activity of *blessing*. It is a psychological procedure as old and as well proven as motherhood.

Blessing is the act of calling forth our noblest qualities to honor the goodness in other people and in situations—noble qualities such as love, joy, wisdom, and compassion. The act of blessing is a powerful one that brings us into contact with the Universal Connection; it liberates our spirit so that it may flow into the physical plane, adding new and healing life to whatever it touches. Through blessing, hate is neutralized by love, sadness is transmuted by joy, and the darkness of our unconscious is brightened by inner light. It is the most healing way we can use our mind.

The act of blessing shifts our attention away from ourself and our self pity; it engages us in the activity of helping others. Moreover, as the energies of love, compassion, and goodwill flow through us during the process of blessing, they clear out the barriers (built by long eons of selfishness) that have obstructed the mind and have made it less than efficient. And so, the act of blessing brings us great personal benefits, too—it helps us overcome our miseries. Of course, that should never be the dominant motive for this activity—our motive must be to become a clear channel for goodwill.

Spurred on by this purpose we can, like Saint Francis, ask to be made an instrument for peace, so that we may sow love where there is hatred, pardon where there is injury, faith where there is doubt, hope where there is despair, and joy where there is sadness.

It is important to bless the people and the situations in our life, just as it is important that the sun shines on the world. The sun shines on our planet continuously through the gloom, rain, and snow which cover its surface; similarly, the inner light of our essence is meant to shine figuratively on and through our personality. It is never stopped by the darkness of our difficulties nor blocked by the storms of our conflict and turmoil. It is stopped only by our lack of recognition and acceptance. Our free-will choice to seek its assistance is necessary before we can express a greater manifestation of wisdom, love, and courage in our life.

The act of blessing recognizes the value of the Law of Consequences, as it operates in our life. We are often unaware of how justly our needs are fulfilled by the Universal Connection. But they are: when we cry out for strength, life gives us problems to solve. When we seek wisdom, we receive perplexing situations to handle. These struggles, when courageously met, help us overcome our weaknesses and fulfill our obligations. And so it is quite realistic to bless these circumstances and the people involved, as a means of releasing further healing and building energies to work with. We can be thankful for these difficulties because of the valuable lessons we have learned from them.

Until we realize the purpose behind such thankfulness and cease to resent our hardships, we will continue to be mired in our problems—or at least the painful memories of them. Even worse, the unpleasant circumstances may recur, because the uncleansed memories of them can act as "bad seeds" for a new crop of woes.

Therefore, we should bless those who hate and condemn us, for they teach us forgiveness, stamina, and faith in ourself. We should bless those who deceive us, for they teach us discernment and the value of honesty. We should bless those who scorn us, for they help us become truly self reliant. We should bless those who act ignorantly, for they teach us the value of wisdom and skill. We should bless those who act in malice, for they teach us the value of kindness and gentleness. We should bless those who grieve excessively over their exaggerated losses, for they teach us to find joy in small things. We should bless those who are impatient and fussy, for they teach us the value of patience and the need for respect for others. We should bless the sick, for they teach us the value of good health. We should bless hostile people, for they teach us the value of affection.

This activity is not especially religious in nature; it is a simple but noble humanitarian act which helps others as it heals our own imperfections. The effort is small, and we risk nothing. Still, as an investment of our time and energy, it has no peer.

Blessing, however, is not a mental magic act that makes our problems vanish. In its fullest, it is an integral part of the constructive work of compensating inequalities and acquiring knowledge and skills in living. It is an active expression of compassion through our reactions to others. It is not something done in the isolation of our room but rather in full contact with the circumstances of life. It reminds us of our personal destiny and of the universal purpose that makes our own efforts worthwhile; it gives us a means for communicating these hidden messages to others.

Many of us cry out for greater understanding of the meaning of life. As we have seen, that can be achieved—by reviewing our life experiences and discerning their purposes. But understanding is not enough: a destiny without fulfillment is worthless. Once we grasp the nature of our duty and the meaning of the disciplinary trends of our life, we must then transmute these insights into acts of goodwill, wisdom, and courage—and we must sow these good seeds so they can help the universe unfold.

BUILDING RIGHT
HUMAN
RELATIONSHIPS

A LIVING ART

Modern man defines his understanding of human relationships in many ways—some useful, others not. Some people, for example, view their relationships as valuable channels for human sharing; others use them to dominate and manipulate people for selfish gain. Some recognize the love, joy, and enlightenment they gain from contacts with their fellow human beings, while others register sorrow, heartbreak, and disappointment. Some comprehend the role their relationships play in encouraging personal and spiritual growth, but others think of them only as random alliances without cause or purpose, devoid of all but a transitory significance.

Perhaps the best way to fully understand the nature and importance of human relationships, though, is to see them as *a living art form*—an art form in which we can all be artists. Viewed as such, our human relationships take on new meanings: they become avenues for the expression of beauty, opportunities for developing our skills in living, and doorways to brotherhood.

In this art form, the "paints" that we apply to the canvases of our lives are the intangible energy streams of love, affection, benevolence, tolerance, charitable goodwill, kindness, tenderness, gentleness, compassion, strength, and understanding. The portraits we create are group portraits: friendships, marriages, business partnerships, and family kinships. And even though our efforts will not be awarded blue ribbons at art shows, they will indeed be recognized—by increased opportunities for growth and greater participation in the collective activities of mankind.

Unfortunately, some of us work at the art of human relationships with no more skill than many modern painters bring to their labors. There are, for example, those artists who stand back from a blank canvas and in a haphazard mood throw buckets of paint upon it. When the resulting chaos of color and shape reaches suitably perplexing levels, they quit and loudly proclaim the result a "work of art." Others turn to "op" art and labor diligently over rigid geometrical designs, eventually producing paintings filled with sterility and coldness—and empty of inspiration. And then there are the ones who splash about in the shallows of pop art, painting soup cans. Of course, none of these rather infantile experiments produces anything of lasting value. Nor do the analogous experiments in the living art of human relationships. It takes more than uninhibited impulsiveness to create meaningful bonds, and likewise more than cold manipulation—or the sloppy sophistication of being "camp."

Still, an artist who knows something of subtle shading, the use of colors, and true inspiration can produce works of lasting value. Similarly, a person familiar with the meaning of human relationships and the use of love, goodwill, and tolerance can create bonds of surpassing beauty and artistry.

In building such a work of living art, it is not

necessary to start with a relationship which already demonstrates a high level of compatibility. Any human relationship—even a bitter conflict or a family situation that is falling apart—can, with patience, love, and intelligence, be turned into one of lasting value. But such expertise in the "living art" cannot be achieved without three basic realizations. First, art is a striving for ideals. Second, art is a dynamic expression of those ideals. And, most importantly, art is the antithesis of chaos.

Art is a striving for ideals. And what are the ideals of human relationships? The principal ideal is that they be *right* human relationships—relationships that express caring, sharing, and goodwill; relationships that help us mutually fulfill our creative purpose as human beings. The Christ summed up this ideal in His statement: "Truly, I say to you, as you do it to one of the least of these my brethren, you do it to me."

Whenever we succumb to self centeredness and separativeness in dealing with others, we lose touch with this fundamental ideal. We begin to think of relationships as vehicles for personal satisfaction and gain, rather than as a wonderful medium for the living art. We overlook the important truth that we are all equally heir to the Father's riches, and must therefore honor the birthright of "the least of these my brethren"—if our own birthright is to have any significance at all.

To be an artist in the field of human relationships, therefore, we must approach our work fully understanding the depth of our ties with other people—with *all* other people. We must recognize the differences that exist among people and take them into account, but we must learn that at the innermost level, all men are created equal. All men and women share the same cosmic purpose, the same evolutionary goals, and the same capacities and opportunities for achievement. When we honor that common heritage in the way we treat others— even the "least of these my brethren"—then we honor the fundamental ideal. A right human relationship, therefore, is one that expresses inspired *brotherhood*.

Art is a dynamic expression of ideals. Relationships are essentially *flows of energy*. The emotions and thoughts which we express and receive in a relationship are energy patterns that flow freely to and fro between the participants of that relationship, thus establishing a bond. This bond *is* the relationship. Each of our thoughts, our emotions, and actions modifies this bond to some degree. Loving and considerate thoughts and actions improve the quality of the bond. Cruelty, jealousy, anger, and hatred pollute the quality of the bond. (Not only do they pollute the bond, but far worse, they also contaminate the pool of energy in which we literally live. Thus, every time we express anger or hostility, it is something akin to dumping raw sewage into a swimming pool in which we must swim.)

Any strong feeling, be it loving or malicious, will intensify the bond. In practical terms, therefore, the goal of human relationships should be the expression of compassion, tenderness, forgiveness, goodwill, gentleness, joy, kindness, mutual confidence, and tolerance. Hatred, selfishness, envy, and anger simply do not serve our best interest. Far from pushing the disliked person *away* from us, as is commonly supposed, they draw him *closer*—thus compounding our dislike. Such negative expressions become vicious, repetitive cycles, until we replace them with more appropriate ideals and become an inspired artist.

Right relationships need not necessarily be free from conflict, as it is conflict which produces harmony and helps us achieve maturity. But they should be free from discord, resentment, and animosity—the adverse personality reactions to conflict. And they should be especially free of the pettiness which ignores the principle of brotherhood and makes excuses for our character flaws. As long as we think that the problems of a relationship are the other person's fault and that it's the other person who must make the changes, then there is no possibility for improving the relationship. The reason why is simple. Such resentments and grudges immediately enter into the flowing stream of energies which *is* the relationship and pollute it. They lower the quality of the energy of the bond, and such a state perseveres as long as resentment remains.

It is because relationships are bonds of constantly flowing energy that they can be improved. It is for the same reason that they can be considered an art form. They are not static; they are not unchangeable. They can be shaped toward perfection.

Art is the antithesis of chaos. Chaos is a state lacking any kind of intelligent structure. Art is the process of resolving chaos into meaningful, beautiful, and structured patterns. Many human relationships of today tend toward chaos; a man and woman marry, for example, and then as the years pass, their marriage decays and falls apart. They have let the energy flows of their bond get out of control; often, the bond was wild and out of control from the beginning.

It is pointless to believe that such chaotic relationships will ever improve "on their own." The production of beauty and order from chaos is *not* an automatic process. Chaos never builds; it destroys. Thus, chaos remains chaos until it is subjugated to the intelligent will of an artistic force. In the realm of human relationships, this means that beauty and order can only be produced by intelligent and loving work on the part of the individuals involved.

Meaningful and right human relationships, therefore, are not accidents. They are not flukes of fate, any more than the masterpieces of Rembrandt were flukes of fate. They are produced through the steady development of skills of living and the careful study of the nature of human bonds—what causes problems, what causes growth, and what the ideal state of human relations is. Then, once these basics are understood, the artist begins the process of molding and creating, working with the energies of his own relationships—carefully, deliberately, and with inspiration. In this way he defeats the forces of chaos and glorifies the process of art—and gradually creates right human relationships with all he meets and knows.

CRUCIBLES OF GROWTH

The ultimate purpose of relationships is to manifest physically the brotherhood which exists already at the innermost levels of humanity. In a more practical and immediate sense, however, relationships serve two important functions: they provide needed roles for various kinds of expression, and they create ideal opportunities for growth.

Let's look first at the roles involved in relationships. These can be lumped into two broad categories: roles in which the two people are recognized as equal partners, and roles in which they are not. In the first category are relationships such as friendships, marriages, and business partnerships. In the second group, the most notable examples are the relationships of parent-child, boss-employee, and teacher-student.

When the nature of any role (and the fact that it *is only a role and therefore not absolute*) is fully understood, generally a good relationship results. But when the role is not understood, trouble can be expected. For instance, even though marriage should be based on shared partnership, it often is not: one of the two becomes domineering, the other submissive, and strain is created.

Furthermore, it must be recognized that our relationships are not static and fixed. The roles we play through our relationships may often change, and we must be flexible enough to change with them. Thus, if a secretary is married to her boss, they must observe the requirements of the boss-employee relationship during working hours, and the quite different nature of the marriage relationship outside of the office. Confusion of the two roles would inevitably lead to trouble, as it often has.

Sometimes the roles of a relationship are reversed, as happened in the case of a high school principal and one of his students. One summer, the principal attended a canoe camp where the student was a trip leader. Assigned to a trip led by the student, the principal unfortunately failed to recognize that he had no authority on this trip, and that his erstwhile student had full authority. He tried to continue playing an authoritarian role, and the result was a constant battle between them.

The key to comprehending the importance of roles within relationships is seeing that roles permit *mutual expression*, and understanding that mutual expression can be far more powerful and productive than individual expression. (Indeed, certain kinds of creative expression are only possible in groupings of two or more.) The nature of this mutual expression naturally varies, depending on the kind of relationship involved:

1. Friendship. This role permits the expression of similar strengths, through the principle of sharing. If two friends experience joy when they are together, they express joy mutually. If they work together in a mental way, by sharing ideas, they express intelligence mutually.

2. Marriage. The mutual expression in this case is much the same as in friendship, but greatly intensified. It is no longer just a case of sharing similar strengths, but of merging them together and truly becoming one. A practical example of this unification is found in child-raising; if the parents are not of one mind in approaching the issue of discipline, their children will quickly learn to play one against the other.

3. Parent-child. The expression is mutual growth. Ideally, the parents realize that they are evolving and becoming better people; they share this growth with their children, who are also growing. These levels of growth are different, but should be in step with each other; if they are synchronized, then there will be the ideal mutual expression.

4. Business partnerships. Here the mutual expression is purposeful achievement. Such partners do

not have to share similar hobbies or interests, but it is important that they express either inventiveness, creativity, or business acumen together. This expression is often complementary in nature, with one expressing inventiveness and the other, business acumen.

5. Boss-employee. This role permits mutual productivity. The more skilled boss guides and supports the employee, and thus certain goals of productivity are achieved.

The second important function of relationships is that they provide ideal opportunities for mutual growth. Some may find this concept difficult to accept, but it is true nonetheless. Unfortunately, we often enter into relationships for incorrect reasons, with unwarranted expectations; then, when we are confronted with reality, we don't like it and withdraw from the relationship. In this way, one of the fundamental reasons for relationships is frequently negated, and much opportunity wasted.

Many of us, for example, seek friendships that will be ego-boosting. We want someone who will praise us, support our delusions, and never muddy the waters of our serene ignorance. But that is a poor substitute for friendship: rather than sharing joy and the exaltation of personal growth, all that is being shared is prejudice, misery, and narrow-mindedness. Just so, we often marry with expectations that are impossible to fulfill; we seek some mythical state of "happiness" based on supposed compatibility and ecstatic bliss.

Much suffering would be alleviated if it were realized that relationships are meant to induce growth. In fact, they are the *perfect crucibles for growth*. A crucible is a container in which ores are melted and blended to produce alloys—metals which are far stronger and more useful than the original ones, and otherwise unattainable. Relationships are like crucibles because we can attain greater strength and become more useful by working through them than we can by following our self-centered impulses. But implicit within the concept of the crucible is a bit of self sacrifice and pressure. The metals must be heated to great temperature; they must be blended and fused. Correspondingly, in right human relationships the ultimate desired state of harmony can only be reached by passing through certain stages of conflict and pressure—a heating up, as it were, that melts down the impurities within the bond. Because so few of us recognize the need for this stage, however, most of us regard its symptoms as a sign of incompatibility and often don't bother to last it out. As a result, we deprive ourselves of the harmony that would surely result.

Growth comes from maturely confronting our weaknesses and transmuting them into character strengths. But we cannot develop strengths from weaknesses until we first recognize the weaknesses. Relationships often provide the only means for identifying our weaknesses (through the evaluation of our reactions to other people). Thus, if a meaningful relationship is to produce growth, it will usually begin by "flushing out" the weaknesses of each of us. The resulting conflicts reveal the areas of personal growth that we must honestly face and conquer. If each of us does sincerely strive to transmute our weaknesses into strengths, then the potential harmony of the relationship will soon be tapped. But if we get mad at each other for "exposing" our weaknesses, then the relationship will produce conflict rather than harmony, and it will decay and collapse.

Not only do human relationships provide the best opportunity for growth, but they also supply the best *motivation* for conquering our weaknesses. To be sure, this motivation means little to someone who is still basically self centered. But as we begin to honor the human potential of others, we come to perceive that the worth of a friendship, partnership, or marriage is far greater than the sacrifice of changing our ways. With this understanding comes the desire to make the required effort.

Thus, one of the purposes of friendship and marriage is to stimulate the growth of maturity. As this happens, it will unavoidably upset the serenity of any relationship from time to time. But does it not make better sense to experience our "growing pains" at the hands of a close friend or loved one, rather than a stranger or someone we dislike? Of course it does, even though we aren't used to thinking in this way. When our character flaws are revealed to us by someone we respect and care about, there is much greater impetus for doing something to improve them. The flaws are also more likely to be exposed with gentleness and kindness, which help ease the pain. In fact, the closer the relationship, the more it should be the focus for this kind of growth, because the potential momentum is greater.

When we understand that we enter into close relationships more for the possibility of growth than for compatibility, then we can begin building our relationships on much more solid foundations. This realization alone, fully worked out and understood, will go a long way toward alleviating the pain and suffering which often accompany relationships.

THE INNER REALITY

In our efforts to build inspired human relationships, it is important to avoid being hypnotized by their superficial aspects. We must see beyond the outer nature of our bonds and consider their inner aspects as well. Only then will we fully see the absolute need for making relationships honest, open, and right, and proceed toward that goal fearlessly and with detachment. People who ignore the inner realities tend either to regard the value of their relationships with cavalier indifference and insensitivity, or to place such false importance upon them that they will try to preserve them at any cost. Family members, for example, are often pressured into making concessions which they know to be wrong, all in the name of "family unity." Similarly, it is not uncommon for passive individuals to meekly submit to conditions of virtual servitude to their spouses in the name of marital unity. Such situations are obviously not *right* human relationships, and they never will become right as long as the people involved willingly let others manipulate and abuse them in grossly unfair ways, just for the sake of preserving the bond. Instead, such relationships become downward spirals of discord.

Another problem arising from a lack of understanding of the inner realities of relationships is the all too common one of friends refraining from making needed suggestions because they do not want to upset—or insult—each other. And so the relationship remains superficial, uncomfortable, guarded, and not very meaningful.

What must be realized is that if a relationship is important, *it will never be broken by right and honest action!* It may be temporarily interrupted, even for several lifetimes, but the bond is never really severed. Only the physical bond is interrupted in the vast majority of instances. The bond of emotional energy (positive or negative) lives on, as does the mental bond. The negativity perseveres in grudges, resentment, intolerance, and the unwillingness to forgive. It will have a degree of immortality, just as long as it remains unresolved. Positive emotions and thoughts—patterns of love, joy, affection, goodwill, and creativity—will endure as well. When the relationship is resumed, the latent problems and strengths surface again, including the potential for harmonious expression (which never perishes). This continuity of the bond occurs regardless of the nature of the interruption.

Relationships are permanent. They transcend time and space. The bond of friendship is as real at distances of thousands of miles as it is at a few feet. It is as real in moments of seeming discord as it is at times of great rapport. Moreover, relationships exist from one lifetime to another. In this fact lies much of the explanation of the seemingly inexplicable aspects of relationships. Strong attraction to certain people is usually the result of an earlier history of relationship. Major conflicts are often the unfinished business of conflicts which were not resolved into harmony in earlier times. Great generosity or loyalty from a friend is likewise the result of favorable patterns of earlier relationships, in most instances.

Consequently, if we wish to practice correctly the fine art of right human relationships, we must keep in mind the permanent aspects of any bond and give them greater weight than the seeming needs of the fleeting moment. How much time is wasted by needless insecurity about the stability of a relationship, when in fact the true bond cannot be broken under any circumstances? How often is the right course of behavior not followed, in false fear that it will terminate the bond? How often are the problems of a relationship not squarely faced, in the mistaken belief that they will be resolved by physical separation? Likewise, how much grief is expended in lamenting missed opportunities or the death of a friend, when the true essence of the relationship has not changed, and opportunity will surely come again?

In fact, it is because relationships *do* transcend time and space (and have an inner, permanent reality) that we can rationally consider the prospect of creating ideal relationships, even in the most difficult situations. A marriage, for example, may be crumbling, but if one understands the immortality of relationships, one can know with certainty that sometime in the future, this relationship *will be harmonized*. The principle of universal order demands it. However, if the potential exists for a perfected relationship eons from now, then that same potential exists for expression right now (within certain restrictions). Understanding this can provide a glimmer of hope, and that hope can provide motivation. The proper motivation, combined with intelligent effort, can produce remarkable results.

STUMBLING BLOCKS

To improve our relationships, we must have the inner ideals of perfection well in focus. But we must also keep in mind the fact that we do not begin with perfection; we begin with imperfection. We start with problems—sometimes very difficult ones—that will not go away until we confront them and mutually solve them. Because the building of right relationships is an art form, we are constantly involved in the critical process of rendering order from chaos. If we ever forget this, we run the risk of being overwhelmed by the chaos. Therefore, it is important to train ourself to discern the major problems that can occur. No good is ever served by ignoring difficulties and pretending that they do not exist.

We have already seen that an improper understanding of the roles of relationships can lead to serious trouble, as in the case of a marriage not founded on shared responsibility. At times, the imbalance in a marriage can be quite obvious, as when one spouse is a crude, insensitive bigot who continually asserts his or her dominance over the other. On the other hand, it can be a more subtle imbalance, as when a man loves his wife very much but in a childish way, placing her on a pedestal and virtually worshipping her. Such relationships may seem good ones for a while, but the imbalances will eventually surface and produce conflict.

In addition, we have seen that problems invariably arise when people approach their relationships with stereotyped expectations and unsound motivation. The couple that is "madly in love" at age twenty will shortly find that an effective and productive marriage requires more of a commitment than just the emotional "high" of being in love. It requires maturity, dedication to ideals, and mutual respect. But the discovery of this reality will unquestionably cause stress in the relationship. Similarly, the couple that marries only on the strength of physical attraction, each believing that the other possesses a mythical sexual prowess, will have to cope with the problem of learning that marriage is not that superficial. Likewise, a person who seeks friendship for the purpose of collecting "debts of gratitude" will ultimately have to face the bankruptcy of his selfishness. And adults who become parents either without thinking about it or for a specious reason (such as providing themselves with an heir) will inevitably have difficulties in their relationships with their children.

Even when we form relationships which allow for mutual expression and mutual growth, however, there can be serious problems. Those that arise will probably be caused by one of three conditions.

1. Fundamental differences in the people involved. While the creation of all men and women was equal, they were not all created as carbon copies. It was the *process* of creation that was equal, not the *products* of creation! There *are* differences, both in temperament and competence.

The world is populated with people of distinct psychological temperaments. Some people tend to be scientific in their approach to life; others tend to be intuitive, mystical, or creative. Some like to work with their hands, building things, while others are very impractical and constantly daydreaming. Some are extroverted; others, introspective. Some will go out of their way for a good fight or argument, while others react uneasily at the slightest trace of discord. All of these forms of human expression are necessary—one is not superior to another. But if we are shortsighted and do not realize that these differences exist, we can misconstrue the attitudes and actions of another person and take them as personal affronts, when they are nothing more than the natural expression of that person.

We can imagine, for example, a friendship between a person of the devotional, religious type and one of scientific, agnostic bent. Unless fanatical, the scientist's skepticism is not a character flaw. Rather, it is part of his basic disposition to be intelligently doubtful. Similarly, the devotional person's religious and mystical fervor is perfectly appropriate—for him. If these two people understand that the beliefs of the one are not insults to the other, then they can probably forge a meaningful relationship. But if the devotee makes it his "duty" to convert the agnostic to religion, or if the scientist makes it his mission to dissect rationally the seeming lack of logic in the beliefs of the devotee, there is going to be serious trouble.

The same kind of conflict can arise in a marriage between a person who loves details and another who is more abstract by nature. After all, this rather simple difference can easily create much difficulty in communication. The two people will look at the same facts and draw totally different conclusions. The person who loves details will proudly present a tabulation of statistics, and the other will fall asleep with boredom. Or, the abstract thinker will become excessively irritated at the other for failing to perceive the true essence of what he's saying.

But it need not be so. The enlightened person realizes that psychological differences can be *harmonized*. They need not be accentuated; they do not have to become wedges that split apart the relationship. Rather, when properly handled, they can stimulate real growth.

How can people work effectively with such marked differences in a relationship? Through tolerance. The devotee and the agnostic must realize that each embodies an important facet of human expression; neither is right and neither is wrong. Each is simply heeding irresistible forces within. Similarly, the lover of details and the abstract thinker must understand that each expresses a valid method of thinking; the one is not superior to the other. They can just do different things with their minds.

This first step of tolerance then sets the stage for harmony. When the devotee learns to blend his religious drive with the investigative techniques of the scientist, and when the scientist learns to blend his rationality with the faith, aspiration, and idealism of the devotee, they will find that their lives have become greatly enriched—and the relationship, too. And, when the lover of details and the abstract thinker learn that they can work together in harmony, rather than in opposition, they will find that the work of each becomes more worthwhile, more complete, and more productive.

It is also important to recognize that there are different levels of competence among people; often we have occasion to form relationships with people of either greater or lesser talent or understanding. If we react adversely to these differences—by envying a person with greater competence, by scorning an individual with less expertise, or by pretending that no differences exist—then great trouble can arise.

These problems can best be handled by treating the other person as we would want to be treated. When dealing with someone who is not as skilled as we, for example, we should adopt the approach of the loving parent, who knows that his or her child is immature and undeveloped, but nonetheless nurtures the latent potential within. However, when working with someone with greater competence, we should imitate the eager child, who seeks to learn as much as possible from the more knowledgeable adult. Under no circumstances should we pretend that these differences do not exist.

2. The misuse of energy. Because relationships are channels for the flow of living streams of energy, many different kinds of energy can flow through them—the energy of love, the energy of wisdom, creative energy, the energy of money, sexual energy, and many others. Thus, there is the potential for misuse of any kind of energy which might be part of a relationship. Obviously, a promiscuous use of energy will create many problems in the relationship.

This problem is most readily apparent in the promiscuous use of sexual energy, which causes many kinds of tension within a man-woman relationship. It often leads to enforced marriages between emotionally unprepared couples. It introduces strain into a marriage when the sexual needs of the partners are on different levels. And uncontrolled sexuality tends to destroy relationships.

But the promiscuous use of money can be as great a problem. In a marriage, if one partner wantonly squanders money without concern for his mate or children, much difficulty can arise. Likewise, if the motive for marrying is to increase one's material possessions, that improper use of the relationship will ultimately produce trouble. In a business partnership, the selfishness and greed of one may create great stress and cause the disintegration of the bond. Even among friends, a person who continually borrows money, pleading great need but never repaying his debts, will eventually place more strain on the bond of friendship than can be indulged.

Just so, the energy of industry and creativity may produce various stresses if not properly used. The businessman or professional who is so driven by his work and his quest for fame that he ignores the demands of his family will eventually come to grief on the home front.

The energies of relationships can be abused in other ways as well. If one partner in a bond is a conceited egomaniac who consistently grabs the spotlight of attention and shoves the other person out of it, this selfishness will damage the other person's self esteem and undermine the healthiness of the tie. Or, if an individual regularly hurts other people as a means of "protecting" his own little domain, he will arouse resentment and fears that will strain his relationships. This problem is frequently found in boss-employee relationships, in which the boss feels threatened by the competence and ambition of those working for him, and becomes obsessed with the effort to put them in an unfavorable light. He may actually feed them false data to work with or misrepresent their efforts to his superiors, in his attempt to retain an "advantage." The resulting harm leads to chaos and confusion, not greater artistry.

Curiously, it is also a promiscuous misuse of energy to withdraw from active participation in a relationship, crawling into a comfortable shell of our own. Shutting the door on others can hurt them as much as overt harm—and destroys a part of our own essential humanity as well.

The antidote for the misuse of energy is behaving responsibly. If we hire an electrician, we expect him to work in a responsible way and not go around shocking people with electrified wires. Such behavior would be an irresponsible use of electric energy. Similarly, whenever we use any kind of human energy, we must use it wisely. We must act responsibly in the relationships we forge.

The heart of behaving responsibly is recognizing the duties inherent in our relationships and working unselfishly to fulfill them. In some cases, these duties are spelled out quite clearly, as in most business relationships. At other times, the duties may be implied rather than stated, as in friendships. Often, a bond will involve both stated and implied commitments, as in marital and parental relationships. The person who tries to shirk his duties or manipulate another person to assume them is not behaving responsibly; he is misusing the energies of the bond. By contrast, the artist of human relationships is a person who is responsive to the true needs of the relationship. He does not think so much about what he can get out of the bond as he does about what he can add to it—how he can enrich the experience of sharing, how he can help the other person in his or her activities, and how he can contribute to their mutual expression. Instead of resenting his responsibilities, he is constantly finding ways to expand them, since that is the key to making the relationship ever more meaningful.

At the same time, the responsible person does what he can to ensure that he does not injure the quality of the bond. He works to clean out his own negative and destructive habits, emotions, and thoughts. He strives for wholesomeness of expression. He makes this effort because he realizes that *he is one of the channels through which the living streams of energy of the relationship must pass,* and if he is unclean, how can the relationship be healthy?

3. A lack of love. The basic energy of relationships is love—not the emotion of "being in love" or the sexual urge associated with "making love," but rather the quality of goodwill-sharing. This quality of love has many derivatives which are the tools used in building right human relationships: affection, patience, forgiveness, benevolent concern, caring, generosity, kindness, gentleness, tolerance, harmony, devotion, and idealism. When these expressions of love are missing in a relationship, difficulty will inevitably brew.

Some people mistake love for possessiveness. They believe that to love a person is to own him. Thus, they view their loved ones and friends as their own personal belongings, like pieces of furniture or objets d' art. Such an attitude is a perversion of the energy of love and will cause conflict. The adjustment of this error lies in realizing, as Edgar Cayce put it, that "Love is giving. Only that you give away do you possess."

A sure sign of a lack of love is any trace of selfishness. It should be obvious that selfishness is one of the largest stumbling blocks to right relationships. When a person uses a relationship to help him manipulate and connive his way to success, a price will be paid in the quality of the bond. Or, when one partner in a relationship sits back and lets the other make all the contributions, sacrifices, and effort, difficulties are inevitable. Mostly, however, the lack of love crops up in the thoughtless, careless responses we make to others. It is expressed in such destructive forms as envy, coldness, rudeness, anger, criticism, harmfulness, insensitivity, malice, ill will, resentment, and bitterness. These adverse forms of behavior undermine the stability of a relationship. They pollute the quality of the bond and drag both parties down into a cesspool of emotional murkiness and squalor from which it is hard to emerge.

The only cure for possessiveness, selfishness, and emotional cruelty is an increase of benevolence. How is benevolence increased? In exactly the same way that any talent or quality is increased—by practicing it. Just as an artist works years and years developing his techniques and mastering his medium, spending many hours every day, so must we work patiently and skillfully to build our talent in expressing benevolence. We must make a concentrated effort to treat others with affection and kindness. We must watch ourself closely, too: when we lapse into undesirable activities—such as being possessive or cruel—we must check that behavior and begin acting once more with compassion, tenderness, and tolerance.

We must especially work to forego any tendency to criticize and hold grudges. Criticism is perhaps the greatest threat to relationships. It is, of course, perfectly acceptable to lovingly offer helpful suggestions to another person. But criticism destroys. It impairs the exchange of love.

Holding grudges is also more serious than many people realize. A grudge creates resentment, which builds as time passes, increasing in strength until it becomes an irrational force within the individual—and likewise within the relationship. It opens the door for anger and hatred to enter. If strong enough, it can entirely block out the light of love. To quote Cayce once more: "To hold grudges, to hold malice, to hold those things that create or bring contention, only builds the barrier to prevent thy own inner self enjoying peace." The cure for such resentment is, of course, forgiveness—giving up the grudge.

Giving up our grudges. Sacrificing our irritation. We *can* live without our hostility—if we really want to. Giving up our anger: that is what true forgiveness is. Through forgiveness, the irritants of a relationship are dissolved, so that loving energy can flow freely between the two people again. Anything short of this adjustment is not forgiveness and will not produce right relationships. As the old cliché says, two wrongs do not make a right. The fact that each person has equal grudges does not create balance.

A good way to achieve balance in any relationship is to begin by making a list of all the grudges we hold against the other person. A list of grudges is not a list of the things that this person does to irritate us. Rather, it is a list of how and why we irritate *ourself*—when in the company of this person. They are our grudges, after all: our problems. Then, once we have compiled this list, we must forgive! This forgiveness must be more than a superficial statement of the moment—it must be a commitment of our whole being to forego any resentment. Hence, it may take repeated effort over a period of several months—daily reaffirmations to ourself that we have truly forgiven this person—in order to completely erase the grudges that have accumulated.

Forgiveness is important work. It opens up much greater potential for love than is possible otherwise. But the work of forgiveness is all too easily sidetracked—for example, by the resentment that "I'm the only one" trying to improve the quality of the bond. "Why do I have to do all the work?" we ask. "Why must I be the one who makes all the sacrifices? Why should my mother-in-law benefit from an improved relationship when she hasn't made any effort to help me?" Such resentment is an insidious illusion which retards any chances for improvement. Underneath it is the selfish assumption that the other person is more responsible for the conflict. Rather than begin the work of forgiveness in good faith and with the expectation that the other person will respond, we selfishly assume that it is the other person's responsibility to initiate the changes we seek.

Such an attitude is seriously out of tune with the rhythm of the universe. The best way to overcome it is to consider carefully these two questions:

1. How many times has someone else made the effort to improve his or her relationship with us? How many times has someone reached out and lent us a helping hand so that we could better ourself? Even if this other person is totally in the wrong—which is unlikely—is it not time for us to repay our debt for the help we have received, by offering to do the work to correct this relationship, without any strings attached?

2. Which is the larger irritant and stumbling block to creating a right relationship: the other person's undesirable behavior, or our stubborn reaction to it?

THE SEED OF BEAUTY

When the resentments and grudges of a relationship have been washed away, it is then possible to begin to see the seed of beauty within the relationship—the potential for a positive, meaningful, and mutual expression. It takes some imagination to glimpse this unmanifested beauty, just as it takes a powerful imagination for the sculptor to visualize the final masterpiece within an uncarved block of marble. But by taking some time to contemplate the meaning and purpose of a relationship, it can be done. Obviously, many of the ideas already put forth in this essay can be used to help structure such a quest for insight. A number of questions can be asked. For example: what human qualities are being developed by each person involved in the relationship? What will be the practical benefits of developing them? What forms of behavior is each person learning to tolerate? And, what mutual strengths will be given greater expression by harmonizing the points of conflict?

It is also important to understand that a right relationship involves the total being of each person. The mind, for example, must be used to perceive the meaning and purpose of a relationship and to work intelligently to improve its quality. It is also used to participate in mutual creative expression. The emotions, on the other hand, are used to express love in the relationship—and love in its many aspects of goodwill, compassion, kindness, and the like should be a part of all human relationships (even business partnerships). It is love, working through the emotions, that increases the strength and stability of the bond. Finally, the physical body is the vehicle through which physical closeness is established, thus manifesting the relationship on the physical level.

If a relationship exists at any of these three levels (mental, emotional, or physical), then it should exist as strongly at the other two levels as well. Often the problem in a relationship is that two strands of the bond are firmly established but the third is not. There may be a strong physical and emotional bond in a marriage, for example, but intense static on the mental level. That static must be removed, of course, before the seed of beauty can be seen.

It should be remembered, moreover, that the personality bond is not the whole extent of the relationship. There is also a relationship between the inner beings of the two individuals—a spiritual bond. It is at this inner level that the seed of beauty for the relationship actually exists, for a right human relationship is one that reflects the brotherhood of the inner beings. It is a relationship through which the inner love, wisdom, and power can shine.

A right relationship is like a serene pool of water reflecting the royal blue glory of the sky. Should the pool be in turmoil and not serene, it cannot reflect the sky above. Therefore, only a right relationship can become an adequate expression of the brotherhood we all share and participate in—at the level of the soul.

When this vision of the ideal is glimpsed, the process of building a better relationship can begin. The word *building* is not used here lightly; the improvement of human relationships is a definite *activity*. It is necessary to expend effort to achieve success.

It is likewise important to use intelligence. Just as a blueprint is needed for building a house, it is also necessary to have a blueprint for shaping the energies of a human relationship into right patterns. Fortunately, there is such a blueprint, one which everyone can use. It is the ideal of brotherhood: "As you do it to one of the least of these my brethren, you do it to me."

Brotherhood is the understanding that each member of humanity shares a common purpose and heritage at the level of the inner being. At this inner level, we are all members of the same group—and that includes the Christ on the one hand and the least of these our brethren on the other. That's the blueprint—the model we should use in building any of our relationships into works of living art. We must strive to let this basic plan for brotherhood, harmony, and unity shine through, not only on the inner levels of our being, where it already exists, but also on the personality levels, where it has not existed.

Of course, one cannot create a work of art without some kind of medium. The painter must have his paints and canvas. The sculptor must have his block of marble. The artist of right human relationships must use his own energies: he must contribute part of himself to every relationship. Thus, he builds with his own physical, emotional, and mental energies—plus the energies of the people he relates to. For no one ever builds alone—the work of creativity is always shared by everyone in a relationship. If that were not so, the resulting relationship would be about as meaningful as a relationship with a brick wall.

It will help here to consider a couple of definitions. *Creativity* is the building of forms of beauty from existing materials and energies. These conditions are certainly inherent within the living art of relationships. *Beauty* is any creation which reflects the glory of the order of the universe. Thus, in a meaningful relationship, we are not just striving for peaceful co-existence, or a truce in the siege, or some limbo state of neutrality. An artistic relationship is one through which the energies of love and wisdom are being expressed, not just occasionally, but as a matter of habit!

Beauty does not spontaneously "happen," however. To work with his chosen medium, an artist uses tools. A painter employs brushes to transfer the paint to the canvas. A sculptor uses chisels to carve away the unwanted stone. Artists in the realm of human relationships must have their tools as well. These tools are caring, true perception, harmony, love, harmlessness, tolerance, and patience. It is through their steady, dedicated application that underlying beauty can be discerned and given life.

The tool of **caring** is used to attune ourself to the humanity within other people; it puts us in touch with the joy, the talent, the genius, the love, the aspiration, and the courage with which they live their lives. By actively caring about others, we support their efforts and nourish their development.

At times, the tool of caring also attunes us to the sorrow and anguish of others, but if we have mastered this tool, we will be able to use it with detachment. Thus, even in those moments of struggle, we will care sufficiently about the growth of our friends to help them overcome their sorrow and re-orient themselves to the inner joy, love, aspiration, and courage they have lost sight of. Without the ability to care deeply about the welfare of others, we really have no relationship with them at all; we may be in close physical contact with them, but emotionally and mentally we are "miles apart."

True perception is another valuable tool. Most of us never build relationships with real people—we build them with our *images* of other people. In our mind, we create papier maché models of what we think the other person is like and then build our bond with that image. Frequently, the other person is not anything like our image of him. Perhaps we formed our papier maché model ten years ago. In all likelihood, this person has changed enormously in those ten years. Still, we have not updated the image. Furthermore, the image we created may have been colored by our own frustrations, hopes, and fears, and in this way distorted. Or, we may have molded our image on partial information, or wrong conclusions, or the opinions of others. Such an image obviously becomes a barrier preventing us from making genuine contact with the other person *as he is.*

To build a right relationship, we must pierce through the illusions we have created and perceive the reality of the other person. We must tear up our papier maché models and evaluate the other person—and our relationship—honestly and without prejudice.

Harmony is like the flame of a welding torch which melts down the differences existing between two people and then joins their energies together in a much stronger bond. Or, to employ a different simile, harmony is like the skillful composer who takes two seemingly discordant tones and plays with them in his mind until he understands their true musical relationship and potential for harmony. Then he uses the tones in that combination, producing pleasing sounds rather than discordancies. If one person in a relationship, for example, is intolerant of loudmouths, and the other person is a loudmouth, it is the tool of harmony that will help the two learn to fit together more perfectly. After all, the loudmouth can help the intolerant person develop tolerance, and the intolerant person can help the loudmouth learn some of the principles of right speech.

Harmony is cultivated by learning to find ways to blend our noblest efforts with the productive labors of others, so that we may achieve mutual goals. At times, harmony is best produced by sharing common interests, but it can also be developed by using our skills and interests to *support* the separate activities of another. The abilities to cooperate and compromise are important elements in harmony.

Love is used to strengthen the quality of any relationship. In the process, it also helps us break down the barriers of our selfishness and thus enter more fully into close ties. As previously stated, this energy of love is not the self-serving sentimentality most people equate it with, nor the emotional "high" extolled in popular songs. Rather, love is a natural response to the humanity within other people. It flows automatically once we have learned to perceive the inner humanity in all—once we have begun to honor the needs, contributions, and inherent virtues of others. And as our "throughput" of love increases, we learn the many ways it can be used to build better relationships: by expressing compassion, benevolent goodwill, generosity, gentleness, tenderness, kindness, and affection. Obviously, the quickest way to develop this particular tool is by cultivating the use of these qualities in our daily life—the qualities of compassion, goodwill, generosity, gentleness, tenderness, kindness, and affection.

Harmlessness is an indispensable tool in the art of building right human relationships. The temptation to hurt someone—even with an unkind word—must always be steadfastly resisted. This guideline applies not just to physical harm, but to emotional and mental harm as well. It applies not only to overt harm, but also to harm caused by failure to live up to one's responsibilities, failure to make needed decisions, or failure to behave in a compassionate, helpful way. There are times, for example, when silence can be painfully harmful.

Such harmfulness sabotages our other efforts at improving relationships. Thus, we must always strive to be *creative* in our relationships, never *destructive*. We must learn to curb our anger, our hate, our jealousy, our vindictiveness, and our pettiness. Harmlessness can best be achieved by honestly facing the times we have hurt others—either intentionally or accidentally—and by carefully considering what forms of behavior would have been more loving and constructive.

We must take care, however, never to let our concern for being harmless degenerate into a negative, passive approach to life, where we are reluctant to do anything at all for fear of hurting someone. Such an attitude is a distortion of true harmlessness, which should be an active expression of goodwill and helpfulness.

Tolerance is an important adjunct to harmlessness. It is the ability to endure the outrages and the cruelties—or merely the silliness and limitations—of another person without striking back in kind. We tend to be intolerant of people who are different, who are foolish, or who hurt us. We must learn, however, that there is never any excuse for being intolerant of someone who is "different"—in race, religion, or anything else. At the inner levels of reality, all men and women have the same origin. Nor is there any excuse for intolerance of the foolish. We, too, are foolish at times. And there really is no reason for being intolerant of those who would hurt us. Because the universe is orderly, just, and benevolent, the meanness of other people produces its own just punishment. We do not have to be vindictive, hateful, and bitter toward others—and if we are, then our relationships with them will be quickly poisoned by our own attitudes (and we will suffer thereby). Instead, we can tolerate the baseness of such people, because we know the universe will respond far more effectively to correct their waywardness than we ever could.

Of course, tolerance always implies certain common-sense rules of thumb: we need not tolerate a situation which endangers our life or the lives of others. Nor is it desirable to become passive and let others manipulate us. But there are times when we must tolerate the impositions, unfairness, and even cruelty of another in order to reap the full growth potential of the relationship. In fact, it is unrealistic to attempt to build *right* human relationships without this ability to endure the impositions or selfishness of others. We are often drawn into circumstances where success can be achieved only through tolerance.

Finally, the tool of **patience** is an important part of the effort. The art of building right human relationships is not mastered overnight, any more than a great drama can be written and staged overnight. Changes occur slowly, and the artist must have the patience to stay with the project until the desired beauty is fully realized.

This tool is more important than might be suspected at first, for the immediate result of any effort to improve a relationship is sometimes more negative than it is positive. In specific, if the *conscious* effort toward improvement is being made by one person alone, it often happens that the other person reacts with greater antagonism than ever. The reason why is twofold. First of all, any attempt to improve a relationship must begin with cleaning out the negativity of the problems. But while this negativity is being flushed away, it flows out of the subconscious through the conscious mind. Thus, the people involved become much more aware of the negativity than before, especially that which has been deeply embedded and hidden from view. It may take several months for all the effluence to be discharged, and during that time the relationship may be quite uncomfortable — as both people react to this flushing out process. But the patient person will realize the need for this cleansing and will not be discouraged. He has glimpsed the seed of beauty and is capable of enduring until it is manifested.

Secondly, the other person may resent the fact that changes are occurring and may try to resist the improvements. This resistance can come even if he is not consciously aware that an attempt to build a better relationship is being made. On the subconscious level, the activity is being perceived psychically. And, if the person is malicious or cruel, he or she may even launch a psychic attack — to try to upset the process of building an inspired relationship.

Such a person will realize that his unfair and unethical domination of the relationship is being halted. His evil consciousness has no desire whatsoever for a balanced and harmonized relationship reflecting the beauty of the divine. Obviously, with such a person a tremendous amount of patience is required. But even in these cases, right human relationships can be established.

One might wonder why we should take the trouble to build right relationships with malicious people. Why offer love, if only hatred will be returned? The answer is straightforward: even malicious people are our brethren. We cannot hope to establish right relationships with the best of our brethren if we are unwilling to do likewise with the worst of our brethren. Moreover, there are wonderful compensations for the effort, for any time we direct love toward another person, there will be a loving response—if not from the other person, then from somewhere in the universe. The Law of Exchange guarantees it. Love is never wasted; every loving act is indelibly imprinted in the memory of the universe. It is never erased; instead, it is strengthened by subsequent acts of benevolence and goodwill. Because love accrues like dividends on invested money, the practice of patience is really a dynamic process yielding great returns.

Tools, of course, are worthless unless used. It is pointless for a person to go to the store and buy the best quality cooking utensils and then go out to restaurants for all his meals. The cooking utensils become nothing more than items of show. Just so, it is pointless for a person to talk knowingly about the tools of caring, true perception, harmony, love, harmlessness, tolerance, and patience, yet never use them to build more artistic human relationships.

As stated, the seed of beauty lies within each relationship. But that seed never becomes the living art of right human relationships until the people involved begin to make the honest effort to create that ideal bond, using the proper tools.

THE DOOR OF BROTHERHOOD

The most obvious benefit of building right human relationships is the joy of seeing beauty emerge from circumstances that have been chaotic. This steady unfoldment of beauty involves more than merely smoothing out problem wrinkles. It is not, for example, just a case of a couple once on the verge of divorce learning to co-exist peacefully "for the sake of the children." Instead, it is the discovery of once-latent dynamic qualities within the relationship, so that the husband and wife are able to work together creatively, inspiring each other in their self development and expression. It means lifting the quality of their bond to the point where they truly become an inspiration to others, a model of harmony between two people. It is a level of beauty and joy which far transcends the stereotyped concepts of marital harmony and bliss.

Nor is it just a matter of reducing some of the tension with people we don't care for very much. On the contrary, it is the dawning of a much better ability to perceive the *humanity* within another person—no matter how poorly he or she may express it—and the charging of our attitudes so that we can properly honor that humanity (even if the other person does not). This aspect of building right human relationships is high and noble work; for it recognizes the dignity of mankind and pays tribute to it—a truly enriching experience. Rather than being snobbish, saying, "That fellow is so hopeless, so dumb," we begin to see the actual nature of his struggle and effort, and the valuable lessons he is learning. We begin to respect him. Rather than playing the bigot, emphasizing the differences between ourself and other people, we choose to emphasize the similarities—the common aspirations, the common hopes, the shared achievements and strengths. Rather than envying another's good fortune or talent, we rejoice in his human potential and honor the progress he has made in developing it. And thus, we begin to understand more completely Will Rogers' statement, "I never met a man I didn't like."

But there are other benefits, too, which come from mastering the art of right human relationships. It lifts the spirit of friendship out of the common expression of "someone I enjoy being with" and redefines it as "someone I enjoy sharing my humanity with, someone who greatly enriches my life, and someone who can be enriched in the same way by contact with me." This transformation greatly intensifies the meaning of friendships. Unfortunately, few people truly taste the full depth and breadth of the experience called "friendship." The others do have friends and enjoy their company, but it is almost because they are expected to. They have no concept whatsoever of the transfiguring depth of true friendship—friendship as expressed, for example, between Christ and the beloved disciple, John. They have never given a second thought to other great friendships on record in the annals of human history: Paul and Timothy; Yogananda and his master; Pope, Swift, Arbuthnot, and Gay; Johnson and Boswell; Helen Keller and Anne Sullivan; and many others. Yet the sublime bonds of these relationships—which transcend the interruptions of birth and death—are merely the rewards for the practice of right human relationships.

Then, too, the mastery of right human relationships allows a person to cope effectively with evil-minded people. This might not seem to be much of a benefit, but it is. There *are* evil people in the world. We often deal with them, like it or not. If we do not know how to handle them, we will end up being manipulated by them. But the master artist of human relationships has gained the knowledge he needs to deal competently with them. He can approach evil and malicious people with pity, compassion, and steadfastness. Confronted with such strength, the evil will eventually be shattered.

Moreover, as the physical, emotional, and mental bonds of a relationship are purified and rebuilt, the artist begins to perceive more fully the nature of the bond that exists at the inner levels of being. Here he finds the prototype for all of the emotional manifestations of love, and learns how to use this prototype to raise the quality of his relationships to entirely new dimensions.

Eventually, the artist also comes to understand that relationships are expressions of the dynamic will of Universal Intelligence. It is the will of God that we form relationships with other people and that we make these right relationships. It is the will of the Life Principle that we become healers of life, creators of life, and participators in life. Through our relationships, we fulfill our duty as healers, by working to harmonize the energies of conflict. We satisfy our role as creators by building relationships which are channels of mutual creative expression. And we live up to our obligation to participate in life by using our relationships to *commune* with all other people.

Communion is not a process of sipping some wine and eating some bread. The ritual is merely a symbol for a much deeper reality. We actually partake of communion through our right relationships with all mankind. Whenever we treat another person as we would treat the Christ, we drink of the wine. Whenever we mutually serve as a channel of creativity with another, we eat of the bread. But whenever we treat "one of the least of these my brethren" in a manner unbecoming Christ, we estrange ourself from His fellowship and His communion.

The essence of communion is brotherhood. Contrary to public opinion, brotherhood is not a utopian goal. It exists right now: brotherhood is a reality on the inner levels of being. Paul referred to it in 1 Corinthians 12 as the "body of Christ" and told us that we are all members of it. As we contemplate this idea, we begin to understand that brotherhood is not a state, it is not a condition. It is a vital, moving flow of energy—the energy which links all humanity together as brothers and sisters. It exists in war as well as in peace. It exists in moments of individual depression and isolation as well as in times of individual exaltation. It exists regardless of whether or not we believe in it. It exists regardless of whether or not we are conscious of it.

To commune with brotherhood—with all humanity—is simple and open to everyone. It is so simple, indeed, that many may not think it worth the effort, but it is. As we relate to our spouse, let us realize that we are communing with all humanity through this bond. As we relate to our parents, let us remember that we are touching the living energy of brotherhood as well. As we relate to our friends, let us recall that we thus link ourself with all people, everywhere and in every epoch, and with Christ Himself. Let us visualize the living streams of brotherhood pouring through us, and in the perfect communion we are celebrating with our loved ones and friends, let us see the reflection and the manifestation of our constant communion with all mankind.

Communing with brotherhood can have special significance when it is a part of the ritual of communion, but it is also an activity which should be a constant part of our daily living. Furthermore, it is something which requires our own initiative and input. Brotherhood, the final glory of right human relationships, is not something which will come in a blinding flash of lightning from above. There will be no trumpet call from the angelic hosts, no parting of the clouds so that brotherhood may descend. It will come through the honest and intelligent efforts of each one of us, as we commune with all of our fellow men and strive to create masterpieces of right human relationships—the living art—in our life.

THE SPIRIT
OF GENEROSITY

GIVING A HAND

There is an old story about a greedy and selfish man who fell into a lake. He did not know how to swim, but he was not far from the wharf, so his rescue seemed certain. Indeed, a number of people rushed up and extended their arms to the struggling man, saying, "Give us your hand." But the fellow did not seem to understand and did not respond to the help. All efforts failed, and the man drowned.

Later that day, one of the would-be rescuers described what had transpired to the deceased man's neighbor, who knew him well. The neighbor shook his head and said, "It's not your fault for not knowing, but you went about the whole rescue effort incorrectly. You see, a selfish and greedy person like my neighbor does not understand the meaning of the word *give*. When you reached out to help him, you should have shouted, "Here, *take* my hand."

Many people do not understand the meaning of the word *give*. They equate it with weakness, with "giving in" and succumbing. Sarcastically and with contempt, these people divide the world into two classifications: the takers and the took. They measure their success and happiness in terms of what they have and what others have not; they spend their time contemplating how much they can get, what they can take, and how much responsibility they can avoid. They view life in negative terms, consequently ignoring the vast abundance of riches and opportunities that is but an arm's reach away—if they would only learn to give.

Giving and receiving are important: they are parts of a fundamental process of life. We live, quite simply, in a generous universe. If we wish to live successfully and creatively within this universe, then we will have to become truly generous, too. For if we do not live the spirit of generosity, then we are out of tune with a basic principle of the universe.

There are times we must give, times we must receive. Frequently, we must both give and receive at the same time. But being truly generous does not come merely by increasing our commitment to sharing. The desire to be generous is important, of course, but it must be complemented by an intelligent understanding of what generosity is and how it should be applied. Unintelligent giving is a waste of time and effort. And misdirected giving—giving with a selfish motive—is a thinly disguised curse.

Indeed, many "gifts" are quite harmful. When we give destructive criticism, it hurts rather than helps. When we give someone bitter opposition, it is an expression of hostility rather than goodwill. Just so, we can give diseases, we can give problems, we can give black eyes, we can give trouble, we can give grief. Through our laziness we can give someone so much work that we cause his eventual exhaustion and collapse. The list could be extended until it became very long.

Other "gifts" are not directly harmful, but nonetheless selfish and misdirected. Conspicuous giving, for example, is really just vanity. And giving with an ulterior motive—giving in order to get—is actually a form of bartering. Neither of these is an example of generosity.

Sometimes we give the right thing but at the wrong time—an instance of unintelligent giving. We may need to give discipline to a child, for example, but if we wait too long to give it, the educational benefit of the discipline may be entirely lost. A classic example of giving the right thing at the wrong time is the tennis fan who shouts a word of praise for a well-executed shot while the volley is still in progress, thus breaking the player's concentration. The praise often causes a subsequent poor shot, instead of rewarding the good one.

The other prevalent instance of unintelligent giving is when we wish to help someone in difficulty but give him the wrong thing. Perhaps we give him money when he needs love and understanding instead. Or, conversely, we give him religious dogma and pompous preaching when what he needs most is some financial support. Still another common example of wrong giving is seen in difficult family situations, when we give someone the attention and indulgence he demands, solely for the purpose of "keeping the peace." If that attention and indulgence cause him to develop poor personal habits, then they are gifts that help no one.

Thus, a study of generosity and its aspects of giving and receiving is worthy of our attention and thought. It is a subject which must be approached with intelligence, else the results will be considerably different than what we had anticipated, perhaps even disastrous. Moreover, we must strive to understand the *purpose* of generosity, for only then will we comprehend the values of generosity and the reasons for giving. Only then will we actually become generous even as the universe is generous.

Once we have understood the nature of generosity, however, we can then work to make it an active part of our daily expression. We can open ourself to the spirit of generosity and let it work through us and move us. In this way we can become familiar with the beneficent impact that intelligent generosity can have upon others—and upon ourself as well. And then whenever we give, whether the gift be money, praise, or a helping hand, we will in a very real sense be giving the love and wisdom of the universe.

AN INVESTMENT IN LIFE

There are three basic aspects of generosity. The first is the inclination to give, but that alone does not guarantee true generosity. Much giving is just thinly disguised selfishness. The inclination to give must therefore be combined with the second element: a willingness to give what we have in abundance. In other words, we gracefully share with others what has been already shared with us. In so doing, we discover the third element of generosity: the need to be motivated by a benevolent intention to help. Giving that originates in other motives— for example, as a result of social pressure (as in much modern "charity")—is just giving and not an expression of benevolence. It is not generosity.

The process of generosity should be thought of as an investment that we make in our life. Like any investment, it is made in the expectation of a worthwhile return, and its success is measured by that return. But the return must not be looked for in selfish terms—by how much *we* will benefit from it (although we surely shall). Rather, we look for the return in the lives of the people we are trying to help with the gift. This investment is much like the investment parents might make in their child by sending him or her to college. They do not expect the child to repay the cost of the education, but measure their investment in terms of what the child can then do throughout the rest of his or her life with that college preparation. All gifts should be measured in this way.

In being generous, we invest ourself, our concerns, and our resources—whatever we have an abundance of. We make these investments in the people associated closely with us, in the people we meet from day to day, in the responsibilities we bear, and in the opportunities that come to us. In true generosity we do not fling our resources indiscriminately to the wind and let whoever happens by pick them up. We choose our investments of time, interest, and concern with intelligent care, to insure that the return will indeed be a profitable one. After all, "as we sow, so do we reap." And if we sow the wind, we will surely reap the whirlwind.

If we give silliness, we will reap indiscretion. If we invest mere sentimentality, we will earn a dividend of superficiality. If we give hostility, we will receive anger and rejection in return. If we invest harsh criticism, we will be judged harshly.

But if we give kindness, we will reap respect and affection. If we give help, we will earn a dividend of friends who are mature, responsible, and able to give help themselves. If we give benevolence and compassion, we will find that people will seek out our company and share their abundance with us.

As with any investment, the investments of generosity require time to mature. The kind word of praise given in a spirit of friendship may be met at first with a rebuff. But the generous person is one who understands the basic principle of exchange and response in the universe and does not quickly panic and try to cash in on his investment. He gives it time to mature and makes the investment large enough to do some genuine good. When it has indeed matured, he wisely reinvests it for still further gain. He never allows his investment of generosity to become static, and thus he practices the wise economy of the inner being.

These investments of generosity are far less speculative and risky than the investments we make with money. We are actually making our investment in life itself, even though the direct recipients of our gifts are friends and relatives and people we know. But since each individual human being is an expression of the One Life, our investment in that person is in truth an investment in the life which sustains us all. It may happen that the individual will squander the praise or the help or the money we give him (or we may think he has squandered it), but our investment is backed by the One Life. An investment in true generosity is never lost, never defaulted. It is the safest and surest investment that can be made.

THE VALUE OF THE INVESTMENT

Generosity is based on the principle of sharing our abundance. The problem is that many people do not comprehend the secrets of abundance. Even people with great abundance—in money, in opportunities, in human qualities, or in friends—often do not understand the secrets of abundance, although presumably they should have gained some experience in the matter.

The great law of abundance is that it must be used, it must be shared with others, it must be reinvested. It must not be hoarded, for it has an inner quality which resists hoarding, and it will eventually destroy the person so foolish as to attempt to hold it all for himself or herself. This secret can be seen quite obviously (and all secrets are obvious to those who care to investigate them) in the hoarding of money. But it is equally visible when a person tries to hoard his opportunities, his friendships, his kindly words, and his human qualities and strengths. The person who has good and trusted friends, for example, but is jealous of everyone else who shares the friendship of these people, will eventually be overwhelmed by his own envy.

Why is this so? The answer is straightforward: the universe's basic preoccupation is with evolving, growing, and expanding in consciousness. Nothing remains static, although it may seem that way on occasion to unobservant eyes. Simply put, the universe is constantly reinvesting itself even as we must reinvest ourself. Thus, any amount of abundance that accrues *must* be used to help create greater abundance. If the human being who has been granted stewardship of the abundance does not work consciously and with generosity to achieve this greater abundance, then life itself will take over and force the issue. In many cases, the person will be stripped of his stewardship until he or she once more demonstrates sufficient responsibility.

Thus, generosity serves a vital role in the art of successful living. As we invest in our life the abundance of dignity, integrity, goodwill, faith, hope, compassion, patience, persistence, and joy that we have achieved through intelligent and loving effort, we are bestowing the richest gifts we can on our friends and loved ones. We are sharing a precious treasure that will nourish the spirits of these other people. At the same time, our generosity also nourishes our own abundance and causes it to increase in degree and quality. Moreover, as we give freely but wisely of our own abundance—whatever it may be—we demonstrate our capacity to work effectively with the treasures of the universe, and thereby open up new opportunities for stewardship of even greater riches.

These ideas may be scorned and ignored by the ignorant, who will dismiss them as impractical or untrue. But any instance of generosity, large or small, sets an important example which is itself a form of sharing, a type of giving. Any reinvestment of our abundance, even when it may be rebuffed by the proud or thoughtless, is an offer that has been made—and further establishes our record as a responsible steward of abundance. Moreover, it is an act that honors the deepest humanitarian principles by which we live, and this produces its own internal reward.

Additionally, in most cases of generosity, our efforts will gradually attract to us those people who will respond favorably to our benevolent and altruistic projections. We will be less bothered by those who would reject us anyway and will be automatically sought out by those who can benefit from what we are offering. Eventually, if our generosity becomes a habit which extends to every facet of our life as a constant presence, we will build an environment in which we are surrounded by loyal friends, delightful people, and favorable opportunities that can help us in fulfilling our work and can assist us in our times of need.

In spite of all these good reasons for making the investment of generosity, however, many people do not make the effort. Some are still too much in the thrall of selfishness, of course, but others are not. They are inclined to be generous, but they do not believe that they have any abundance to give from! Having created a self image of impoverishment and worthlessness, they underestimate their own value and the investments they might make. Many goodhearted people fall prey to this illusion. The first step toward becoming more generous, therefore, must be to examine our own abundance or potential abundance—and see how it can be invested in life. Basically, there are four kinds of gifts by which we can invest our spirit of generosity: the investment of our human qualities, the investment of right speech, the investment of right service and right action, and the investment of material gifts. Each deserves to be examined in detail.

The Investment of Human Qualities

These are the famous "treasures of heaven" and are at once the easiest and the most difficult to give. They are the easiest because every day affords us ample opportunities to be generous with them, but they are the most difficult because we must first acquire the qualities ourself in some measure of abundance before we can share them with others.

This acquisition does take more effort, skill, and aspiration than does the mere accumulation of material wealth. It requires *commitment*.

Put in a slightly different way, these gifts are the gifts that the "Good Samaritan" gives to his fellow traveler for psychological and emotional succor. These qualities can be partially enumerated as follows:

1. *Goodwill* This is the capacity to respond favorably to the *best* within other people, recognizing that they have flaws and deficiencies but choosing not to dwell on these weaknesses or do anything which might augment them (such as paying too much attention to them). Rather, the spirit of goodwill sees the many good qualities in other people and emphasizes them, trying to help them nourish those qualities and strengths and thereby grow. This is the gift of goodwill, and by generously projecting this attitude to the people we are associated with—including the people in our past—we gradually build an aura that is dynamically positive. It will dominate our speech and action, and thus lend sincerity and integrity to what we do. And the people around us will respond favorably to this aura; we will build a reputation as someone who is friendly and trustworthy. Goodwill is *not* flattery, which is unwholesome and selfishly motivated; rather, it is a commitment to the growth and development of others and the generous expression of this commitment to those people. And it reaps great rewards for us. For example, in the art of skillful communication, it builds a psychological tone of trust and respect—it breaks down the barriers of suspicion and hostility in other people. In turn, this allows us to act with less opposition from others and

attain our goals with greater effectiveness.

2. *Dignity.* This is the recognition of the divine spark within ourself and within all people. Having acknowledged the dignity in ourself and in our fellow man, we invest this quality by treating others with respect, not condescension; by refusing to engage in petty behavior; and by acting nobly in life. We understand the importance of our relationships and treat them as hallowed communions—which is what they should be. Thus, the gift of dignity in any relationship lifts its quality to a new plateau and lets it become expressive of greater potential. And the response, of course, is that others begin treating us with dignity as well.

3. *Patience.* When investing patience, we cease putting so much weight on temporary feelings that might arise in our day to day dealings with others— moments of anger, fanatical loyalty, undue excitement, fear, and so on. We become more deliberate, sensible, and aware of the larger pattern of events: the long-term view which can overshadow any temporary fear, doubt, frustration, or the like. Thus, we are able to endure temporary moments of irrationality in others—instances of bad manners, rejection, and selfishness. We endure them not in a spirit of "sacrifice" or indulgence, but rather because we are aware of the significance of the larger picture. We patiently point out the dimensions of that larger picture, and in the process the other person becomes aware of it as well. The reward that we reap for this particular investment is the ability to complete the projects we embark upon, rather than having them founder on the rocks of impatience.

4. *Integrity.* This is the state of interior wholesomeness, inspired by our deepest humanitarian

principles. Many people lack such integrity and are instead characterized by interior chaos—no coherent set of principles, no structured format of behavior. The generous investment of integrity is made through the consistent and loving application of our deepest principles to every situation we encounter. When dealing with a person who lacks integrity, for example, we do not suddenly abandon our own ideals to deal with him on his level of intimidation, manipulation, and dishonesty. Rather, we remain steadfast in our inner convictions, while taking care not to be deceived. In this way, we demonstrate the value and the advantage of integrity. The reward that we reap is a gradual increase in integrity in those close to us, which of course makes our own expression of humanitarian ideals much easier.

5. *Faith*. This is an inner conviction that constructive and redemptive changes can occur in time, within ourself and within others as well. Goals can be reached, and the healing force within each person will gradually bring improvements. The knowledge of this is the basis of faith. And when we generously radiate this faith toward all that we meet, it becomes a great and good gift. This inner conviction serves the purpose of actually triggering that healing force and releasing it, so that the other person will indeed mature and reach the goals he has set. Faith extended to others forms a bridge of living energy which keeps open our own channels of courage, wisdom, and compassion until our goals have been reached. And if we give the gift of faith to others, then under the law of compensation we, too, will receive faith. We will meet people who will encourage us by having faith in our efforts. In this way, the bridge of living energy is extended.

6. *Hope*. The quality of hope derives from the realization that there is structure and purpose in life—that life is worth living. Our efforts are meaningful, our labors are rewarded. There are many times when the gift of this realization to others is invaluable. Certainly when a friend or acquaintance has lost his or her hope, the generous person will share his own measure of hope with that person and restore what has been lost. This can be done through verbal sharing, through action, and through thought. But the person who is truly generous will share his hope at all times, thus reinforcing the innate hope of others and helping to keep them aware of the meaning and purpose of life.

7. *Serenity*. The serene person is one who has attained a useful measure of poise, peace, and detachment. In the face of emotional disturbance and turmoil, he can remain calm and composed, in full control of himself and the energies of the situation. This is not a state of indifference, but rather one of dynamic involvement. A serene individual is able to understand why the turmoil at hand developed and what good can yet be wrought from the situation. The influence of such a person on others can often be remarkable; it can calm panic, inspire nobleness and dedication, and teach self control. Thus, it is a priceless gift that frequently influences the flow of events and lives. Of course, the greatest reward that comes to the giver of serenity is the swift staunching of disturbances which arise, thereby preventing the unpleasantness of being sucked into chaotic situations.

8. *Joy*. By expressing joy, we charge the atmosphere around us with a kind of infectious glow that helps lift the spirits of others and ourself as well. It

is an almost magical antidote for despondency, doubt, and apathy. It lifts us into a state of mind that is more alert, more responsive, more sensible, and better able to transcend external fears and worries.

9. *Graciousness*. Grace is an active attitude of appreciation and gratitude for the good works of others and life itself. Thus, the person who has become somewhat aware of grace will share it with others in a thoughtful and appreciative way. He will not insist upon fanatical independence, but will graciously allow others to do good works and "favors" for him (without in any way becoming a parasite). In this way, he gives them opportunities for expressing themselves. Moreover, the gracious person responds with appreciation and dignity to the humanity in those favoring him. And he is able to bestow his own gifts to others without any trace of irritation or condescension, and this stimulates a wholesome reaction in them. The rewards for the investment of graciousness are the deeper ties of friendship that result from it.

10. *Persistence*. This is the courage to endure until jobs are finished, responsibilities met, and goals achieved. It is one of the greatest investments we can make in our livingness and is especially important within the context of groups, for it is often the persistent person who holds a group together, inspires it, and motivates it onward to achievement. Persistence is the mark of the courageous person who is able to sacrifice temporary good feelings and well being for a greater reward in due time. It is the gift of leadership and is therefore rewarded by further and more significant opportunities for leadership.

The Investment of Right Speech

Much of what we give is given through the words we say—and the words we do not say as well. Thus, our use of the spoken word is an investment in life, and an excellent channel for our generosity.

The gifts of the spoken word are gifts that have immediate impact. They can be bestowed in a formal context, as in a public speech, or in an informal, casual way, as in the conversation of two friends. These gifts can be made to one person or to many. But the impact is swift and often easily judged, by observing the feedback. Thus, if our words produce a favorable reaction, in all likelihood the gift has been a good one. On the other hand, if the words are met unfavorably, then we must analyze the gift we have given. It may have been an improper gift, one that hurts; it may have been a good gift, but spoken at the wrong time; or it may have been a well-intentioned gift that was given with a poor choice of words.

Obviously, close observation of the verbal gifts we give to others will help us practice being a generous person. And, if we are to achieve true generosity, we must be very careful to invest in right speech.

What is right speech? It is the recognition of the power and impact of the spoken word and the resolve to use this force only for creative purposes, in loving ways. It is furthermore the abstinence from those forms of speech that will hurt another person and interfere with his or her growth, from all forms of speech that are a waste of time (and therefore not creative), and from all forms of lying.

Thus, the generous person investing wisely in life

shuns all gossip and harsh and unfair criticism. He does not say anything that will hurt another person, either directly or behind his back. He refrains from wild, speculative talk—especially speculation about the character of other people. Nor does he tacitly approve of others engaging in such gossip or criticism.

In addition, he eschews flattery and sycophantic slavering—the telling of untruths for the purpose of impressing another person. Some people might think of flattery as a form of gift, but it is a gift that is no more inspired than the gift of a match to a pyromaniac. It misleads and often causes a person to become overly confident in an area of life in which he has not actually achieved competence. Flattery, therefore, is unfair to the person involved—and even more unfair to all the rest of us who must deal with him.

Indeed, the generous person will avoid making *any* comments that might mislead another person. He will never be deceitful or dishonest—not even in seemingly insignificant ways. Some people, for example, are fond of posing as experts in fields in which they do not have expert knowledge—aspects of life in which they do *not* have an abundance and therefore should not be giving. The generous person does not play such games. What purpose would it serve for him to give directions when he himself does not know the way? His directions would only mislead. In this, and many similar instances, it is best for the generous person to remain silent.

In fact, silence is often an ideal gift, a perfect investment in right speech. Certainly when we might mislead or are tempted to hurt, then silence is clearly the preferable alternative. But silence can also be a constructive aspect of right speech. When someone is tired and wishes to relax, any form of speech from others may be an unwanted intrusion. Silence would be a precious gift rewarded with gratitude. Or, when a person is deeply involved in concentrating on a creative project, the ideal form of right speech may again be silence.

Silence is especially appropriate whenever the full truth would be painful to bear, as in many situations involving interpersonal relationships. Perhaps an obnoxious neighbor invites us to dinner but we decide to decline his invitation rather than endure his company. If the neighbor then asks us why we are not coming, it is *not* necessary to spell out the whole truth and give him a detailed accounting of his obnoxious behavior. That would be cruel. But neither should we lie. The *generous* use of right speech would be a graceful exit line such as "We simply can't make it," and then silence.

Similarly, when we know something that another person does not know, but is making an effort to find out on his own, it is hardly generous to blurt out our knowledge unless we are asked for it. We must remain silent, even when we wish to impress the other person with our greater knowledge. To give a simple illustration of this, if someone is working on a challenging mental puzzle that we have already solved, he does not care to learn the answer from us, unless he becomes totally stumped. The "gift" of the answer would be inappropriate and would jeopardize our friendship. The gift of silence is the generous one.

This rule of thumb can be applied to the process of human growth as well. Many lessons of life can be most effectively learned by others if we let them learn through their own efforts, rather than from our learned explanations. Of course, it is equally true that there are times when a helpful word will greatly assist a person in learning a lesson, and in such a case silence would not be right speech. So, right speech actually involves knowing when to say something and when not to. Making this distinction requires much practice and experience. It is not always an easy decision.

When a helpful word can be given, because we are speaking from the abundance of our wise experience and because it is the correct time to make such a comment, then it is a priceless gift. It is clearly an expression of right speech, and the reward is significant. It is the reward that any true teacher comes to understand: the joy of observing another human being grow and mature in right and proper ways.

Thus, one of the ideal ways in which the spoken word can be a useful gift is *education*. This is an investment of the abundance of our knowledge and wisdom in other people, be they children or adults. Another ideal use for the spoken word is *inspiration*. The generous person will often use the words he or she speaks to stir up other people to slough off their indifference and increase their own involvement and investment in life. This kind of generosity tends to create an environment of active people who inspire one another through their own deep interest in life.

The simplest gift of the spoken word, however, is to support and compliment others. The generous person does not mince his words of praise; instead, he takes care to highlight the achievements and qualities of others with the words he speaks. In no way is this flattery. Rather, it involves being alert to the true achievements that others make, the generous favors they do for us, and the praiseworthy qualities they display, conspicuously complimenting them at appropriate times. It means graciously thanking them for service rendered.

The value of this particular investment is immeasurable. Such kindness begins to show us the nature of our true relationship with others—and with all humanity. It opens for us a glimmer of the reality of brotherhood. And as our generosity with praise and support becomes a constant habit, the glimmer begins to glow more brightly and transform our entire life and attitude.

The Investment of Right Service

The heart of life on the physical plane is activity and "doing." It is not enough just to understand the principles of generosity; we must also perform generous acts. It is not enough only to make generous statements; we must supplement them by acting generously. Indeed, to be truly generous, we must seek to act generously in every aspect of our activity: in our work, our relaxation, our family life, and what we do for the good of mankind.

The main inhibitions to right service are thoughtlessness, selfishness, and a lack of awareness of the real benefits of helping others. Thoughtlessness is a problem because it has never occurred to many people that they could give generously of their time and energy to help others. They are insensitive to the needs and feelings of others and fail to recognize their obligations and opportunities to assist. These people usually busy themselves with being superficially nice, almost as a substitute for rational behavior. Selfishness, by contrast, is the problem of being too concerned with satisfying personal desires, to the exclusion of paying any attention to fulfilling the basic responsibilities of being a part of the human race. In fact, selfish people usually regard others as some kind of a burden to be avoided. The third problem, the lack of awareness of the benefits of service, is due primarily to inexperience. Once a person begins making the investment of generous service this inhibition rapidly disappears.

Actually, none of these inhibitions would pose much of an obstacle if we fully comprehended the meaning of the injunction, "Do unto others as you would have them do unto you." We need to interpret this principle in a personal light: for example, if we consider it valuable to *receive* a helping hand when our assigned tasks are more than we can handle alone, is it not equally important to be ready to *give* that kind of help to others when they are overburdened? Is that not what generous service is? Similarly, if we considered it beneficial as a child to *receive* guidance and friendship from wise adults, then should we not—as adults—*give* guidance and friendship to children?

The Golden Rule has been invoked so many times throughout the ages that many people now consider it trite. But trite or not, it is nonetheless the central thesis of right service. The ideas and principles of right service may be well-worn, having been thoroughly explained by wise individuals in the past, but that merely underscores their importance. What is needed now is not so much further explanation, but rather further *practice*.

Right service need not be dramatic or spectacular—and seldom is. To perform right service, we do not have to abandon our lifestyle and become a missionary in deepest, darkest Africa. For most of us, that would be counter-productive. We can find ample opportunities for right action and service within the context of our neighborhoods, our friends, our home life, and our careers. The way to begin is by asking ourself: "What kinds of service would I appreciate having others do for me?" Once we have contemplated our answer thoroughly, we can then reverse the roles by asking ourself: "How can I wisely and generously do similar things for them?" Right action is no more difficult than that and can begin quite humbly, as generous service to one or two. As we gain skill in that service, we can then gradually extend the sphere of our activity to include more and more. Indeed, true generosity implies this sort of expansion of qualities and service, for it must be harmonious with the evolution of life and consciousness in the universe.

Naturally, the reward for the investment of service is that others begin responding in kind, as indicated in the Golden Rule. The response, however, will not always be an exact accounting; if we help someone solve a difficult personal problem, that person may not be able to repay the favor directly. In fact, it is unlikely, for solving personal problems apparently is not his forte, and the gift of generosity is always made from one's abundance. Indeed, he may not be able to repay us in any way. But the repayment will come—perhaps through a different friend or new opportunities for growth.

An investment in right action brings with it another dividend, too. Service is the gateway to all growth and spiritual unfoldment. As we are generous with our time and energy in helping others, we invoke the opportunities that will make us better people: the chance to develop our mind, the occasion to increase our intuitive and psychic abilities, and the opportunity to expand our understanding and nurture our spirituality.

The Investment of Material Goods

Generosity of money and accumulated goods is of undeniable value, but again, it is an investment which must be made intelligently, lest the result be undesirable. First, we must check our motives to be sure our intention for giving is benevolent. After all, while the gift of material goods is often a generous act, there are times it is not: we might, for example, have an old chair that we dispose of by giving it away. This is hardly an instance of generosity. The person who receives the "gift" is probably being more generous than we, for he is sparing us the cost of having our junk hauled away.

In other cases, the motive for giving money and goods is not true generosity but rather exhibitionism—the desire to demonstrate to the world that we are indeed generous, even though we are not. Thus, we make a loud and visible display of our giving, making sure that our name is inscribed on a plaque or listed in the newspaper. This is not an investment in life—it is an investment in publicity and self aggrandizement. To be sure, something worthwhile may be done with the money we have given, but nonetheless *this is not generosity*.

Second, we must ascertain in advance whether our proposed gift is actually needed and will be used beneficially. Otherwise, it will not be a true investment—just a waste. For instance, our gift may only serve to support the laziness and irresponsible habits of the other person. That would not serve a constructive purpose and therefore our gift—even though benevolently motivated—would have no meaning in the universe. Only where there is purpose can there be meaning.

Of course, generosity with money is not limited to traditional "gifts." Many of our ordinary dealings with money and goods are suitable areas for our generous investment in life. An employer, for example, can be generous in his determination of fair wages for his employees, and in this case he is certainly not making a traditional "gift." But he is giving a gift of his humanity, for the wages he pays must be used by his employees to support their physical life. Likewise, an individual selling his or her home can strive for generosity in the way he handles the negotiations with the buyer—not that he will "give" the house away for a ridiculously low price, but that he will approach the negotiations with a spirit of fairness to settle on an equitable figure. The seller who tries to gouge the buyer (or vice-versa) is not living the spirit of generosity.

Even the taxpayer can pay his taxes with generosity. In this case, the amount of taxes does not change, for that is determined by mathematical formula, but the attitude does. Instead of whining and complaining about the amount of taxes and how hard it is to compute them, we can start to view our taxes as a generous investment in the protection, the achievement, and the future of our country. We can see the payment of taxes as a guarantee of our freedom, a participation in a vast public endeavor, and an involvement in the purposes of the inner spirit of our country.

The key to using material wealth as the means of our investment in life is to perceive the purpose of the investment. When we can do that, then our use of money will indeed be generous. And the reward will be the receipt of even more wealth, for we will have demonstrated our wisdom in handling material goods.

ACTIVATING THE UNIVERSE

In true giving, the personal factor must be de-emphasized and given only secondary importance. It will be present, of course, because only as individuals can we give, and only as individuals can we receive. But we must hold this personal factor at bay and not let our attempts at generosity be motivated by selfish desires to manipulate others. It is not generosity, for example, to make a gift to someone so that he will be beholden to us. That is just spiritual blackmail, and it will backfire. The reward for it is ingratitude.

Selfishness often creeps into giving. It is not uncommon to run across a self-styled "spiritual" leader who will advocate giving up all of one's personal belongings and money as a means of attaining spiritual grace, and then suggest with a straight face that these goods be given to him! Also common are the cheap metaphysicians who talk and talk about how we "grow by giving"—because they themselves are "on the take."

These are merely sophisticated beggars, and supporting their addictive habit is not part of true generosity, which must always be grounded on the bedrock of wisdom as well as benevolence. Nor is this beggary and spiritual blackmail limited to the monetary aspects of giving. Often these people affect a cloying degree of niceness, not because they value being nice, but because they want others to indulge them. This kind of niceness always carries with it a price tag: "Since I am being so nice, the least you can do is give me such-and-such." The emphasis is always on the word "me," and the concept of generosity is lost in the process.

By contrast, real giving is first, a recognition of a need in someone else or in some situation; second, a recognition of our ability to be of help; and third, a recognition of our willingness to subordinate personal welfare to provide that help. Real generosity is basically altruistic; it is pursued without much thought for the kind of reward that will be forthcoming. We may well be rewarded—indeed, the basic nature of the universe and its law of compensation *guarantee* that our acts of generosity will be repaid, somewhere, somehow, sometime. But the motive of genuine generosity is never tinged with greed. Where there is greed, there is no generosity.

The act of true generosity is inspired by our values and our deepest humanitarian impulses. As these well up from our inner being, they effectively subdue our personal interests. And as they rise and spur us on to generosity in thought, word, or deed, these impulses generate within us a joy which is an immediate reward far superior to anything achieved by the selfish individual. After all, we have recognized our deepest humanitarian obligations, we have fulfilled those obligations, and therefore the spirit radiates joy into the personality. As the old platitude puts it, "A good deed is its own reward."

There will also be secondary, more material rewards coming to us—money, friendships, opportunities, and so on—but these must not dominate our thinking. Knowing these secondary rewards will inevitably come gives us a basic trust in the nurturing capacity of the universe, and this is most valuable. We must have this trust in order to make a complete commitment to being generous. But once we have made the commitment, we must no longer be motivated by secondary benefits.

As the personal factor in generosity fades, we begin to comprehend that we never stand alone in the universe. Rather, we are always close to riches far beyond measure—in the "heaven within." This understanding comes first as a brief glimpse, but as it grows, it greatly enhances the entire procedure of generosity.

The glimpse will not grow, however, unless we actually *demonstrate* these treasures in our livingness and givingness. Only then do we become an active participant in the universe. We have to *stir up* the universe by acting; we have to *stir up* the universe by investing ourself favorably in our opportunities and responsibilities. The universe is by nature generous. But that generosity can only be tapped by us and made practical in our life when we *individualize* it—when we express it through our own acts and attitudes and words.

It may seem odd that only as the personal factor fades can we individualize generosity and make it personal. But this, of course, is one of the mysteries of individuality. As selfishness and vanity lose their grip on the personality, then the true self can begin to express itself. The heaven within becomes bound to earth and releases its treasures as an inevitable expression of its nature.

By acting generously, we activate the universe, and its riches become a potent force in our life. Our initial glimpse of the "heaven within" grows, and we begin to understand that the principles of altruism are well-founded, indeed. Then, as our generosity matures, we discover another facet of the act of giving: *we are not the only giver!* Our own capacity to give is fed by a hidden source—the great abundance of life that we tap within ourself. We also learn that it is this hidden source that responds to us—usually through the actions and attitudes of others—when we share our abundance of wisdom, love, talent, and physical goods with our brothers and sisters.

Of course, the person who has not learned to activate the universe will often fail to grasp the meaning of altruism. He will doubt its validity and fear that being generous will result in a loss for himself. If he has money, he will fear that others or life itself will take it from him and make him a pauper. So he hoards his possessions suspiciously. If he has good ideas, he fears that others will take them and use them for their own benefit, not his. So he does not share them. Seeing life as an adversary, he limits the sphere of his activity by the defensive posture he takes. His fears build a wall around him that keeps people out, but also keeps all of life out, locking him inside. Instead of discovering the riches of the universe, he sinks into a sorry state of impoverishment.

Such skeptical and ungiving people invoke a similar response in others—they are distrusted, ignored, and met with indifference. They stand out as people who take all they can get and give only what they must, and even that reluctantly. And so they are shunned. Obviously, the loss due to such an attitude is immense.

And so pointless! The imagined sacrifice of generosity is just that—imaginary. The only time the universe requires a person to sacrifice what he has is in order to receive something much better in its place. Thus, the view that being generous is a sacrifice involving risk to our security is distorted. It is the stuff that prison walls are made of—prisons of the soul.

Ironically, the poor giver is often a poor receiver as well. He may be able to grab and take, but he does not know how to receive. When the universe spreads its magnificence before him, he does not have the eyes to see it. When a fellow human being offers him needed help, he scorns it and rejects it, for fear of losing his independence. When a friend pays him a compliment, he does not know how to accept it graciously and stumbles over it awkwardly, making a fool of himself. Having never invested himself in his fellow human beings, he does not comprehend the value of the investments they offer to make in him—or the value of accepting them. He pridefully turns them down.

Ultimately, one of the rewards of giving is learning the lesson of receiving. As we become generous, our hearts are opened to receiving the riches of the universe. Some of these treasures come to us through our links with the inner life, but many come through the ministrations of others. Once we might have rejected these gifts because of the isolating curse of pride, but we now have clearer insight into the purposes of giving and receiving. So we open our heart and receive. And in so doing, we once more give something quite valuable.

BEING GENEROUS

We give from our abundance: this is true generosity. We do not sit down and eat a full dinner and then scatter the leftovers and crumbs to the needy. The generous person gives what he values most, and in so giving, doubles its value. That is the meaning of making an investment, is it not?

Nor is generosity something to be reserved for only one part of our life. To be successful in this enterprise, we must act with a generous heart, a generous mind, and a generous hand. Each of these is something that can be developed over a period of time, if given conscientious attention.

In order to develop a generous *heart,* we must drill ourself to notice that people are much better than they sometimes act. They may behave in unpleasant ways, but we train ourself to observe the good within them, struggling to rise to the surface as they do the best they can in spite of the difficulties they face. We look beyond the external conflict and with goodwill observe the inner purposes at work. We develop our empathy, so we can more fully extend compassion, patience, and faith to others who may be crabby or irresponsible. From the heart, we generously nurture the good elements within others and seek to help them recognize and respond to the blessings in their lives.

In this way, we become like the loving, wise parent who knows that his or her child will frequently pass through moments of great immaturity. But the parent does not take these moments as personal insults and thereafter withhold his or her love. On the contrary, the wise parent redoubles his investment of hope and faith in the child during those times and thereby generously helps the youngster grow in maturity.

When we can extend the same goodwill to all people, then we have developed a truly generous heart—a disciplined ability to *not* respond with hostility, anger, or irrationality when someone else is acting in those ways toward us, but rather to respond with serenity, dignity, and love. In this way, we force the other person to come up to our level of maturity (because we refuse to stoop to his), and this, too, is one of the hallmarks of a generous heart.

The generous heart is characterized by wisdom and is skilled in the art of living. It is *not* a sentimental heart or one that thinks that the answer to all problems is an overdose of sweetness and niceness. Nor is it permissive. Rather, it is faithful to its highest principles and is guided by them. Avoiding all pettiness, the generous heart emphasizes the important issues of life. For this reason, it finds it easy to ignore the minor flaws of people and their broken-record complaining. It focusses on what is being achieved and encourages further achievement through verbal and tacit support and judicious praise (not flattery). Similarly, it always gives the benefit of the doubt and scrupulously avoids gossip or fault finding in others.

In developing a generous *mind,* we must discipline ourself to overcome our usual emotional reactions to difficult and adverse situations and replace that emotionalism with calm reasoning and accurate perception. We must try to understand the underlying causes of someone's upsetting behavior and thus make good sense of what is happening. This takes effort and dedication, but that is why it is a worthwhile gift. In this work, we must *listen* to people, both physically and intuitively, and in this way ferret out the good reasons for respecting them and helping them. We must never indulge, but instead strive to comprehend. We must creatively seek out areas for mutual improvement.

The generous mind seeks to understand how it fits into the universe—and how others fit in as well. It tries to learn how it can more successfully honor its inner potential and obligations. It actively looks for responsibility—and for ever better ways of fulfilling it. Therefore, the generous mind is never critical, nor does it exhaust itself in creating clever defense mechanisms to protect itself from the rest of the world. It does not make excuses or rationalize its behavior. Rather, it looks for and defines the substance of life—our deepest humanitarian principles—and it searches for ways to express that substance. It involves itself in the realm of ideas and shares these ideas freely with others, so they may benefit from them and be stimulated to work in the realm of ideas as well. It stands up and honors the principles it holds dear and defends those same ideals in others when they come under attack. It generously gives support to people who are working effectively in the sphere of the mind—especially those who are living quiet lives of unsung heroism.

To develop the generous *hand,* we must do much more than just exchanging gifts at Christmas or contributing to charities when the volunteers knock on the front door. We must develop an appreciation for good service. The important rule here is that true service is never indulgence of others—a handout that will simply support the laziness or irresponsibility of the other person—or a mere satisfaction of petty wants. *It must be real help!* It must be a response to an actual need—and a response that will further the inner purposes of the recipient of the gift.

Sometimes real service is not at all what the other person is looking for. To be helpful, we occasionally have to issue constructive criticism, be disciplinary, or stand firm and say, "No! I'm not going to support your bad habits." It would hardly be generous service to buy a bottle of wine for an alcoholic, even though he may desperately want it. Just so, there is nothing ungenerous about saying no to someone who is making a shambles of his life and asks for your support—even though he may try to make you feel guilty about not helping him.

The generous hand is most often extended in some form of education. The selfish, ungenerous person may give a "less fortunate" person a sum of money in the hopes that he will be satisfied and go away and stop pestering him (or annoying him with guilt). But the generous person will see the real need and respond to that with genuine help. This help may not involve money at all. Usually, it is a kind of teaching which will let the individual become more in tune with his own potential, and thereby achieve a greater degree of personal efficiency through his own efforts. Such real education is priceless and is based on the principle that it is more important to teach a person to fish than it is to give him free fish.

The generous hand also supports and assists, gladly contributing a full share to the work that must be done, whatever that is. It seeks out meaningful activities and then devotes its time and energy and, when necessary, its material resources to them. But it never makes the mistake of substituting money for the contribution of time and energy. Our own involvement with the sustaining power of the universe is the motivating force for the generous hand. Our generous use of money can often wisely complement our own personal involvement and make it more effective, but it should never replace it. And indeed, it cannot.

Above all, the generous hand gives most effectively by setting a good example—by demonstrating to perfection its innermost humanitarian principles. Offering constructive criticism to another, for example, can be a generous act. But our generosity will be increased if we can reinforce our verbal suggestions with a proper example in our own life—an example that can be observed and repeated by the person we are helping. Part of developing a generous hand, therefore, requires correcting our own flaws, weaknesses, and bad habits. For whatever our example is, we will surely give it.

SHARING IN THE ONE LIFE

The more we participate in the generosity of the universe, the more we come to realize that there is only One Giver and that we are all channels for His beneficence. It is the great abundance of life in and around us that is the real giver. And just as it is our own abundance which provides the initial motivation for our generosity, so it is this greater Abundance that motivates all giving in the universe. As we become skilled at "stirring up" the universe through our individual acts of generosity, we begin to see that this is so.

Naturally, the One Abundance can flow through

any and all human beings. If one person can tap it, so can the rest of us—if we just take the time to make the effort. And the more we recognize the nature and the blessing of generosity within ourself, through our own acts, then the more we will recognize it in others. We will begin to see no real difference between the acts of generosity of others and our own. Rather, we will see the real similarity—the fact that all individualized expressions of generosity are gifts of the great Abundance in and around us.

By participating in this dynamic action of generosity, we open ourself more and more to *both* giving and receiving. Both of these functions of generosity increase together, for the doorways for giving and receiving are actually the same doorway. We may be individually giving or receiving at any one moment, but the difference lies only in our perception. In either case, it is the One Abundance that is giving. Thus, the doorway of generosity is a somewhat unique door: it does not open and close. It is always open! It is always giving: sometimes directly through us, at other times through the ministrations of others.

In simplest terms, therefore, giving and receiving are one and the same. The duality and the differences disappear, and we are left with the reality of the One Life. The generous person participates in this One Life in whatever way is appropriate at any point in time. At times, he will give fully and without reserve; at other times, he will receive—also fully and without reserve.

There is just One Life, one nurturing Life. All that this Life creates is continuously sustained and nourished by this giver of life. Through our intelligent giving and receiving as human beings, we share in the majestic sweep of the One Life. We become aware of a universal activity and make it our activity as well, by sharing our newly acquired abundance with all others. This, of course, is a great stimulus to fostering the spirit of brotherhood among men and women. Indeed, generous sharing is an essential part of the fabric of brotherhood.

If we can make the principle and the reality of brotherhood a dynamic factor in our mind and heart and all our acts, then the spirit of generous sharing will become an integral feature of our consciousness. We will come to experience the knowledge that every act of thought, feeling, and service carries with it a response—a response determined by the nature of our intentions and the quality of our acts. And if we are truly generous with life, then it will respond with many good favors and opportunities, which will help lift us to our rightful spiritual status as proper sons and daughters of God, blessed with His rich, divine inheritance.

As He gives, so we can give.

And as we do, we begin participating more fully in life—the inner life of our own higher self and the inner life of the cosmos at large.

JOY

SOMETHING EXTRA

A recurring theme in many old parables and scriptures is that the Lord of the Universe has spread a magnificent banquet for us all, a board laden with ambrosia and nectar of the highest quality. All of us are invited, but few actually do partake in the feast. That's because there are *two* halls in which the feast is being served. One is real and the other is counterfeit, but the illusory banquet is sufficiently impressive that the vast majority of people mistake it for the real one. They are quite content with it, even though the food is neither nourishing nor satisfying. It does not occur to them that they have settled upon their lowest expectations, and have thus deprived themselves, by not thinking, of the real feast. They are dimly aware that they have been promised a certain something extra in life, but they believe that they have found it—notwithstanding the fact that they still hunger and thirst, even in the midst of seeming plenty.

In the art of human living, there are many qualities which give a wholly new dimension to life when we learn to express them: peace, harmony, love, wisdom, and beauty, to name a few. But there is one which deserves special consideration, for it is an essence which can justifiably be called the ambrosia and nectar of mankind. It is a certain "something extra" unknown to the average man or woman, but nonetheless a quality which will transform the life of the individual who begins to express it. It lifts life out of the realm of the humdrum, the ordinary, and the uncreative into the sphere of the harmonious, the purposeful, and the productive. It adds a new sparkle, a new enthusiasm, and a touch of good humor. It helps us become more mature and capable of expressing confidence in the purposes of life, even when the tides of events may seemingly be flowing in opposing directions. It is the quality of *joy*.

Undiscerning people trapped in the hall of the illusory banquet have no real understanding of what joy is. They believe that the "something extra" of life can be found in the conventional state of good feelings. They talk profoundly about "bliss" and smile wanly, convinced that they have found something worthwhile—as they sup and sip from nothingness.

Joy cannot be known in the hall of illusion, for it exists only in the banquet of reality. It can, however, be cultivated by those who wish to do so. Indeed, the cultivation of joy is well worthwhile, for joy is indispensable to the art of living. It is a celebration of intelligent involvement in the universe: of creativity, of healing, of participating with the One Life. But it must be properly understood if it is to be developed. For joy is an intangible quality which exists independently of mankind in the universe, although it can be contacted by men and women and blended into their lives. It has a reality of its own; it is not the invention of mankind, nor is it the conjuration of man's imagination.

This notion may be upsetting to those who believe that they can create their own universes in their imaginations—who think that whatever they happen to believe in is right for them. This is an interesting theory, but hardly one that matches reality. Such people generally assume that joy is just the same thing as happiness or feeling good. They lead bland, lukewarm lives—uninspired, unfulfilling, and lacking in any real achievement. But they desperately want to believe that they have accomplished something of importance in their pursuit of mediocrity, so they talk loudly about their great feelings of bliss and peace, hoping someone will believe them and help sustain their somewhat fragile illusion.

It is an error to blur the distinctions between joy and the emotional states of happiness and feeling good. It is just such careless thinking which leads us into the hall of the counterfeit banquet in the first place. And once we find ourself there, there is only one way we can find the way out: through more careful and precise thinking. We can begin by comparing the three states of happiness, feeling good, and joy.

Happiness is a state of emotional contentment. Most people would define it as the absence of hardships and problems, and therein lie the roots of illusion. Happiness has no real substance—it is most often just a neutral state in which the emotional waters are calm for a period of time. Of course, happiness is sometimes produced by participation in activities one likes, but such instances are only of secondary importance. After all, if a person is disturbed by some problem in his life and racked with worry and fear, then the mere involvement in a hobby or activity which he traditionally likes will not lead to happiness. So, for most people, the state of happiness is essentially the state of "not being unhappy." And it is a fragile state, for it is not based upon the fundamental realities of the universe, but rather upon the evanescent likes and dislikes of the individual's personality. Happiness tends to be sentimental in character, heavily colored by selfish interests and personal prejudices, lacking any real depth or foundation. Made of superficialities, it crumbles under the touch of the person who grabs for it and tries to hold on to it. It is never permanent; the first problem that arises will shatter it.

Feeling good is an illusion of the same magnitude. Feeling good can be defined as the quest for pleasant emotional sensations, which are sought in a variety of ways: through the "ultimate" experience of sex, the "ultimate" empathy of watching a soap opera, the "ultimate" high of taking drugs, and so on. In each instance, the individual is seeking an outside stimulus which will make a strong impact upon his or her emotions and produce an artificial sensation. Such sensations literally induce a massive commotion in the individual's emotional body (as seen clairvoyantly)—a commotion which most closely resembles utter chaos but which nonetheless seems to appeal greatly to many people. The state of feeling good can, of course, create a feeling of happiness for the short duration of the sensation—a happiness which may indeed linger for awhile after the sensation ceases. But eventually the repeated quest for the pleasure of feeling good will lead to emotional exhaustion, intense unhappiness, and depression.

Both happiness and feeling good are emotional

states—states of being focussed on the astral or emotional plane. They are emotional responses to outside events and stimuli and are thus entirely dependent upon the nature of one's experiences at any point in time. If all is going as hoped, then happiness and good feelings result; if not, then frustration, despair, or grief are sure to ensue. In either case, the need for happiness and good feelings becomes an addiction, and the individual's center of consciousness becomes focussed almost exclusively on the emotional level. While the unimaginative would undoubtedly disagree, it is nonetheless an occult truism that the emotional plane is the very heart of the banquet of illusion. The individual who pursues happiness and good feelings becomes entrapped in that illusion, believing them to be the "something extra" he has sought. As a result, his life remains incomplete.

Manifestly, the quest for happiness and good feelings is *not* enough to fulfill the purpose of our humanity. After all, a certain kind of happiness is sometimes achieved by people in most repulsive ways. It is known that Adolph Hitler was quite happy after the Nazi victory over France. Similarly, malicious gossips seek their emotional highs in the titillation of dragging the good names of other people through mud and slime. It would be hard to argue with any conviction that such states of happiness and feeling good lift up the human spirit or contribute to the advancement of mankind.

In contrast, the genuine "something extra" is a quality which is greater than both happiness and feeling good. It is a state of being which does not find its impetus in emotional sensations or any external events. It does not fade during periods of unpleasant circumstances and hardship; it does not wither in the face of opposition or bitterness. It does not prey on the misfortunes of others, nor spring from the wells of selfishness or personal prejudice. Rather it is an abiding presence which is entered into only when one begins *sharing* in Universal Consciousness. It is not the expression of a need (as is happiness), but rather an expression of fulfillment.

While happiness and feeling good are emotional *reactions* to the events which happen to us, the bonafide "something extra" is a creative energy which molds, shapes, and above all else *acts*. It pushes outward from within, as an impelling force which permeates the whole being of an individual. It is not just an indifferent state of not having anything amiss, but also a dynamic, affirmative state of knowing that there is meaning and order in the universe, that we are sharing in that universe, and that this is right and proper, fundamentally good. In short, it is a celebration of the reality of life, both individual and universal.

Such, then, is **joy**. It is neither an emotion nor a feeling, but rather a universal quality which links us with all other universal expressions of life—when we express it. It has its origins and existence in the realm of the mind, in the banquet of reality. It is part of the landscape of the mental plane, and as such is a reflection of the bliss of the atmic plane (to use occult terminology). Joy, therefore, is a mental energy, an expression of the principle of will. It is life-giving, vibrant, and vital. It dances and flickers about like the flame of a candle, full of radiant energy.

Joy is a very busy kind of energy, almost always

associated with achievement. It expresses itself through activity, not through immobility, passiveness or rest. This activity of joy is a point which must be stressed, for many spiritually motivated people have formed entirely mistaken impressions of joy. They believe that joy is some sort of mystical stupor of ecstasy which more closely resembles catatonia than activity. In large part, this misunderstanding is the result of observing the Oriental gurus who have become so popular in this country today, and who are often received without intelligent examination. To the Easterner, joy is usually associated with being very "nice" in the conventional sense—extremely placid, always smiling, and quite harmless. Of course, there may be virtue in this state compared to what these people would be like otherwise, but it has nothing whatsoever to do with being joyful. Typically, the person who follows the Oriental regime becomes dull, listless, humorless, and incoherent. Joy is not dullness! It is the expression of creative achievement. Joy is not listlessness! It is a state of great activity. Joy is not humorlessness! The primary hallmark of joy is an excellent sense of humor that snaps, crackles, and pops with wit. Joy is not incoherent! It is a function of the mind and thrives only where there is clear perception and the capacity to discern reality.

Part of the problem lies in most people's lack of knowledge of the higher realms of human existence. A common misconception, for example, is that the nirvanic (atmic) state of bliss is a completely passive loss of identity in a vast ocean of consciousness. Nothing could be more removed from reality, however, for the inherent nature of the atmic plane is intelligent activity. Thus, bliss is the epitome of human involvement. And since joy is a reflection of bliss in the mind of mankind, then obviously intelligent achievement is the very heart of this "something extra."

Indeed, the most notable examples of joy confirm this basic principle. There is, for instance, the dramatic story of Archimedes, the Greek mathematician and inventor. Archimedes was asked by his friend Hieron II, king of Syracuse, to test the purity of a gold crown. Hieron had given gold to a smith for the purpose of making the crown, but began suspecting that the smith had cheapened the purity of the gold with silver. At first, Archimedes was at a loss as to how to conduct such a test. But the needed flash of insight came to him as he stepped into a tub filled with water at the public baths. He observed that the bulk of his body displaced some of the water in the bath, causing it to spill over. He then calculated that the amount of water displaced was equal to the bulk of his body; furthermore, as silver is lighter than gold, a pound of silver will be bulkier than a pound of gold and will therefore displace a greater amount of water. The ingenuity of this simple test for the purity of gold delighted and thrilled Archimedes, and he jumped out of the bath shouting, "Eureka! Eureka!" In Greek, that expression means, "I have found it!" In his enthusiasm, he forgot to dress himself and ran naked through the streets of Syracuse with only one idea in mind: to go home and test his inspiration. This he did and found that Hieron's suspicions were well-founded: the crown was not pure gold. It can be imagined that this discovery did not cause the smith any measure of joy, but Archimedes' delight was obviously unalloyed. He had accomplished something of great moment and importance, and the thrill of creativity rushed through him like a mighty current. He was overwhelmed by the power of his insight, was lifted up to a wholly new level of vision and comprehension, and momentarily became oblivious to everything lesser.

An even more spectacular example of joy can be found in the book of Genesis. Here the mathematician and inventor is not Greek, but Universal: He is God. The richness of joy permeates the entire process of Creation, as told symbolically in this account. Consider, for example, the passage: "And God said, 'Let there be light,' and there was light. And God saw that the light was good." Hidden within these few words is a great revelation of the nature of joy, which can be seen by anyone with eyes to see. God saw that what He had made was good, and He rejoiced in His work; He delighted in His creation. And this joy spurred Him on to further creativity; the joy at the end of the first day led Him to pursue His work on the second day, which built momentum for the third day, and so on through the whole process. It is joy which characterizes the tempo of God's work, right up to the end of the sixth day, when He created man and woman in His own image and saw that His work was *very* good, and blessed His entire creation. Indeed, the mood of joy is so very much present in this divine act of creativity that one is almost tempted to believe that the godly image from which the pattern of man and woman was drawn was the *image of joy!*

Of course, few of us are inventors like Archimedes, and none of us is the Universal Mathematician. But while our own personal manifestations of joy may not be as memorable as these two examples, it is nonetheless important that we, too, can learn to express joy through our own achievements, big or small. And when we have tasted joy and learned what it is, we can then weave it into the fabric of our life and make it an integral part of our being. For joy is not some rare essence that can only be captured in peak moments in the bathtub or at the Creation of the world. Instead, it is an enduring, active force which can be known and expressed every moment of a person's life, bubbling up from the clear springs of humanity within. If we are to be artists of life, we cannot choose to turn our artistic ideals on and off depending on the vagaries of the moment. We must strive to express the highest degree of art every moment of every day. Thus, joy must become a constant presence for us, a constant though spontaneous dwelling in enthusiasm, delight, and vitality which can help us face the difficult and despairing moments of life as well as help us celebrate the moments of great breakthrough.

Joy heals, joy lifts up, joy harmonizes. It can be found wherever human life is found; it can be expressed in any circumstance, in any surroundings. It can be learned by the person who feels stuck in a dreary, uninspiring job in an office with drab walls, as well as by the person who has just the kind of job he or she prefers. It can be expressed by the housewife who has to diaper babies' bottoms and scrub floors, as well as by the person who leads a free and independent life. It can be known by the blue collar worker and the white collar worker equally; it is not the privilege of any segment or class of society. It can be known by the minister in his pulpit, by the teacher in his classroom, by the psychiatrist at his desk, and by his client on the couch. And when joy is expressed, it transfigures what once might have been dull and uninspiring; it gives new life, new purpose, and new fulfillment. The office worker who discovers joy begins to find new possibilities and new satisfaction in the same job he once considered a dead end; he feels less restricted and more in harmony with his mates and superiors. The housewife who trades in her complaints for joy begins to find new significances and rewards in the raising of children and the management of a household.

No, joy is not happiness; it is not just a mirthful response to what is happening to us. It is truly a "something extra" which lifts us out of the merry-go-round realm of illusion into clearer perception, into greater fulfillment. Nor is it an abstract imagining of poetic minds; it is real and has substance. It is a tool for active participation in daily life and can be cultivated by anyone interested in learning the art of living. And the reward for the effort is great and good, for the reward is a seat at the feast in the hall of reality, the feast of ambrosia and nectar.

Anyone who has tasted and sipped of the essence of joy knows that it is a sustaining force of rare degree. It is indeed food, but no ordinary food. It lifts up the heart of mankind and gives new purpose; it infuses the mind of man with new inspiration. It makes the mortal immortal.

DELIGHTENMENT

Joy can perhaps be best defined as *the delight in achievement and accomplishment*. The accomplishment can be big or small; if it is genuine, it will bring joy. When a person is just beginning to learn to express joy, this delight in accomplishment will probably only occur as the result of his or her own achievements, and possibly the achievements of friends and colleagues. Later, as the individual develops a more universal consciousness and a greater awareness of joy, he will begin to express joy simply because humanity itself is growing, maturing, and accomplishing worthwhile goals. The awareness of the achievements of mankind becomes a constant realization for him, and thus even in moments that lack personal accomplishment, he can be filled with joy.

It is, however, important to have a true understanding of what achievement and accomplishment are. An individual can conceptualize a new idea, but that by itself is not an accomplishment. The idea must be *produced*—it must be made manifest and given shape, color, and function. And, it must be shared with others. Then and only then will it become an achievement which can be delighted in and rejoiced about.

Ultimately, as we grow in spiritual wisdom, we begin to see that the one great achievement of life is enlightenment. And so we set about perfecting the art of living, and as we do, our understanding of joy acquires new significance. We begin to discover that in this art, every day can bring fresh achievements of great value; thus, every day can bring new joy. Soon, and in very practical terms, joy does become a constant sharing in universal consciousness; it becomes a habitual mood with which we greet every moment.

In this fashion, we quickly grow into what should truly be called a state of *delightenment*—a wonderful state of delighting in our constantly increasing enlightenment and the constantly increasing enlightenment of all mankind and civilization. This is joy: a state of being lit up with life, of shining that light into the whole world, and of delighting in the recognition of the light in all forms of life everywhere. Delightenment is the gift of the Midas touch—not to turn everything we touch into gold, but to touch everything we can with the sparkling effervescence of joy.

It should be obvious, then, that joy is actually a mood of the inner being, of the soul. It is ever the soul that delights in achievement, it is ever the soul that perceives human growth and is pleased. Of course, a mood of the soul is something quite different than a mood of the personality. Moods of the personality, such as happiness, fluctuate and vary. They are caused by reactions to the moment. By contrast, moods of the soul are constant states of realization—unshakeable and real.

In other words, at our innermost levels of being, we are constantly expressing joy. Life may be hellish in the outer realms of the personality, but nonetheless the soul knows joy. The soul knows delightenment.

Why? Quite simply, because joy is a *natural state of existence* at the inner level of being, just as having a heart and a brain is a natural state of existence on the physical level. Joy is part of the basic equipment of the inner being, and this is true for an unadvanced person as well as for a highly developed being. Any entity (in this case, the soul) that can create such a complex mechanism as even a primitive human personality is obviously capable of expressing great joy. For joy is the natural product of perfectly understanding the nature of our identity and our relationship to other life in the universe. It is the product of perfectly understanding our purpose and work and of making the effort to fulfill that purpose. The soul has this basic self realization and therefore knows joy.

Thus, our capacity to know joy and to express delightenment will depend to a large degree upon our understanding of the role we play in life (as a personality) and upon our contact and rapport with the inner being, our soul. It will also depend upon our level of enlightenment and upon the true comprehension of our self identity. And, it will likewise depend upon our ability to delight in the wisdom and benevolence and smooth functioning of the world.

Joy grows as our understanding of ourself and of the universe in which we live grows. But there is another requirement as well. Joy grows as we achieve greater expression of the inner purpose of our being at the level of our personality. In other words, even though joy is a quality of the soul, it nonetheless constantly seeks to be grounded in the physical and the emotional realms of the personality. In partially enlightened people, the manifestation of joy will occur only from time to time. In fully enlightened people, it will be a constant expression. But no matter how little we have been expressing joy until now, we can resolve to strive for its full expression in our daily life.

An important point to inject here is that many people express joy without being aware of any conscious contact with their soul. After all, only a very small number of people have conscious awareness of being in contact with their soul. In comparison, the number of people who express joy at least occasionally is much greater. Actually, any expression of joy should be seen as evidence that some kind of direct contact does exist between the soul and the personality, and as evidence that the soul approves of and rejoices in at least some part of the effort the personality is making.

Thus, while joy is a mood of the soul, the only effective measuring stick for deciding how much joy we express is the personality. We must try to decide how much of the joy of the soul is seeping through the personality into expression—and what we can do to open up the personality for a greater expression of this something extra of delightenment.

It would be impractical to list here all of the possible ways of manifesting joy in physical expression. All events of life contain the seed for the expression of joy. It is perhaps most natural to express joy after making some great mental discovery, or in the process of traditional creativity—writing, painting, sculpting, acting, dancing, or whatever. But the richest possible expression of delightenment, of course, comes in perfecting the art of living. Can there be a better way of displaying joy, for example, than by delighting in the building of a right relationship with another human being—a vital relationship which will inspire both people to greater growth, maturity, and love? Or, can we imagine a more satisfying form of joy than the delight gained in finding meaning and purpose in some aspect of life that other, less inspired people find dull? It is a real achievement to be able to take a seemingly menial task—either at work or at home—and transform it into something that expresses our humanity and ingenuity. Such achievements inevitably trigger joy, by evoking a deeper interest in the way the world works and in the way that consciousness expresses itself.

Any effort at improving one's life is an excellent way of stimulating joy. The achievement of a certain amount of detachment, for example, is a cause for great rejoicing and will invoke the delight of the soul in the success of the personality. The successful elimination of a distressful habit pattern and its replacement by a better one is likewise a cause for celebration. The development of a new skill or talent—be it playing the piano, improving concentration, or developing a new degree of intuition—will similarly produce joy.

A growth in maturity, a deeper understanding of the purposes of mankind, a greater ability to think—all of these will prove torchbearers for joy. And so, even though we do not all have the opportunity to be an Archimedes or a Rembrandt, we all do have the opportunity—the option, to be more precise—to become master builders of right relationships, master craftsmen of inspired living, and master draftsmen of perfect habit patterns. In other words, we all have ample opportunity to make delightenment a reality in our lives—simply by expressing it. We do not have to wait for it to "magically" appear (so that we may be joyful). Waiting for joy is a fruitless process. We find joy by *putting* it into our life, by engaging in activities that draw a joyous response from the soul. We become joyful by *filling our life with joy.*

THE WAYS JOY WORKS

Happiness could be called "an end in itself," to use a common phrase. It culminates an effort. Joy, however, should be called "a beginning in itself," for it is much more than just pure delight. It is a living energy which marks the beginning of innovation and further growth. It does not merely celebrate a certain accomplishment, but also leads on to further evolution, further advancement, and further achievement. Joy releases a quality of life which permeates consciousness and works toward a transformation of understanding, skills, and talents. This quality of life, which is really a derivative of the will to live, produces a number of important effects within us which are worth examining in some detail. They can be catalogued as follows:

Joy is a motivator. It fills us with enthusiasm. Its presence causes us to delight in the work we are doing. In this way it builds momentum to give us the initial desire to begin a creative project (for example, in the art of living), and it keeps us on the job once we have begun to work. Without joy, we need some kind of artificial stimulus to get us to work and to keep us going—a stimulus such as money or fear.

Of course, joy is not motivation itself; it is a mood which releases motivation and indicates to us what the innermost motive for the art of living is. But that inner motivation cannot be tapped and known by a human being except through the development of joy.

It seems to be popular in this modern day to belittle the worth of work and proper motivation. The "work ethic" is abused; it is not *chic*. But then again, that may explain why being *chic* is so often a joyless state.

Joy is a healing force. It is the mood in which the soul created the personality, and it is likewise the mood in which the inner being goes about the work of healing the personality, when that is necessary. Again, it is not precisely joy that performs the healing work, but the entire healing process is greatly augmented by the presence of joy. This holds true for healing not only the physical body, but the emotional body and the mind as well—every aspect of the personality.

On the mental level, an inflow of joy tends to stimulate the mind and make it more alert. The apathetic mind, for example, will find a powerful antidote in the stuff of joy. Similarly, the mind which has been imprisoned by illusion will find that the process of cleaning out the debris of old thoughtforms proceeds far more quickly when approached with joy.

On the emotional level, joy tends to heal depression and despair. The state of being downcast, grim, and excessively sober about life is actually a state of joylessness. If a person who is afflicted by depression would open himself up to the presence of joy, then much of the feeling of defeat and despair could be alleviated. The pattern of constantly wallowing in the depths of negativity would be broken up by the act of reaching up to higher levels of awareness.

Physically, the person who has learned to express joy will on the average be less vulnerable to illness and better equipped to overcome that which does come his way, for he has a more thorough understanding of the meaning and purpose of all aspects of his life. The person who can grasp the hidden purposes being worked out by an illness will be better able to overcome it quickly than the individual who sees sickness as just a meaningless (and threatening) event in his life.

On every level, the healing flow of joy cleanses the personality; it breaks up the logjam of piled up thoughts and conflicts in the subconscious. It relieves our mental indigestion and constipation. In this sense, the healing aspect of joy acts as a lubricant which oils the mechanism of consciousness. It keeps us from overheating, it smooths away the roughness of life, and it cuts down on the friction which is a part of everyday living. In general, it makes us more efficient.

Joy is a balancer. It is a sure indicator of proper perspectives; it is a compass which always lets us step back from the full flush of our activities and see all of the alternatives. It leads us out of the hall of the banquet of illusion into the hall of the feast of the real. It produces the balance and poise which give us this kind of detachment. And in the process, joy relieves stress of all kinds. Stress is merely the result of imbalance. With the return of balance, stress is eliminated.

One of the clearest examples of how joy can be used to restore balance in a person's life is the effectiveness of humor in relieving stress. Humor is one of the principal hallmarks of joy; the joyful person always has an abundance of wholesome, good humor, which aids him in keeping his life in balance. In difficult situations, the gift of humor helps him avoid being carried away with the emotions of the moment; it helps remind him of the larger principles upon which he bases his life. For instance, it often occurs that two people become embroiled in an intense argument over an issue that is quite silly. In the heat of their emotions, they lose sight of the essential silliness of the argument, and the conflict becomes bitter. However, if one of them can catch himself and realize that the difference is being carried to absurd extremes—and that the whole scene is quite foolish and laughable—he can avoid being sucked into the full emotionalism of the argument. He can step back sufficiently to be able to chuckle at the obvious absurdity of the situation, and may often be able to succeed in getting the other person to see the humorous aspects of their conflict as well.

Joy can provide just that kind of balance. As our appreciation and expression of joy increases, so does our sense of humor and the ability to use it in this manner. Naturally, this use of joy is a most valuable tool in the art of living, and one which can be applied in many ways—not just to end a silly argument. The capacity to laugh at ourself and at the situations we must face is a great gift and a sure sign of maturity. It is frequently our rescue and our salvation.

If we find ourself suddenly filled with great fear, for example, but can step back enough to see the ludicrous nature of our fear (and all fears are ludicrous), it will then be possible to laugh gently at ourself and banish the fearfulness from our mind. Laughter is a mighty weapon; it literally destroys any negativity on contact. Similarly, if we find ourself depressed, we can take a moment to contemplate how utterly absurd it is ever to allow ourself to be depressed, even for a brief minute. There is so much beauty and joy and awe-inspiring glory in this universe of ours that it is absolutely comedic that we should be so silly. And so, having been guided back to our senses by recalling the presence of joy, we laugh at ourself gently and restore our equilibrium.

Of course, this matter of laughing at ourself requires a delicate and proper touch. It would be harmful to be cruelly sarcastic of ourself, for instance. Rather, we must learn that balanced ratio of good humor and intelligent insight which is so marvelously portrayed by the fairy sprite Puck in Shakespeare's *A Midsummer Night's Dream*. In this play, Puck has the assignment of helping the various mortal lovers stay out of serious mischief and yet fall in love with the persons they are supposed to marry—not an easy task at all. The result is confusion, heated emotions, intrigue, and—eventually—success. Puck finds humor in it all, saying: "And those things do best please me / That befall preposterously." He also learns a thing or two about the human condition and sums it all up in his classic statement: "Lord, what fools these mortals be!"

Let this be our motto, then: "Lord, what fools we mortals be!" When we start to succumb to despair or fear, or strife of any kind, let us remember this phrase and repeat it as though it were a mantra. In this way, we can attune ourself once more to the constant presence of joy and let it flood our whole awareness. Thus, we restore balance.

It is natural for men and women to be foolish every now and then, so there is really no cause for shame and despair—these are just absurd reactions. Rather, we must laugh a little at our grimness and excessive seriousness, shake our heads bemusedly, and then get back to the task at hand. The joyful person can do this much more easily than the joyless one.

Joy is an integrating force. It harmonizes the diverse aspects of the personality, so that they cohere and function in unison. Such harmonization is of great significance, as it is the key to maturity and mental health. Without it, the personality would have no chance to become strong and dynamic. But joy does more than just integrate the different elements of the personality. It also integrates the harmonized personality with the soul, and it is this integration which eventually produces enlightenment. Joy stirs up within us our deepest intellectual and spiritual capacities and links them with our daily functioning vehicles for thought, feeling, and activity. Gradually, it attunes the outer vehicles with the inner capacities, until they become one and the same, united. Joy makes our emotions and thoughts and physical bodies receptive to inner inspiration and also causes us to continually "ground" the inner inspiration through the outer personality. In this way, it forces the integration of the soul and the personality.

Of course, this dramatic-sounding process actually works out in many ordinary ways. We may, for example, achieve a good measure of integration through something as commonplace as an absorbing hobby. The pursuit of the hobby causes us to seek the inspiration of the inner being—its guidance and creativity. And the time we spend engaged in the hobby gives the inner being the opportunity to ground itself through the mind, the emotions, and the physical body. It is for this reason that hobbies frequently play an important role in our mental health and growth. For many people, their hobbies are the only aspects of their lives in which they permit joy to well up from within. Thus, the hobbies provide the sole opportunity for integrating the personality.

Naturally, the wise person will see that these principles of integration can and should be applied to every aspect of life. In other words, he will try to express joy as a constant presence.

Joy is a vitalizing force. The acts of rejoicing and enjoyment are not just releases of pent up feelings. They are actually bursts of new life and vitality. It is this new energy which fuels continued innovative efforts. Joy, therefore, is an important aspect of creativity.

In fact, the mood of joy is the mood of creativity. After all, joy is a mood of the soul. And what does the soul do? It creates. It creates the physical body, the emotions, and the mind, and it sustains this threefold personality throughout life. It also creates the conditions that the personality must work with in its life—the opportunities, the handicaps, the good luck, and the obstacles. It does all this with the ultimate goal of being able to create a personality which is capable of demonstrating the joy, the love, the wisdom, and the light of the inner realms of existence.

The roots of all creativity are found within, in the region of the soul. Our acts of creativity are born deep within us, at this level of abstract being. Here the first flash of inspiration is conceived and begins to take shape as a practical expression. As an idea, it remains for awhile at this level, building up intensity. It is at this point that the vitalizing capacity of joy becomes important. The soul's mood of joy infuses the creative idea with certain potent life energies which give it the dynamic push to seek manifestation. In this sense, joy is very much like a flame that produces not only light but also heat. Not only does joy create a sense of delight at the potential of this new creative idea, but it also generates the energies which will transform the potential into manifestation.

Once the creative idea has gestated in this fashion, it then begins flowing downward into the personality with great power—assuming that we are open to creative inspiration and have removed all roadblocks in the subconscious which might otherwise interfere. The inspiration enters the mind and becomes known consciously to us as an idea. If the idea is welcomed, then over a period of time it becomes clothed with mental energy, taking shape more definitely in the mind's eye. But with this creative inspiration also comes the same mood of joy which infused the idea with life at the level of the soul. The joy protects and nourishes the creative idea as it is being translated in the mind, and helps condition the mind to work with the new idea. It tends to produce in us a sense of enthusiasm—the enthusiasm which will give us the motivation to initiate this creative project.

As this occurs the idea is precipitated also into the astral body, causing an emotional reaction. We form either a like or a dislike for the idea; if the former, we then begin building up a strong desire to see it through to manifestation. The basic stimulus of this desire is, of course, the steady pressure of the joy of the inner being. Finally, even the sluggish physical mechanism is stirred into action, and the creative idea finds complete manifestation on the physical plane—as a novel, a painting, a new invention, an improved relationship, a fresh approach to raising children, a new understanding of other people, an additional use of intuition, or whatever it may be.

In this way, the inner being uses the quality of joy and the process of creativity to add new life to the personality, to introduce new vitality and inspiration into its daily affairs. Creativity is not just a process of rearranging existing variables—it is innovation, the production of something better. Working creatively with the emotions, for example, is not just a question of rearranging emotional hang-ups and problems so we can live with them more easily. Emotional perfection is not achieved by repressing our worries and fears through hypnosis, nor by releasing our hates and frustrations through screaming and pounding and wailing. Nor is it just a bland state of emotional calmness which really amounts to being an emotional eunuch. True creativity goes much deeper. It is analogous to the work of the village smithy, standing at his forge, melting ingots of iron and then hammering that red-hot iron into entirely new forms of practical use. We must take the raw material of our emotions and traits, melt it in the forge of our creativity with the heat of our joy, and then hammer the red-hot essence into wholly new expressions of love, affection, tenderness, and kindness which are appropriate for our relationships, our needs, and our life. We must then express these pure emotional forms in our life, striving as we do to express also the joy with which we created them. We must use them as powerful tools for communicating with others, for helping others to see more clearly, and for touching others with hope, compassion, and inspiration.

Nor does the creative use of the mind have anything to do with being a better sophist than others or being able to manipulate the thoughts of others. Rather, it involves being able to illuminate our thoughts with a much higher quality of life, and being able to mold mental energy into precise forms which can serve as vehicles for the constructive use of the mind: for healing, teaching, and inspiring.

At the end of the creative process, the vitalizing quality of joy most naturally expresses itself as a celebration of the achievement, and this then prepares the way for further creativity. No constructive, affirmative act in this universe is ever wasted or forgotten; every achievement we make in our life opens the door for a greater inflow of the vitality of life into our own consciousness. It is this new inflow of life, indeed, which gives us great delight and makes us want to shout with Archimedes, "Eureka! Eureka!" It makes us want to rejoice, to shout from the top of the mountain that we have reached a new peak. This urge to celebrate should not be repressed: it should be given vent. For it signifies the birth of a new measure of life—a measure of life which will have a profound impact upon what we are able to achieve in the future.

BECOMING JOYFUL

Any effort to increase our understanding and expression of joy must begin where joy exists—on the mental plane. In other words, we must begin by *thinking*. And, as much as possible, we must try to think as the soul thinks, for joy is a fundamental mood of the inner being.

But what should we think about?

In the first place, we should think about those aspects of our life which are causes for rejoicing. In all likelihood, we will have to start by throwing out and revising a large number of basic assumptions about our life in order to do this, because many of us—having never thought about joy before—would immediately conclude that there is little if anything *worth* rejoicing in. We are still stuck in the banquet of illusion. But in point of fact, each one of us can find many, many aspects of life worthy of our delight.

Then we can add to that the contemplation of how the inner being views and regards our life. What is the inner being's purpose? What is it trying to accomplish? How is it seeking to express greater joy? Again, we will have to be prepared to revise many of our thoughts and attitudes if this particular line of thought is to succeed. After all, very few of us are used to thinking—we have just been reacting emotionally all of our life. That will not suffice if we are seeking to become joyful. We must start using our minds. We must escape the bewilderment of illusion.

To this activity we can eventually add another: the contemplation of the purpose and role of mankind, and the realization that our participation in the activities of mankind enriches our own life and gives us joy. To be effective, we will have to broaden our perspectives and overcome our selfish limitations. We will have to give up our prejudices and our stereotyped notions. All of these thought-forms will have to be cleared away, so we can indeed begin thinking. Then we can start considering how much mankind as a whole is growing, and in this way we can begin delighting in these accomplishments as well as our own. In doing this, it is important not to get sidetracked and bogged down in the mass consciousness of fears, hatreds, and worries that afflict the average person in the world today. Again, these are illusions and emotional reactions. Rather, we must see the advancements in human caring, in international rapport, in science, in education, and in the many, many other fields in which there have been significant achievements in the last few hundred years.

Obviously, the success of this thinking will depend to a large degree upon our ability to think about these issues with detachment—with the poise of the soul. The mastery of the practice of detachment is a necessary first step to becoming joyful.

But abstract thinking by itself, while a good beginning, is not enough. It merely prepares the mind to handle joy. We must also seek to be more innovative in our life, knowing that it is through the activity of achievement that joy finds expression. Of course, this does not mean that we must rush out and join a painting class or start writing poetry. Creative expression can indeed be found in such traditional forms of art, but we must always remember that the most important area of creativity is the art of living. This is an art that uses our moods, emotions, thoughts, habits, relationships, and spoken words as the raw materials for creating masterpieces of beauty. It is an art that finds inspiration in the circumstances of our life as they exist now—the conditions of our work, the nature of our home life, the inner content of the subconscious, and so on. Perhaps these conditions do not seem very artistic at present, but that is precisely why they are such apt vehicles for increasing our creativity and thus our joy. They can be *made* artistic.

By deliberately trying to make the variables of our life creative, we can succeed in becoming joyful. There really is no other way. If we have an unpleasant job, we do not become joyful by quitting the job and trying to find one that suits us better. There is no joy in running away from situations we cannot handle or in avoiding people we dislike. Joy always comes through achievement—by taking a difficult job and making it satisfying, by discovering a creative way of improving our relationship with someone we have not liked, or by putting joy into aspects of life we once thought joyless. And joy only comes through individual self initiative. It is not given to us by angels blowing golden trumpets—it is released by our own efforts. We must blow the trumpets ourself!

Most importantly, however, we must seek to enjoy life in all its aspects—even the trials, the struggles, and the crises. We must try to make delightenment a general attitude with which we meet every event and every moment of our life.

There is more than one way to walk down a road. We can walk straight and uprightly, sure of our footing, with dignity, grace, and joy. Or, we can stumble clumsily along, like a drunk. Even worse, if we break a leg, we have to limp along, propped up by crutches. Just so, there is more than one way to tread the path of personal growth and enlightenment. We can approach our growth with eagerness and joy, delighting in every step of the way and never letting obstacles or adversity either slow the pace or dim our joyfulness. Or, we can become very serious and stamp out every trace of humor and levity. We can plod along with heavy foot, talking grimly of the terrible struggle we are undergoing, about the "dark night of the soul" we are facing, about the crosses we must bear, and so on. We can become obsessed with suffering and in the process suffer immensely. Or, worse yet, we can put on a very sour countenance, whining and moaning about every step we take. We can complain about all the evil around us—especially the evil in others; we can jabber foolishly about original sin and fire and brimstone. We can, in short, succeed in making our pathway a living hell.

The road of whining and moaning is a grossly unintelligent way to tread the path; it is a regression, not a progression—a dehumanizing curse upon mankind. But in truth the road of the self-styled martyr and sufferer is not very much better. It, too, is an unintelligent approach which impedes growth more than it encourages it. And yet there are many good people who have devoted themselves to the eventual goal of enlightenment who have not learned the dangers of this path. They consider it a spiritual virtue to deny themselves, to be contrite to the point of groveling, and to be perfectly miserable most of the time. They have not learned the virtues of expressing joy.

We do not tread the pathway for ourself alone. Our progress makes it easier for those who will follow us at a later time—and there are billons yet to come—to find the path and make their progress. If we litter the pathway to enlightenment with the beer cans of our suffering, with the plastic wrappers of our depression, with the garbage of our adversity, and the broken glass of our excessive seriousness, we will be doing those who follow a great disservice. Not only will they have to make their own effort, but they will also have to pick up our litter! Nor is this description just a clever metaphor. There *is* a pathway, and it does collect and permanently record our attitudes and moods. We leave indelible marks along the way.

To put it quite plainly, an emphasis upon struggle, hardship, and suffering is incompatible with true growth and spiritual realization. As Saint Francis de Sales said it, "A saint who is sad is a sad saint." Groveling has no place in the thinking of a person sincerely interested in perfecting the art of living.

It may be objected by some that such an attitude is unrealistic, that there *is* suffering along the way; there are obstacles to be overcome and adversity to be faced. There are temptations and trials. The dark night is an undeniable experience which all must face.

True. But each of us has the option as to how we will face these obstacles. It is possible to see an obstacle ahead and weep with despair. But it is also possible to see the same obstacle and react with great joy, knowing that the obstacle presents a challenge which will help us develop talents and strengths which can then aid us in treading the pathway more rapidly. Obviously, this is the healthier response.

Thus, it is important to cultivate a joyful outlook as we proceed along the way. Not only will it make our efforts easier, but it will also greatly help those who are yet to come. For, rather than leaving behind us litter which might cause some of them to stumble and fall, we are leaving behind us little lights that will help them see more clearly where the path begins and where it leads. We are leaving behind guideposts and helpful assistance. And that in itself is a form of constructive achievement.

Therefore, let us not begrudge what we must do. Instead, let us wade into it with enthusiasm, delighting in our opportunities to contribute to the growth of mankind. We must not sulk in the face of adversity, but instead rest cheerfully in the assurance that "my yoke is easy, and my burden is light." We must stand confident in our joy and let others see it. It is far healthier to skip and dance our way merrily along the path—even if we may be accused by some of being irreverent—than to plod along solemnly as though the full weight of the world were on our shoulders.

Truly, Isaiah knew whereof he spoke when he said: "With joy you will draw water from the wells of salvation." There is no other way.

WORTHY OF IMMORTALITY

The rewards of joy are many. One of the greatest is that joy helps lead us out of the hall of illusion into the hall of reality. Joy helps us put our life into better perspective; we begin to see more clearly the gains we have made, the opportunities which have opened up for us, the good people we are friends with and the good times we have shared with them, and the capacity we have built up for expressing our inner humanity. We begin to think.

Then, too, joy is a signal of the satisfaction of the inner being. Happiness comes with the fulfillment of the desires of the personality. Joy, on the other hand, comes with the fulfillment of the will of the soul. Thus, the surging up of joy from within is a sure indication that the soul is pleased with what the personality has accomplished, just as God was pleased at the end of each day of Creation when He gazed at all that He had wrought and sighed: "It is good." Can the personality ever hope for any greater reward than a sign that its inner being is pleased?

Moreover, as we develop our joyfulness, we enlarge our capacity to share in universal consciousness. We begin to understand that when we are joyful we are in a very real sense giving voice to God's delight in the world. We embody the abstract and give it form, so that others may see it, too. In truth, joy is not personal at all; it is universal. It is God's joy, not ours alone.

This universal awareness can greatly enrich our life. The light in which we delight lets us see the light which surrounds us on all sides—the light in other people, the light in other dimensions, the light in all of life. We spontaneously begin to see the nobility and perfection inherent in all life, in ourself, and in God's design for us. We become conscious of the growing presence of universal awareness in our hearts and in our minds. We develop the eyes to see, the ears to hear, the mind to know, and the heart to feel.

On the personality level, the joyful person is rewarded in many ways. He begins to extend the scope of his joyfulness in all directions. Whereas once he knew joy only under certain conditions and at certain times, he begins to express joy more constantly. He comes to find joy in the smallest of things—even the least important occurrences of life. It is not just when he discovers a great mathematical principle or achieves a major goal of life; it is also when he meets other people, when he goes to work in the morning, when he travels, when he relaxes—in short, in the ordinary course of daily life. He finds joy in commonplace circumstances not because they give him joy, but because he puts joy into everything he does. The joy is *within him,* and thus all of the circumstances of his life reflect that joy.

As a person becomes more joyful, his sense of humor deepens and becomes more ever-present, keener, and more refreshing. With it also comes greater flexibility and resilience; he is less rigid than before. He can bend rather than break—he is more tolerant and understanding, better able to withstand difficulties. Joy gives him a protection for the work which must be done, a shield against all the dangers that must be faced. The art of living does require facing our weaknesses and overcoming them, making the imperfect perfect. Without joy, we might well be overpowered by our weaknesses and imperfections. But with joy, we have the capacity and support to succeed.

And last but not least, joy is the "something extra" which lets us partake of the feast that has been prepared for us—the banquet of ambrosia and nectar. In Greek mythology, ambrosia and nectar are the divine food and drink upon which the gods sup. By becoming joyful, we can share in this abundance, too, and it can sustain us. But it can do even more. For, according to mythology, ambrosia and nectar have a hidden power: the power to keep a corpse from decay. In other words, they bestow immortality.

Joy bestows immortality upon us. Not immortality of the physical body, of course, for that will invariably die. Who would want to keep his physical body for all eternity anyway? Rather, joy lets us create manifestations of life that are *worthy* of immortality.

Worthy of immortality! How much of our lives are worthy of immortality? Immortality is not a gift bestowed on us on some mythical judgment day in the sky. It is an accomplishment which is earned through diligent effort. We achieve immortality by creating works that are worthy of lasting forever— for all eternity. These works are not physical works, of course. Rather, they are masterworks of human consciousness and talent: works of love, kindness, gentleness, affection, beauty, hope, faith, perception, aspiration, courage, strength, understanding, and many other humanistic qualities. These are the raw materials from which the *important* works of mankind are created. And when we have created a perfect expression of any of these qualities and skills, it then becomes a *permanent* part of our consciousness—and an inspiration for those who follow.

It is not the physical work of great people, after all, that lingers on (although it may be preserved for awhile); it is the quality of their consciousness. It is not the actual physical labor of Albert Schweitzer in his hospital in Africa, for example, which still exists. It is the quality of his love, his compassion, his dedication, and his intelligence. And those qualities are immortal—they will continue to inspire humanity long after the hospital is gone from the face of the earth.

This is, of course, the supreme creative effort— the effort to make something that will endure for all time. We build the best we can. Many times the results are quite remarkable. They endure for hundreds of years before we realize that we can do even better. And so we tear down and start all over again, from scratch, but with a better understanding of how to proceed. Thus, the next effort comes a good deal closer to being worthy of immortality. In this way, the process continues.

It is the nature of creation that only the good things—the very best of the best—will achieve immortality. All the rest—the cheap, the counterfeit, the seedy, the evil—will be torn down and destroyed sooner or later, to make way for better efforts. At the same time, however, it is also the nature of creation to encourage us to realize our role in this process and participate in it—as did Schweitzer and many, many others.

That is the true meaning of joy. It encourages us to participate in the effort of creation—to become worthy of immortality. It encourages us to partake of the feast in the banquet hall of the universe.

Jean-Yves Pecollo

La sophrologie
CHEMIN VERS LA CONSCIENCE

© Éditions du Rocher, 1989

INTRODUCTION

A sa naissance, l'homme possède un capital. Ce capital est constitué pour une part d'un savoir inné, stocké dans une mémoire héréditaire et cellulaire et, pour une autre part, d'un énorme potentiel de développement, activé par le pouvoir de mémorisation. Cette capacité d'acquérir de nouvelles connaissances différencie l'homme des autres espèces animales qui semblent emprisonnées dans un déterminisme fonctionnel.

Utilisant, dès son premier souffle, son savoir inné, l'homme avance dans sa vie, jour après jour... progresse pas à pas comme un explorateur découvrant un espace encore vierge. Chaque pas qu'il fait conditionne les suivants, chaque jour est une nouvelle aventure. A tout instant une question se pose, une situation se propose, une réaction s'impose. La réponse fournie, l'attitude adoptée seront fonction de l'expérience innée ou acquise. Problèmes et solutions, vécus et mémorisés, viennent grossir les bagages du voyageur... sa connaissance s'élargit, sa conscience se modifie... et la route continue...

Ainsi, d'expériences en expériences, se forme puis se transforme, tout au long de la vie, le « monde intérieur ». Etrange et fascinant monde du dedans qui fait de chaque homme un être unique... un *individu*. Domaine privé où se mélangent simplicité et complexité, certitudes et doutes, unité et diversité, vie et mort. Ici se trouvent enfouis, au plus profond et au plus secret de l'iceberg, les motivations de nos actes, le centre réel, la source de toutes nos vies – instinctive et volontaire, végétative et motrice. Mais si profond qu'il soit, ce jardin secret est *manifestement* présent dans nos faits et gestes quotidiens. C'est-à-dire qu'il se *manifeste* par nos actes, nos attitudes et nos pensées. Il induit nos découvertes et nos révélations. Il protège en même temps qu'il limite notre liberté individuelle.

Depuis toujours, en Occident comme en Orient, des générations de philosophes, théologiens, sociologues, psychologues, neurophysiologistes et généticiens sont parties à la découverte de cet espace humain.

L'hérédité culturelle et le mode de fonctionnement de la pensée occidentale ont poussé nos chercheurs vers une voie rationnelle, ne s'écartant pas des chemins de la sacro-sainte logique. Depuis l'Antiquité, de très nombreuses théories furent élaborées visant à expliquer le comment pour comprendre le pourquoi. Il y eut le temps de la métaphysique religieuse, des théologiens et des philosophes. Puis vint l'ère des psychologues et des cliniciens. Entre leurs mains la recherche s'est vite orientée vers une action thérapeutique : démonter, pour mieux les connaître, les mécanismes de la machine humaine – d'abord au niveau des structures organiques et maintenant au niveau des structures mentales... Et nos pensées, nos désirs, nos peines et nos pleurs se trouvent traduits en termes de chimie intra et intercellulaire. Si bien qu'à nos troubles profonds, qu'à nos incertitudes de vie, qu'à nos angoisses d'exister nous sont proposés des remèdes à la formule de plus en plus complexe et de plus en plus ciblée. Le courant scientifique a eu le mérite de nous libérer des institutions religieuses qui, par la tyrannie de leurs dogmes et l'arbitraire de leur croyance, enchaînaient l'homme au poteau de l'intolérance. Mais, comme tous ceux qui prennent un pouvoir sans partage finissent par en abuser, la pensée rationnelle est devenue à son tour institutionnelle, dogmatique et intolérante. Jetant l'anathème sur toute forme de pensée naissant hors de son courant, elle préside, dans l'arbitraire de ses certitudes, à une forme de dictature intellectuelle. Cet état de fait a comme conséquence dommageable de couper notre société en deux groupes :

Ceux qui croient savoir et ceux qui pensent ne rien pouvoir. Les premiers, en vertu des pouvoirs qui leur sont conférés, sont devenus sectaires et interventionnistes; les seconds, en vertu du savoir qui leur est retiré, se sont rendus, corps et âme. Dans nos sociétés le savoir induit le pouvoir, le pouvoir impose le respect, le respect se confond trop souvent avec soumission et abandon de soi.

Cependant un nouveau courant apparaît et de plus en plus nombreux sont les thérapeutes qui prennent conscience de la limite de leur grand art : s'ils détiennent le *savoir soigner*, le *pouvoir guérir* appartient à leur patient.

En Orient, et depuis des millénaires, existe également un même élan vers la conquête de ce monde intérieur mais la démarche est différente. Par une attitude plus réflexive et méditative, la révélation intuitive remplace la vérification scientifique et l'expérimentation par le vécu vient authentifier et développer la connaissance.

Le corps, dépassant la notion simpliste de « contenant », est considéré comme le siège – le temple sacré – de l'âme et de l'esprit. Ces trois facettes sont en étroite relation et forment un ensemble unique : l'être humain. Cette approche uniciste et globaliste de l'homme est fondamentale pour comprendre les philosophies et les religions orientales.

Sur terre, l'homme est en **devenir** et se doit de

vivre dans l'harmonie l'alliance sacrée Ame-Esprit-Corps. En japonais Do signifie le chemin à suivre pour parvenir à la réalisation de cette alliance, à l'illumination (SATORI) et cette racine se retrouve dans certains arts martiaux comme le Kendo (escrime au bâton), le Judo, le Sado (Cérémonie du thé), le Kado (arrangement des fleurs) et aussi le Kuyndo (tir à l'arc). Un très grand cérémonial entoure ces activités – qui ne rentrent pas dans le chapitre des « sports et loisirs »! – qui conduisent à l'harmonisation globale par le contrôle du geste effectué en pleine conscience de sa portée sur le plan symbolique.

Les conceptions orientales et occidentales avec leurs qualités et leurs défauts respectifs se sont longtemps heurtées et paraissaient contradictoires et inconciliables. Mais il est heureux de constater que, depuis quelques années, les différentes voies de recherche semblent parfois converger et que les échanges entre savants de toutes origines, cultures et religions se multiplient. C'est par ces échanges (où chacun apporte sa façon de lire l'Univers de l'homme) que l'on peut progresser dans la Connaissance.

La Sophrologie qui, par définition se propose d'étudier la conscience de l'homme, se situe au carrefour de ces multiples formes de pensées. Ecole scientifique en permanente évolution, elle offre une synthèse entre le courant phénoménologique et mystique de l'Orient et le courant pragmatique et expérimentaliste de l'Occident.

Sur le faire-part de naissance de la Sophrologie figurent aussi bien des méthodes inspirées de la philosophie du Yoga, du Zen ou de la Méditation transcendantale que des techniques héritées de l'Hypnose ou de la Relaxation de Schultz. La Sophrologie a comme champ d'investigation la conscience humaine et comme hypothèse de travail que cette conscience subit tout au long de la vie des modifications (plus ou moins importantes selon l'impact de l'événement vécu) dans un sens positif d'adaptation ou dans un sens négatif de détresse. De ce fait, l'Ecole sophrologique s'intéresse à *tous les moyens connus ou à venir* permettant de mieux connaître et de renforcer la conscience de l'homme. Sont dignes d'intérêt tous les chemins qui, dans un but thérapeutique, pédagogique et prophylactique, aboutissent à une plus profonde connaissance de l'homme, ce curieux animal si complexe !

Essayons, pour nous faire une pâle idée de cette complexité, de nous représenter un volume sphérique dont la surface serait composée de multiples facettes : il y a toujours une face opposée à celle que l'on observe, si bien que, lorsque nous éclairons une face, l'autre, cachée, est forcément dans l'ombre ! Quand nous considérons les facettes de surface, nous ne pouvons pas voir les profondeurs obscures du volume ! Et le tout se complique encore car ces divers éléments s'enchaînent dans une dynamique de vie, s'interactivent et évoluent dans le temps et dans l'espace subissant d'inévitables influences !

On comprend dès lors mieux combien il est difficile, pour ne pas dire impossible, de saisir toutes les composantes qui définissent l'espace humain et combien il devient nécessaire et urgent de prendre en compte et de réunir les connaissances apportées aussi bien par l'observateur qui, dans une approche purement scientifique, se situe *hors* du volume (enquête objective : l'homme objet de l'étude) que par l'expérimentateur qui, dans une approche phénoménologique, se place *dans* le volume (enquête subjective : l'homme sujet du vécu).

« La vie de chaque homme est un chemin vers soi-même, l'essai d'un chemin, l'esquisse d'un sentier... Chacun de nous est un essai de la

nature dont le but est l'homme. Nous pouvons nous comprendre les uns les autres, mais personne n'est expliqué que par lui-même. » (Hermann Hesse, *Demian*. 1925.)

Ces quelques extraits du prologue du roman d'Hermann Hesse pourraient servir à définir le sens et le but de la Sophrologie en même temps qu'ils pourraient résumer l'objet même de ce présent ouvrage. En effet, qui est mieux placé que l'individu lui-même pour partir à la conquête de cet espace intérieur?... Partir à la rencontre de cet Etre qui habite au fond de lui!

Que l'option initiale soit thérapeutique, pédagogique ou prophylactique, la Sophrologie proposera toujours cette démarche primordiale : commencer le chemin qui conduit à la rencontre de soi et à la reconnaissance de sa réalité agissante. La conscience individuelle grandit et s'éclaire à chaque pas fait dans cette direction... Conscience sophronique qui reconnaît en son centre une zone virtuelle de rencontre et d'intégration des différentes composantes qui définissent un être, endroit idéalisé où peuvent se vivre les notions d'unicité et de globalité de la personne humaine.

Nous avons tous été confrontés à la multiplicité et à la diversité de nos actions et de nos réactions, souvent surprenantes, face à des stimulations extérieures, et parfois déroutés par l'aspect non conforme des réponses fournies! Chacun d'entre nous a érigé par réflexe d'autodéfense, d'autoprotection, un système de *cloisonnement* intérieur interdisant ainsi la liberté d'expression à telle ou telle « part de soi ». Nous reviendrons sur cette notion de cuirasses intérieures mais sachons dès maintenant que cette attitude de défense dite de « l'autruche » est absurde et dangereuse car nous ne pouvons pas interdire les réactions profondes et, en supprimant leur intégration consciente, nous risquons de produire soit des réponses rentrées (maladies psychosomatiques) soit des réponses qui vont s'extérioriser d'une façon peu contrôlée (comportement dévié).

D'ores et déjà peut être introduite l'idée de dialogue. Dialogue intérieur. Echanges intimes permettant une intégration consciente des différentes réponses composites. Mais pour qu'un dialogue efficace et authentique puisse s'installer, il faut au moins deux conditions de base :

– **Premièrement, du calme.** Comment peut-on discuter avec un ami dans le bruit et l'agitation ? Toute technique sophrologique commencera donc par de la relaxation.

– **Deuxièmement, une libre circulation** des informations, avec deux corollaires :

• Apprendre les différents langages et savoir les entendre.

• Lever les obstacles internes freinant la communication. (Cette deuxième condition est résumée par les concepts d'harmonisation et d'intégration.)

L'être global comporte trois grands aspects, trois plans :

– *Le plan physique*

C'est le monde du réel, son langage est sensation et ses motivations relèvent de l'instinctif. Sa représentation symbolique est le **Carré.**

– *Le plan psychique*

C'est le monde du symbole, son langage est sentiment et ses motivations sont d'ordre affectif. Sa représentation symbolique est la **Croix.**

– *Le plan spirituel*

C'est le monde de l'imaginaire, son langage est silence, ses motivations prennent source dans la conscience individuelle (idéaux philosophiques ou religieux). Sa représentation symbolique est le **Cercle.**

Le carré, la croix et le cercle, symboles fondamentaux, seront repris et expliqués. Ils serviront de titres aux différents chapitres de ce livre. Il est curieux de constater qu'ils servaient déjà, dans le chinois ancien et là sous forme d'un idéogramme, à représenter l'homme sain, debout entre ciel et terre.

Que l'un des trois plans s'hypertrophie ou que l'autre s'asphyxie... et le déséquilibre apparaît avec son cortège de conséquences négatives. Le grand dessein de l'homme est de tout faire pour préserver l'harmonie entre les différentes facettes de sa personnalité.

Pour parvenir à ce but, de très nombreuses techniques sophrologiques peuvent être utilisées (nous en décrirons certaines dans le chapitre sur le sport). Une d'entre elles revêt une importance particulière, c'est pour cette raison qu'elle servira de référence, dans ce livre, à la démarche sophronique : *la Relaxation Dynamique de Caycedo*.

La Relaxation Dynamique de Caycedo

Un grand nombre de nos contemporains, plongés dans une vie dont la « gestion » est souvent épuisante, éprouvent une certaine difficulté « à être » et quelle que soit la forme que prend ce

malaise existentiel, celui-ci est toujours lié au même problème de fond : une ***dysharmonie***.
- Dysharmonie de **moi** dans le rapport à **soi**.
  - « Je ne suis pas fier de moi... »
  - « J'aurais dû mieux faire... »
  - « Je suis fatigué. » « J'en ai marre, je m'ennuie... »
  - « Je suis laid... trop gros... », etc.
- Dysharmonie de **moi** dans le rapport aux **autres**.
  - « On ne me comprend pas... On ne m'aime pas... »
  - « On se moque de moi... On m'en veut... »
  - « On m'oblige à faire ceci. On m'empêche de faire cela. »
  - « Les gens sont fous ! »
- Dysharmonie de **moi** dans le rapport à **l'univers**.
  - « Je n'ai pas de chance... Je ne crois en rien... »
  - « Les événements sont contre moi... Ma vie est inutile. »
  - « Je suis né sous une mauvaise étoile. »
  - « Qu'est-ce que je fais sur terre ? »

Toutes ces expressions qui traduisent une discordance ont un dénominateur commun :

Moi

C'est à partir de ce point central, « le centre des centres », que se pose la problématique de la relation à soi-même, aux autres et à l'environnement naturel et culturel.

« Je suis le centre, le foyer, la source sainte,
D'où torrentiellement s'élance tout désir... »
Novalis

Vouloir renforcer ce « soi », c'est d'**abord** prendre conscience que le « moi » existe! Voici défini le **premier degré** de la Relaxation dynamique. C'est à partir de cette connaissance de notre intimité que s'élabore notre individualité, dualités indivisibles dont les différentes composantes s'harmonisent et concourent à la réalisation d'un ensemble fort. Nous serons alors invité à méditer sur cette organisation homogène qui évoque et même provoque l'idée **d'unité et d'unicité, de cohérence, de stabilité** et **d'équilibre,** grâce à la perception de la corporalité à travers les sensations récupérées lors d'exercices respiratoires et à l'occasion de certains gestes symboliques dont la répétition amène la conscience à vivre le sentiment d'harmonisation de l'ICI ET MAINTENANT, instantané de vie qui s'enchaîne et s'inscrit dans une dynamique globale du devenir.

Une fois ce « travail » réalisé, nous pourrons établir le contact avec les différents environnements. De *sujet* de notre concentration, nous deviendrons *objet* de la relation qui nous unit au monde. Plus contemplative ou expectative, cette attitude définit le **deuxième degré** de la Relaxation Dynamique. Nous vivons dans un monde dont nous avons une représentation subjective. Par des processus mentalement vécus d'intégration à *quelque chose d'autre, nous prenons la forme d'autre chose,* ce qui nous donne accès à la connaissance de la place que nous occupons nous-même dans notre monde de représentation. En d'autres termes, nous prenons de *la hauteur* par rapport à la situation de vie que constitue l'image de moi dans l'univers. Par ce regard d'intégration, se développent alors lentement les concepts vécus **d'accord et d'unisson, d'appartenance et d'alliance,** ce qui permet de prendre *objectivement* conscience de notre relative *subjectivité* et de nous débarrasser de la surcharge angoissante qui endeuille nos relations avec le monde. « JE » devient l'image de l'objet que le regard contemple et la conscience enveloppante prend note que « celui-ci » peut apparaître sous un angle nouveau quand il est vu de « l'extérieur ».

On comprend qu'il soit absolument nécessaire, avant de pouvoir prendre cette distance par rapport à soi, d'avoir assuré et ancré ce « MOI » dans une corporalité pleinement prise en conscience lors du premier degré, sous peine de prendre cet autre, qui n'est autre que moi, pour un **étranger.**

Les exercices du premier degré, par une attitude d'intériorisation et de concentration et par le mouvement corporalisé d'intrusion, nous placent en situation de percevoir le « monde du dedans ». Le deuxième degré, par une attitude d'extériorisation et de contemplation et par le mouvement mental d'extraction, nous place en situation d'apercevoir ce que nous percevons du « monde du dehors » et comment celui-ci peut nous percevoir.

Le **troisième degré** nous place en situation de... non-situation. Dans la vie courante (qui nous fait courir!) il est devenu obligatoire de s'entourer de repères et de références. Nous avons pris l'habitude, par nécessité, de rendre *signifiant* l'environnement pour le comprendre, l'aimer ou s'en protéger. Nous verrons qu'ici nous entrons dans un monde de non-repère, de non-référence et de non-signifiant pour « demeurer immobile, à écouter (le silence)... c'est la tranquillité de l'axe au centre de la roue... L'axe qui avance avec la roue, mais ne tourne jamais. » (Charles MORGAN, Fontaine.)

Peut-on parler alors de... Liberté? Non.
Peut-on parler alors de... Eternité? Non.
Peut-on parler alors de... Absolu? Non.

Là où nous en sommes, il n'y a ni texte ni prétexte, ni phrase ni mot car tout cela n'est que trop signifiant. Nous sommes EN silence, EN solitude, EN dehors, EN méditation. A ce moment le sophrologue-accompagnant cesse son « terpnos logos explicatif » et chaque individu se présente alors seul devant « le grand chemin », abandonnant toute vanité et toute attente (notions appartenant au monde du signifiant).

Ecoutons encore le poète TAGORE (Poème 44, Offrande lyrique), nous dire comment,

> « De l'aube au crépuscule, je reste devant ma
> [porte ;
> je sais que soudain l'heureux moment viendra
> [où je verrai.
> Cependant je souris et je chante, tout soli-
> [taire. »

Mais pour cela,

> « Mon chant a dépouillé ses parures. Je n'y
> [mets plus d'orgueil.
> Les ornements gêneraient notre union.
> Ma vanité de poète meurt de honte à ta vue. »

Cette expérimentation vécue du non-moi évoluant dans un espace au-delà du « trou noir » du cosmos tangible et perçu, sort, pour le moins que l'on puisse dire, de l'ordinaire. Doit-on y rester ? Bien sûr que non.

Revenir dans notre réalité subjective quotidienne et coutumière est le but du **quatrième degré** de la Relaxation Dynamique. Nouvellement décrit par Caycedo, il est à mes yeux, de toute première importance. Il s'inscrit dans la suite logique de l'évolution de chaque individu à qui il permet de « boucler la boucle » et de « redescendre sur terre » pour vivre sa vie au quotidien, vie dépouillée de vanité et d'angoisse futiles. Il est dit que « la culture c'est ce qui reste quand on a tout oublié ». Il en est de même pour le travail réalisé en sophrologie et plus particulièrement par la Relaxation dynamique

Le plus important est ce qui en *reste*. Ce quatrième degré est là pour prendre conscience que

« quelque chose, quelque part en nous, a bougé » et pour entretenir la flamme qui a été allumée. Flamme, sublime symbole de la verticalité, qui se dresse en notre conscience, réchauffe notre corps et fait vivre « debout entre ciel et terre » un devenir qui se situe au-delà de l'immédiatement perçu. Ce n'est pas un retour à la « case départ » mais une intégration de la quotidienneté qui sera perçue avec un autre regard. Car quand le regard sur moi change, c'est mon regard sur les autres, sur les choses et sur les liens qui m'unissent au monde qui change. « Je suis (autre) au monde qui se redécouvre et que je pénètre. »

Dans l'univers privé de l'homme plusieurs mondes cohabitent, régis chacun par des lois et des règles spécifiques. Notre façon de vivre les a cloisonnés, rendant difficiles les échanges d'informations... Mondes « clos par nécessité ».

L'un de ces mondes (symbolisé par le Cercle) est le monde informel de l'espace métaphysique. Situé en dehors du temps et de l'espace, il abrite, développe et fait vivre l'idée d'un Dieu, de l'Infini, de l'Eternité. Ici le langage est silence, prière et méditation : c'est le monde de la spiritualité et de la foi. Ici, *premièrement* je crois, et si mon corps vit cette imprégnation, c'est secondairement.

Ce monde peut parfois être opposé à celui de la logique, de l'intelligence rationnelle, du modèle mathématique. Les problèmes posés, soumis aux raisonnements et aux preuves, sont standardisés. C'est le lieu des lois universelles de la physique et de l'expérimentation scientifique. C'est un espace de vie mécanique, technique et robotisé où il faut faire « marcher ses cellules grises ».

Champ de bataille et de compétition, c'est le monde froid, distant, sans imaginaire et sans émotion, où chaque problème devrait trouver solution et où chaque solution se doit de trouver une application. C'est un endroit où l'homme est impliqué avec sa rationalité (Carré). Dans nos pays à grand développement technologique, ce côté « efficace » de l'individu a été considérablement amplifié, souvent même hypertrophié. Cette trop grande spécialisation, cette très sélective orientation ont pour conséquence dommageable un appauvrissement de l'autre facette :

Le monde de l'affectivité (que symbolise la Croix) et celui de l'émotion primaire ou de la sensation (représenté par le Carré). Pourtant ils sont là, bien en nous et occupent une place et une fonction importantes. L'un, celui de l'affectivité, renferme notre « corporalité » (corps en relation avec le psychique) et toute notre histoire individuelle, l'autre est l'expression du corps physique, avec sa mémoire propre et ses motivations instinctives. Ce pourrait être le monde du « cœur » et celui du « ventre » que l'on oppose à celui de la raison ! Notre erreur, bien souvent, est de vouloir appliquer des solutions faisant appel au rationnel pour résoudre des problèmes intéressant le « monde du dedans ». Ici le langage est vibrations, la logique est tout autre. Alors il ne faut pas s'étonner si « ça ne marche pas » !

Par ce versant, nous sommes en fait en prise directe avec une autre vérité, plus profonde, plus intime, plus authentique : nous sommes en contact avec notre **corps vécu** qui vibre au même rythme que nos émotions et nos sentiments.

La sagesse populaire a su traduire cette réalité dans le langage usuel : « Avoir la peur au ventre »... « la joie au cœur »... « trembler d'émotion. »

Peur, angoisse (qui prennent à la gorge), tristesse et souffrance (qui font pleurer), joie et bonheur (qui déclenchent des rires), tous les vécus sur le plan psychique ou mental auront toujours des répercussions corporelles. De même, toute expérience, positive ou négative, laissera une trace au niveau de la conscience, en la renforçant ou en la fragilisant.

CORPS ET ESPRIT SONT ÉTROITEMENT LIÉS DANS UN MÊME PROCESSUS DE VIE.

Les trois facettes, les trois mondes qui composent l'être humain doivent tendre vers l'**équilibre** et l'**harmonie**.

Pour atteindre cet équilibre, il est indispensable de lever les barrières qui isolent les trois étages afin d'établir une communication, une interrelation pour aboutir enfin à cette vision globale de l'homme, à cette unification si nécessaire à sa santé. C'est là un des buts prioritaires de la Sophrologie : l'homme total, harmonisé qui, partant du bas, s'élève vers son Cercle puis revient vivre sa vie en pleine conscience.

« Le travail de base consiste à (...) desserrer l'étranglement des cuirasses, à prendre conscience de l'obligation du corps, du fait concret de la relation à lui-même, de la joie de vivre quotidienne, du goût de notre corps vis-à-vis de lui-même, du plaisir, de la découverte de la rapidité des phénomènes d'ordre physique (le grounding = enracinement). »

Le docteur Jean-Pierre Hubert a raison de souligner, dans son livre *La Relaxation dynamique*, l'importance qu'il y a de commencer par... le début, c'est-à-dire de commencer par prendre conscience de la présence de son corps, de comprendre et d'organiser son « Carré ». Ce n'est qu'à partir de ce travail de base, réalisé, entre autres, lors du premier degré de la Relaxation dynamique de Caycedo, que l'on peut envisager un progrès d'éveil et partir à la conquête de soi. Les deuxième et troisième degrés vont ensuite apporter un renforcement de la « Croix » et du « Cercle »... pour retourner, par le quatrième et dernier degré vers la base vécue en toute conscience. Ce quatrième degré, nouvellement introduit dans la Relaxation dynamique, résume cette notion fondamentale d'unicité de l'Etre Humain. L'homme est UN et INDIVISIBLE et l'unité psycho-physique doit se concevoir dans un concept d'harmonie.

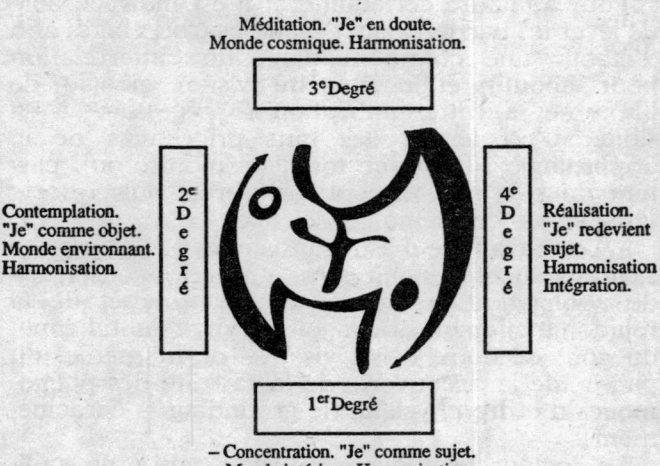

L'HOMME SAIN EST HARMONIE

Méditation. "Je" en doute.
Monde cosmique. Harmonisation.

3ᵉ Degré

Contemplation.
"Je" comme objet.
Monde environnant.
Harmonisation.

2ᵉ Degré

4ᵉ Degré

Réalisation.
"Je" redevient sujet.
Harmonisation
Intégration.

1ᵉʳ Degré

– Concentration. "Je" comme sujet.
– Monde intérieur. Harmonisation.

Ce sigle montre l'évolution proposée par la Relaxation dynamique qui part du « Carré », suit le chemin de la « Croix », s'extasie dans le « Cercle » pour réintégrer le carré avec une conscience à la fois harmonisée et renforcée.

Ce présent ouvrage va s'articuler autour des notions exposées dans cette introduction. Ainsi, le premier chapitre contient les éléments de base de la Sophrologie :

Les définitions essentielles.

Les notions de schéma corporel et d'images mentales.

La relaxation sophronique : la Relaxation rapide et contrôlée.

Puis, nous détaillerons, en trois chapitres, la démarche sophronique en suivant le chemin des trois degrés de la Relaxation Dynamique de Caycedo :

Le Carré et le premier degré

avec les notions de concentration, désir et volonté.

La Croix et le deuxième degré

avec les problèmes de la perception sensorielle et intuitive.

Le Cercle et le troisième degré

avec les différentes approches orientales et occidentales.

Ensuite nous tenterons de voir **les principes de base de la conscience humaine** par quelques notions simplifiées de neurophysiologie et une approche de la suggestion.

Enfin, nous prendrons comme exemple concret l'adaptation des techniques sophrologiques **au sport et à la compétition.**

PREMIER CHAPITRE

APPROCHE GÉNÉRALE

Définitions essentielles
La Relaxation rapide et contrôlée
Les images mentales
Le schéma corporel

DÉFINITIONS ESSENTIELLES

Il est important de s'entendre sur les termes usuels employés en Sophrologie et de les définir de la façon la plus claire et la plus simple possible. Les définitions de base citées entre guillemets sont extraites du *Lexique de Sophrologie et des termes usuels* de Jean-Pierre Hubert.

Du grec SOOS (harmonie), PHREN (esprit), le terme de Sophrologie pourrait être traduit par « Science de l'esprit serein ».

« C'est une école scientifique, fondée en 1960 par A. Caycedo et qui s'applique à l'étude de la conscience humaine dans les modifications des états de conscience, les modifications des niveaux de vigilance et les moyens de produire ces modifications. »

Dans une perspective naturelle, la conscience se modifie par adaptation et réaction à deux processus fondamentaux que nous développerons plus loin : la *suggestion* et l'*expérimentation*. Cette maturation de la conscience passe par des modifications, plus ou moins contrôlées et plus ou moins durables, de son état. On admet, d'une façon générale, comme pouvant conduire à une modification de l'état :

Les grandes émotions (peur, colère, joie...).
Les manifestations pathologiques (maladies mentales, angoisse, phobies, etc.).
Les grands syndromes douloureux.
La méditation, la prière, la rêverie poétique...

Caycedo a défini trois possibilités existentielles de la conscience : la conscience **pathologique,** la conscience **ordinaire** et la conscience **sophronique.**

Quel que soit l'état considéré, la conscience connaît plusieurs niveaux échelonnés de l'hypervigilance au coma! Parmi ces différents niveaux, deux seront particulièrement intéressants dans le travail sophronique : **l'hyperéveil** et le niveau **sophroliminal,** aussi appelé « zone X ». Il est très utile de bien saisir cette différenciation entre états et niveaux de la conscience pour comprendre la démarche sophrologique.

La sophronisation

1. Induction

Objectivée dans le schéma de base par la ligne A-B, l'induction est le processus par lequel la conscience voit son niveau se modifier. Dans la plupart des cas, ce changement de niveau s'obtient par la relaxation neuromusculaire, ce qui entraîne une baisse de la vigilance et conduit vers un niveau proche de celui du sommeil : **le niveau sophroliminal** (N.S.L.). Les moyens d'induction sont très nombreux et variés mais relèvent schématiquement tous des mêmes techniques de détente musculaire et de focalisation (concentration) sur le corps ou sur une image mentale. Le sujet sophronisé [1] apprend, dès ce stade, à participer à cette

---

[1] Est dite sophronisée toute personne qui, pendant la sophronisation, vit un état de conscience sophronique. L'aptitude à être sophronisé est indépendante de toute considération religieuse ou raciale, sociale ou culturelle et de tout niveau intellectuel. En dehors de certains cas bien précis, nous pouvons admettre que tout individu est « sophronisable ». L'apprentissage des techniques sophrologiques exclut toute attitude d'assisté, mais demande au contraire une participation pleine et entière, une présence effective et volontaire. Le sophronisé – appelé aussi « élève » – garde et exploite sa personnalité, sa volonté et sa propre

modification de niveau – et plus tard, à la conduire lui-même – en prenant en conscience les phénomènes qui en résultent, de façon à être capable de les reproduire ultérieurement en complète autonomie.

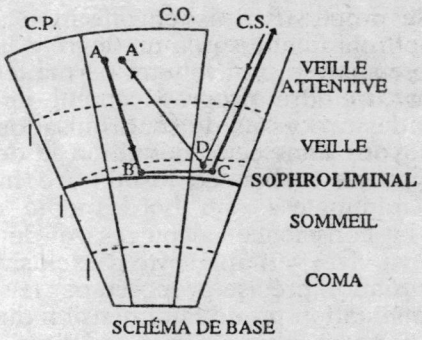

SCHÉMA DE BASE

2. Niveau sophroliminal

« Terme qui désigne les limites diffuses qui séparent les niveaux de veille des niveaux de sommeil. Le contrôle de ce niveau permet les modifications allant de l'état de conscience ordinaire à l'état de conscience sophronique (...). Ce niveau sophroliminal, appelé aussi niveau " X ", ouvre les portes à une communication beaucoup plus profonde avec le subconscient et l'inconscient. » Mis en relief par le processus de la sophronisation, ce degré d'éveil de la conscience est naturel ou physiologique puisqu'il est « traversé » au moins deux fois par jour : une fois au moment de l'endormissement et une autre fois au moment du réveil.

---

sensibilité. Il va apprendre, guidé un certain temps par le sophrologue, à se mieux connaître et à mieux se comprendre et à se respecter, développant ainsi le contrôle et la maîtrise de soi par soi. Ce n'est qu'à cette condition que l'apprentissage en sophrologie est véritablement efficace. Sans cette adhésion la Sophrologie perdrait tout son sens !

3. Conscience sophronique

Définie par Caycedo comme l'une des trois possibilités offertes à la conscience, « cette appellation désigne d'abord la situation spéciale que vit le sujet pendant le processus de sophronisation allant du niveau sophroliminal jusqu'à un degré d'hypervigilance. C'est aussi un nouvel état permanent que le sujet peut atteindre progressivement grâce à la répétition des processus de sophronisation ».

Nous voyons dans cette définition le dessein de notre approche : abaissée jusqu'à ce niveau de vigilance minimale (« au bord même du sommeil »), la conscience, débarrassée de pensées parasites, va vivre, en une sorte d'exclusivité absolue, une situation précise proposée par le sophrologue. Cette situation prend la dimension du réel par la perception des phénomènes qu'elle déclenche. En effet, l'idée maîtresse de toute sophronisation est l'*expérimentation phénoménologique* (conscience sophronique, éveillée au vécu du ou des phénomènes présents « *ici et maintenant* »). La situation qui naît, se réalise et évolue lors de cette phase d'activation intra-sophronique, laisse dans la conscience du sujet une trace durable. Le devenir de ces traces successives est lié à la capacité d'auto-entretien de l'état sophronique (et non de l'autosophronisation !) de l'individu lui-même. Il y a bien dans la démarche de la Sophrologie *une mise en cause personnelle, une volonté profonde libératoire et responsable*.

De ce fait on pourrait inclure dans la définition de la conscience sophronique une capacité de contrôle et de maîtrise de soi qui s'accroît en même temps que se développe, chez la personne sophronisée, le champ de conscience, c'est-à-dire l'étendue des phénomènes conscients.

Sur le schéma de base, cet état est parcouru par

la flèche ascendante qui, partant du point C, s'élève vers un niveau théoriquement illimité en conscience sophronique.

4. Désophronisation

Phase terminale de la sophronisation qui permet le retour à l'état de conscience ordinaire, c'est-à-dire le retour à la vie quotidienne (ligne D-A', sur le schéma de base). Il est intéressant de s'apercevoir que cette désophronisation n'est pas un retour au point de départ, mais qu'il y a entre A et A' un progrès, une avancée vers l'état de conscience sophronique. Pendant la sophronisation, la conscience s'est renforcée et s'est *enrichie de l'expérience acquise par l'expérimentation*. Tout l'art de la désophronisation auto ou hétérodirigée consiste à garder en mémoire le bénéfice de ce vécu privilégié. Le passage du point A au point A' peut être considéré :

en sophrothérapie, comme la résolution du problème en cause;

en sophropédagogie, comme préparation progressive au vécu positif d'un événement déterminé;

en sophroprophylaxie, comme un pas vers un état de conscience sophronique permanent.

En outre, la relaxation physique ayant été très profonde durant la séance, il convient de remettre en tonicité l'ensemble du corps. Assimilable au processus du réveil après le sommeil naturel, cette reprise en main de l'activité physique s'accompagne d'une élévation du niveau de vigilance. Eveil physique et éveil mental doivent se faire en harmonie, en totale conscience du mouvement et de la mobilisation de l'énergie nécessaire à ce mouvement. Cette attitude favorise grandement l'intégration du **schéma corporel, base de l'équilibre et du renforcement du Moi.**

Il faut bien comprendre que la mise en relaxation et la remise en activité du corps et du mental relèvent toutes deux de la même capacité de contrôle et de maîtrise de soi, capacité qui se développe par l'attention dirigée sur la perception du corps lors de ces deux périodes. Il apparaît alors comme évident que cette phase de désophronisation revêt une importance capitale et qu'elle doit être conduite avec beaucoup d'application.

Dans les premiers temps de l'apprentissage, les séances seront donc généralement divisées en trois parties égales, en durée et en importance : l'induction, l'activation intra-sophronique et enfin la désophronisation.

- L'induction par laquelle la conscience accède à un niveau proche de celui du sommeil. Les techniques utilisées font référence à la **relaxation.**

- L'activation intra-sophronique par laquelle la conscience accède à un vécu, expérimentant dans l'**ici et maintenant** les phénomènes perçus. Les procédés employés font appel aux **images mentales.**

- La désophronisation par laquelle la conscience accède à un niveau de vigilance et d'éveil élevé avec une expérience positive durable et présente dans la vie de tous les jours. Cette phase développe la notion de **schéma corporel.**

Relaxation, images mentales et schéma corporel seront les trois principaux axes du travail d'éveil de la conscience sophronique.

LA RELAXATION RAPIDE ET CONTRÔLÉE

Relaxation, détente, repos. Mots usuels, mots à la mode, mots pour rêver! Mais quel contenu ont-ils? Sommeil, sieste, vacances... « Relaxation » en passant dans le langage courant a été quelque peu vidé de son sens. Elle n'est pas faite que de farniente, d'indolence ou de moments d'apathie. La relaxation est un *acte*, une manifestation de la volonté, une *démarche personnelle*.

Le dictionnaire donne de ce mot deux définitions :
- Le fait de détendre, de desserrer les tensions corporelles.
- Le fait de relâcher – dans le sens de libérer – un prisonnier.

Dans une relaxation bien conduite et bien comprise, nous devrons donc à la fois détendre, desserrer toutes les tensions musculaires et ainsi libérer les tensions mentales prisonnières, détenues dans nos pensées, par notre cerveau. La relaxation pour bien être doit être psychique en même temps que physique : effacer, gommer, supprimer tous soucis, peurs, angoisses enfermés dans notre mental pendant que, par le repos, notre corps fait le plein d'énergie et de force vitale.

Il existe plusieurs méthodes donnant accès à l'état de quiétude. Parmi elles, la plus connue et la plus utilisée en sophrologie est le training autogène de Schultz qui date du début de ce siècle.

Cette méthode consiste, en son cycle inférieur, en un entraînement échelonné sur plusieurs degrés, chacun comportant un exercice qui, par la perception d'une sensation spécifique, permet la mise en évidence de sa capacité de contrôle des tensions.

- *Sensation de pesanteur*

« Mon bras droit est lourd... tout à fait lourd... agréablement lourd... plus le bras se détend, plus il devient lourd... Maintenant mon bras gauche est lourd... Je prends conscience de la pesanteur, de l'attraction terrestre... » Progressivement la sensation de pesanteur s'étend à l'ensemble du corps.

- *Sensation de chaleur*

« Ma main droite est chaude, très chaude, de plus en plus chaude... un rayon de soleil réchauffe ma main qui se détend... Puis ma main gauche devient elle aussi agréablement chaude... »

Les sensations seront vécues de plus en plus nettement et globalement au fur et à mesure que la relaxation s'installe. Les stades suivants sont consacrés à l'activité cardiaque (« mon cœur bat, calme et fort dans mon thorax... »), à la respiration (« quelque chose de calme et de tranquille respire en moi... »), au plexus solaire (source de chaleur et d'énergie).

Le dernier exercice incite à vivre la sensation de fraîcheur au niveau du front... « Je sens une brise légère rafraîchir mon front... »

La sophronisation de base emprunte, lors de l'induction, certains exercices à cette méthode. Moins directive, la relaxation sophronique demande une plus grande prise de conscience de l'état de détente et, de ce fait, permet un vécu réel et profond de sa relaxation.

« J'accueille et recueille dans ma conscience toutes les sensations venant de mon corps détendu... Je suis présent dans le phénomène relaxation que je perçois et comprends. »

Comprendre le phénomène relaxation!

Pour essayer de comprendre ce qui se passe pendant cette période d'induction qui conduit à une relaxation globale, il faut partir du concept général de la relation corps-esprit. Notre cerveau, siège du mental, est tenu en éveil par les stimulations qu'il reçoit des différents récepteurs sensoriels répartis dans l'ensemble du corps et qui ont pour mission de fournir le maximum de renseignements sur :

- le monde extérieur, par l'activité de nos sens : vue, odorat, ouïe et toucher. Ce sont les sensations *extéroceptives*;
- le « monde intérieur », par la présence de capteurs situés d'une part au niveau des muscles, tendons, articulations, etc. (sensations *proprioceptives*) et d'autre part, au niveau des organes internes, appareils circulatoire, respiratoire, digestif, etc. (sensations *intéroceptives*).

En fonction de ces stimulations, le cortex renvoie une réponse sous forme de stimulation centrifuge qui maintient une certaine tonicité neuromusculaire. A ce circuit « somato-psycho-somatique » s'ajoute un autre type de réaction ayant pour point de départ une activité cérébrale (ou mentale) essentielle ou primitive avec toujours son cortège de réponses corporelles. C'est le sentiment qui s'objective dans la relation psychosomatique : la peur qui fait trembler les jambes, la timidité qui fait rosir les joues, etc. Les interrelations qui s'installent ainsi entretiennent un processus qui peut tendre vers un état de tension extrême ou alors vers une détente de plus en plus grande. C'est ce système qui prime lors de la relaxation avec une potentialisation de l'effet par une prise de conscience de la **spirale descendante.**

Partant d'un simple relâchement musculaire

(repos) et d'une diminution des stimuli extérieurs (pénombre, insonorisation ou musique répétitive), nous obtenons d'une façon automatique une baisse du niveau de vigilance donc, en retour, un début de détente neuromusculaire. A partir de là s'induit une véritable relaxation mentale et physique amenant la conscience jusqu'au niveau sophroliminal.

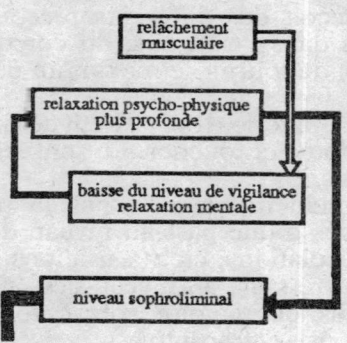

Détente globale par relation psychosomatique

La prise de conscience, dans le travail sophronique, rend le processus reproductible à volonté, de plus en plus rapidement, et ce, quel que soit le niveau de tension du départ. C'est en quoi la relaxation de type sophronique est considérée comme un acte volontaire avec une décision au départ, une exécution consciente ayant pour finalité un résultat tangible vécu par la perception des sensations présentes.

Dans les schémas qui suivent, nous voyons l'éveil cortical (nombre de points) diminuer proportionnellement à la baisse des stimulations centripètes – extérieures et intérieures. Elles-mêmes sont, par effet rétroactif, de moins en moins fortes par apaisement centrifuge, d'origine corticale.

Mais, même au plus profond de la relaxation,

des sensations existent encore (le corps est toujours présent !) et celles-ci – parfois très nouvelles – sont d'ailleurs fort intéressantes car elles fournissent de précieux renseignements sur l'état de relaxation corporelle. L'attitude sophronique d'écoute attentive et bienveillante de son corps détendu permet d'en prendre conscience, de les mémoriser afin de pouvoir les reproduire chaque fois selon l'envie... ou le besoin.

A) *La relaxation est absente.*
Niveau de conscience : *veille attentive.*
Etat physique : *eutonique à hypertonique.*

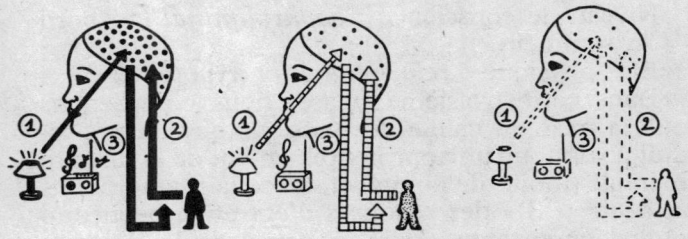

1 = Stimulations extérieures : sensations extéroceptives.
2 = Stimulations intérieures : sensations proprioceptives (muscles, tendons...).
3 = Réponses centrifuges (cerveau => corps) qui alimentent par effet de feed-back les tensions intéro et proprioceptives.

L'activité cérébrale (représentée par les petits points) est entretenue par des stimulations de tous ordres, normales dans un niveau d'éveil ordinaire : d'une part extérieures et d'autre part d'origine interne ou iatrogène comme les pensées, les soucis, etc. Cette activité cérébrale entretient, en réponse, une certaine tension corporelle, objectivée sur le dessin par la flèche « 3 » épaisse.

B) La relaxation commence.
Niveau de conscience : *veille.*
Etat physique : *détente.*

C'est l'état de départ. Dans cette deuxième phase, nous opérons une baisse des stimulations extérieures, moins de bruits, lumière tamisée, paupières fermées, etc. Automatiquement se produit une sorte de « mise en veilleuse » de l'activité corticale (diminution du nombre de points) et donc une baisse sensible des réponses centrifuges des tensions corporelles (flèche « 3 » moins épaisse).

C) La relaxation est maintenant globale, physique et mentale.
Niveau de conscience : *sophroliminal* (au bord du sommeil).
Etat physique : *relâchement et hypotonie.*

Dans cette troisième phase, nous comprenons que la mise au calme des tensions physiques produit à son tour un approfondissement de la détente mentale (moins de points) et, de ce fait, nous avons la flèche « 3 » des réponses d'entretien beaucoup moins importante. Ainsi, à partir de la décision volontaire de se mettre en relaxation, s'enchaîne un processus, que l'entraînement va rendre quasi automatique, de « descente » en une profonde détente *et* physique *et* mentale.

**La relaxation devient un acte,
le résultat d'une démarche volontaire.**

Dans les applications de sophropédagogie, par exemple pour la préparation aux examens, à la compétition sportive ou dans certaines techniques utiles aux vendeurs, il sera toujours possible d'arrêter cette spirale inductive, quel que soit le palier atteint, modulant ainsi la *profondeur*, la *direction* et donc la *rapidité* de la relaxation.

A cet effet nous avons mis au point, avec les

étudiants et les sportifs, une méthode de **relaxation rapide et contrôlée** permettant d'obtenir une « défatigabilité sélective » au niveau de telle ou telle région du corps et une « défatigabilité nerveuse » afin d'effacer les surtensions émotionnelles, mentales et intellectuelles.

La possibilité de moduler et adapter son état aux circonstances à vivre est déjà une réponse positive aux stress trop importants occasionnés par des événements « chargés ». Elle aboutit à un état permanent de maîtrise de soi tout en étant parfaitement compatible avec une vie active et dynamique, car elle donne un sentiment de sécurité et de sûreté de soi par une meilleure « mise en jeu » de ses capacités physiques et intellectuelles.

Apprendre la relaxation!
La sophrorelaxation rapide et contrôlée

La technique que nous allons décrire est donnée à titre d'exemple. Elle comporte tous les éléments d'un apprentissage : explications, expérimentations et mémorisation. Nous verrons aussi qu'elle fait appel à deux notions fondamentales qui seront reprises plus loin : la perception du *schéma corporel* et l'élaboration d'*images mentales*.

La relaxation est un acte et comme tout acte, pour bien le réaliser, il faut l'apprendre. L'apprentissage proposé se fait en trois étapes. Chacune représente un degré d'intégration des phénomènes présents. N'oublions pas que la sophrologie ouvre la conscience en stimulant la perception des phénomènes. Pour comprendre la progression nécessaire, nous pouvons nous représenter
> **la relaxation comme un chemin ou une route,**
> **permettant d'aller d'un niveau d'éveil quelconque**
> vers le niveau sophroliminal
> ou niveau de détente profond.

C'est un chemin et, pour le parcourir chaque fois plus sûrement et plus rapidement, il faudra connaître trois choses :

1° Où aller, donc définir le but à atteindre.

2° Par où passer, donc jalonner la route de repères.

3° Prendre un moyen de transport.

Définir le but

Lors de ce premier contact avec la relaxation, le « travail » consiste à guider son corps, depuis « l'état de départ » jusqu'à la détente globale.

1° Ce chemin qui se fait en relâchant chaque muscle du corps, du front au bout des pieds, n'est réalisable qu'avec notre participation consciente et volontaire. L'effet de l'induction en spirale (voir explication pages précédentes) se produit et la seule occupation est de laisser faire, de *lâcher prise*. C'est une attitude qui n'est pas aussi évidente que cela car certaines résistances peuvent se manifester. Il faut également bien savoir que ce *lâcher prise* n'est pas un abandon de soi, une perte ou une absence à soi. C'est tout le contraire, chaque pas que l'on fait sur ce chemin est un pas fait en parfait contrôle de soi.

2° Une fois arrivé au but fixé – la détente parfaite du corps et de l'esprit –, il est important de *prendre en conscience* des sensations libérées par la relaxation. L'écoute attentive de son corps relaxé est très instructive.

Les sensations qui parviennent à la conscience qui s'éclaire sont de coloration et d'intensité peu coutumières. Nous avons pris l'habitude de ne considérer notre corps que lorsqu'il nous envoie des sensations fortes et généralement négatives (fatigue musculaire, douleur...).

**N'attendons pas que notre dent soit en rage et notre foie en crise
pour nous mettre à l'écoute attentive et douce de ce qui se passe dans le « monde du dedans ».**

Que dire des sensations de la relaxation ? Rien... Rien avant qu'elles se manifestent et que nous les ayons perçues, vécues.

**Chacun a ses propres sensations.
Il n'y a pas de relaxation stéréotypée.**

3° Maintenant que la relaxation a libéré ses sensations et que celles-ci ont été perçues par la conscience, il va falloir les mémoriser.

La mémorisation fait partie de la sophronisation. Or notre cerveau mémorise d'autant mieux qu'il peut traduire ce qui se propose à lui en image mentale. C'est pourquoi le sujet sophronisé est invité, une fois la détente obtenue, à transformer l'ensemble des sensations ressenties en une image mentale.

Cette image est, bien entendu, laissée au libre choix de chacun. Image de la relaxation représentée en un « tableau » correspondant à une image réelle ou inventée, cela n'a aucune importance.

A cette image, sophroniquement créée, se trouve associé l'état de détente globale. Le but du chemin est maintenant objectivé et pourra être, lors des prochaines inductions, imaginé facilement... dans une volonté d'autoconduction de la relaxation.

Pour un exemple concret, prenons un extrait du terpnos logos d'une séance :
- ... « Vous êtes parfaitement détendu, les muscles sont relâchés,
- les sensations de la relaxation parviennent nettement
- à votre conscience attentive... et
- je mets dans ma tête, devant mes yeux, en projection mentale
- l'image d'un voilier dont la silhouette blanche

– se découpe sur un fond de mer bleue... »

L'image mentale de ce bateau devient *votre* image référence à laquelle seront associées *vos* sensations de bien-être. **Vous venez d'imaginer (transformer en image) votre relaxation.**

L'expérimentation de l'état de relaxation, par la perception et la mémorisation (résumées par le mot « vécu ») des sensations, enrichit la conscience d'une expérience de contrôle de soi. Cette nouvelle expérience ne peut que favoriser les prochaines tentatives tout en rendant le sujet de plus en plus autonome.

Mise en place des repères

Cette image référence (le bateau, dans notre exemple) est maintenant utilisée pour faire plus rapidement le chemin qui conduit vers la détente. Voici le déroulement, pas à pas, de ce que nous pourrions considérer comme une deuxième séance :

1° Avant que ne commence le mouvement mental vers le « bord du sommeil », il est indispensable de « revoir » l'image afin de définir le but à atteindre. Ainsi, dans les premières minutes, le candidat à la relaxation tentera de reprendre en conscience cette image mentale de détente et de repenser aux sensations vécues lors du dernier « voyage ». Cette démarche facilite la mise en place de la « spirale descendante », stimule la concentration sur le résultat à obtenir en même temps qu'elle encourage la décision de commencer.

2° La concentration de l'attention est augmentée également par une écoute sélective de la respiration, sans la modifier mais au contraire, « en se plaçant en spectateur ou en témoin de l'activité naturelle du corps », dans une sorte de constat de l'état de départ. Puis la route commence, chaque muscle est relâché, l'induction en spirale se déroule... et le « bord du sommeil » est atteint.

Ici, la conscience, débarrassée des pensées et images parasites, peut diriger son regard intérieur vers différentes zones du corps, zones qui serviront de repères ou d'étapes. Ces repères sont au nombre de trois.

a) Le visage

De très nombreuses sensations peuvent se révéler dans une écoute attentive du visage détendu. Par exemple :
– pesanteur dans la mâchoire inférieure, lourdeur dans les paupières;
– légère sensation de chaleur au niveau des joues, lèvres comme plus épaisses, etc.;
– mais surtout toute une série de sensations très fines, très subtiles et privées au niveau de la peau du visage dues au relâchement progressif des dizaines de muscles de la face.

Le premier repère entraîne un état de calme diffus

b) Bras, dos et jambes

Ces régions corporelles ont été choisies comme deuxième repère sur la route qui conduit à la détente car elles présentent deux principales caractéristiques :
– Nous avons généralement un bon contrôle de ces muscles par toute l'activité quotidienne. (Certains même en ont une parfaite maîtrise, comme les sportifs ou danseurs.) Il est relativement facile de « s'adresser » mentalement à ces zones qui sont largement représentées au niveau des aires cortica-

les. Le schéma du corps est présent dans le cerveau.

– Elles sont responsables du plus gros des sensations proprioceptives et donc leur relaxation va diminuer le nombre des stimulations entretenant l'éveil cortical et entraîner par ce fait une baisse du niveau de vigilance. Par le simple (!) relâchement de muscles des bras, dos et jambes, un pas important est fait en direction de la détente globale.

Les sensations libérées sont généralement très nettement ressenties :
– pesanteur ou attraction terrestre,
– chaleur (paumes des mains) par dilatation des petits vaisseaux sanguins,
– picotements au bout des doigts, impression d'onde,
– de courant d'énergie (parfois le long de la colonne vertébrale), etc.

Encore une fois, l'important est de recueillir dans sa conscience des renseignements sur son corps au repos.

Le deuxième repère conduit à la relaxation musculaire

c) Le ventre

Troisième et dernier repère avant le « bord du sommeil ».

Les muscles du ventre relâchés redonnent au corps sa respiration naturelle. La respiration abdominale, de même type que celle du dormeur, est la preuve objective que le niveau sophroliminal est atteint. Elle symbolise le calme intérieur et signifie donc que les tensions profondes sont atténuées.

Par la respiration du ventre, calme, souple, au rythme lent et régulier, le corps montre son apaisement en même temps que ces messages de « paix intérieure » montent vers les centres plus évolués du cerveau et favorisent la baisse du niveau de vigilance. Le vécu sophronique de la respiration tranquille assure une sorte d'auto-entretien de la détente et met la conscience en présence de la quiétude que procure l'harmonisation de soi.

• Harmonisation dans les relations de soi par rapport à soi. « En moi rien ne vient troubler mon bien-être. Je me sens en confiance. »

• Harmonisation dans les relations de soi par rapport au monde. « Rien autour de moi ne peut déranger ma tranquillité. Je suis en confiance. »

Le troisième repère symbolise la détente totale psycho-physique

Les types de respiration

Dans ce dernier degré d'apprentissage de la Relaxation rapide et contrôlée, nous mettrons en place quelques moyens d'atteindre ces différentes étapes avec efficacité et rapidité : deux types de respirations contrôlées spécifiques à chacun des deux premiers repères.

Pour le premier, la relaxation du visage, nous emploierons la respiration dite « des trois étages », c'est-à-dire que l'ensemble de l'appareil respiratoire participe au mouvement de la respiration : le ventre, le thorax et les épaules.

Ce mouvement respiratoire ample s'exécute en trois temps. Après avoir soufflé, nous inspirons profondément par le ventre puis nous remontons l'air au niveau du thorax et enfin dans les épaules. Là, sans bloquer, sans effort, nous « suspendons » l'inspiration (comme le temps peut suspendre son vol...) quelques secondes, dans une apnée inspiratoire. Nous soufflons longuement, en contrôlant l'expiration, « comme en soufflant dans une paille », et en dirigeant mentalement le souffle vers la région du corps dont nous désirons maîtriser les tensions. Cette respiration étant associée à la relaxation des muscles du visage, nous proposons la manière suivante de procéder :

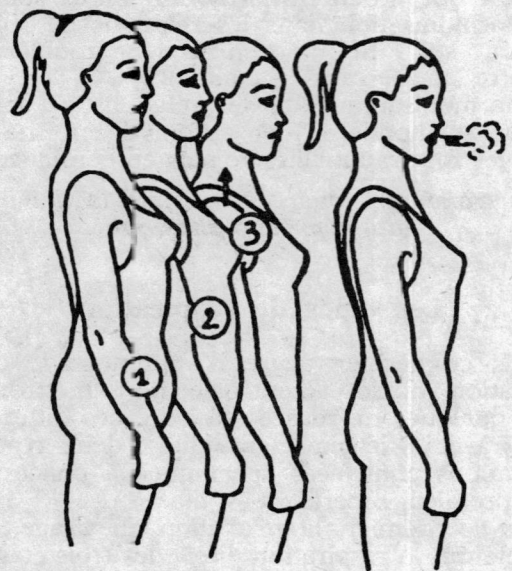

Ventre Thorax Epaules   Souffler

Respiration des « trois étages »

Ventre + thorax + épaules... apnée... expiration « vers » le front, les yeux, les paupières... Respiration libre... vécu des premières sensations... ventre + thorax + épaules... apnée... expiration de relaxation des muscles des joues, autour de la bouche, de la mâchoire inférieure... respiration libre... vécu des sensations complètes.

Quand le but d'un mouvement respiratoire est

de détendre, le temps de l'inspiration est raccourci et celui de l'expiration lente est rallongé. Nous verrons que pour une dynamisation, nous inverse-

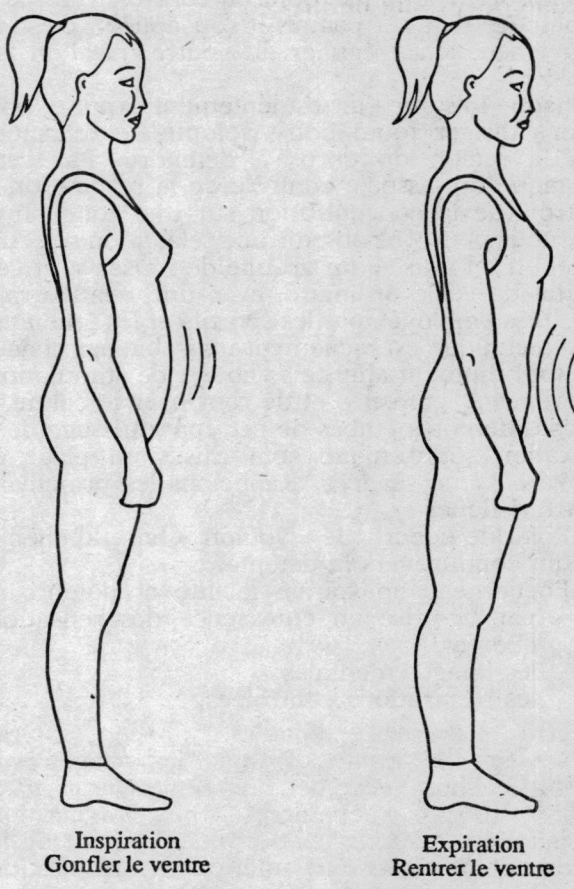

Inspiration
Gonfler le ventre

Expiration
Rentrer le ventre

Respiration abdominale contrôlée

rons ces différents temps, en particulier celui de la rétention d'air en inspiration sera plus important.

Pour le deuxième repère, la relaxation des bras, jambes et dos, la respiration conseillée est une respiration abdominale dont on contrôle rythme et amplitude. Il n'y a pas arrêt (ou apnée), c'est un mouvement lent, régulier du ventre que l'on **fait** respirer.

Chaque fois que l'air est lentement expulsé, nous devons diriger toute notre volonté de relaxation vers la région du corps à détendre. Par cette technique qui associe contrôle de la respiration et contrôle de la concentration sur une zone physique, nous pourrons obtenir une relaxation sélective de tel ou tel muscle ou groupe de muscles, et ceci en état de veille ordinaire, avec une relative rapidité. Très employée par les sportifs et les étudiants, cette technique est facilement utilisable par chacun et à tout moment afin de se libérer de stimulations superflues et parasites et de retrouver le calme.

Les différentes étapes de cet apprentissage de la relaxation sophronique sont mises en place en quatre ou cinq séances. Rappelons les principales caractéristiques :

> Point de départ : le « vouloir » faire le chemin qui conduit vers la détente.
> Phénomène en spirale facilité et potentialisé par la prise en conscience des sensations libérées,
> les images mentales,
> les respirations contrôlées.

LES IMAGES MENTALES

« Outre qu'il a la fonction d'un organe d'attention locale, le cortex sensoriel a aussi pour fonction d'emmagasiner les impressions passées. Celles-ci peuvent venir à la conscience sous forme d'images, mais plus souvent elles demeurent hors du champ de la conscience. Elles forment ainsi des modèles organisés de nous-même que nous pouvons appeler des schémas. Ces schémas modifient les impressions amenées par les influx sensoriels afférents, de telle manière que la sensation finale de position ou de localisation au moment où elle parvient à la conscience est chargée d'une relation à quelque chose qui s'est passé antérieurement. » (HEAD) (1)

L'imagerie mentale, très facilement repérable par le rêve du dormeur et la rêverie du poète, est aussi présente dans l'activité cérébrale du philosophe, du scientifique et du manuel. Les images mentales constituent un véritable langage de la conscience. Elles servent de référence dans l'analyse d'une situation et induisent, par là même, notre comportement de réaction.

Le terme « image » est pris dans un sens large. C'est l'ensemble du savoir organisé qui réside dans notre cerveau et dont nous disposons pour comprendre ce qui se passe en nous-même et dans notre environnement. Les images pourront être de type visuel (le plus fréquent) mais également de

(1) Citation extraite du livre : *La Relaxation Dynamique*, J.-P. Hubert.

modalité sensorielle différente, auditive, olfactive ou tactile selon la prédominance perceptive du sujet. Par exemple, un non-voyant fabriquera plus facilement une image mentale d'un bruit (éclat de rire, musique, etc.) qu'un peintre ou qu'un cinéaste qui donnent une préférence à l'image visuelle.

La formation puis la réapparition de l'image mentale est en relation avec le mode perceptif individuel mais également avec l'intensité émotionnelle de l'événement vécu. En effet l'émotion, au sens large du terme, (c'est-à-dire l'ampleur des modifications organiques et leur diversité) est mobilisante : elle favorise la prise en conscience de la situation vécue ou suggérée en faisant réagir un plus grand nombre de neurones cervicaux. Traductrice puis inductrice d'un état comportemental, l'image est toujours présente pour globaliser, englober et mémoriser tous les éléments inclus dans la situation.

L'activité d'imagerie mentale peut à elle seule déclencher une somatisation de l'état émotionnel qu'elle a mémorisé lors de sa formation initiale. Cette réponse somatique à l'image a été mise en évidence par l'enregistrement électromyographique des modifications spécifiques de certains muscles de la face (muscles de mimique) différentes selon que la situation imagée représentait des sentiments de joie (rires) ou de chagrin (pleurs). De même lorsque des sujets phobiques sont invités à imaginer leur peur (représentation mentale de la situation de détresse), on enregistre des modifications de leurs rythmes cardiaque et respiratoire.

L'évocation d'une image fortement chargée en affectivité peut déclencher un état émotionnel comparable à celui suscité par la perception de l'événement réel. En d'autres termes, par évocation d'une image ou par suggestion d'un événement, nous retrouverons dans l'organisme tous les mécanismes neurophysiologiques mis en jeu, à l'origine, lors du déroulement et du vécu de l'expérience de référence.

Ainsi, par suggestion sophronique, peuvent être mises en place certaines images mentales « positives » en relation avec l'évocation d'une situation précise traumatisante (par exemple une phobie). Au moment où le sujet aura à vivre cette expérience précise, ce sont elles qui vont prévaloir et, se substituant ainsi aux images « négatives » antérieurement mémorisées, vont modifier la réponse comportementale.

Cette capacité naturelle de la conscience s'avère très efficace pour résoudre certaines situations qui apparaissent comme négatives et qui engendrent un comportement inadapté. Au lieu de laisser naître, d'une façon incontrôlée, des images mentales inhibantes et désagréables, les structures mentales pourront « sécréter » d'autres images auxquelles est associée une attitude plus responsable donc de plus grande maîtrise.

Prenons l'exemple de ces premières séances consacrées à l'apprentissage de la relaxation de base.

Le relâchement musculaire progressif libère certaines sensations dont le sujet doit prendre conscience pour les mémoriser afin de pouvoir les reproduire à volonté. Le « travail » du sophrologue, lors de ces séances, a pour but de mettre l'individu en présence du phénomène de relaxation. Le « travail » du sophronisé consiste alors en une activité d'imagerie mentale (libre ou dirigée) de façon à concrétiser le sentiment de détente qui naît (par exemple, l'image d'un édredon lourd et chaud si les sensations perçues sont lourdeur et chaleur). L'état sophronique et la suggestion favorisent l'association image-sensation et permettent sa mémorisation. Plus tard, et selon le désir du sujet, la réactualisation de cette image (édredon) facilitera la détente en entraînant avec elle les sensations qui lui sont liées. De ce fait, l'image mentale associée, par cette action sophronique, sert de support à l'idée de relaxation et lui permet d'être vécue comme une réalité.

Nous pourrions également citer le cas de cet étudiant que j'ai eu l'occasion de préparer à une intervention chirurgicale grave par la sophrologie. Lors des premières séances, vivant en état sophronique les sensations de calme et de paix profonde, il leur a associé l'image d'un bateau à voile sur fond de mer bleue. L'entraînement progressif a rendu cette image mentale utilisable pour une auto-induction de l'état de relaxation. Ceci lui a permis de vivre les jours et les nuits précédant l'opération avec beaucoup de sérénité et de confiance.

Huit à dix mois plus tard, présentant des concours d'entrée aux grandes écoles, cette technique mentale de contrôle de soi lui a donné la possibilité d'affronter les épreuves avec une parfaite maîtrise de son état émotionnel. Les insomnies fréquentes précédant les examens ont été supprimées et juste avant les différents écrits et oraux, ces images mentales, de bateau et de mer bleue, rapidement évoquées lui ont permis de calmer ses esprits et de remettre de l'ordre dans ses idées et dans sa mémoire. Ce jeune homme est devenu maintenant un ingénieur à très hautes responsabilités et continue à se servir de ce « petit truc » chaque fois qu'il doit prendre des décisions importantes.

Le deuxième cas qui me revient en mémoire est celui d'un adolescent qui avouait des relations amicales rendues très difficiles en raison de sa grande timidité : chaque fois qu'il se trouvait en présence de jeunes filles de son âge, il bégayait et une forte transpiration lui donnait les mains moites... et la poignée de main désagréable. Par la technique dite de somatisation positive, il a pu associer à l'image choisie par lui (le soleil) une sensation de chaleur au niveau de la gorge et dans les mains. Lors de ses premiers contacts avec la situation réelle, il a dû faire « l'effort » de penser à ces images mentales et d'en ressentir les effets bienfaisants puis après quelques expériences positives, de nouveaux schémas se sont mis en place, supportés par de nouvelles images mentales de réussite et les symptômes psychosomatiques de sa timidité ont progressivement disparu... et, par la suite, sa timidité elle-même !

Pour être efficaces les images mentales doivent être, dans le travail sophronique, associées à un comportement positif de calme et de contrôle mais également liées à un stimulus conditionnel. Il s'opère alors un véritable changement d'attitude par substitution d'images.

Ce fait est particulièrement mis en valeur dans la préparation à la naissance. Ce jour-là, toute une série d'images mentales vont remonter à la surface. Certaines d'entre elles peuvent être chargées d'affects négatifs (peur de la douleur, angoisse de malformations du nouveau-né, etc.) et perturber très fortement le vécu de la naissance. L'événement, qui ne devrait être qu'heureux, devient un moment difficile avec dans la tête des images porteuses d'émotions « débordantes » qui se somatisent par une douleur accrue et mal supportée. Par la préparation sophronique, les images mentales associées, élaborées et mémorisées lors des séances, vont se substituer aux « idées noires » généralement véhiculées et vont pouvoir influencer favorablement le vécu et donc le comportement de la future mère.

Les images mentales résident dans les structures corticales sous la forme de graphes – voir pages 231 et suivantes – qui se constituent à l'occasion d'une expérience ou d'un apprentissage. Les premiers graphes qui se formeront, dès le début de la vie, seront donc en relation avec les premières expériences, c'est-à-dire la perception du corps. Ils restent potentiellement actifs, et représentent le *schéma du corps*. Schéma, bien entendu évolutif au cours des années, qui est à la base des rapports que tout individu entretient avec lui-même. Il est indispensable que le schéma corporel soit bien intégré dans la conscience de chacun... C'est à ce titre qu'il occupe une place primordiale dans la démarche sophronique.

LE SCHÉMA CORPOREL

Nous sommes des « *enfants de divorcés* ». Divorce entre le corps et l'esprit. Divorce entre l'homme et la nature. Comment en sommes-nous arrivés là ?

Logique, objectif et scientifique, l'homme occidental, confiant en ses découvertes, ses outils et sa technologie, a offert son corps-objet aux « gens de la science ». L'anatomiste l'a dépecé, disséqué, objectivé. Comme sur une carte d'état-major, le corps s'est retrouvé divisé en régions et en quartiers, avec des noms savants et des trajets décrits. Sur ces planches d'anatomie, se trouve dessiné, en belles couleurs, un « écorché » avec des muscles, des artères et des veines mais sans âme et sans conscience :

Le corps s'est dépersonnalisé...

Le physiologiste a cherché à comprendre le pourquoi et le comment des mécanismes de la vie. Le corps a pris petit à petit l'allure d'une machine compliquée avec ses rouages parfois mystérieux mais que la science perce chaque jour davantage. Alors furent inventés des cœurs et des reins artificiels, des circulations de remplacement et des respirations de substitution... A quand l'intelligence artificielle implantée dans une conscience électronique ? Sur ces schémas de montage l'organisme se démonte et se remonte, se démontre et s'explique :

Le corps s'est standardisé...

Le médecin, avec dans une main des pilules et dans l'autre un bistouri, est devenu le réparateur-dépanneur de cette machine humaine... selon le schéma de montage! Les anomalies de fonctionnement ont été répertoriées, les diagnostics et les traitements se sont affinés et sont appliqués selon une nomenclature si précise qu'il est actuellement question d'informatiser et d'automatiser entièrement la thérapeutique : à partir d'un questionnaire, les signes cliniques sont « rentrés » dans l'ordinateur et en quelques secondes apparaissent les examens complémentaires à effectuer conduisant, selon les résultats, à un diagnostic et à une thérapie...

Le corps s'est déshumanisé...

Il faut savoir que la science a pour objectif la compréhension et la domination (dans la mesure du possible) du monde matériel. Vouloir sans adaptation appliquer ses principes à l'être humain, c'est réduire ce dernier à de la simple matière! L'erreur est évidente, l'impasse est inévitable!!! Je peux vous assurer (et vous rassurer?) que vous n'êtes pas que matière organique... Il y a en vous une composante immatérielle qui limite (et en même temps dépasse) l'approche trop scientiste de l'action thérapeutique.

Il serait bien évidemment stupide et dangereux de rejeter en bloc les formidables progrès réalisés dans le domaine de la médecine. C'est incontestablement par cette approche rationnelle et systématique des maladies que certaines d'entre elles ont été totalement résolues, et le nombre de vies humaines sauvées par nos médecins occidentaux impose le respect et l'admiration.

Il me souvient à cet égard d'une anecdote significative rapportée par un de mes amis gynécologue-accoucheur. Il était parti, avec un groupe de spécialistes, en voyage d'étude en Chine. Voulant profiter de la chance d'être en relation avec les plus hauts responsables du Service de maternité de Pékin, les médecins français ont, bien sûr, demandé certaines précisions sur l'efficacité de l'acupuncture – considérée en France comme une médecine dite parallèle – et ils ont passé leur temps... à répondre aux questions posées par les médecins chinois sur les techniques d'anesthésie péridurale utilisées en Occident! L'intérêt des Orientaux pour cette technique (qui soulève tant de polémiques ici) est compréhensible car elle autorise une anesthésie partielle tout à fait confortable en préservant l'éveil et la conscience du sujet. Je sais bien que « nul n'est prophète en son pays » et que ce qui existe « chez les autres » est toujours mieux mais, n'en déplaise aux orientalistes occidentaux exclusifs, il faut se garder des attitudes extrémistes qui prennent l'allure d'une sorte d'idéologie! Nos chercheurs et nos cliniciens méritent bien une « médaille d'or », même si, comme toute médaille, celle-ci comporte quelque revers. Un des principaux inconvénients de cette « hypermédecine » par trop mécaniste est d'avoir laissé le champ libre à une tendance opposée « hyperpsy », elle aussi parfois extrémiste, qui déverse à flots des théories de substitution quelque peu parapsychologiques ou ésotériques, pures et dures, abstraites et sans **ancrage corporel.**

D'un côté, **le corps s'est dépersonnalisé,**
tandis que de l'autre,
la Personne s'est décorporalisée.

Le bon choix est, c'est évident, le juste milieu qui permet d'utiliser la très haute technologie tout en prenant en considération la notion fondamentale d'**unicité de l'Etre.** Cette alliance est urgente et la philosophie générale de la Sophrologie y conduit.

Prenons garde de ne pas considérer notre corps comme une machine que l'on ignore quand tout va bien et qu'un dépanneur-réparateur, appelé en urgence, tente de réparer en cas de problèmes! Ne soyons pas les locataires de notre « *maison intérieure* » mais bien des propriétaires responsables de nous-même!

Dehors, il y a bien sûr trop de lumières, trop de bruits, trop de mouvements, trop de violences... et ce monde nous attire jusqu'à nous dissoudre, nous accapare jusqu'à l'épuisement, nous fascine jusqu'à l'éblouissement qui conduit à l'aveuglement. N'attendons pas que notre foie soit en crise ou notre dent en rage pour nous soucier de leur existence!

Dedans, le monde qui nous habite est fait de nuances douces, de lumière tamisée... alors, assourdis par le tohu-bohu extérieur, le calme et les sensations discrètes ne sont plus perçus et ce monde du dedans devient silence puis absence! Nous commençons par nous éloigner de nous-même et, égaré dans la jungle de la vie, nous finissons par nous perdre totalement.

La société, en s'organisant, nous désorganise!

L'urbaniste a construit des usines et des villes autour de ces usines, puis des villes dans les villes, colonisant la campagne et la forêt. L'homme se retrouve enfermé dans de véritables prisons avec des interdits, des obligations et des emplacements réservés : emplacements pour manger, pour dormir, pour travailler... lieux réservés où l'on doit circuler, endroits où l'on doit stationner. Dans le nouvel environnement de l'homme il n'y a plus de chemins creux, de gibiers à chasser et de fruits à cueillir pour se nourrir, mais des avenues, des immeubles et des magasins.

Il n'y a plus de chants d'oiseaux mais le bruit des motos. Il n'y a plus d'arbres et de fleurs mais des panneaux et des poteaux!... et le pauvre petit arbre du square qui abrite les jeux des enfants de la ville fait plus pitié qu'envie et son ombre est dérisoire tant les tours qui l'encerclent sont immenses.

Le corps s'est dénaturé...

Cette distance prise avec la Nature est du même principe et de la même gravité que celle prise avec notre corporalité. Une alliance plus forte avec la Nature pourrait conduire à une rencontre avec nous-même, à un recentrage, à un ancrage dans notre corps vécu comme un concept de base. Sophrologie et Ecologie, dans cette optique, semblent partager la même ambition de prévention : retrouver, pour la défendre et la protéger, la Nature qui est en nous et celle qui nous environne.

- ... « Je suis dans cette Nature qui est en moi...
- En parfaite harmonie, en totale communion avec les éléments
- naturels qui m'entourent... Je suis moi-même un élément
- naturel de cette Nature... Un élément naturel de cette Nature.... »

Ce sont là des phrases suggestives que l'on rencontre souvent dans des séances de Sophrologie. Elles mettent l'accent sur l'indispensable intégration de l'homme dans son environnement naturel dont il tire énergie et calme.

Des structures particulières de notre cerveau autorisent la mise en route d'un pilotage automatique. Certains de ces automatismes sont en place depuis notre naissance – et certainement avant! – et règlent notre vie instinctive. Ils prennent, par exemple, en charge l'« équilibrage » très complexe des tensions musculaires permettant la station debout ou assise, la marche ou la course, le saut, etc. Ils assurent aussi les premiers réflexes de succion du nouveau-né puis, plus tard, ceux de la mastication. En fait, ces automatismes nous facilitent la tâche en nous donnant la possibilité d'effectuer une foule de gestes sans avoir besoin de mobiliser notre attention, libérant ainsi nos facultés mentales, intellectuelles ou physiques.

Certains autres ont été mis en place après apprentissage. C'est ainsi que nous pouvons écrire, parler ou conduire une voiture, d'une façon quasi automatique. L'acquisition de ces réflexes nous permet, encore une fois, d'agir sans l'intervention constante et consciente de la volonté. Ce mode de fonctionnement définit pratiquement toute l'activité quotidienne et habituelle. L'homme passe le plus clair de son temps dans cette sorte de ronronnement de routine confortable et très pratique !

Mais que les partisans de ce moindre effort prennent tout de même garde ! En effet, que penser du commandant de bord d'un avion qui, par manque de connaissances, serait incapable de reprendre en main les commandes de son appareil au moment d'une quelconque difficulté ? Comment imaginer que seul le « pilote automatique » puisse résoudre un problème imprévu ? Nous sommes dans les mêmes conditions : nous avons mis notre vie sur des rails, et, automatisant certains gestes, nous avons purement et simplement abandonné les commandes. Comment s'étonner, dans ces conditions, si parfois il nous arrive de « perdre les pédales »... de cette commande ? Faisons en sorte de ne pas avoir à nous reprocher, un jour, devant une situation non prévue, une incapacité (par manque de connaissance) à reprendre le contrôle de soi avec pour conséquence une dérive vers un état de détresse.

Dans le renforcement de la corporalité, la sophropédagogie et la sophroprophylaxie apportent une aide précieuse par le *vécu du schéma corporel*. Certaines techniques appropriées (en particulier la Relaxation Dynamique de Caycedo) développent et renforcent l'image du corps et établissent une interrelation puissante entre le corps et la conscience. Dès les premiers instants, la sophronisation permet un vécu existentiel des sensations naissant de la relaxation physique : premiers pas feutrés dans le « monde du dedans »!

- ... « Mon corps ressemble à une ville endormie... tout est calme et tranquille...
- la respiration est profonde et régulière... Je l'écoute...
- j'écoute, je vois, je vis mon corps respirer...
- je suis présent en conscience dans le phénomène respiration par la perception des
- sensations qu'il me procure... Je prends conscience des rythmes naturels de mon corps
- ... des rythmes naturels de la Vie... Je laisse venir, sans effort et sans retenue, toutes les sensations intimes, personnelles...
- et quelle que soit la sensation, je l'accueille et la recueille dans ma conscience...
- Sensations venant de mon corps détendu dont je perçois pleinement la présence... sa forme... son volume... son poids... que je vis sous forme de sensation d'attraction terrestre...
- Ce corps que j'ai su mettre au repos, je le réécris dans ma tête, je dessine mentalement la carte de mon corps... etc. »

Alors naissent et se développent une foule d'impressions subtiles, fines et nuancées venant des muscles, des ligaments, des organes... Le corps nous parle de lui, nous parle de nous et enfin nous prenons le temps de l'entendre, nous savons l'écouter ! Entre le corps et la conscience, un dialogue s'établit.

- « ... J'ouvre à mon corps les portes de ma conscience.
- Je donne à ma conscience l'accès à mon corps... »

Il faudrait insister et insister encore sur l'importance du schéma corporel et de son intégration au niveau de la conscience. Etre « bien dans sa peau » est l'essentielle condition de départ pour réaliser l'harmonie entre soi et son environnement.

La plupart des philosophies orientales apprennent à vivre la conscience universelle à travers la conscience du corps. Le monde cosmique dans toute sa dimension métaphysique est présent à l'intérieur du monde organique où l'infiniment Grand et l'infiniment Petit communiquent dans un même élan de Vie.

Il n'est de plus cruelle absence que l'absence de son corps ! Et pour qu'aucune situation ne nous place « hors de nous » ou nous « fasse sortir de nos gonds », il devient urgent de partir à la découverte, à la connaissance, à la conquête (reconquête) de notre corps par la prise en conscience de sa corporalité. Faute de quoi nous ne sommes plus maître chez nous, maître en nous, maître de nous.

DEUXIÈME CHAPITRE

LE CARRÉ

**Le contenu symbolique
Premier degré de la
Relaxation Dynamique de Caycedo
Les états de l'attention
L'expression du désir
et l'exercice du vouloir**

LE CONTENU SYMBOLIQUE

Le Carré est la représentation symbolique du monde terrestre. A la différence du Cercle qui, comme nous le verrons, montre l'aspect dynamique, éternel et céleste de l'Univers, le Carré désigne la *chose réalisée, finie et définie*.

Il faut mettre des minuscules aux mots nature et homme, signifiant ainsi la matérialité de l'objet : c'est l'objectif à atteindre, le terme de la transformation et de la concrétisation de l'Idée et signe, par sa forme dessinée, « l'absolument beau en soi » (Platon). Par le Carré sera donc reconnue la totalité du monde créé, visible et saisissable par la conscience et l'intelligence de l'homme.

Dans de nombreuses civilisations (chinoise, chrétienne) le cosmos est en Carré : la terre, le ciel et les étoiles apparaissant ici dans leur réalité physique.

Le Temps et l'Espace prennent par ce symbole une dimension et une mesure définissables. Certains cherchent dans la perfection du Carré la preuve de l'existence de Dieu et souvent la Maison de Dieu a une architecture carrée. De même, dans les églises et temples, les ouvertures peuvent présenter la forme d'un carré dont un des côtés est arrondi; ainsi le Cercle surmonte le Carré, Dieu est partout présent ici-bas, le Créateur et sa création sont liés, la « quadrature du cercle » est envisagée dans l'union mystique du Ciel et de la Terre.

Au Carré se trouve liée toute la symbolique du chiffre **quatre** utilisé pour signifier le solide, le tangible, le concret. C'est ainsi que la terre est divisée en *quatre* parties, *quatre* horizons montrés par les *quatre* points cardinaux symbolisés par les *quatre* branches de la Croix. La terre est alors appréhendée comme un carré et l'expression « envoyer des messagers aux *quatre* coins du monde » traduit la notion totalisante du symbole. De même l'Univers est soutenu par *quatre* piliers, *quatre* saisons divisent l'année, *quatre* éléments composent le monde et la lune présente *quatre* phases.

Partant de cette notion première de représentation de ce qui est créé et visible, et terrestre, le Carré se charge de diverses significations souvent opposées.

Il devient le symbole de la mère, de l'enracinement, de l'hérédité, de l'esprit terre-à-terre, du « bon sens paysan ». C'est également le corps (ou plus exactement la région abdominale du corps), là où naissent et se libèrent les pulsions instinctives mais aussi là où elles se trouvent enfermées et étouffées. Le centre d'énergie vitale, le courage et la force se situent, chez les Japonais, en cette zone abdominale : le hara.

De la force physique et noble à la puissance militaire, il n'y a qu'un pas... et le Carré a vite représenté la puissance sociale, financière et phallique.

Dans une certaine mesure, le Carré peut aussi symboliser la fonction de l'hémisphère gauche du cerveau. Il sera alors synonyme de la certitude, de l'expérience scientifique et de l'intelligence raisonnée. Dans ce sens, notre civilisation occidentale a poussé l'individu vers un développement exagéré du « Carré » en mettant en relief l'aspect rationnel des choses, le côté cartésien du raisonnement, l'approche matérialiste de la vie. Comme tout ce qui est excessif, cet état de fait est devenu négatif. L'instinctivo-moteur qui régit les réactions du « Carré » s'est quelque peu emballé et l'homme qui a su, en partie, résoudre ses peurs ancestrales se retrouve maintenant certes un homme civilisé mais toujours traqué par la... civilisation ! Pour reprendre l'idéogramme de base, la caricature de l'homme occidental pourrait être représentée comme ceci :

La dysharmonie est évidente : trop stimulé par tous les problèmes matériels et concrets avec une approche souvent limitée au seul souci de paraître, le Carré s'est hypertrophié !

La solidité n'est qu'apparente et comme le chêne dans la fable de La Fontaine qu'un orage déracine, cet homme-là, dont la Croix et le Cercle ont été « sacrifiés » au profit du Carré, ne pourra peut-être pas toujours résister, et, un jour, devant une situation plus stressante qu'une autre, il se trouvera peut-être lui aussi désarçonné !

L'équilibre et l'harmonie présentent une structure beaucoup plus stable et préservent ainsi bien mieux la santé !

Dans les propos qui intéressent la sophrologie, le Carré est le symbole du corps réagissant à des mobiles vitaux (ou étant interprétés comme tels) et agissant selon des motivations instinctives. Il est tout à fait important, pour une plus grande compréhension de la réalité corporelle, réalité agissante lors de chaque situation de vie, de commencer par une intégration consciente de la corporalité. Nous pourrions dire aussi, de commencer par libérer, dans une écoute consciente, le dialogue entre le corps et l'esprit en apprenant à respecter le langage de chacun : *sensations* d'un côté, *images mentales* de l'autre. Et pour que s'établisse une intercommunication authentique, il faut savoir faire taire les informations parasites, faire taire tous les messages dus aux tensions inutiles : c'est le but de la *relaxation sophronique*.

PREMIER DEGRÉ
DE LA RELAXATION DYNAMIQUE

La conscience éclairée

L'une des principales idées intégrées par la Sophrologie est que l'homme est en *devenir*. C'est-à-dire que chaque individu vit sa vie sous forme évolutive et dynamique ou, plus justement, doit vivre la forme évolutive et dynamique de sa vie. Le chemin de la vie est un axe, l'axe de la vie est un chemin de « croix ». Les faits et gestes, les actes et les paroles qui font l'extraordinaire et le quotidien de l'existence (ce que les Orientaux appellent le Karma) dirigent nos pas. Nous allons dans une direction.

La pièce se situe au moment d'un de ces pas.

« Je » est l'acteur principal de cette scène. « Je » vit. L'unité de temps est une tranche de vie : un battement de cœur, une heure, une vie, qu'importe ! « Je » est DANS la pièce et le seul temps est le *ici et maintenant*. L'acteur (celui qui fait acte) doit être avant tout « bien dans la peau » du personnage. Première mise en scène, première mise en situation.

Traduit en termes de sophrologie, cela revient à dire que la priorité est donnée à la relation au corps, à la prise de conscience de sa corporalité, le personnage en l'occurrence étant sa propre personne. Le monde intérieur doit être un monde libre dans lequel circulent sans obstacle les informations venant des différentes zones de localisation et des centres d'intégration. Les stimulations répétées engendrées par certains gestes et exercices respiratoires de ce premier degré vont permettre de révéler les trois grands axes existentiels et référentiels de l'individu.

1. Premier axe : la référence émotionnelle dont l'expression somatique passe par la région centrale du corps, région séparée en deux par le *diaphragme*. La prise en conscience, par activation, de ce grand muscle respiratoire va favoriser l'intégration de certains « vécus », non conscients et non résolus, qui sont restés bloqués soit sous la forme figée de la somatisation, soit sous la forme larvaire de l'émotion première.

Au-dessus du diaphragme, se trouvent signifiées toute l'activité de relations à autrui (ou à l'événement extérieur) et leurs résonances privatisées ; c'est une activité de type thalamique (voir page 226). C'est dire que l'appareil respiratoire devient un appareil de communication, d'expression de l'émotion.

Nous allons vers l'objectivation corporalisée et visible du « ressenti », visible de l'extérieur comme de « l'intérieur ». Par l'intermédiaire des modifications de la respiration, nous prenons contact avec la réalité du sentiment et nous le disons sans mots. Mais le langage du corps est pauvre, il ne peut exprimer que des changements et leurs intensités. Seule la manifestation est prise en compte et retenue : par exemple, le blocage respiratoire est le même devant une frayeur, une douleur ou un grand plaisir. Le principe émotionnel n'est pas toujours divulgué et se retrouve alors « refoulé ».

> Noyé dans la réponse, **le corps a perdu la raison...** primitive de son émoi.

Au-dessous du diaphragme se trouve le ventre.

Univers obscur, symbole refuge des deux plus anciens et plus partagés archétypes qui soient : l'angoisse essentielle d'*être au monde* et celle de mourir de faim. Inquiétude sourde, diffuse, résidant dans « les tripes ». Cette peur ancestrale, archaïque et animale de ne plus « être au monde » ou de mal être au monde, dirige l'instinctivo-moteur de l'hypothalamus vers des attitudes réflexes de survie. Vouloir enfermer cette crainte inhibante dans un compartiment étanche d'un corps cloisonné (nous avons employé, quelques pages plus haut, l'image « d'un monde intérieur aux différents étages « clos par nécessité »!) ne résout en rien le problème et laisse planer la menace de la voir un jour imploser et envahir notre vie. Il faut la libérer ou plus justement s'en libérer.

> N'aie pas peur, éclaire le profond de ton corps
> Vois le plus sacré, le plus secret de ta mémoire
> Secrète. Et regarde l'envers du miroir.
> Je te dis : « L'envers de la vie n'est pas la mort. »
>
> Eclaire le fond de ton âme, n'aie pas peur
> De ses ombres troubles; n'aie plus peur de ta
> [peur.
> La nuit a toujours une étoile pour lueur.
> Vois le noir et sa lumière. Crie et pleure.
> Je te le redis : « Ecris et crie et pleure... »
>
> Pars en dedans de toi et refais le chemin.
> L'enfant qui naît, naît du noir vers la lumière,
> Toi, laisse hors de tout « ça » ta part de Demain,
> Je te dis : « Respire. Inspire. Expire ton Hier... »

Ainsi s'exprime le poète.

2. Deuxième axe : la référence sexuelle par laquelle sont appréhendées grand nombre de situations. C'est également une zone manifestement refoulée et dont l'éclairage suscite parfois quelques troubles. Temple sacré dans lequel la Vie se régénère et par lequel se vit la « petite mort ».

Nous lui avons imposé le secret et l'avons rendue muette en dépit de l'envie. Nous l'avons « dénaturée » et rendue compliquée en dépit du désir. Nous avons voulu, contre nature, étouffer l'émotion première de l'instinctivo-moteur pour la rendre secondaire à des motivations plus dignes.

La lumière se tamise, les yeux se ferment et le regard intérieur, au moment de l'extase, trop « honteux » de ce corps à corps, se voile et se détourne... lève les yeux vers le ciel, la morale est sauve! Mais le regard n'a pas vu la bouche qui s'ouvre, la peau qui transpire, le cœur qui bat.

Alors le corps, las de dire sans être entendu, reprend ses plus primitives émotions, enclave ses plus pures sensations et érige ses frontières.

Volets clos et paravents séparent désormais Epicure de Platon. L'intention se dissout dans trop de prétention

Les zones corporelles de ces deux axes référentiels sont mises en évidence par plusieurs gestes et exercices respiratoires inspirés du Raja Yoga. Dresser une sorte de nomenclature des exercices de ce premier degré me semble totalement inutile car pour les comprendre il faut les vivre en présence d'un sophrologue accompagnant. Cependant, nous allons essayer d'en montrer deux qui me paraissent de la plus haute importance et d'en expliquer les principes de base.

Exercice respiratoire n° 1. 3e geste du protocole établi par Caycedo.

Debout, les jambes légèrement écartées, les pieds bien en contact avec le sol. Les muscles sont relâchés, les bras ballants le long du corps. Les yeux fermés.

En un mouvement lent, empreint de concentration et d'harmonie, nous levons les bras au-dessus de la tête, tête que nous penchons en arrière dans une inspiration profonde. Les mains jointes (comme dans une prière) sont ensuite ramenées pour venir bloquer les narines dans un effort (sans violence) de rétention d'air. Vient alors la phase de libération. Libération des bras en les projetant en avant. Libération de l'air en soufflant fortement par le nez et en imprimant une sensible poussée au niveau de l'abdomen (rentrer le ventre au moment de l'expiration). Libération du dos en se laissant aller en avant, les bras pendants. Perception de la sensation de lourdeur. Puis retour à la position du départ et vécu des sensations présentes que nous « récupérons », que nous recueillons dans notre conscience qui s'éveille dans l'écoute de ce monde intérieur.

Cet exercice disloque tous les cloisonnements mis en place par nos différents systèmes de défense lors de nos confrontations avec les situations coutumières de la vie. Il éveille d'importants centres d'énergie (Chakras) et libère ainsi cette énergie intérieure globale (Kundalini, dans le yoga) dans un but d'harmonisation et d'intégration de soi.

Le **1ᵉʳ chakra** (Muladhara), entre la racine de l'organe génital et l'anus, point de départ de la Kundalini, de forme **carrée**, en relation avec la

terre, de couleur jaune et assurant la fonction de l'**odorat.**

Le **2ᵉ chakra** (Swadishtana), au niveau du plexus lombaire, en relation avec l'**eau** assurant la fonction du goût et en forme de croissant de lune.

Geste Nauli. 14ᵉ geste du protocole, deuxième partie.

Debout, les jambes pliées, les mains calées en appui sur les genoux, les pieds bien à plat. Recherche de la position d'équilibre.

Puis inspirons profondément et soufflons en *rentrant le ventre*. Rester en apnée expiratoire et exercer des *pressions dans les muscles abdominaux* (tension de la paroi abdominale, brassage). Au bout du souffle, sans jamais vouloir « dépasser ses limites », nous reprenons notre respiration quelques instants et nous recommençons deux fois ce geste.

Par ce geste, nous entrons en dedans de nous-même. Notre conscience des sensations éclaire l'obscurité que notre culture et notre oubli ont jetée sur cette partie profonde de notre corps : le ventre. Ici, nous sommes en présence de souvenirs archaïques relatifs aux bases mêmes de la vie. Le ventre utérin et le ventre sexuel apparaissent et libèrent leurs forces enfermées. Formidable énergie fœtale dirigée vers le devenir individuel et inépuisable énergie sexuelle au service du devenir de l'espèce.

Le dialogue qui s'établit à ce moment entre le

corps et la conscience (dialogue qui se situe, bien sûr, hors discours oral ou écrit!) donne à ce geste valeur d'expérimentation du moi profond et insu, expérimentation parfois douloureuse et difficile à assumer mais qui finit par nous faire accéder à une sorte de certitude existentielle de vie manifestée par l'énergie libérée et perçue.

> « ... Le monde chancelle
> lorsque je tiens de mon passé
> de quoi vivre au fond de moi-même. »

Qui pourrait mieux que le poète (1) traduire ce qui se passe au moment précis de ce geste dont les origines se perdent dans la nuit des temps et que Caycedo a su mettre à la portée de notre vécu.

3. Troisième axe : la référence intellectuelle dont le siège se localise dans la zone frontale située entre les deux yeux. (Le troisième œil et l'œil de Civa.) Dans le yoga, cette région s'appelle Trikuti et correspond à l'Ajna Chakra ayant pour fonction la volonté, la décision et la détermination. C'est par ces aspects que l'Homme se différencie des autres espèces animales et peut prétendre à la conscience. On pourrait comprendre cet endroit comme le symbole de l'intégration des phénomènes vécus au niveau du corps, de leur contrôle et de leur maîtrise. Est-il en corrélation avec le cerveau droit? Je pense qu'il est encore un peu tôt pour l'affirmer, bien que de nombreux arguments puissent venir étayer cette hypothèse. Quoi qu'il en soit, c'est évidemment une zone de toute première importance qu'il convient de stimuler, d'éveiller par certains gestes. La Relaxation dynamique a inclus à cet effet l'exercice du **tratac.**

L'exercice du tratac se pratique debout. Projeter

---

(1) Paul CHAULOT, *Jours de béton*, édit. Amis de Rochefort. Extrait de *La Poétique de la rêverie* de Gaston Bachelard.

le pouce en tendant le bras devant soi et en fixer un point quelconque. Ensuite, tout en gardant le regard sur le même point du départ, il faut ramener le pouce en direction du front ce qui entraîne une convergence centrale des yeux vers cette zone et un dédoublement de l'image du pouce, comme si le pouce venait stimuler la région de l'Ajna Chakra.

Ces différents exercices – il y en a dix-huit en tout – ont une grande valeur d'éveil. Ils actionnent certains centres en libérant leurs potentialités et agissent comme des agents évocateurs (ou provocateurs!). Chaque geste, chaque type de respiration provoque, évoque et exalte des sensations particulières qu'il convient, par une écoute attentive, de « récupérer » dans la conscience qui s'éclaire.

Cette phase dite de « récupération » est le moment le plus important, moment où s'installe le vrai dialogue avec le corps. C'est ce temps, ce tempo de la matière profonde que le sophronisé doit retrouver, recréer dans une lecture lente, indéfinissable trame du temps qui se repose et d'un présent qui tente un devenir.

L'écho venant des profondeurs de nous-même résonne d'autant mieux que nous sommes capables de nous mettre au calme.

L'état de détente est souvent assimilé à une sorte de somnolence avec abandon de son corps et absence de sensation : ici, nous nous apercevons que la relaxation peut être obtenue dans un contact préservé et réservé à l'écoute de la musique du corps, que celle-ci soit écrite en largo ou en fortissimo. Musique qui se fait de plus en plus harmonieuse au fur et à mesure que la conscience se met en accord avec son corps. Musique dont les accords traînent encore longtemps, longtemps après que les gestes ont disparu.

La présence à soi-même jointe à une relaxation à partir de cette présence constitue la base indis-

pensable, **la trame à partir de laquelle la conscience sophronique se construit.**

L'une des grandes qualités de la Relaxation Dynamique est de permettre, à partir de la méthode de base, une adaptation ciblée sur les préoccupations de tout un chacun. C'est précisément au moment de cette phase de récupération que le sophrologue-accompagnant intervient et dirige son « discours » (terpnos logos) en fonction du but visé. La méthode globale admet ainsi des techniques additionnelles.

Au cours de presque vingt ans de pratique de la Sophrologie, aussi bien en groupes qu'en séances individuelles, je me suis aperçu qu'un grand nombre nos contemporains partageaient deux grandes préoccupations :

Améliorer les facultés de concentration
 ou « les degrés de l'attention ».

Savoir libérer la volonté
 ou « l'exercice du vouloir ».

Le premier degré inclut « normalement » des exercices de concentration; cependant, l'importance de ces notions et leurs applications pratiques quotidiennes méritent un développement plus grand.

LES ÉTATS DE L'ATTENTION

Nous avons tous eu l'occasion de constater que notre attention peut présenter alternativement plusieurs états. Ils sont au nombre de quatre. La rêverie, la distraction, la concentration et la focalisation. Chacun a son importance et son utilité, le problème réside dans le contrôle de ces degrés, en particulier ceux de la concentration et de la focalisation.

La rêverie

C'est en quelque sorte un peu de vacances que l'esprit s'accorde... parfois sans autorisation! En pleine évasion, il vagabonde à la manière d'un papillon attiré par d'invisibles parfums de liberté sauvage... Rêve éveillé et libre qui efface progressivement la réalité extérieure et le monde s'estompe et s'oublie.

Cette attitude, bien connue – et recherchée – par les poètes et autres artistes, favorise l'élaboration de nouvelles images mentales ou de nouveaux concepts. La rêverie est une des forces les plus dynamiques de la conscience. Une force de création où l'imagination devient un élément moteur du développement psychique.

Par la rêverie nous nous détachons progressivement des pesanteurs de la trop fade quotidienneté et la conscience rêvante donne au monde imaginé une double réalité : la réalité d'un passé qui se réactualise dans le désir présent et la réalité d'un présent qui se colore aux couleurs de l'« à-venir » désirable. Ici l'être de rêverie devient en même temps qu'il fait devenir l'univers que son imaginaire construit. Par cette concomitance, il y a symbiose entre le créant et le créé. Par cette symbiose, il y a harmonie : « Le rêveur et sa rêverie entrent corps et âme dans la substance du bonheur. » Cette force créatrice de la rêverie est une aptitude naturelle de la conscience. Elle nous habite même si parfois nous l'avons réduite à de courts instants de rêvasserie. Elle nous accompagne depuis notre enfance. Nous verrons dans le chapitre réservé au deuxième degré de la Relaxation dynamique comment la réveiller. Mais avant, lisons encore Bachelard nous dire que « ... dans ses solitudes, dès qu'il devient maître de ses rêveries, l'enfant connaît le bonheur de rêver qui sera plus tard le bonheur des poètes ».

La distraction (1)

Cet état de dispersion de l'attention peut être défini comme le résultat d'un manque d'intérêt suffisant pour un objet ou une situation extérieure. L'activité cérébrale passe d'un sujet à l'autre, sans raison apparente, par simple association d'idées. Cet état préside à une période de repos après un long effort ou à un état d'indifférence à un sujet précis. Cet état de vagabondage qui capte, sans les trier, un trop grand nombre d'informations est préjudiciable à tout apprentissage et en particulier à la perception concentrative des sensations corporelles libérées lors des exercices du premier degré.

Ici l'esprit non fixé, non captivé reçoit d'une façon aléatoire un certain nombre de stimulations

(1) Se reporter au chapitre « Sport » pour les schémas et les applications concrètes.

extérieures et son activité « volage » est sous la dépendance de « rencontres aléatoires » avec quelque chose qui se passe dehors ou quelque image mentale surgissant de nulle part.

La concentration

Comme son nom l'indique, la concentration est le résultat de l'élimination de tout ce qui est superflu ou inutilisable. Il y a donc un tri qui s'opère, consciemment ou non, réservant ainsi un espace mental le plus large possible au traitement d'une situation **A** donnée. Sont alors rendues insignifiantes certaines stimulations extérieures (bruits, mouvements, etc.), certaines sensations intérieures (proprio- et intéroceptives) et inopérantes certaines pensées, idées ou images privées.

La situation **A** étant polymorphe et composée d'un nombre important d'éléments, la concentration se traduira par un état de l'attention relativement large, pour ne pas se priver de tous ces importants renseignements aidant à la compréhension puis à la mémorisation de la situation globale **A**. Ce rétrécissement relatif du champ de conscience peut se faire automatiquement dans la mesure où **A** présente un intérêt certain et il se maintiendra tant que l'intérêt persistera.

Il est possible, je pense, d'avancer la constatation suivante : la concentration est obtenue, non pas *sur* un objet, mais bien *grâce* à l'attirance exercée par tous les paramètres constitutifs de la situation globale.

L'état de concentration est le résultat d'une non-dispersion.

Mais si l'objet n'est apparemment pas captivant ou s'il perd son attrait en cours de route, la distraction revient inévitablement. Comment faire pour retrouver cet état de non-dispersion ?

Si **A** a perdu de son charme, il est inutile d'essayer de lui en redonner. Il suffit, tout simplement, de supprimer la distraction qui survient, en portant son attention, son intérêt sur autre chose et *grâce* à ce nouveau pôle d'attraction, l'état de concentration se retrouve. Par exemple, la respiration... En modifiant légèrement son rythme et son amplitude pendant quelques secondes, nous arriverons très facilement à éliminer pensées ou sensations parasites.

Une fois la « non-dispersion » obtenue, nous pourrons tranquillement substituer à la situation respiration, la situation **A.** Je suis presque tenté d'écrire : « Et le tour est joué ! » Cette capacité est très facilement accessible avec un peu d'entraînement. Le plus difficile réside dans le fait de prendre conscience que notre esprit commence un mystérieux voyage et d'avoir la volonté de résister à « l'appel des sirènes ».

La focalisation

C'est à partir de cet état de concentration induit *sans effort* que va se faire le mouvement de focalisation. L'attention se dirige vers un point bien précis, un objet faisant partie de l'ensemble **A** et va le considérer en toute *exclusivité*.

Pour comprendre ce qui se passe à ce moment-là, observons une personne qui lit. Son attitude générale reflète l'intérêt qu'elle porte à sa lecture. Le livre est à bonne distance de ses yeux et les agitations extérieures ne semblent pas la déranger outre mesure : elle est dans ce qu'elle lit, dans la situation globale proposée par le sujet de son ouvrage. Si c'est un roman, elle suit avec intérêt l'histoire et se laisse aller à vivre les images mentales qui surviennent spontanément. Si la lecture est plus studieuse, son esprit se livre aux différents phénomènes d'association et « accroche », à ses circuits déjà en place, les éléments lus.

Puis soudain, un détail est plus difficile à intégrer. Regardez alors son comportement : elle change de position, se rapproche du livre, l'entoure même parfois de ses bras, elle fronce les sourcils comme pour mieux diriger son regard qui devient exclusif. Elle transporte toute son attention vers ce problème à résoudre dans un mouvement *volontaire de focalisation*, soutient cette tension mentale pendant un instant, puis se recule, reprend son attitude initiale et poursuit sa lecture. Ce faisant, elle retrouve l'état de concentration premier.

Durant un apprentissage, la focalisation de l'attention exigera toujours cette démarche voulue de mouvement vers un point particulier et précis qui présente un intérêt ou une difficulté quelconque. L'hémisphère gauche du cerveau est réputé être spécialisé dans ce genre de travail. Si, jusque-là, l'état de concentration large avait été obtenu par la participation *conjointe* des deux hémisphères, maintenant il est seul à agir pour analyser, intégrer et mémoriser la nouvelle donnée. Son activité de focalisation terminée, il redonnera au cerveau droit le soin de rétablir l'état de concentration.

Pour se trouver « en prise directe » avec un fait qui mérite toute notre attention, il est beaucoup plus facile de partir de l'état de concentration large que de l'état de distraction totale. L'effort de « rétrécissement » du champ de conscience est moindre et, quand la focalisation est terminée, le sujet conserve une bonne attention. Le couplage concentration-focalisation donne à la fois une meilleure « vue d'ensemble » du problème (cerveau droit) et un regard aigu sur un détail à mieux comprendre (cerveau gauche).

Imaginez que vous devez explorer, avec une lampe torche, une pièce plongée dans l'obscurité. Si vous réglez votre lampe en un faisceau lumineux puissant mais étroit (focalisation), vous éclairerez seulement un détail et vous n'aurez de l'endroit qu'une connaissance partielle, petit bout par petit bout, sans comprendre l'ensemble. En revanche, en éclairant d'un faisceau large, vous pourrez avoir une idée de la pièce, tout en sachant qu'il est toujours possible de diriger ensuite un éclairage plus intense sur une partie. De même que l'on dit « qu'un arbre peut cacher la forêt », la focalisation d'emblée sur un élément peut déformer l'ensemble du problème et nuire à la compréhension et à la mémorisation.

Rêverie, distraction, concentration et focalisation sont autant « d'états d'esprit » naturels correspondant à des degrés spécifiques de mobilisation de l'attention. Chacun a son utilité et son charme. Il faut seulement savoir contrôler le passage de l'un à l'autre, **dans les deux sens.** Si pour les uns, le mouvement de polarisation, allant du général au particulier, pose quelques problèmes, pour d'autres, c'est exactement l'inverse. Ils restent « polarisés », ils n'arrivent pas à se distraire de leur travail. Quelques expressions populaires traduisent ces préoccupations :

- *Dans le sens d'une difficulté à la concentration :*
  « J'ai les idées ailleurs », « je rêvasse, je pense à autre chose ». Se « mettre » au travail... Se « pencher » sur un problème.
- *Dans le sens d'une difficulté au repos ou à la distraction :*
  « Je ne fais que penser à mon problème », « je n'en dors plus la nuit ». Etre complètement « polarisé ». « Besoin de se changer les idées ».

Le contrôle de ces différents niveaux est expérimenté dans toute sophronisation de base mais aussi dans le premier degré de la Relaxation dynamique servant de support aux exercices stimulant la volonté.

EXPRESSION DU DÉSIR
ET EXERCICE DU VOULOIR

Le vouloir, la seule expression de la Volonté.
La Volonté, la seule expression de la Liberté.
Le monde intérieur est un monde de tempêtes. Nous vivons toute chose et son contraire. Que naisse l'envie et aussitôt apparaît le manque. (Que naisse le manque et aussitôt apparaît l'envie!) Les dualités entre le cœur et la raison, le conscient et l'inconscient (le su et l'insu), la liberté et l'obligation (le vouloir et le devoir), le travail et le loisir, moi et les autres, etc., entraînent un état permanent de tensions internes.

Comment repérer le désir dans la foule des obligations, comment vivre le calme dans la nécessité d'efficacité, comment se laisser aller au sentiment d'amour sincère dans un monde que l'on dit sans pitié mais qui a remplacé l'amour par... la pitié! Comment penser à soi sans être égoïste, comment penser aux autres sans se perdre ou se noyer.

Le fait qu'il y ait en toute chose le pour et le contre, que les médailles aient toujours un revers et les miroirs toujours deux faces, crée le doute et altère le pouvoir de décision. Alors deux clans se forment, le clan des passifs qui ne font plus rien « puisqu'ils vont, dans un sens, mal faire » et le clan des agités qui font à leur fantaisie « puisque, quoi qu'ils fassent, ça sera mal ». A quelle espèce appartenons-nous?

A celle de ceux qui privilégient leur instinct ou

leurs pulsions, sans réfléchir aux conséquences de leurs actes, les « moi-je » qui ont rangé le doute inconfortable dans un tiroir et qui se disent « fonceurs »? Qui s'imposent en s'opposant?

A celle de ceux qui, troublés par l'incertitude et leur incapacité à décider, délèguent leur vouloir et adhèrent à la foule des « sans opinion » gouvernée par le Grand Maître, « ON », où, par besoin de sécurité, toute personnalité est anéantie et se fond dans une attitude d'assimilation et d'identification à ce fameux ON qu'il est d'ailleurs souvent impossible de définir. Mais qui est ce ON? Personne ne le sait vraiment, mais je sais que « on » va me juger donc je fais ce que « on » me dit de faire.

De la désujétisation dans les mots naît la déresponsabilité dans les actes en même temps que meurt l'expression verbalisée du désir.

Le « je dois » s'impose prioritairement au « je veux » au point qu'il se produit souvent une confusion entre les deux formulations pour arriver à la contradiction suivante :

**A de la volonté celui qui fait ce qu'il... DOIT
et non ce qu'il... VEUT.
Le sens du devoir prime
et supprime le sens du vouloir.**

L'idée même du devoir contient les notions d'obligation et donc de punition ou de récompense décernées, d'obéissance « sans soupir ni murmure » et donc de non-liberté. Devant le devoir à accomplir, le chemin, même s'il est ardu et astreignant, a l'avantage d'être tracé. Contrairement aux apparences, il est plus « facile » d'aller dans le sens de ce que « je dois » faire car la motivation (moteur des actes) est fournie en même temps que l'itinéraire. Tandis que le vouloir, le vrai et l'authentique vouloir, celui qui émane du plus profond de nous, nous **trouve et nous laisse libre.**

Suivons Paul Chauchard quand il écrit :

« La fausse sagesse moraliste nous imposait l'inhumaine suppression des désirs : par une mauvaise réaction ignorante nous en concluons qu'il faut se laisser aller aux désirs, alors que la dimension pleinement humaine n'est pas de dire l'homme un être de désirs, mais un être capable de contrôler sagement, de gouverner ses désirs afin d'en faire un instrument d'épanouissement et non de déchéance. La volonté ne consiste pas à se priver de bonnes choses [...] elle consiste dans la lucidité contrôlée du gourmet. »

Sachons, sans fausse pudeur, rattacher à la notion de volonté les concepts de désir, d'envie et d'autosatisfaction (dans le sens de satisfaction de l'ego, le moi étant le sujet qui désire et non l'objet des désirs). Cette capacité à vouloir est, pour tout être humain, une qualité résidante mais malheureusement trop stagnante et même parfois étouffée car entachée de péché culturel ou social. Un enfant **qui veut** est dit capricieux et l'éducation lui enseigne très tôt que « dans la vie, on ne fait pas toujours ce qu'on veut ! », ce qu'il finit par traduire par « dans la vie, on ne fait jamais ce qu'on veut » et le désir devient coupable. Un adolescent **qui veut encore** est menacé de se voir refuser l'accès au monde des adultes pour manque du sens du devoir. Un adulte **qui veut toujours** est accusé de vanité ou d'orgueil, d'insouciance ou de manque de responsabilité et quelquefois même, comble du comble, de manque de volonté.

Il est grand temps de redorer le blason de la volonté et de remettre au goût du jour la fameuse formule de nos parents : « Quand on veut, on peut ! »

Il faut relancer la mécanique du vouloir.

De même que pour avoir de « gros biceps », il faut s'entraîner en soulevant d'abord des haltères modestes, de même avant de vouloir grand, il faut savoir vouloir modeste pour entraîner sa volonté à s'exprimer.

La première démarche à réaliser est de faire taire ce vouloir volontariste et culturel, expression du « cerveau gauche » (nous verrons comment et pourquoi), qui agit « a contrario » de la nature humaine et qui se verbalise par des contresens. La sagesse populaire fait souvent dire : « Il a voulu trop bien faire et il s'est trompé. » Au départ de l'action était un mauvais vouloir, né dans l'agitation et le trac de ne pas pouvoir, activé par des motivations non authentiques et dévié par l'ambition de réussir et de prouver, à l'arrivée se trouve alors un acte manqué !

Pour bien vouloir, pour accéder au « bon vouloir », il faut avant tout vouloir se mettre au calme. En sachant calmer nos tensions internes, musculaires et mentales, en sachant mettre le monde intérieur en harmonie, non seulement nous exercerons ainsi notre volonté mais, en plus, nous nous mettrons en condition pour vouloir plus loin et plus grand.

La philosophie orientale enseigne que c'est en « ne voulant pas », au sens commun, que l'on parvient à « bien vouloir ». Tout au long de ces pages, nous verrons comment la sophrologie a su adapter certains principes de base de ces philosophies millénaires à l'esprit occidental et comment, par son approche globale de l'être, par sa méthode, par ses techniques et les exercices proposés, elle permet d'accéder à une plus *grande connaissance de soi*.

La volonté authentique et profonde, celle qui s'oppose au volontarisme imposé et culturel, se développe et se définit dans le calme et la quiétude du « monde intérieur ». Cette sorte de volonté se retrouve à l'état pur dans la **foi.** En acceptant une version laïque de la foi, nous retrouvons par exemple, dans l'expression populaire : « La foi soulève des montagnes », l'idée dynamique d'une force agissante.

Le philosophe et moraliste Confucius disait, 500 ans av. J.-C. :

> « Un homme sans foi :
> je ne sais ce qu'il faut en faire.
> Un grand char sans joug,
> un petit char sans collier,
> comment le faire avancer ? »

La volonté est résidante. Elle s'exprime par l'action, à l'occasion d'une action. Il faut prendre conscience que nous sommes capables de vouloir et d'agir dans le sens de notre désir. Laisser sa volonté s'exprimer en termes simples et la voir se réaliser naturellement sont deux conditions presque suffisantes pour amorcer le mouvement de conscience vers la confiance en soi. La volonté au naturel. Sans peur. Sans doute. Sans violence. La vraie volonté n'admet ni l'inquiétude ni la violence. Elle est détruite par l'un et par l'autre.

Au début du courage se trouve la peur, le courage est une qualité pour la surmonter. Au début du vouloir se trouve le doute, la volonté est une qualité pour résoudre l'incertitude. La peur est nécessaire à l'expression du courage. Sans elle, plus besoin du courage. L'affirmation : « Il a du courage car il n'a pas peur », ne veut rien dire ! Le doute nourrit et renforce la volonté ; il oblige à faire un choix. C'est à partir de ce moment que se met en route la mécanique du vouloir.

L'exercice du vouloir consiste à choisir, à définir son désir.

Le désir est la version émotionnelle de la volonté.

Le vouloir porte en germe une promesse d'action.

La route ne s'arrête pas là, au contraire, elle commence ici. Mais au moins nous savons vers où nos pas doivent nous conduire même si nous ne savons pas encore quel chemin suivre. Mais que le chemin soit long, les pas nombreux, qu'importe! le vouloir s'est exprimé. Le mouvement a commencé. Le « reste à faire » est une question de réalisation, de concrétisation et de finalité.

Simone de Beauvoir nous dit que « c'est le désir qui crée le désirable, et le projet qui pose la fin ». Traduisons : Cessons de « mettre la charrue avant les bœufs » et de vouloir ce qui est culturellement désigné comme désirable, car cela revient à dire que le désir est secondaire au désirable. Au contraire. Laissons, dans le calme et la paix intérieure, notre volonté nous montrer le « voulu », le vrai voulu. Alors, et alors seulement, posons-nous l'absolue question : « Que dois-je faire? » C'est-à-dire envisageons le processus de réalisation, définissons notre projet. **Imaginons la fin et débutons l'action.**

L'imagination est le contenu de la volonté en même temps qu'elle la contient. L'imagination fertilise le champ de la conscience, fait éclore nos désirs et les regarde devenir. L'imagination éclaire comme un soleil peut éclairer, guide comme une étoile peut guider, conseille mais aussi trahit comme une amie peut trahir, par erreur. C'est pourquoi le doute essentiel est toujours là pour réactiver le vouloir, vivifier le désir et relancer l'action. L'action qui dans ce sens pourrait se définir, à l'exemple de Bergson, comme un cheminement qui s'enroulerait autour de « L'Elan vital », axe d'Energie qui va de Moi à l'image idéale de Moi. L'imagination se met ainsi au service de la volonté et nous pouvons alors ajouter que :

se « pré-voir », c'est déjà vouloir.

Lors de la Relaxation dynamique n° 1, la mise en place du vouloir apparaît à la lumière de certains exercices originaux (intercalés entre les gestes de base) qui mettent en évidence les différentes phases de son expression. Nous allons en donner les grands principes, étant bien entendu que, dans la pratique, ils se décomposent en plusieurs séquences.

La volonté, sous peine de se voir réduite à une simple velléité, doit être liée à l'action et l'action est le résultat de toute une série de modifications qui convergent vers le but voulu. Avant que s'enchaînent les multiples changements, il faut « s'assurer » (comme un alpiniste qui assure son ancrage avant de progresser dans son ascension). Le point de départ est donc, impérativement, un « *constat d'être* ». La mise en situation consiste en une prise de conscience des sensations liées à la situation initiale. Il y a les sensations premières, celles qui s'imposent d'évidence et les sensations secondes qui n'apparaissent que dans une attitude de concentration. (Attitude stimulée tout au long de ce premier degré.) Après la mise en situation, intervient la décision et le vouloir prend forme :

- Dans l'intention, c'est le **projet** (l'imagination).
- Dans la réalisation, c'est **l'action** (motivation).
- Dans l'expérimentation, c'est **l'analyse** (mémorisation).

Voici, à titre d'exemple, comment nous procédons dans la pratique de la Dynamique I : sophronisation de base debout, les jambes légèrement écartées, les bras le long du corps, les yeux fermés.

« Dans cette position, bien en équilibre, je vais détendre mon corps. La relaxation est déjà **l'expression de mon vouloir.** Je veux mettre mon corps au calme et pour cela je détends les muscles du visage (front, yeux, etc.). Puis je relâche les épaules et les bras... »

Chaque fois que nous détendons un muscle ou un groupe de muscles, essayons d'être « présent » (concentration) dans cette partie du corps que nous contrôlons. La relaxation est un peu comme une vague qui envahit tout le corps, relâchant sur son passage chaque fibre de chaque muscle.

« Je laisse aller le dos en ne gardant que la tonicité nécessaire à ma position... J'accompagne mentalement cette vague de détente jusque dans mes jambes et ne conserve que la tonicité nécessaire. »

Cette démarche volontaire de mise au calme permet de saisir en conscience les phénomènes de la relaxation. (Étude phénoménologique qui caractérise la sophrologie.)

« J'ouvre à mon corps les portes de ma conscience. Ma conscience peut alors vivre sans retenue la situation relaxation dans sa globalité.

« Je perçois le phénomène naturel d'attraction terrestre et la sensation de pesanteur dans les bras et les mains. Je vis le poids du corps au niveau de la plante des pieds...

« Je ressens et prends conscience de ce que je ressens. **Je suis et prends conscience que je suis.**

« Je remarque qu'il est possible d'accéder à une certaine harmonisation et le sentiment de bien-être est le résultat de ma volonté de calme. »

Ensuite nous portons notre attention sur des sensations plus discrètes (attitude de focalisation), mais tout aussi parlantes, qui accompagnent la relaxation et qui participent à la prise en compte de la situation.

« Je me mets à l'écoute de mon corps : tonicité résiduelle due à ma posture, la présence des vêtements, l'évidence de la respiration, son rythme, son amplitude, les caractéristiques de l'air inspiré. La respiration est automatique : je me rends compte que mon corps respire et cette activité est libre de toute intervention de la volonté. »

Nous allons pouvoir modifier cette respiration, c'est-à-dire exercer un contrôle volontaire. Que la respiration soit abdominale (respiration sophronique) ou totale (faire monter l'air inspiré de la région ventrale à la région thoracique haute : respiration des « trois étages » – voir pp. 44 et 45, que son rythme soit lent ou au contraire très rapide, cela n'a guère d'importance ici. Ce qui importe c'est de *prendre conscience* du pouvoir de décision et du pouvoir de réalisation de l'acte voulu.

« Toute prise de conscience est un accroissement de conscience, une augmentation de lumière, un renforcement de la cohérence psychique » (Gaston Bachelard).

« A partir de ce calme résidant, je fais le projet de modifier ma respiration... Je choisis de faire une respiration... Je choisis de faire une respiration totale et mentalement je me prépare à l'action... J'imagine mon ventre prendre l'air, puis mon thorax se gonfler et s'élargir et enfin l'air sera retenu quelques instants au niveau des épaules. »

« Je devance les sensations perçues, sensations d'étirement, de plénitude, d'élargissement. »

« En réalisant l'acte désiré, je vais à la rencontre de mes " pré-visions ". Toute ma volonté est dirigée sur la réalisation de cet acte et je laisse au repos les muscles qui ne participent pas au mouvement volontaire. »

« JE VAIS DROIT AU BUT
et j'en retire une simple joie. »

Puis nous mémorisons, grâce à la perception consciente des modifications engendrées par le geste, le maximum de renseignements sur l'état de notre corps. Ceci participe à l'expérimentation du vouloir avec ses composantes : projet, réalisation, conséquences. Ainsi, de l'expérimentation vécue, nous aboutissons à l'expérience. La conscience s'en trouve renforcée et enrichie, la confiance en soi revient. La mécanique du vouloir est en marche.

Le premier degré de la Relaxation dynamique nous offre un exercice d'une très grande portée symbolique : *Le geste karaté, ou geste de la cible.*

Ce geste est effectué en synchronisation avec la

respiration. Au moment d'une inspiration profonde nous élevons le bras en fermant le poing, rétention de l'air en rapport avec la concentration de l'énergie puis expiration forte (parfois sous forme d'un cri) en même temps que nous projetons en avant le bras et le poing. Projection vers... une cible que nous avons mentalement dessinée devant nos yeux. Cette cible peut contenir certains aspects négatifs de notre personnalité (problèmes, défauts, manies, tics, phobies, etc.) que nous désignons volontairement comme objets de dysharmonie. Nous pouvons également laisser la cible se peupler d'images surgissant des couches profondes et révélant une part de notre insu. (Cette dernière version peut conduire à certaines révélations sur nous-même et de ce fait avoir une grande portée analytique.) Le but de cet exercice est double :

exprimer ces « choses » à rejeter, les « cibler »,
c'est-à-dire les ramener en conscience,
exprimer la volonté de s'en défaire.

Partant des principes de base de cet exercice, il est possible d'en faire une adaptation quelque peu différente de façon à mieux mettre en valeur les forces du vouloir et de les diriger, dans un regard positif, vers une acquisition. Les modifications apportées se réfèrent à la démarche du kuyndo (tir à l'arc) qui considère *l'intention* comme étant le premier mouvement mental nécessaire et obligatoire et l'action comme étant le résultat concret de la volonté donc secondaire. Il s'agit avant tout de savoir diriger sa volonté vers..., la flèche ne fera que suivre le chemin tracé. Il y a concentration mentale absolue sur l'essentiel et la conscience sait voir le bras, l'arc et la flèche, la cible dans un alignement parfait et elle seule peut intégrer, dans ses tenants et aboutissants, la dynamique complète du mouvement. Toute action se compose de plusieurs phases ou séquences. De la bonne exécution de ces séquences va dépendre le résultat final. Il est tout à fait fondamental de bien comprendre cela et de réaliser chaque phase de l'action avec le plus d'application possible sans se laisser influencer par l'envie de réussir. Encore une fois, ne mettons pas la charrue avant les bœufs et gardons tout notre désir intact dans la réalisation de ce tout petit « ici et maintenant » dont la perfection va préparer l'« ici et maintenant » suivant... jusqu'à la réalisation finale de notre projet toujours en conformité avec le vouloir initial.

Exerçons notre vouloir, notre désir de réussir, dans chaque « ici et maintenant » qui compose l'action globale. C'est bien là le meilleur moyen de réussir... finalement.

Dans l'exercice que j'ai donc mis au point et que je propose sous le nom de « **exercice du vouloir** », la cible imaginée est une « vraie » cible avec un « vrai » centre et l'action globale est décomposée en séquences en synchronisation avec un mouvement respiratoire complet afin de symboliser les limites de chaque « ici et maintenant ».

Debout, les yeux fermés, la tête droite.

a) Pendant une inspiration profonde et complète (respiration des « trois étages »), nous tournons la tête vers la droite ou la gauche pour concentrer toute notre volonté sur une cible imaginée à « portée de flèche ». Puis, la tête revient en position droite.

Dans cette première séquence, nous objectivons notre désir qui, par le pouvoir de l'imagination, devient un projet.

b) Inspiration... nous présentons « l'arc » à bout de bras... Expiration.

L'attention (attitude concentrative) est stimulée dans ce geste qui doit être exécuté en prenant conscience que l'ensemble de l'action est lié à cette première « façon de s'y prendre ».

c) Inspiration... Position de l'archer qui arme son

arc et mobilisation de toute notre énergie, de toute notre capacité à vouloir... Expiration.

C'est la phase dynamique, active, de toute action. Nous voici dans l'« ici et maintenant » de la réalisation proprement dite pendant laquelle nous devons assurer un bon ancrage sur terre et une stabilisation de la région Hara (bas du ventre).

d) Inspiration... Nous tournons maintenant la tête vers la droite (en direction de la cible mentale)... Rétention de l'air et nous envoyons la « flèche » vers le but à atteindre... Expiration alors que nous ramenons la tête droite, les bras en croix.

C'est un moment difficile à « gérer » : il est déjà trop tard pour espérer et encore trop tôt pour regretter. La « flèche » est partie et rien ne peut ni l'arrêter ni modifier sa direction. « Les dés sont jetés. »

e) Inspiration... Nous ramenons maintenant l'arc

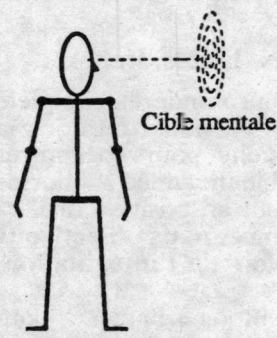

Tête tournée sur le côté, yeux fermés, jambes légèrement écartées. Symboliquement marqué par une respiration totale, nous vivons ici un "Ici et Maintenant" pendant lequel notre désir devient projet.

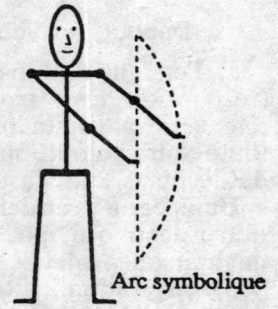

Bras tendus en avant. Concentration sur le geste à faire en excluant, dans cet "Ici et Maintenant", toute autre considération.

Position classique de l'archer qui arme son arc.
Phase dynamique. Grâce au bon ancrage sur la terre, notre énergie intérieure va pouvoir se libérer. Comme le fauve qui ramasse ses forces avant de bondir.

Position les bras en croix.
La flèche est partie vers son but.

Nous ramenons la tête à droite.
Bras en croix, nous respectons quelques instants de silence intérieur.
Ensuite nous replierons l'arc...
L'action est terminée...

virtuel en position centrale... expiration alors que nous laissons tomber les bras le long du corps dans une attitude de relaxation.

Nous sommes alors invité à vivre, dans l'intimité de notre conscience, la joie d'avoir su vouloir, d'avoir pu réaliser notre désir dans la plus

pure concentration de chaque « ici et maintenant ».

L'exercice est répété trois fois. Au début, le centre est laissé vide. J'insiste sur le fait que l'important est de savoir mobiliser toutes ses forces mentales, de laisser exploser sa volonté à l'état pur. C'est ce premier mouvement qui permet de mettre en marche la mécanique du vouloir. L'objet du désir est secondaire au désir et prend forme grâce à notre capacité d'imagination. Ce n'est donc que dans un deuxième temps que nous mettrons au centre de la cible l'image de l'objet de notre vouloir. Alors notre conscience ne se laissera plus berner par la grande supercherie qui consiste à chercher d'abord l'objet et à le vouloir ensuite. Faisons de notre désir une réalité avant de peupler ce désir de réalités concrètes.

Nous pouvons alors réfléchir à cette phrase de saint Ignace de Loyola (fondateur de l'ordre des Jésuites) :

**Fais toute chose *comme si* son exécution
ne dépendait que de toi
et *comme si* son résultat
ne dépendait que de Dieu.**

Vivre le désir et libérer
la force du vouloir qui conduit à sa réalisation,
c'est faire un pas important vers l'harmonisation.

Vivre le désir réalisé c'est libérer
la « Croix » qui vibre en soi...

Vivre sa Croix c'est être prêt à aborder...
les exercices du deuxième degré...

RÉSUMÉ DU PREMIER DEGRÉ
DE LA RELAXATION DYNAMIQUE

Attitude générale

- Position debout, les yeux fermés.
  (Sauf dans le dernier exercice de relaxation récupérative.)
- Attitude mentale de CONCENTRATION.
- Approche perceptive de la corporalité.
- « Je » est le sujet, « Je » est dans le corps.
- Expérimentation de la capacité à vouloir.
  (Technique personnelle et facultative.)

Buts poursuivis

- Lever les blocages internes.
- Harmonisation du monde intérieur.
- Améliorer la relation à soi.
- Développer le schéma corporel.
- Augmenter la volonté.
  (Pouvoir de décision et pouvoir de réalisation.)

TROISIÈME CHAPITRE

LA CROIX

**Le contenu symbolique
Deuxième degré de la
Relaxation Dynamique de Caycedo
La perception du monde
L'intuition**

LE CONTENU SYMBOLIQUE

La Croix réunit le Cercle et le Carré. Par sa position intermédiaire, elle donne à la Terre une connotation de mystère et, en mettant une majuscule à la Nature, va au cœur de la nature même des choses et des hommes. Elle est alors la représentation du « monde intérieur » de l'être, de l'affectivomoteur.

Par la Croix se trouve ainsi signifié le « contenu » en interrelation avec l'extérieur : elle s'inscrit dans le Cercle qu'elle divise en quadrants mettant ainsi le temps à la portée du vécu. En réunissant les extrémités de ses branches, elle dessine le Carré mettant ainsi de l'émotion dans le geste. La Croix est toujours à l'intérieur et contient le Centre du Carré et le Centre du Cercle. Sa fonction est donc la synthèse et la mesure :

« En elle se joignent le Ciel et la Terre... En elle s'entremêlent le temps et l'espace... De tous les symboles, elle est le plus totalisant... Elle est le symbole de l'intermédiaire, du médiateur... » (Introduction au monde des symboles de Champeaux (1).)

La Croix est la marque tracée et objectivée du *perpétuel mouvement* allant de l'intérieur vers l'extérieur et retournant au Centre.

Ecoutons Novalis, poète romantique du XVIIIe siècle, nous dire :

---

(1) Cité dans le *Dictionnaire des symboles*, Editions Robert Laffont.

> « Je suis le centre, le foyer, la source sainte
> D'où torrentiellement s'élance tout désir,
> Et vers quoi tout désir, divers quand il se brise,
> Finit par revenir, apaisé, se rejoindre. »

Dans la religion chrétienne, la Croix s'est évidemment fortement chargée en représentations diverses et les significations rendues par ce symbole religieux sont variées, telles que : rédemption par le sacrifice, protection par la puissance (d'origine céleste ou divine). Dans cette tradition la Croix cristallise l'espérance du croyant de voir unis le Ciel et la Terre, Dieu et les hommes, l'universalité absolue et l'universalité relative. Ainsi il n'est pas étonnant que l'image du Fils de Dieu (fait homme) mort sur la Croix soit si fortement chargée et qu'elle concrétise l'idée abstraite de la foi, de l'espoir d'un devenir.

C'est le chemin par lequel l'homme terrestre et mortel peut accéder au ciel et à l'éternité : *le chemin de la Croix* ou le *Chemin de Croix* !

Cette image religieuse donne accès, par la notion archétypale d'ascension, au schème de la verticalité.

Ce symbolisme se retrouvera aussi dans la flamme, la flèche, l'arbre et d'une façon générale, tout ce qui peut être **axe central.** C'est ce que précisent d'une part le globe surmonté d'une Croix polaire, identifié par les alchimistes au creuset générateur et d'autre part le signe du mercure, la Croix supportant le Cercle qui concrétise la régénération intérieure (yoga).

Citons encore Novalis, en exemple de la Croix représentant le Chemin intérieur qui mène vers Dieu :

> « Mais la Croix, qu'il a érigée
> En protection pour chaque cœur
> ....

L'Arbre de grâce, approche-le,
Ecoute en toi l'appel secret :
Une flamme en vient qui se lève
Et dévore le mauvais rêve.
Sauvé, tu seras par un Ange,
A nouveau tiré sur la plage,
D'où tu contempleras, là-bas,
Tout joyeux la Terre promise. »

Dans le complexe unitaire de l'Etre humain, la Croix se trouve située dans la partie intermédiaire du corps, poitrine, thorax et bras, et conserve donc toutes ses valeurs symboliques. Il est tout de même curieux de constater que c'est au niveau de cette région du corps que certaines de nos émotions primaires ou archaïques et que quelques-unes de nos pensées se transforment en sentiments ressentis car somatisés. Ici se trouve le cœur, siège de l'affectivité et de l'amour, mais aussi centre énergétique, moteur de l'impulsion dynamique, responsable des échanges intérieurs et de la régénération en relation étroite avec un autre centre, l'appareil respiratoire considéré comme lieu principal d'échanges avec le monde extérieur et en particulier avec l'environnement humain. Ce besoin de communication avec les autres se trouve représenté par les branches horizontales de la Croix. Ainsi, comme l'Arbre de vie, la Croix appelle à vivre les deux notions qui sont propres à l'homme :

Par la **verticalité**. Mouvement vers Dieu
    et accession au principe d'**Eternité**.
Par l'**horizontalité**. Mouvement vers l'Homme
    et accession au principe d'**Humanité**.

La connotation quasiment mystique de la fonction respiratoire, avec le *Respire*, le *Souffle*, le *Verbe*... de même que l'attitude adoptée par le prêtre dans ses prières incantatoires, « les bras en croix », les yeux tournés vers le ciel, rend signifiant le symbole de la Croix, lui donne la dimension de la réalité vécue... Réalité vécue qui se retrouve dans les expressions communes comme porter sa croix, vivre sa croix qui révèlent l'espoir que par l'acceptation de ses ennuis l'homme trouve le chemin du devenir... gagne son paradis par sa vie sur terre!

Dans une approche globale de l'être humain, la Croix correspondrait aux manifestations comportementales, c'est-à-dire aux manifestations de la relation corps-esprit, ou encore à la réalité psychosomatique négative ou positive qui préside à la manière d'être dans la vie. La Relaxation dynamique de Caycedo, par son deuxième degré, permet une harmonisation entre d'une part le Cercle et la Croix et d'autre part la Croix et le Carré en favorisant et en renforçant les voies de communication entre l'étage de *l'affectivo-moteur* et l'étage de l'instinctivo-moteur que constitue, comme nous l'avons vu, le Carré.

Nous comprenons alors mieux l'intérêt des différents exercices du premier degré qui permettent de libérer les zones de blocage : la région diaphragmatique et celle de la nuque et du cou. Par cette libération, la Croix peut redevenir l'endroit par lequel « transitent » les informations corporelles. Elle peut jouer pleinement son rôle de réunion et d'intégration des différentes motivations vécues au niveau des zones archaïques : ventre et région sexuelle.

Le « cœur » comprend les raisons du corps que la raison ne peut pas comprendre! Les pulsions instinctives et inconscientes passant par la Croix trouvent et se colorent de sentiments humains. Elles peuvent aussi enrichir la conscience d'un sujet éveillé (par l'écoute attentive) à ce qui se passe dans des zones qui, d'ordinaire, échappent à la perception consciente.

DEUXIÈME DEGRÉ
DE LA RELAXATION DYNAMIQUE

Conscience éclairante

La première étape nous a permis de rentrer en contact avec notre corps, de le libérer de certains blocages afin d'harmoniser ce monde intérieur que nous habitons. Nous l'avons perçu « par en dedans » pour mieux le sentir vivre et vibrer. La seconde étape va nous amener à le regarder vivre. L'attitude mentale est contemplative et « je » est l'objet sur lequel le regard va se poser. Après avoir répondu à la question : « Qui suis-je ? », nous allons envisager le « je » sous l'angle nouveau du : « Que suis-je ? » En fait, nous tentons ici l'expérience de **l'objectivité.** Il est important de bien comprendre ce mouvement ascensionnel de la conscience. Avant de poursuivre, nous allons essayer d'expliquer notre démarche en prenant un exemple... bateau.

J'étais sur un voilier, naviguant au gré des flots et des vents. Puis j'ai appris à mieux connaître mon embarcation. Je l'ai visitée de fond en comble, j'ai vu la quille profonde et le pont en surface. J'ai manœuvré les cordages, compris l'utilité du gouvernail pour me diriger et garder le cap. Je l'ai senti vibrer sous la bise et gîter sous la tempête. Je connais ses points faibles et ses qualités. Maintenant, je fais corps avec mon bateau. Dès lors, je vais pouvoir monter en haut du mât principal et regarder. Un bon capitaine doit savoir être tout à la fois timonier et hunier. Et là-haut, en prenant de la hauteur, je m'aperçois que je peux voir certaines choses qui m'étaient encore inconnues. (Il est vrai que lorsqu'on est DANS la situation on ne peut tout voir!) Installé à la hune de mon bateau, la première chose que je vois, c'est moi. Je me vois naviguant. Etrange impression d'être et de se voir en train d'être! Puis mon regard embrasse l'immensité environnante. Les limites étroites que m'imposait la vague immédiate ont disparu. Je suis au milieu d'une vaste étendue, peuplée d'autres bateaux et la vague que je croyais énorme n'est pas plus grande qu'un clapot, vue d'en haut. Je peux aussi – et je dois dire que j'en suis tout ému – voir la trace laissée derrière moi. Une belle écume blanche qui montre la route déjà faite. Quelques instants, je me laisse bercer par les souvenirs d'hier. Mes premiers virements de bord, le jour où j'ai « dessalé », et aussi cet autre jour où, découragé, j'ai voulu « affaler » la grand-voile. Dans ce sillage tout est marqué, je peux relire ma vie de navigateur mieux que dans le livre de bord. Je sais que depuis, j'ai acquis de l'expérience. Expérience que je contemple d'en haut... Mais le voyage n'est pas fini. Devant moi, le temps et l'espace m'attendent. Ils m'attendent pour se matérialiser. J'entrevois qu'il existe une autre dimension, ailleurs, que la « dimension cachée » de l'être humain. L'immensité intime de mon bateau prend une autre grandeur et je me mets à aimer l'infiniment petit de son habitacle... Mais il est grand temps maintenant que je reprenne la barre, que je retrouve mon « carré » de navigateur. Je sais que je garderai au plus profond de ma mémoire l'incroyable vision de moi et de mon bateau, vus d'en haut.

Le deuxième degré nous incite à ce genre de voyage. Poser un autre regard sur nous-même ou plus justement nous regarder sous un angle différent. Voir la place que nous occupons au milieu de nos références et la place que nous donnons à ces références.

La conscience sort du jeu et regarde jouer l'Autre (qui n'est rien d'autre que moi!). Une zone étrange **présente** dans notre conscience qui **contemple** le spectacle du « Je » en pleine **représentation.**

L'Homme est un fait social, un fait relatif. Certains philosophes ont donné à ce « monde du paraître » une connotation négative laissant entendre que ce Moi s'éloigne ainsi du Soi et s'épuise dans l'incessant besoin à vouloir paraître autre. Ils considèrent avec dédain et ironie cette façade artificielle derrière laquelle se morfond et meurt d'ennui l'authentique personne. Le dédain est une arme défensive et l'ironie une arme offensive maniées par ceux qui ont peur d'eux-mêmes. Je pense qu'il faut avoir un peu plus de respect pour cet *animus* placé en première ligne dans la confrontation avec l'environnant. Matière psychique d'être-au-monde, matière plastique douée d'une extraordinaire énergie d'adaptation et d'évolution, cette part-de-Soi est là pour assimiler toutes les expériences existentielles. C'est un acteur actif. Laissons-la jouer son rôle et agir, tout en prenant garde de ne tomber dans le piège, tendu à tout acteur, de l'identification au personnage. (Piège dénoncé par Jung comme étant une des causes des troubles de la personnalité si le Moi s'identifie trop à certains archétypes et prend alors une personnalité usurpée.) Un des meilleurs moyens de prévention contre cette déviation est précisément un regard lucide, une conscience éclairant la grande scène de la vie.

Ce mouvement de « torsion » qui consiste à placer la conscience en marge de son corps passe par l'étape (indispensable au début) de concentration sur un objet, l'image d'un objet. (La « prise » de l'image d'un objet dans le champ de la conscience est un exercice déjà pratiqué dans le premier degré, deuxième partie.) Puis par un phénomène d'assimilation se produira une véritable identification à l'objet au point que le corps deviendra lui-même objet de la contemplation. Essayons de voir le processus mental qui préside lors de chacune de ces phases.

1. Concentration sur un objet

Disons tout de suite que cet objet est choisi, donc il ne peut pas être neutre. Le choix est totalement libre, cela peut aller de quelque chose à quelqu'un. (Toutefois, dans les premiers temps, je conseille de choisir un objet naturel comme une fleur ou un arbre. Prendre une personne existante est plus difficile à « manier » et risque de dévier le vécu de la séance.) Quoi qu'il en soit, cet objet **inanimé** se transforme en un objet « **in anima** ». La rencontre avec l'objet dépasse le simple phénomène de la concentration et amène à vivre l'attitude de contemplation et même de méditation. Mais avant d'envisager ces thèmes, revenons à la prise de l'objet car nous mettons ici en action le processus fondamental de l'imagination qui permet la libération de l'image mentale. L'image mentale est l'ensemble du savoir organisé et mémorisé dont nous disposons sur cet objet que nous désirons **recréer** mentalement. Cette somme de connaissances définissant l'objet relève aussi bien de l'approche rationnelle que du regard intuitif. C'est dire que nous aurons une participation des deux hémisphères cérébraux pour cerner le problème, chacun apportant des données intéressantes. Le cerveau gauche précisera les caractéristiques se rattachant à la logique de l'objet, le cerveau droit libérera l'esthétique de l'objet.

Certaines personnes ont une étonnante facilité à voir les images mentales, d'autres au contraire, s'épuisent et se dispersent dans l'effort de concentration et n'ont pour résultat qu'un voile noir devant leurs paupières fermées où « dansent des taches de lumière sans forme ». J'invite ces personnes à ne point se concentrer avec obstination sur l'objet encore absent du champ de la conscience mais de laisser les sensations se concentrer elles-mêmes et prendre forme.

L'image mentale ainsi référencée, non seulement apparaîtra sans effort mais le dialogue indispensable à la méditation aura déjà commencé. Les créations imaginatives, même les plus inattendues, ne sont jamais des inventions pures mais elles prennent source dans les expériences perceptives résidant dans la mémoire. Toute image mentale est extraite de notre environnement perceptif, elle était donc déjà constituée et caractérisée. Notre imagination ne fait que la reconstituer et la rendre présente dans notre esprit. A cet égard, elle prend valeur de symbole par la rencontre qu'elle propose entre le sujet et l'objet.

2. Contemplation de l'objet

La fonction de l'imaginaire n'est pas une manière de **voir** mais bien une manière de **vivre,** en organisant ses relations avec l'objet. C'est là, bien sûr, l'attitude de l'artiste, poète ou peintre, qui échange sa propre intimité avec celle de l'objet.

« L'imagination est aussi indispensable que l'œil pour prendre conscience de la réalité. » C'est en revivant les sensations relatives à l'objet que l'image viendra, quelquefois sous une forme visuelle mais le plus souvent sous la forme du **sentiment** que nous sommes en présence de l'objet choisi.

Le pas que nous faisons vers cet objet, le regard que nous posons sur lui sont d'authentiques gestes d'amour. Nous nous donnons à lui, en même temps qu'il se donne à nous. Il n'est plus ce qu'il paraît être mais il apparaît tel qu'il est : l'image que nous avons créée, l'image de notre désir. Maintenant que l'image est présente et que nous sommes présent à l'image, nous nous laissons aller à une lecture lente de ce qu'elle nous offre. L'image a la puissance d'un poème. Si nous acceptons son action captivante, sa force envoûtante, tout notre être vivant, tout notre être rêvant nous est rendu, se distillant à travers le filtre d'une lointaine mémoire. L'image est alors poétiquement vécue car elle est vécue avec toute l'affectivité qui fait vibrer la *croix* du rêveur. La vie s'écoule goutte à goutte, chaque goutte est une seconde d'éternité qui, au centre de l'image, vient éclairer la conscience d'une belle lumière. La conscience du sujet devient à son tour conscience éclairante qui, tranquillement, enveloppe toute chose d'une douce lueur. Au féminin. A la manière d'une lune, en *anima*. Nous entrons en état de rêverie poétique, rêverie sophronique avec l'image comme compagne de notre solitude et notre conscience qui veille comme la flamme d'une chandelle. La langue française manque, à ma connaissance, de mots pour désigner ce rêveur en éveil et de verbes pour dire ce mouvement de conscience vers d'autres lieux. Rêvasser est impropre. Par sa connotation de paresse, ce verbe indique une attitude statique et non dynamique. Une sorte de dérapage incontrôlé de l'attention et de la concentration. C'est un verbe utilisé par le « cerveau gauche » qui tente, par une moquerie dédaigneuse, de masquer son incapacité à l'évasion volontaire et qui prétend que « la Muse a mérité les insolents sourires et les soupçons moqueurs qu'éveille son aspect » (Vigny). Mais laissons l'animus qui a besoin des choses et des gens pour exister et revenons à notre rêveur.

La contemplation est un pur acte de conscience où se retrouvent le désir originel et le mouvement vers l'accomplissement de ce désir. L'image est comme un miracle qui cherche à se définir et qui se réalise dans sa rencontre avec le rêveur.

> « Je mets une pomme sur ma table.
> Puis je me mets dans cette pomme.
> Quelle tranquillité (1) ! »

En un survol distrait, ce genre de phrase frise le comique. Mais dans une lecture approfondie, dans une lecture lente où chaque mot est rêvé, où chaque geste est mouvement, qu'en est-il exactement ? Qu'advient-il de ce « je » promu par miracle au rang de noyau, sinon une conscience qui rêve son devenir ? Qu'advient-il de ce fruit qui, par le même miracle, se retrouve habité, sinon une conscience qui enveloppe le « je » ? La rencontre de ces deux intimités se fait en toute tranquillité et c'est là que se réalise le vrai miracle de la rêverie sophronique. Rencontre totale, exclusive, privée entre deux êtres, entre deux mondes, entre deux vies, entre deux eaux, deux eaux tranquilles, deux eaux vives. Après cette approche pendant laquelle l'objet se livre et le sujet se délivre, survient la fusion. Fusion de deux noyaux, fusion nucléaire étincelante. Il y a intégration. C'est la troisième dimension de ce mouvement de conscience.

---

(1) Henri Michaux. Cité par G. Bachelard, « La Terre et les rêveries du repos ».

3. Identification à l'objet

Pour Milosz, « il y a image quand il y a transformation de l'imaginant. Au niveau de l'image vécue, la relativité du sujet et de l'objet est totale. Les distinguer, c'est méconnaître l'unité de l'imagination ». La notion d'unité et d'unicité qui unit le rêveur à son image fait que l'imaginant devient l'imaginé. L'identification à l'objet est une identification de principe. Il y a échange entre deux êtres de leur « principe d'être », de l'essentiel d'être. C'est en allant ainsi à sa source que nous pouvons comprendre et accepter le monde. Mais c'est aussi en nous mettant « à la place des choses » que nous pouvons regarder le **principe essentiel de notre propre être au monde.**

Cela revient à ce que Kant nommait la connaissance de l' « en-soi », connaissance à laquelle notre système de références sensorielles habituelles ne donne pas accès. Et Patañjani nous dit que, dans l'état de transcendance, « l'esprit s'identifie à l'objet brut de telle façon que l'objet continue d'exister en lui-même, hors d'atteinte des ondes mentales de nos propres réactions... »

Le très grand communiant avec les objets, Alain Bosquet (*Poèmes*, Un. Gallimard.) nous dit, dans un de ses « écrits en marge du poème » :

> Table, dis-tu?
> Avant de l'accepter,
> Je veux savoir ce qu'est son acajou;
> avant son acajou,
> son paysage;
>   avant son paysage,
>   Les deux yeux qui le guettent;
>   avant les yeux,
>   ce qui les autorise
>   d'être des yeux.
>   Table, dis-tu?

Détruis-la, pour qu'absente
je veuille en faire
une vraie table ;
    à l'origine elle était soie,
    grenouille, verbe
    ou musique très douce.
Pour la comprendre,
je vis en table,
je suis la table.

La finalité de cette démarche d'identification se situe au-delà d'une curiosité intellectuelle ou mentale. Elle nous donne accès à une authentique manière d'être. Une manière simple d'être bien.

Ce simple bien-être nous est donné par la rêverie sophronique dans l'unification vécue avec le monde. Il est d'évidence. Il est là, ce bien-être, sans provocation et sans référence au monde extérieur, ancré dans le plus profond et dans le plus archaïque de notre être. Et dans la plus petite de nos cellules, l'archétype de la vie ronronne et fait le gros dos. L'anima s'étire, s'étale et se réchauffe à la chaleur de la fusion. Le monde est en nous et nous sommes monde.

« Le monde est corps humain, regard humain, souffle humain, voix humaine. » (G. Bachelard.)

Et la conscience, qui est une conscience d'être, enveloppe de son regard éclairé l'être que je suis et qui est **au** monde, qui est **du** monde, qui est **dans** le monde. A partir de cette tranquillité harmonisante nous pourrons aborder un autre type de rêverie, que permet l'imaginaire libéré : voyage dans l'espace, voyage dans le temps. Nous parlerons des voyages dans le temps et, en particulier, vers l'enfance dont nous réveillerons les principes assoupis.

VOYAGE VERS L'ENFANCE

Et dire que nous avons tous joué
  dans les jardins de l'Enfance!
Et dire que nous avons tous vécu
  l'origine de la vie!

Au début du chemin, nous étions une flamme, une flamme qui veut. Regardez ce très jeune enfant qui, des bras de sa mère aux bras de son père, ose son premier pas. Cet enfant va vers son demain. Quelle formidable leçon de volonté que ce premier pas incertain. Quel beau vouloir que ce vouloir qui dépasse la crainte immédiate et qui pousse à agir. Aller devant, aller en avant, bras ouverts et cœur exposé, tenter l'expérience du moment présent. Enrichir le monde de sa présence, s'enrichir de la présence de l'univers puis continuer toujours devant, toujours en avant. Etre vivant, quel émerveillement. Devenir, quelle belle histoire racontée au présent. Devenir qui? Devenir quoi? Qu'importe! **Vouloir devenir est l'essentiel. Devenir est un désir.** Grandir et grandir encore et rêver que l'on devient grand. Grand comme le monde rêvé que l'enfant rêve de conquérir avec comme atouts sa belle confiance et sa naïve insouciance.

Et dire que nous avons tous rêvé notre demain!
Et dire que nous avons tous vécu la naissance
  [de notre vie!

Regardez ce jeune enfant qui joue. Il joue ce que son imaginaire lui permet d'être. Il est ce qu'il rêve d'être, sans compromission et sans restriction. L'imagination fertilise ses actions en faisant éclater les barrières et les limites. Et dans le nouveau monde qu'il se crée, même au milieu d'autres compagnons de jeu, il est seul. Il est seul pour réaliser son désir d'être. La solitude de l'Enfance est une solitude de fait. Comment peut-il communiquer, comment peut-il expliquer? et à qui? L'Enfance se raconte-t-elle à celui qui s'en est éloigné! Alors la solitude se peuple d'images, images qui prennent forme et se mettent en scène. L'enfant est dans sa fable. Fable qu'il se raconte, en solitaire, et dans laquelle maman, papa, moi et les autres prennent place, une place de rêve, sous des aspects de rêve. Et le monde change de dimension, il prend sa vraie grandeur. Un Petit Homme, du haut de ses trois pommes, voit toujours grand. Et tant que les adultes lui laisseront le droit de rêver et de vivre ses rêves en paix, il verra grand et pur. Jusqu'au jour où la phrase fatidique « cesse donc de rêver et fais tes devoirs » arrêtera tout net sa rêverie d'enfant et le plongera dans le monde social, un monde déjà fait et qui l'attend de pied ferme. Plus tard, au midi de sa vie, l'homme, devenu raisonnable et raisonnant, lassé de cette distance à lui-même, reprendra ses désirs, rallumera sa flamme et re-créera le monde, dans la même solitude d'antan. **Il rêvera son enfance.**

Voici donc le voyage proposé : revivre ici et maintenant l'état de conscience de l'enfance. Avec le principe essentiel du désir de devenir, de toujours aller devant. Nous retrouvons dans quelque recoin d'une vaste mémoire le vouloir pur et fort qui nous animait alors. A l'époque où le temps n'usait pas encore notre vie mais lui donnait un sens.

Les souvenirs d'enfance ne sont pas des souvenirs d'enfants, mais sont les éléments d'une mémoire qui nous situe en amont de nous-mêmes.

Le regard sophronique rend contemporaine la primitive énergie et rend vive la flamme qui devient. Sous la pile de ses devoirs énormes, le Petit Homme, haut comme trois pommes, dormait. Ses rêves étaient devenus des rêves de dormeur qui n'exprimaient que des regrets. Maintenant il se réveille et ses rêves sont des rêves de rêveur qui éveillent le désir. **Le chemin qui conduit vers l'enfance débouche sur demain et nous appelle à vivre.** C'est ainsi que « au bord de cette eau tranquille », si chère à Bachelard, et qui repose en chacun de nous, Novalis entrevoit que « la nuit des temps se rajeunit » et qu'« aux claires sources irisées » le « vieux désir » est comblé.

La détemporalisation des états sophroniques pousse le voyageur au-delà des heures carrées et la trace de sa vie est vécue au présent de même que sont vécus au présent les projets qui déjà se dessinent. Nous retrouvons, tout vibrant en nous-même, le merveilleux étonnement de notre prime jeunesse, étonnement d'être en même temps que de toujours devenir. Novalis nous dit que « tout commencement effectif est un deuxième moment ». C'est en rendant *affectivement* effectif le commencement de notre vie intime que nous pourrons nous placer au début de ce deuxième moment, de ce deuxième mouvement vers notre avenir.

Souvenons-nous du langage que nous comprenions alors, souvenons-nous que nous comprenions au-delà des mots. L'enfant qui vit pleinement son enfance vit en alliance avec l'univers. Il est l'ami de l'oiseau, de la fleur et du vent. Il sait leur parler et les écouter. Dans sa poitrine tour à tour se lèvent et se couchent le soleil et la lune. Ses yeux ont le regard des dieux, le regard des poètes, le regard de ceux qui aiment. L'enfance est tout amour et bien-être et si parfois, par un heurt avec la matière pesante de l'existence, un « gros chagrin » fait couler quelques larmes, ces larmes sont chaleureuses. De chaudes larmes qui font briller les yeux quand l'amour divin s'essaye à devenir humain. Un amour qui déborde, qui s'exprime et qui attend. Un amour au pouvoir magique qui fait fondre la carapace d'en face.

Grâce à l'enfance, nous savons que l'amour est communicable. Grâce à l'amour et au travers de l'état d'enfance retrouvé, deux consciences aimantes communiquent. Sans discours. Parfois un mot suffit, comme peuvent suffire une larme ou le geste d'un ami.

Dans cette démarche vers l'enfance nous retrouvons le même processus d'identification vécu avec l'image mentale d'un objet. Et cette identification à l'enfance passe aussi par les phases de concentration (sur un fait de jeunesse, par pure mémoire) et de contemplation (par le regard bienveillant sur ce que nous fûmes). Puis, après avoir dépassé le concret de nos souvenirs, avoir soupiré nos regrets et transcendé la nostalgie du temps passé, nous atteignons la source « d'où torrentiellement s'élance tout désir ». Notre conscience d'aujourd'hui se laisse imprégner et vit l'état de conscience de l'enfance. Quand cette primitive conscience se retire pour nous rendre à la vie, elle laisse derrière elle en « cadeau » son pouvoir d'émerveillement, son enthousiasme, son imagination potentielle et ses projets. Toutes ces innombrables richesses font la qualité d'une conscience sophronique.

La rêverie sophronique vers l'enfance, en provoquant l'indispensable rencontre intime, nous rend à nous-même. De ce dialogue aux naïfs accents de sincérité, notre conscience de base, quelque peu épuisée dans les combats quotidiens, boit, au bout de l'horizon de la mémoire, une gorgée de soleil et retrouve la force de la jeunesse. « Si jeunesse savait, si vieillesse pouvait », dit-on! Mais une

« vieillesse » qui sait vivre son enfance latente est une vieillesse qui peut... toujours vouloir et qui, grâce à l'expérience acquise, sait mieux vouloir... encore.

Dans le deuxième degré de la Relaxation dynamique, tout voyage dans le temps et dans l'espace, mentalement vécu, se termine toujours par une reprise en conscience de la réalité du maintenant, réalité concrète perçue par et dans le corps. Lui aussi a vécu l'état d'apesanteur de l'enfance libérée du pesant fardeau du rituel social. Il a senti dans ses artères, dans ses muscles et dans son cœur la force du désir retrouvé. Lentement et profondément, il a respiré la liberté et le premier bonheur de vivre. Et ce corps heureux, nous le reprenons, un peu comme nous retournons à la maison après une longue randonnée. Avec le plaisir tout neuf qui résonne encore. Comme il est bon, en récompense d'une grande marche sophronique dans un coin de forêt encore inexploré de conscience troublée, d'arriver enfin à l'orée du village et...

> « De laisser mon âme communier
> avec le silence s'harmoniser.
> Quelque chose de sourd me fit penser
> qu'enfin, ici, ma route s'arrêtait.
> Le doux regard des basses maisons
> dont la lueur disait l'éternité
> ravivait en moi la Belle Saison
> de mon enfance jamais oubliée.
> Je n'avais jamais vu ce village
> qui semblait surgir du fond des âges,
> mais à la fumée calme des toits,
> je disais : " Ici, je suis chez moi. " »

Ce retour vers le corps est véritablement un retour « chez soi », un retour à la maison. Il s'agit de se retrouver en place et de savoir que, de cette place, le monde est toujours accessible. L'univers attend, nous attend. Tout naturellement, il s'offre à notre perception. Le monde environnant se fera monde imprégnant dans la mesure où nous nous ouvrons à lui. Un peu à la manière d'un rayon de soleil pénétrant qui éclaire la pièce d'un parfum de jardin.

LA PERCEPTION DU MONDE
CAPACITÉ FONCTIONNELLE DES SENS

Prenons conscience de la situation d'un individu. Le voilà sur terre avec autour de lui tout un univers, immense et complexe. Un univers peuplé d'un nombre incalculable d'éléments divers dont certains peuvent représenter un danger pour lui. Entre son monde intime et cet environnement : un système de perception pour lui permettre d'évaluer les différentes situations. Ainsi vont se structurer, à partir du point central que représente le sujet, des zones allant en s'élargissant. Ces espaces proxémiques (dont parle Edward T. Hall) dépendent des modalités fonctionnelles des organes des sens. La proxémie la plus étendue est définie par la portée du regard ou par la perception auditive. Entrant dans ce cercle, l'élément considéré s'approche du sujet : la vision est de plus en plus nette jusqu'au moment où, la distance étant trop courte, la vue se trouble. Un deuxième espace proxémique s'ouvre, celui délimité par la zone du toucher et il faut avoir déjà établi des rapports de confiance pour admettre l'élément étranger dans cette région si proche. Si ce n'est pas le cas, la surprise motivera sans aucun doute des réflexes d'autodéfense (fuite, recul ou attaque). Puis, ayant franchi ces barrières successives, l'élément (qui n'est plus étranger) peut espérer un contact plus étroit, pénétrer dans la zone proxémique intime et être perçu, par exemple, par les papilles gustatives.

Nous placerons volontairement l'odorat en dernier. C'est un sens à part. Il intervient dans les systèmes de perception de tous les cercles proxémiques et renseigne sur des choses qui peuvent ne pas vraiment exister mais qui... « flottent dans l'air » !

L'ouïe et la vue

Pour notre vie de relation, dans la panoplie des instruments naturels mis à notre disposition pour comprendre le monde, ce sont les plus importants. Ils permettent d'agrandir l'espace perceptif. En effet, nous ne pouvons sentir, goûter et toucher que des éléments relativement proches alors que nous pouvons entendre et voir ce qui peut être plus éloigné.

L'espace auditif et l'espace visuel peuvent être appréhendés de deux façons. D'une façon passive, c'est entendre et voir et d'une façon active, c'est écouter et regarder. Personne, à ma connaissance, n'a dénombré l'incroyable quantité de sons divers qui arrivent aux oreilles et la quantité encore plus grande d'images qui viennent stimuler la rétine. Devant cette somme d'informations auditives et visuelles, nous devons faire un choix, une **sélection.** Cette sélection peut se concevoir comme une sorte de programmation du cerveau à ne tenir compte que de certains signaux, programmation par automatisme (culturel ou inné) ou par éducation (vigilance sélective). Nous ne voyons et n'entendons pas tout ce qui peut être entendu ou vu et, à la lumière de cette règle générale, nous pouvons dire que chaque individu remplit son espace environnant d'éléments qui lui sont propres.

Ceci a des conséquences très importantes et permet de comprendre le comportement d'un sujet face à une situation donnée, comportement qui pourra étonner son voisin qui n'en aura pas du tout la même approche. Considérons, par exemple, deux personnes qui marchent côte à côte dans une rue commerçante.

Ces deux personnes sont des individus et donc, par essence même, différentes. Augmentons encore la différenciation : il y a un homme et une femme, l'un est plus âgé que l'autre et ils n'ont pas la même activité professionnelle. On pourrait penser qu'ils ont au moins un point commun : le lieu, c'est-à-dire la rue qu'ils parcourent ensemble. Eh bien non! Si nous leur demandons de « raconter » leur chemin, nous comprendrons que chacun a perçu des éléments très différents. En entrant dans le schéma stupide de la trop classique discrimination sexiste, disons que la jeune femme a repéré les boutiques de mode « avec dans la vitrine, une ravissante petite robe », elle a remarqué aussi que le boucher faisait une promotion sur la viande, etc., et noté l'architecture particulière des maisons. L'homme, lui, aura enregistré tout autre chose et peut-être n'aura jamais vu le magasin de mode ni l'étal du boucher mais aura remarqué la magnifique voiture garée, une librairie, un magasin de sport et... les vieilles maisons.

Leurs témoignages respectifs révéleront que, bien qu'ensemble, ils n'étaient pas *vraiment* dans la même rue. Les caractéristiques architecturales seront le seul endroit de rencontre, où ils pourront *vraiment* communiquer. C'est-à-dire, abandonner leurs différences et poser sur l'environnement deux regards convergents. Là encore, verront-ils les mêmes détails? Ce n'est pas si sûr. L'un, plus technique, aura son regard intéressé en premier lieu par la poutraison apparente, l'emplacement des chéneaux ou la qualité des tuiles. L'autre, plus esthétique, sera attirée par l'allure générale de la maison, la décoration florale des fenêtres ou la chaleureuse quiétude qui s'en dégage.

Passons au-delà de la caricature propre à tout

exemple, pour revenir à l'essentiel et dire que la prise de vue et la prise de son ne dépendent pas des organes récepteurs mais bien du preneur de son ou du cameraman. C'est bien au niveau du cerveau que le spectacle de « son et lumière » prend forme et nous ne retenons de ce spectacle que ce qui est déjà, pour nous, signifiant. Le cerveau est bien l'organe essentiel de la vue et de l'ouïe... finalement. Il va décoder les informations captées au niveau de la périphérie, leur donner un sens et une valeur afin de les rendre intelligibles. Au départ, n'existent que des bruits et des silences, des lumières et des ombres qui, en arrière des récepteurs sensoriels, vont s'ordonner et prendre forme.

En d'autres termes, nous devons admettre que pour bien entendre et bien voir, il faut d'abord comprendre, et tout ce qui n'est pas compris (dans le sens de « compris dans » un ensemble de mémoire) restera non vu et non entendu ou nécessitera un apprentissage.

Il y a ainsi, et selon les expériences antérieures, interprétation – donc lecture subjective et soumise à l'erreur – du monde extérieur. Devant un objet ou un son, le cerveau devra faire un énorme travail d'ordonnancement (1) avant de rendre son verdict.

Quelle rassurante facilité de voir une chaise quand l'objet présenté correspond aux normes mémorisées et de pouvoir tranquillement déclarer : « Ceci est une chaise ! » Mais que celle-ci soit montrée repliée et de profil, alors l'objet (qui pourtant est toujours une chaise) risque d'être vu très différemment. Les yeux détectent quelque chose, le cerveau, qui ne peut pas re-connaître la chaise présentée sous cet aspect, reste aveugle.

---

(1) Définition du Larousse : Déclenchement et contrôle de l'avancement d'une commande à travers les différents services de fabrication, depuis sa mise en œuvre jusqu'à l'expédition au client.

Inversement, si le cerveau cherche du regard une chaise, les yeux ne verront pas l'objet s'il est différent de la forme préconçue. Il va falloir réapprendre cet objet et sa nouvelle image et la laisser se graver dans un ensemble de neurones corticaux ou plus exactement, dans un sous-ensemble de neurones que Jean-Pierre Changeux (1) nomme **« objet mental »**.

L'objet mental peut être défini comme une entité, physiquement créée, résultant de la mobilisation (entrée en activité) simultanée et transitoire d'un grand nombre de neurones pouvant appartenir à des régions du cerveau différentes et ayant des « singularités », des fonctions spécifiques. (Est-ce là la traduction physiologique des archétypes que Jung considère comme préexistant à toute forme de pensée et se comportant comme une véritable préprogrammation à travers laquelle prend forme l'idée ?) Cette *assemblée de neurones*, dont les activités se conjuguent (pour cause de même motif) d'une façon occasionnelle et corollaire, forme ainsi un graphe. Ces circuits peuvent, lors d'une stimulation sensorielle due à une présence extérieure (visuelle, auditive ou, par extension, une situation plus globale), s'organiser en un percept primaire, c'est-à-dire en un graphe spécialisé, en relation et en prise directe avec l'objet extérieur. En termes peut-être plus faciles, nous pouvons dire qu'il faut avoir déjà l'idée de ce que l'on peut voir pour pouvoir le voir.

On comprend maintenant mieux pourquoi l'homme dont les neurones corticaux renferment « l'objet mental » d'une voiture a eu, dans la rue, son regard préférentiellement attiré par cet objet et non par la robe en vitrine dont le percept primaire lui faisait défaut. En bref, pour avoir une bonne vue des choses, il ne suffit pas d'une acuité visuelle

---

(1) Neurophysiologiste, auteur de *L'Homme neuronal*, Fayard.

de dix sur dix, mais il faut aussi avoir, au niveau des neurones du cerveau, des structures d'accueil organisées aptes à reconnaître, à accepter, à comprendre ce qui est regardé.

Toutes ces notions, quelque peu ardues, je l'admets volontiers, nous éloignent seulement en apparence de nos préoccupations de cette fin du deuxième degré de la Relaxation dynamique. En effet, c'est par la connaissance, même sommaire, de ces processus de fonctionnement de base que nous pouvons aussi prendre conscience de notre relativité à l'environnement, de cette absolue subjectivité que nous apprenons à considérer... objectivement. Alors, après un voyage mentalement vécu vers de lointains rivages, quand « je » retrouve sa place, osons nous regarder. Quel est le percept primaire qui correspond à l'être que nous sommes ?

Comme le navigateur que sa conscience a hissé en haut de son mât, à la hune de son bateau, tentons le regard sur nous-même, regardons-nous, voyons-nous. Peut-être pourrons-nous, à notre égard, changer nos circuits, modifier les structures d'accueil et installer de nouveaux graphes.

Qu'un événement négatif et par trop marquant laisse en nous une mauvaise impression, une trace néfaste et notre regard sur les choses de la vie risque de changer et notre comportement de s'en trouver altéré. Sans chercher forcément, dans une approche psychanalytique, la ou les raisons originelles du trouble (de la vue!), ce second degré de la Relaxation Dynamique en multipliant et en favorisant les contacts avec nous-même, permet finalement une rencontre avec cet *être percevant* avec qui nous partageons notre intimité.

125

Le toucher

Un troisième sens nous permet de comprendre le monde immédiatement environnant : le toucher. Il existe également deux façons d'entrer en contact tactile, le toucher actif et le toucher passif (le fait d'être touché) qui déclenche la plupart du temps des réactions réflexes. Nous nous intéressons au toucher actif qui correspond à une exploration des éléments se trouvant « à portée de main ».

Disons-le tout de suite, le toucher est un acte d'amour. (Remarquez l'effort qu'il faut faire pour rentrer en contact de peau avec quelque chose de répugnant !) L'exploration tactile nous donne une foule de renseignements utiles à la compréhension globale de l'objet ou de l'être. Le poids, la forme, la texture de surface ainsi que la température sont déjà des éléments fort instructifs pour nous faire une idée très précise des relations que nous pouvons entretenir avec ce que l'on touche. Le toucher est un geste affectif, un geste d'affection, un élan vers...

Observez le comportement de personnes passionnées de vieux meubles chez un antiquaire : elles ne peuvent s'empêcher de toucher les meubles et les objets qu'elles aiment et qu'elles trouvent beaux. Qui peut acheter un bibelot, par exemple, sans le toucher d'abord ? Cela est si vrai que certains commerçants sont obligés de mettre dans leur magasin : *Défense de toucher*. Ils s'assurent ainsi peut-être contre la détérioration ou la casse de l'objet mais aussi ils suppriment immanquablement une possibilité de dialogue émotionnel, de contact affectif, et même inhibent le désir d'appropriation de l'objet, prélude à l'achat.

La notion de propriété est sous-tendue dans l'acte de toucher. Un objet qui se trouve « sous la main » est un objet que l'on aime bien et surtout dont on aime bien se servir à sa convenance. C'est quelque chose que l'on contrôle, que l'on maîtrise, que l'on possède. Quelque chose ou quelqu'un. Cette appartenance à... est exprimée symboliquement dans le « main dans la main » et le « bras dessus, bras dessous » des couples amoureux. Et la main d'un père ou d'une mère posée sur l'épaule de son enfant signifie : *Je l'aime, je le reconnais faisant partie des miens, c'est* **mon** *enfant.*

Dans certain milieu politico-diplomatique, l'estime que l'on porte au visiteur officiel (ou au pays qu'il représente) est proportionnelle à la durée et à l'intensité du contact établi – on pourrait presque dire, à la surface corporelle touchée! Poignée de main « froide », puis simplement chaleureuse et encore très amicale où les quatre mains entrent en contact et longtemps, et enfin la tape sur l'épaule et même l'accolade. Parfois, on va jusqu'à mettre en relation la surface de la peau des joues!

Toucher, c'est *recevoir* et *donner* le temps du contact. Toucher, c'est donc échanger, *s'échanger* dans le présent. Un **instantané** pendant lequel communiquent et communient deux êtres affectifs et qui apporte un grand nombre d'impressions ressenties physiquement et parfois d'une façon violente. Mais pas toujours conscientes. Souvent les messages passent par la porte de l'insu, à l'insu du receveur comme du donneur. N'étant pas analysés logiquement mais émotionnellement, sont-ils reçus et recueillis par le « cerveau droit »? Difficile à dire. Quoi qu'il en soit, ils participent très activement à la perception de l'autre; ils sont à la base de la rencontre. Lors d'une première rencontre, les contacts par le toucher activent l'émotivité et l'affectivité (positive ou négative), ensuite ils en sont les témoins, les révélateurs.

On ne peut connaître (et pourquoi pas, aimer) *vraiment* quelqu'un ou quelque chose qu'après l'avoir touché. Qu'après avoir partagé son **intimité** et offert la nôtre. Voici peut-être l'essentiel de l'acte de toucher : **échange instantané et corporalisé entre deux intimités.**

Et la première intimité à connaître, c'est sa propre intimité. Le premier corps à toucher, c'est son propre corps. D'abord se connaître et reconnaître la présence de ce Moi intime puis ouvrir un dialogue et le laisser se « dévoiler ». Un des exercices du deuxième degré est réservé à ce contact avec son corps. Oser toucher son corps, simplement, librement... « se prendre en main ». A ce moment, la conscience est au « bout des doigts », elle nous *enveloppe* des pieds à la tête. La pudibonde retenue culturelle s'efface, quelques barrières s'effondrent. La rencontre se produit : je suis **là**, je suis **ici**, je suis **maintenant**. Je suis « étant », je suis vivant.

Le goût

Si nos capacités à voir, à entendre et à toucher nous renseignent sur la provenance des choses, leur saveur nous révèle leur **intimité**. En effet, quand nous goûtons, nous sommes en contact étroit. En relation gustative avec un objet (ou un être), non seulement la frontière de notre cercle proxémique immédiat a été franchie, mais en plus nous permettons l'intrusion, l'introduction dans le monde vraiment privé. Avec peut-être la notion freudienne de possession, voire d'assimilation par digestion après pénétration. Ce sens perceptif est très tôt développé chez l'Homme puisqu'il est déjà efficace *in utero*. En effet, le fœtus a une relation gustative avec le milieu amniotique utérin et le nouveau-né réagit au goût du lait de sa mère, goût qui peut varier selon la nourriture maternelle.

Les cinq saveurs de base se retrouvent dans la sucrerie, la salaison, l'amertume, l'acidité et la fadeur, cependant les notes de bon ou de mauvais goût sont variables selon les individus. La perception consciente, l'appréciation de la saveur d'un aliment est éminemment culturelle. Il ne semble pas qu'il y ait un bon ou un mauvais goût universel. Certains animaux (les chiens, par exemple), avant de prendre la nourriture, commencent par la sentir (premier filtre préventif contre l'intoxication alimentaire), si celle-ci n'a pas d'odeur particulière, ils la goûtent et la rejettent si la saveur n'est pas référencée (stockée en mémoire). Cette aptitude, si elle a existé chez l'homme, n'est guère mise en application (sauf dans des cas extrêmes) et l'alerte sera beaucoup plus olfactive ou visuelle que gustative.

La saveur d'un aliment persiste assez longtemps après son ingestion ou son rejet. C'est dire que la saveur participe au souvenir laissé : c'est une trace. Les références au goût seront là en témoignage d'une sensation passée, déjà vécue... qui laisse un arrière-goût! Sur le plan analogique, on peut constater que :

– Le sucré est assimilé aux bons souvenirs de situations vécues en anima, douces, intimes, presque maternelles et toujours positives (de nombreux poètes parlent du « goût sucré de l'enfance » et si la lune avait une saveur, elle serait sucrée).

– Le salé correspondrait à l'animus, plus vif, plus dynamique, en dehors de la routine (mettre un peu de sel – de piquant – dans la vie! une histoire salée! etc.).

– L'acidité fait référence au mauvais caractère (prix Citron décerné, à Roland-Garros, au joueur de tennis le plus désagréable!) et à la méchanceté voulue (une parole acide n'est pas particulièrement aimable!).

– L'amertume dit bien ce qu'elle veut dire et exprime le regret ou le remords, la déception et même le chagrin. Vous le voyez, nous goûtons le monde qui nous entoure et chacun est invité au Grand Festin de la Vie.

De la même manière que la qualité gustative d'un aliment n'est pas une qualité a priori mais une appréciation a posteriori, nous prenons conscience qu'aucune chose n'est fondamentalement bonne ou mauvaise, tout dépend de la façon dont nous allons l'apprécier. Nous sentons là l'absolue relativité des choses et donc le caractère subjectif de notre jugement. Subjectivité totale qui préside à notre rencontre avec le monde environnant et qui souligne l'intervention constante du Moi-Sujet dans le dialogue qui en résulte. La pseudo-objectivité, ou plus justement l'objectivation (manifestations corporelles, par exemple) est secondaire à l'intégration de l'événement (le vécu), cette vision étant elle-même, en partie, en relation avec les expériences précédentes (mémoire).

L'odorat

Notre civilisation occidentale a laissé encore, heureusement, subsister quelques parfums! Sachons nous laisser réveiller par l'odeur d'un bon café ou d'un pain brioché. Sachons nous laisser toujours émouvoir par les parfums qui donnent aux choses une valeur. L'odorat montre le sens des choses car il nous renseigne sur leur provenance. **L'odeur est en elle-même une mémoire.** Une mémoire qui réveille une autre mémoire. Qui n'a pas été mis en présence de son enfance en respirant l'odeur d'un encrier ou d'un cartable? Qui n'a pas revécu ses premiers printemps en sentant l'odeur des foins fraîchement coupés? Même en n'ayant jamais vécu à la campagne. Quelqu'un qui n'a jamais senti les embruns iodés de la vague océane saura les *re-connaître* dès la première fois.

Les odeurs sont en mémoire, semble-t-il.

Les odeurs naturelles pourraient être une forme de mémoire archaïque, héritée d'une lignée remontant à la nuit des temps. Quand nous « sentons les choses », nous sommes en confiance car en pays de connaissance.

Qui se laisse respirer livre son secret, qui parfume l'air dévoile son mystère. Rien ne peut être *sentimentalement* connu si son odeur nous est soustraite.

Une multitude d'expressions populaires traduisent l'importance de l'odorat : « *Sentir* le vent tourner »; « *Sentir* que quelque chose ne va pas » et après avoir « *reniflé* un mauvais coup », annoncer que « ça *sent* mauvais! ». Ne pas pouvoir *sentir* quelqu'un parce qu'il est « *puant* » ou, au contraire, se *sentir* en confiance pour traduire son alliance et son bien-être. De même, ne dit-on pas que Untel est en « *odeur* de sainteté », etc. Nous sentons le monde et nous nous sentons dans le monde.

Nous sentons bien que ces expressions intègrent au senti une connotation irrationnelle : le « flair » avec ce que cela comporte de mystérieux! Une sorte de sixième sens, sans organes perceptifs, ou plutôt se servant de tous les systèmes de perception : l'intuition.

L'INTUITION

Les cinq sens « classiques » que nous venons d'étudier donnent du monde environnant une approche concrète et rassurante. Ils réconfortent les adeptes de saint Thomas qui ne croient que ce qu'ils voient.. « Cette table existe parce que je la vois, je la touche, je peux la soulever et la déplacer en exerçant sur elle une force que je peux calculer... etc. » Ces cartésiens bon teint ne se doutent sûrement pas qu'ils sont, pardonnez-moi de le dire brutalement, pauvres, bornés et bernés! Pauvres car, se fiant seulement au tangible et au raisonnable, ils s'écartent de leurs richesses intérieures : imagination et intuition; bornés, dans le sens de limités, parce que enfermés dans les limites de la perception sensorielle immédiate et de leur faculté à comprendre ce qu'ils perçoivent (capacité cognitive); bernés par cette perception sensorielle qui n'est en fait qu'une activité d'interprétation subjective conditionnée par leurs propres attentes et références personnelles.

Le dictionnaire donne, par une de ses phrases lapidaires dont il a le secret, une définition de l'intuition qui mérite d'être analysée :

Saisie immédiate de la vérité, sans l'aide du raisonnement.

Sans l'aide du raisonnement... Le raisonnement n'est pas la seule voie d'accès à la vérité. Pascal nous dit que « la raison est une méthode lente et tortueuse par laquelle ceux qui ne connaissent point la vérité peuvent la découvrir ». Les étapes qu'impose la démarche logique sont autant d'obstacles qui éloignent du but et risquent soit de nous arrêter en chemin, soit de nous dévier de notre route. Cette idée sera reprise dans le troisième degré de la Relaxation Dynamique. Sortons du paysage glacé, figé et limité par la pensée rationnelle et sachons nous laisser emporter, hors des horizons définis, par les souffles intérieurs de l'intuition. Nous découvrirons certainement une autre vérité ou, tout au moins, la vérité sous une autre forme, et notre regard gagnera en lucidité et en créativité.

Très souvent, au point de départ de la découverte scientifique se trouve une intuition (... pas toujours avouée par le chercheur), comme une conviction, une certitude intime d'être sur la bonne voie. Et la démonstration logique, secondaire à la découverte, sert de caution et de moyen de communication à cette idée lumineuse qui-vient-d'on-ne-sait-où et qui fait crier : « Eurêka! »

Mais il n'est nul besoin d'être Archimède pour bénéficier de révélations soudaines. L'intuition accompagne tout un chacun et intéresse les problèmes les plus concrets aussi bien professionnels que privés. Comment pourrait-on expliquer ce mode de perception très spécial qui s'amuse à défier la logique ? Difficile à dire, mais nous pourrions imaginer le scénario suivant :

Situation de base. Au cours des nombreuses expériences apportées par la vie au quotidien, le cerveau est capable de stocker un nombre immense de renseignements de tous ordres. Véritable banque de données situées pour une grande part dans une zone mémoire à l'insu de l'activité consciente. Ces différents graphes résident dans des niveaux de structures mentales parfois profonds et sont prêts, par stimulation directe, par analogie évocatrice ou par la force de la pensée réflexive à s'organiser en percepts primaires, images ou concepts généraux.

Situation de départ. Un problème est à « l'étude ». Les structures corticales du chercheur s'enrichissent d'un maximum de renseignements : de nouveaux graphes se constituent et se combinent à d'autres déjà présents. Certains d'entre eux vont correspondre à la solution souhaitée : la question trouve sa réponse. La résolution du problème en question peut passer par deux voies différentes.

– L'activité cognitive consciente (réflexion, raisonnement, comparaison...) va permettre de résoudre la question posée. Les différentes étapes du chemin raisonné sont bien définies (bien qu'elles puissent être souvent très rapides) et elles apparaissent en conscience claire dont le maître d'œuvre est le « cerveau gauche ». Mais parfois les références connues ne suffisent pas et les réponses ne sont pas satisfaisantes... On tourne en rond... On est bloqué... etc. Tout se passe comme si les schémas mentaux n'arrivaient pas à trouver la bonne combinaison d'assemblage, schémas dont la réflexion volontaire a eu cependant pour avantage d'en « réveiller » les graphes.

– Période de gestation ou de maturation. Elle débute au moment où l'activité de réflexion s'arrête pour raison de repos ou de « saturation ». Mais le travail du cerveau ne cesse pas pour autant. La sagesse populaire nous enseigne que « la nuit porte conseil » ! Les éléments de réponse se combinent et ceux-ci peuvent parfois être « réveillés » par un déclic fortuit (dont l'origine est souvent inattendue) et s'organiser en images mentales. On dit alors que « la solution me vient à l'esprit et s'impose à l'évidence ». Imaginons une assemblée parlementaire débattant d'un problème épineux. Chacun donne son avis, développe ses arguments qui vont dans le sens exclusif de ses concepts de base. Tous ces discours, induits par un postulat a priori, divergent et ne peuvent apporter aucune solution consensuelle. Au milieu de ce tohu-bohu, un homme écoute, silencieux. Il prend des notes et retient chaque argument présenté. Sans idée préconçue, il tente de faire la synthèse des divers raisonnements... et finalement trouve une réponse intéressante. Dans le brouhaha général, personne ne peut (ni ne veut) entendre ce qu'il dit... Quand enfin le calme se rétablit, sa voix apparaît claire... On applaudit et tout le monde se met au travail pour voir comment appliquer cette solution lumineuse. Cet homme est-il plus intelligent que les autres? Pas forcément! Il a tout simplement su assembler les différents avis émis pour créer une solution originale qui ne peut se manifester que quand l'agitation et même la fébrilité engendrées par la recherche disparaissent.

C'est ce qui se passe dans le cerveau : pendant l'exploration du problème plusieurs voies sont tentées, plusieurs arguments sont exposés. La nuit, le repos, ou la relaxation viennent faire la tempête. Alors s'ouvre la deuxième voie d'accès... la voie intuitive qui se définit comme une activité cognitive inconsciente, à l'insu du sujet. La pensée logique s'ordonne à partir de ce que l'esprit conscientise à l'instant de la réflexion alors que la pensée intuitive se nourrit d'éléments non accessibles à la conscience claire mais qui, acquis par le biais de perceptions infraliminaires ou de processus conceptuels inconscients, ont été mémorisés parfois bien longtemps avant. Et si nous n'avons pas en nous la réponse directe au problème posé, nous avons cependant tous les éléments pour fournir une réponse adaptée. A un moment non prévisible, ces éléments vont s'organiser pour former, « en un éclair », la solution attendue, intuitivement.

Il faut savoir se tenir prêt à entendre cette « voix

intérieure », être capable de la rendre consciente. Secondairement, nous pourrons soumettre cette réponse intuitive à l'épreuve de la réalité et au raisonnement. L'intuition d'une solution ne survient que très rarement chez quelqu'un qui n'a aucune connaissance rationnelle du problème. Il y a plus de probabilités pour qu'une découverte intéressante sur le cancer surgisse, un jour, sur le mode intuitif dans le cerveau d'un médecin ou d'un biochimiste que dans celui d'un peintre ou d'un ingénieur en bâtiment. Mais il est aussi possible que cette découverte jaillisse alors que le chercheur est en train d'écouter une musique ou d'admirer les mouvements de la vague.

De Bach qui prétendait jouer « les notes dans l'ordre où elles ont été écrites » à Mozart qui dit que « écrire mes musiques ne me prend guère de temps car tout est achevé d'avance », tous ceux qui ont exprimé cette idée parlent de la spontanéité en même temps que de la globalité de l'intuition. Toute tentative pour utiliser *volontairement* l'intuition est vouée à l'échec. La pensée intuitive se manifeste d'elle-même et généralement à un moment de relâchement des tensions intellectuelles et rationnelles. Cependant, s'il n'est pas possible de déclencher sur commande l'activité intuitive, il est intéressant de savoir retrouver les conditions physiques et mentales qui la favorisent.

Une des premières conditions est d'apprendre à considérer l'intuition comme faisant partie intégrante de l'activité mentale; ne plus la rejeter sous prétexte qu'elle n'a pas de logique apparente; ne plus la vivre comme naïve, puérile et indigne (de nos brillants cerveaux!) parce qu'elle se livre, comme la vérité, toute nue.

Certaines techniques proposent des méthodes afin de libérer le mécanisme imaginatif. Elles reposent sur un principe simple mais fondamental : ne jamais préjuger le bien-fondé des réponses émises. Il faut laisser libre cours aux associations d'idées qui surviennent, aucune d'entre elles ne doit être considérée a priori comme hors sujet ou inadaptée au problème posé. L'exercice n'est pas facile! Il faut se garder de toute critique, de tout jugement... apprendre à se « laisser dire » sans s'écouter parler... apprendre à laisser le stylo courir et la feuille se remplir sans se corriger... En bref, s'exprimer sans autotrahison, sans déguisement et sans vanité. Alors peut émerger du plus profond des couches profondes, la solution espérée que notre fatuité à vouloir tout expliquer par les sacro-saintes lois de la logique n'avait pas pu (ou pas su) rendre accessible.

Quand un problème quelconque est soumis à l'analyse rationnelle et consciente, l'esprit humain, même occupé à d'autres tâches, est capable de poursuivre le traitement de la question sur un mode inconscient ou insu. N'ayant plus de censeur sensitif et émotionnel ou de « directeur de conscience » pour le contrôler, il va pouvoir agir librement et faire intervenir certains paramètres qu'il n'aurait jamais osé intégrer consciemment. Libéré des « lourdeurs administratives » de la pensée formelle, il devient « esprit d'entreprise », « esprit de synthèse » et « esprit créateur »!

« L'expérience m'a appris, écrit le poète Housman, à surveiller mes pensées quand je me rase le matin, car dès qu'une rime me trotte par la tête, ma peau se hérisse et le rasoir cesse d'agir. »

Certains auteurs ont lié intuition et conscience corporelle et pensent que, pour développer les capacités intuitives, il suffit d'apprendre le langage du corps. Bien que trop limitative, cette idée semble intéressante à considérer. En effet qui mieux que le corps peut reconnaître la présence de la pensée vraie... quand celle-ci naît dans l'espace intime du « monde intérieur »? Le langage du corps et son écoute attentive constituent l'un des grands axes de la démarche sophrologique, c'est donc naturellement que l'intuition sera abordée dans l'entraînement général. Se manifestant par le corps, elle peut être assimilée à l'instinct. L'instinctivo-moteur du Carré dont nous avons parlé dans le précédent chapitre peut alors se comprendre comme une motivation intuitivement vécue à accomplir certains actes nécessaires à la survie de l'individu ou de l'espèce. Et, il faut encore le dire, cette écoute passe obligatoirement par une relaxation, c'est-à-dire une mise au calme des tensions surajoutées qui, par leur présence trop forte, occultent la « musique du dedans » !

La saisie immédiate de la vérité peut aussi se manifester par le sentiment. Emotion primaire capable de faire vibrer la Croix, le sentiment naît, selon Caycedo, de la répétition des sensations. Le second degré de la Relaxation dynamique donne accès au vécu (imprégnation de la conscience) du sentiment d'harmonie et d'alliance avec l'essentiel. Véritable embrasement de la conscience par la certitude intuitive d'être bien... ou tout simplement d'être ! Libérée et intégrée lors des différents exercices proposés, cette impression de plénitude éclairante pourra, un jour, par la grâce d'un déclic fortuit, être reconnue quand la vérité surgissant de nulle part nous saisira... L'intuition et le cœur ont-ils les mêmes raisons que la raison ne peut qu'ignorer ?

Le processus intuitif de la pensée préside à plusieurs capacités de la conscience :

- Découverte et créativité.
- Evaluation et orientation (spatiale et même sociale).
- Perspicacité et compréhension de la globalité d'une situation ou d'une personnalité.
- Prédiction et illumination.

Ces deux dernières capacités introduisent le chapitre suivant sur le troisième degré de la Relaxation dynamique de Caycedo. En effet, nous apprendrons comment, dépassant les limites de la pensée logique, transcendant l'absurde nauséeux du doute, la conscience libérée prend le chemin intuitif qui conduit à la rencontre de ce qui ne peut être dit, vu, entendu, compris.

Ce n'est que par l'intuition – c'est-à-dire par la saisie immédiate (et globale) de la Vérité – que la conscience peut atteindre, et vivre, ce que le Cercle symbolise.

RÉSUMÉ DU DEUXIÈME DEGRÉ DE LA RELAXATION DYNAMIQUE

Attitude générale

- Position assise (sauf en début de séance).
- Yeux fermés.
- Attitude mentale de contemplation.
- Essai de « décorporalisation ».
- « Je » est objet du regard.

Buts poursuivis

- Harmonisation avec le monde extérieur.
- Amélioration de la relation de Soi avec les autres.
- Développement de la perception par la prise en conscience de nos sens.
- Libération du sens intuitif.

QUATRIÈME CHAPITRE

LE CERCLE

**Le contenu symbolique
Réflexions sur la méditation
Troisième degré de la
Relaxation Dynamique de Caycedo**

LE CONTENU SYMBOLIQUE

Si un symbole est susceptible de réveiller un archétype fondamental, c'est bien le Cercle. Il contient toute une série de signifiants comme Perfection et Pureté – Homogénéité et Globalité – Puissance et Force Spirituelle – Temps Absolu et Mouvement Universel – et, par voie de conséquence, le Ciel et l'idée de Dieu.

Le cercle est la seule figure géométrique qui admette un centre parfait équidistant de tous les éléments de surface. Ce centre, représenté par un point, symbolise la concentration de toutes les forces composantes. Mais ce point central est également un cercle et admet donc, lui aussi, un centre... le centre de ce centre étant encore un cercle... etc. Ainsi, chaque cercle est la représentation étalée d'un point qui est la représentation concentrée d'un autre cercle. Dans le bouddhisme zen, ces différents cercles concentriques sont autant d'étapes de perfectionnement intérieur et d'harmonisation de l'esprit. Il en découle une notion de hiérarchie, non pas pyramidale et figée mais, au contraire, circulaire et dynamique. Le chemin qui mène au Centre des centres est sans fin et sans vertige : chaque point permet la contemplation du monde dont il est le centre et fait vivre la sensation de globalité, d'épanouissement et de force vitale.

Le cercle exprime par sa géométrie la notion de mouvement universel, sans début ni fin. Il permet de mettre en image le concept abstrait d'Eternité, de Temps Absolu qui cohabite en nous avec la perception concrète du temps mesuré. Sont ainsi représentés les grands cycles biologiques, dans ces mouvements perpétuels où « rien ne se crée, rien ne se perd, tout se transforme... ». Chaque chose dans la nature a son propre rythme d'évolution et de transformation et rentre dans un cycle à période de révolution déterminée constituant un temps relatif, ce mouvement circulaire étant lui-même rattaché à un autre cycle à période plus élevée... etc. Nous trouvons cette organisation en cercles imbriqués, où chaque élément participe au Mouvement global, dans la représentation du système solaire avec les différentes planètes qui gravitent autour d'un centre, ce système n'étant qu'un élément dans la galaxie.

Le Ciel, archétype du schème essentiel de l'ascension et de la verticalité, englobe, bien entendu, le système symbolique binaire Lune-Soleil. Ce modèle signifiant, obéissant à la loi de correspondance, induit et révèle plusieurs notions (les signifiés).

Lune	Soleil
Réflexion	Emission
Apprentissage	Enseignement
Passivité	Action
Silence	Parole
Attente	Décision
Féminin	Masculin
Façon d'être	Manière de paraître

La liste de ces dualités pourrait être longue. Dualités qui ne doivent pas se concevoir comme des notions séparées et en opposition (l'excès de l'une entraînant le défaut de l'autre) mais bien comme des éléments complémentaires et unifiés.

La voie de la sagesse paraît être indiquée par la résultante des forces opposées et intégrées.

Le Cercle définit une entité, une globalité et, de ce fait, va symboliser dans de nombreuses civilisations et religions la notion d'universalité et d'unicité de l'univers. C'est dire qu'il représente le Ciel et sous-tend l'idée de Dieu. Entourant le visage de certains personnages, le cercle symbolisera la Connaissance, la Pureté, l'alliance avec Dieu.

Dans l'idéogramme chinois, le **cercle est ouvert.** Cette ouverture montre l'interrelation entre l'homme et l'univers par l'intermédiaire de sa conscience. Interrelation, c'est-à-dire relation dans les deux sens : la conscience de l'homme contient une parcelle d'éternité mais, également, l'homme, par sa conscience, participe à la dynamique cosmique. Aucune Vie n'est inutile puisqu'elle est dans le cercle et intègre donc un courant universel.

Ce symbole se retrouve dans les faits et gestes quotidiens et se manifeste par de très nombreuses expressions :

– Le cercle familial où se vivent les sentiments d'amour et de filiation, d'appartenance. On est dans le cercle et en étroite relation avec les êtres qui le forment.

– Le cercle d'amis où se manifestent les sentiments de sécurité et de solidarité. Ce cercle est plus large et sert de système tampon entre l'individu et l'environnement lointain.

– Le cercle qui entoure, dans un texte, un mot important.

– Le cercle qui délimite la cible dont le centre seul constitue l'objectif, symbolisant ainsi, dans le Kuyndo (tir à l'arc), la démarche de concentration sur l'essentiel.

RÉFLEXIONS SUR LA MÉDITATION

Mille fois, tout au long de ce livre, nous avons parlé du système de références qui permet à chaque individu de faire une lecture intelligible des événements de sa vie. Nous avons vu, à la fin du dernier chapitre, comment notre expérience s'organisait en schémas directeurs dans notre cerveau et faisait de nous des êtres prédisposés à voir et à comprendre telle chose plutôt qu'une autre. Ici, dans ce troisième degré, nous allons envisager une manière différente de se présenter au monde et de se représenter le monde par une tentative d'abolir tout ce qui, sous des aspects sécurisants, nous limite et nous aliène.

Les critères qui avalisent le jugement que nous portons sur nous-même, sur les autres et sur notre environnement font toujours appel soit à notre mémoire soit à notre capacité d'anticipation, c'est-à-dire sont liés à la notion de temps. En figeant le temps, en fixant nos rapports dans un instantané absolu de l'*ici et maintenant*, ces critères s'effondrent ainsi que s'évapore notre tendance au jugement.

Quelle que soit notre mission sur terre, quelle que soit l'importance donnée à nos motivations, à nos projets ou à notre environnement quotidien, nous sommes sur une sorte « d'arrêt sur image », une tranche de vie unique qui voit chaque élément s'unir à l'ensemble pour former un tout. C'est peut-être à ce moment-là que se manifeste l'archétype de la globalité universelle et cosmique (dont nous sommes issus et non extraits) et que représente le symbole du Cercle.

Approche du Zen

Le chemin que nous tenterons de suivre dans ce troisième degré est emprunté au ZEN. Et malgré les énormes difficultés qui surgissent à chaque mot, il est, semble-t-il, indispensable d'en parler en essayant de définir ce que peut être l'esprit du Zen.

Qu'est-ce que le Zen ? Il est impossible de répondre à une telle question car le Zen, par essence même, ne peut pas être contenu dans une réponse aussi complète et détaillée soit-elle. Le Zen représente le côté « inexprimable » de la réalité. Le Zen va à la rencontre du monde absolument concret dont l'absolue présence lui suffit pour exister. Le fait qui éclaire l'esprit zen n'a nul besoin de référence pour être en vie, nul besoin de logique pour être compris, nul besoin de mots pour être transcrit. **Il est, c'est tout!**

La méthode zen consiste à diriger le regard sur le fait lui-même et non sur les effets qu'il peut produire sur nous. La démarche, qui représente un apprentissage de plusieurs dizaines d'années, conduit à démanteler les filtres intellectuels et émotionnels placés entre la réalité et le sujet afin d'entrer en contact direct avec cette réalité d'une façon pratique et personnelle. Tous les systèmes, qu'ils soient philosophiques ou dogmatiques, ne sont que des *moyens* pour approcher la réalité. En passant par eux, en privilégiant ces moyens de connaissances, en les intercalant entre la réalité et nous, nous multiplions les obstacles et nous nous éloignons du but.

L'esprit se noie et se perd dans le labyrinthe des concepts et finit par ne considérer comme essentiel que le fait de sortir de ce labyrinthe et de s'en réjouir dans une sorte d'autosatisfaction stérile. La démarche zen va donc consister à **chercher à connaître la réalité des choses et non point à re-connaître qu'une chose correspond à la réalité.** Car cette dernière attitude consisterait à faire passer l'objet de la connaissance à travers les circuits mentaux (intellectuels ou émotionnels) existant déjà, à en faire l'analyse par comparaison ou analogie et à le décréter vrai ou faux, bon ou mauvais (selon les références utilisées) ou même à nier son existence si l'objet ne « correspond à rien » !

Chercher à connaître la réalité des choses est un chemin plus difficile à suivre mais qui conduit le sujet au cœur même de l'objet et qui permet un vécu authentique, une connaissance personnelle et privée, hors des schémas standard et donc a fortiori non communicables par les voies classiques du langage symbolique. Pour cette raison, on dit que la connaissance zen est :

> Une transmission spéciale en dehors des Ecritures,
> Ne dépendant ni des mots, ni des lettres,
> Destinée directement à l'esprit de l'Homme,
> Pour voir en sa propre nature [1].

Pour arriver à démanteler le carcan de la sacro-sainte logique et à faire taire les débats affectifs internes, les maîtres zen emploient une méthode de questions et de réponses pour surprendre et désorganiser complètement les circuits existants. La technique utilisée consiste à pousser l'adepte hors de ses **références sécurisantes** et à l'amener finalement à **douter** de son propre mode de pensée. Voici par exemple une question posée par le maître Wu Tsu :

« Une vache passe par une fenêtre. Sa tête, ses

---

[1] Extraits de *L'Esprit du Zen*, Alan W. Watts, Dangles.

cornes et ses pattes passent aisément, seule la queue ne passe pas. Pourquoi ? » Ou encore :

« Il y a très longtemps, un homme enferma une oie dans une bouteille. L'oie grandit sans cesse, de sorte qu'un jour il lui fut impossible de sortir de la bouteille. L'homme ne voulut ni briser la bouteille, ni faire de mal à l'animal. De quelle manière procéderiez-vous si vous deviez sortir l'oie de la bouteille ? » Il est évident que des problèmes de ce genre n'admettent aucune solution logique.

Et pourtant, par réflexe, c'est bien avec l'intellect qu'ils seront d'abord traités jusqu'au moment où l'intellect se trouvera dans une impasse totale, au bord du gouffre, à cet endroit où le monde des conventions est prêt à s'effondrer et à laisser la place au doute.

Un doute absolu quant à sa capacité à résoudre, par son intelligence rationnelle, ces énigmes qui représentent un véritable défi à la logique et que le Zen nomme le **Koan** (ou Kohan). Il faut bien reconnaître que tous ces Koan sont en fait le reflet du grand Koan de la vie. De la quotidienneté de la vie qui nous apporte chaque jour son lot d'incertitudes et de doutes, qui nous met en position de vivre toute chose et son contraire et qui altère, par là même, notre capacité à vouloir.

Un doute absolu donc, qui oblige l'esprit à partir à la recherche d'une autre voie. Une voie plus directe, plus dépouillée, plus **intuitive.**

Au bout de ce chemin se trouve peut-être un tout autre regard. Et une certitude. A la manière d'une évidence. A la manière aussi d'un plongeur qui remonte à la surface et qui, à bout de souffle peut enfin respirer, l'expérimentateur se trouve alors libéré des mailles du filet dans lequel il était enfermé et qui l'empêchait de voir. Maintenant et ici, en un instant, en un éclair, comme lors de la première bouffée d'air qui nous fait sortir d'un monde pour rentrer dans un autre. C'est l'Illumination ou *Satori*.

L'authenticité du Satori se révèle par l'absolue certitude de sa présence et sa fragilité est extrême. Un rien le détruit. Que le doute apparaisse et il s'évapore. Que le désir naisse de le retenir et il s'échappe aussitôt. Qu'une seule parole soit prononcée et il s'éteint immédiatement. Rien n'est plus fragile que cette **rencontre** avec la réalité. Rencontre **solitaire** de deux solitudes, de deux « *nature-de-Bouddha* » qui, en fait, n'en font qu'UNE car la nature-de-Bouddha est indivisible. Ce contact direct, sur le mode intuitif, sans limite et sans doute, peut se produire après une longue méditation sur un Koan mais aussi à propos d'un geste banal de la vie quotidienne. C'est ainsi que (Suzuki, D.T., *Essai sur le Bouddhisme zen*) le maître zen P'ang s'écrie :

> Quelle merveille surnaturelle !
> Et quel miracle que ceci !
> Je tire l'eau, je porte le bois !

Dans cette célèbre petite strophe se trouve, à mon sens, résumé l'essentiel de la démarche zen : prise directe avec la vie de tous les jours, avec ses fastidieuses besognes « terre à terre », ses innombrables obligations, ses peines et souffrances imbéciles et pour couronner le tout, l'inéluctable moment où il va falloir terminer une vie sans avoir jamais eu l'impression de l'avoir vraiment commencée. Absurde vie. Incompréhensible vie. A quoi bon continuer, j'ai envie de m'arrêter ! Alors le Zen répond : **« Continue d'avancer, c'est la devise de la vie, et le Zen est la religion de la vie. »**

Mais comment aller jusqu'au bout du chemin quand l'Absurde nous attend à chaque croisement ? Comment « *imaginer Sisyphe heureux* » ? Connaissez-vous le destin de Sisyphe ?

Approche occidentale philosophique

Sisyphe avait déplu aux dieux. Il était trop méprisant envers eux; il avait une passion pour la vie et haïssait à ce point la Mort que Homère raconte qu'il avait réussi à l'enchaîner. Ceci, bien sûr, outragea Pluton : Zeus envoya le dieu de la Guerre délivrer la Mort de son vainqueur. Après encore quelques duperies, les dieux se fâchèrent. Ainsi, il fut décidé que Sisyphe serait expédié aux Enfers. Voici donc le début de l'histoire. Albert Camus nous la raconte avec un immense talent. Par respect et admiration pour le prix Nobel – qu'il me paraît inconvenant de tenter de plagier –, je me permets de reproduire ici, fidèlement, quelques passages de son texte.

« On a compris déjà que Sisyphe est le héros absurde. On ne dit rien sur Sisyphe aux Enfers. **Les mythes sont faits pour que l'imagination les anime.** Pour celui-ci on voit seulement tout l'effort d'un corps tendu pour soulever l'énorme pierre, la rouler et l'aider à gravir une pente cent fois recommencée; on voit le visage crispé, la joue collée contre la pierre, le secours d'une épaule qui reçoit la masse couverte de glaise, d'un pied qui la cale, la reprise à bout de bras, la sûreté toute humaine de deux mains pleines de terre. Tout au bout de ce long effort mesuré par l'espace sans ciel et le temps sans profondeur, le but est atteint. Sisyphe regarde alors la pierre dévaler en quelques instants vers ce monde inférieur d'où il faudra la remonter vers les sommets. Il redescend dans la plaine.

« C'est pendant ce retour, cette pause, que Sisyphe m'intéresse. Un visage qui peine si près des pierres est déjà pierre lui-même! Je vois cet homme redescendre d'un pas lourd mais égal vers le tourment dont il ne connaîtra pas la fin. **Cette** heure qui est comme une respiration et qui revient aussi souvent que son malheur, cette heure est celle de la conscience.** A chacun de ces instants, où il quitte les sommets et s'enfonce peu à peu vers les tanières des dieux, il est supérieur à son destin. **Il est plus fort que son rocher.** [...] La clairvoyance qui devait faire son tourment consomme du même coup sa victoire. [...] A cet instant subtil où l'homme se retourne sur sa vie, Sisyphe, revenant vers son rocher, contemple cette **suite d'actions sans lien qui devient son destin.** Lui aussi juge que tout est bien. Chacun des grains de cette pierre, chaque éclat minéral de cette montagne pleine de nuit, à lui seul forme un monde. La lutte elle-même vers les sommets suffit à remplir un cœur d'homme. **Il faut imaginer Sisyphe heureux.** »

Le *mythe de Sisyphe* pourrait être un des Koan du Zen. Ne trouvez-vous pas que ce héros de l'absurde ressemble à l'oie enfermée dans la bouteille ? Comment sortir de la bouteille (qui représente bien sûr les circonstances et obligations de la vie), comment se soustraire à cette tâche stupide et sans but ? Deux questions identiques et peut-être une même voie pour répondre. Suivons encore Sisyphe. Il est seul avec son rocher. Il est seul dans son travail futile. La souffrance, que l'Absurde et Inhumaine Décision exacerbe, le conduit finalement au-delà de l'immédiat. « Toute la joie silencieuse de Sisyphe est là. Son destin lui appartient. Son rocher est sa chose. » Il devient le maître de sa vie, comme il fut le maître de la Mort.

Il faut imaginer Sisyphe libre. Il n'appartient plus aux dieux puisque la punition qui se voulait aliénante se trouve être libératoire. Il a tué Dieu ou plus exactement, il s'est libéré de l'image-référence de Dieu. Ainsi le maître zen Lin-chi dit :

> « Si vous rencontrez le Bouddha, tuez-le ;
> si vous rencontrez le Patriarche, tuez-le ;
> Tuez-les tous sans hésitation,
> car ceci est l'unique voie de la délivrance.
> Ne vous laissez pas entraver par le moindre objet,
> mais dominez-le, passez et soyez libres. »

Ces paroles très violentes ont été prononcées pour mettre en garde de ne jamais confondre Dieu lui-même et la représentation de Dieu (même si celle-ci est parfois nécessaire pour commencer à faire le premier pas qui mène vers Lui). De même, dit encore Camus, l'homme absurde, quand il contemple le tourment, fait taire toutes ses idoles. C'est-à-dire qu'il n'accepte plus de placer sa conscience sous le joug d'un quelconque système de références et n'ayant plus aucun rapport avec quoi que ce soit qui montrerait un chemin, c'est donc en solitaire qu'il aborde le silence de la route.

C'est peut-être à ce prix ou à cette condition que l'homme accède à cette dimension supérieure de la conscience qui libère une part de vérité. Richard Byrd décrit cette perception intuitive qu'apporte l'illumination :

« ... L'unité de l'homme et de l'univers ne fit pour moi plus aucun doute... Ce que je ressentais transcendait ma raison, plongeait au cœur même de ce qui désespère l'homme et le laisse désemparé. (L'univers) cessait d'être un grand chaos. Et l'homme faisait partie de plein droit de ce cosmos, au même titre que le jour et la nuit. »

Lors de ces expériences de modification d'états de conscience par la méditation qui pousse hors des frontières limitatives de l'apparence, il semble que la conscience délivre d'une façon globale et indivisible la connaissance du Tout. Comme si le savoir résidait dans la conscience et qu'il surgissait, venant de « l'intérieur » mais cependant suggéré par une voie arrivant du dehors. Peut-on voir dans cette alchimie cosmique la consécration de l'union de l'homme et de l'Univers ?

Approche occidentale religieuse

Le caractère quasi obligatoire de faire sortir ses pensées du mode rationnel et émotionnel pour entrer dans le silence (absence de références) et la solitude qui en découle, semble être partagé par tous les ascètes, quelles que soient leur religion ou leur origine. Se libérer de toute concupiscence antécédente et conséquente, se libérer des faits et de leurs effets, est également une priorité et une condition nécessaire chez les ascètes chrétiens qui proposent depuis deux millénaires (!) une voie de purification très proche de celle des ascètes bouddhistes. Mais leur mouvement, leur marche vers la **rencontre avec la nature-de-Dieu** ont été masqués par le sectarisme des théologiens et des scientifiques.

En Occident, les scientifiques sortirent vainqueurs de cette rivalité et en jetant une ombre épaisse sur les expériences de méditation religieuse se sont, du même coup, privés d'une très riche source de connaissances sur la conscience humaine, et sans le moindre soupçon de regret, s'en vont chercher au Soleil-Levant ce qu'ils auraient pu trouver tout à côté. Voici d'ailleurs quelques citations relevées dans le livre de Georges Pégand, *Christianisme à cœur ouvert*, et qui sont, à mon avis, en parfaite relation avec ce que nous avons dit sur le Zen et avec ce que nous dirons sur le troisième degré de la Relaxation dynamique.

• « Un cheveu suffit à brouiller le regard, un simple souci à détruire la solitude **car la solitude est dépouillement des pensées et renoncement aux soucis raisonnables.** » (saint Jean Climaque.) *Il faudra se souvenir de cette phrase lorsque nous* *reparlerons du silence dans les exercices que nous ferons en Sophrologie.*

- « Il est indispensable, aussitôt que l'on se rend compte des pensées, de les retrancher sur-le-champ. » (Hésychius.)
- « Ne laisse jamais un objet sensible ou mental extérieur ou intérieur, s'inscrire ou se dessiner dans ton esprit. L'esprit a une faculté naturelle d'imagination et se **laisse aisément marquer par l'objet de ses désirs** chez ceux qui n'y prennent pas garde. Le souvenir même des objets marque le sens de l'esprit et le porte aux imaginations. **Il ne faut rien admettre avant que soit venue l'heure de l'apaisement** des passions. » (Grégoire le Sinaïte, † 1346.)

En actualisant les termes, ce sont des phrases dignes d'un traité moderne de Sophrologie et qui témoignent de l'extraordinaire connaissance intuitive des phénomènes neurophysiologiques de l'activité mentale que peut apporter une expérimentation méditative.

Si dans cette introduction au troisième degré de la Relaxation Dynamique nous avons cité certaines sources d'inspiration religieuse (orientale et occidentale) et philosophique, c'est uniquement pour tenter de montrer que l'état de conscience (ou état d'esprit) recherché dans cette démarche sophronique est universellement partagé et ceci depuis toujours et dans toutes les civilisations.

Mais cette quête de l'essentiel, au-delà des limites étroites des références sociales ou logiques, peut se faire en dehors de toute idée religieuse et de toute idéologie philosophique. Il est nécessaire que le lecteur comprenne qu'il n'est nul **besoin d'être un grand croyant ou un grand philosophe pour vivre pleinement ce qui est proposé lors de ces séances.** Alors tentons de faire ressortir de ce qui vient d'être dit les points intéressants dans cette attitude globale du troisième degré.

1° **Nécessité de faire taire les a priori.** Pour cela, dans la mesure du possible et quelle que soit la méthode, abolition des réflexes émotionnels et intellectuels.

2° L'état de méditation qui en résulte serait **une sorte d'attente,** humble et sereine, que le contact direct se produise, que la fusion se réalise. Cette attente, qui est une expérience qui ne peut être que personnelle, donc sans comparaison possible, est forcément **solitaire et silencieuse.**

3° Survient alors, parfois, l'Illumination, le Satori, l'Extase, l'Inspiration. Il y a présence de l'Autre, échange d'intimités. Le dialogue est intuitif, il se fait sans mot. C'est comme une stupéfaction, une sidération. Lisons Lao-tseu, cité par Jean-Pierre Hubert dans la *Relaxation Dynamique* :

> « On regarde mais sans voir on l'appelle Invisible
> On écoute sans entendre on l'appelle l'Inaudible
> On palpe sans atteindre on l'appelle Imperceptible
> Voilà trois choses inexplicables
> Qui confondues font l'Unité... »

Purification de l'être par la méditation (comme les ascètes chrétiens ou zen), dépassement de soi par une conscience transcendantale (comme Sisyphe heureux et libéré) ne sont pas les seuls chemins qui mènent à la rencontre. Pour ce voyage au-delà de l'image immédiate, une autre voie peut être proposée. Il ne faut pas s'en priver car elle est loin d'être mineure :

Approche universelle poétique

Il en est de même pour l'amour et la poésie : il y a, sinon des degrés, tout au moins des objets différents. On fait plus facilement cent pas pour l'amour d'un gâteau qu'un seul pour l'amour de Dieu. Mais ce seul pas mesure tout un chemin, celui qui mène à la rencontre. Laissons aussi de côté ces poèmes de cent vers, laborieusement assemblés et dont le seul souci est de bien faire rimer toujours avec amour, ils sont à la poésie ce que la rêvasserie est à la méditation : une grimace. Rêvasser et rimailler sont deux expressions d'un voyage, peut-être aux confins du vécu, mais qui reste toujours signifiant d'une référence intellectuelle ou émotionnelle.

Le poème est deux choses en même temps, une première chose secondaire et, secondairement, une autre chose première.

Le poème est une mémoire puis une attente.

Le poème est une mémoire, *la* mémoire vivante d'un événement. En ce sens, le poème n'a pas besoin de références pour exister : il *se* suffit à lui-même. Il commémore et, comme un sobre monument ou une discrète plaque, il en dit plus qu'un long discours. Mais il ne dit rien sur l'événement, et il s'y rattache, s'y reporte sans le rapporter. Il est dit que le poème est un jaillissement, « un pur jailli », une sorte d'éblouissement de la mémoire, de vertige de la mémoire au moment même où celle-ci bascule dans la non-mémoire, dans le non-encore-su. Alors le poème est solitaire. *Il ne peut être que solitaire.* Singulier (sans concupiscence antérieure). Et, au moment où il naît, au moment où il jaillit, *il ne peut être que silence* car il advient dans une apnée du souffle, du verbe, du langage et de la mémoire.

Le poète Paul Celan dit que « le poème est solitaire. Il est solitaire et en chemin. Celui qui l'écrit l'escorte jusqu'au bout. Par cela même, et dès maintenant, ne voit-on pas que le poème a lieu dans la rencontre, dans le secret de la rencontre ? Je pense que c'est depuis toujours une espérance du poème, de parler comme si c'était *au nom d'un autre*, qui sait, peut-être, **au nom d'un tout autre**... Le poème séjourne ou espère un mot qui renvoie à la créature. »

Un jour l'esprit, poussé, aspiré par je ne sais quoi, s'engage dans une impasse, bute quelques instants sur l'obstacle du vécu et soudain la dernière barrière vole en éclats. L'esprit part alors dans une aventure singulière. Au-delà des symboles et des mots, il est en chemin vers la rencontre avec tout autre chose, avec l'autrement-dit. Derrière la dernière porte qui cloisonnait l'esprit, se trouve le poème. Prêt à surgir, à la manière d'une goutte d'eau qui naît de la vapeur invisible. Il est déjà là, dans une rupture du langage, telle une pensée en suspens, en suspension dans l'air. Celan dit encore : « Le poème serait donc parole d'un seul ayant pris figure, présent et présence du plus intime de son être. »

Le poème est, secondairement, une autre chose. Il est une attente. Il va, peut-être, devenir parole d'un tout autre, d'un autre seul. Dans *La Poésie comme expérience*, Philippe Lacoue-Labarthe écrit :

« Telle est en somme la " solitude " du poème et ce qui l'oblige, [...] non pas à inventer un langage singulier où à constituer de toutes pièces un idiolecte, mais à **défaire** le langage (sémantiquement et syntaxiquement), à le désarticuler et à le raréfier, à le couper selon une prosodie qui n'est ni celle de la langue ni celle de la poésie antérieure, à le condenser, jusqu'à atteindre ce noyau dur, cette sourde résistance à quoi l'on reconnaît une voix singulière, c'est-à-dire départagée de la langue et du langage. »

Ceci se traduit par la nécessité de désorganiser les structures mentales préétablies (dont le langage et la syntaxe sont les principaux emblèmes) de façon à nous amener à être autrement. Non pas à penser autrement mais bien à vivre quelque chose d'autre avec une conscience qui s'éveille.

Jaillissant d'une énigme, le poème reste une énigme. Il ne dit rien, il ne révèle rien au passant sourd et aveugle. *Exactement comme une phrase du Koan!* C'est pour cela que le poème est une attente, l'attente d'une autre rencontre avec quelqu'un de tout à fait autre. Et à cette condition (pour répondre à la question posée par Celan lui-même) « le poème devient le poème de quelqu'un qui est en train – encore en train – de percevoir, qui est tourné vers ce qui est en train d'apparaître, et qui interroge cette apparition, lui adresse la parole; cela devient un dialogue ». Je pense que nous pouvons ajouter que, comme la vapeur invisible s'élève de la goutte d'eau, de ce dialogue jaillira une nouvelle pensée, une autre rencontre, un tout autre poème. Car ce dialogue, comme l'œuvre poétique qui l'alimente, est lui aussi singulier.

> Petit poème
> de Rien ne
> cherche pas à partir
> Il est en
> train de te faire
> sien.
>   Petit poème du non-dire
>   ne te dans l'éloquence
>   noie pas
>   il est en
>   train
>   – tes plus purs silences –
>   de lire.

Bien que, d'une certaine façon, la méditation poétique puisse libérer le regard et enrichir la conscience, certains trouveront qu'il manque à l'attitude ou à l'acte poétique (le poème) le support essentiel de la corporalité. Ou, en d'autres termes, que le poème et la poésie ne débouchent pas sur un autre mode de vie, sur une autre façon de conduire sa quotidienneté. Peut-être. Cependant, il faut dire, et redire encore, que le troisième degré n'est pas une copie conforme du Zen, mais (et justement parce qu'il est en Sophrologie) que ce troisième degré admet et même recherche toutes les formes qui convergent vers les mêmes effets : donner à l'esprit la possibilité d'escalader la montagne des obligations, de se soustraire aux repères de l'intellect et de l'émotionnel et de se retrouver solitaire et silencieux marchant à découvert sur le chemin qui conduit à la rencontre avec **la nature de soi-même.** Et qui, du moine zen, de l'ascète chrétien, de Sisyphe ou du poème ouvrira un authentique dialogue avec l'intéressé? Lui, et lui seul (parce que solitaire) peut prétendre répondre.

TROISIÈME DEGRÉ
DE LA RELAXATION DYNAMIQUE

Conscience en « lumière noire »
Etat modifié de la conscience :
la méditation

Venons-en maintenant à ce troisième degré qui représente le point culminant de l'évolution proposée par la Relaxation dynamique (mais non le point final !) et regardons ce vers quoi nous mènent les gestes, les postures et les différents exercices.

1. Debout devant un siège.
Les yeux fermés. La respiration se fait par le bas du ventre (la vessie). Au début, les mains sont croisées dans le dos puis elles sont croisées sur le bas du ventre. Les mains se soulèvent et s'abaissent au même rythme que la respiration. Si bien qu'au bout d'un moment on ne sait plus qui, des mains ou du ventre, respire. Le premier doute, la première incertitude apparaît. Peut-être voit-on arriver, déjà, les prémices d'un démantèlement de nos habitudes.

2. Assis.
Recherche d'une posture confortable de relaxation. Les yeux sont fermés, la relaxation s'approfondit. Ici, nous appliquons ce qui a été appris dès les premières sophronisations de base : le « *lâcher prise* » ou le « *laisser faire* ». Cette attitude qui s'éloigne des références sociales (qui réclament au

contraire du « maintien » pour ne pas se laisser aller!) est une entrée progressive dans la phase de méditation avec le corps. **Rencontre** avec le corps naturel, avec ce qu'il y a de naturel en nous.

3. Recherche de la posture dite automatique.

C'est une posture d'équilibre autour de la zone Hara qui devient le véritable centre du corps. Les mains posées l'une sur l'autre sont positionnées à ce niveau. Là, nous adoptons la *sophro-respiration synchronique* (inspiration-rétention – expiration-rétention). De par la relaxation, tout le haut du corps, et en particulier la tête, épouse le même rythme et nous vivons ce balancement lancinant, **en dehors de toute idée de temps.** Nous sommes en présence de l'essentiel de nous-même : notre respiration, notre corps, notre vie en relation avec la terre. Ainsi, doucement, les yeux s'entrouvrent, laissant filtrer un monde d'ombres et de lumières.

- « Les bruits sont là et je ne les entends plus;
- les odeurs sont là et je ne les ressens plus;
- les formes sont là et je ne les regarde plus.
- Je vais, au-delà du signifiant, à la recherche de la Réalité.
- Le monde, dont la présence est contemporaine à ma présence, n'est pas là pour être compréhensible ou émouvant.
- Il est là tout simplement parce qu'il offre son intimité et que je lui offre la mienne. » (Rencontre poétique.)

Comme le faisaient les premiers ascètes chrétiens, nous abandonnons nos concupiscences antécédentes et conséquentes et nous nous livrons à la méditation par la simple invocation du nom : **nature.** Chacun vivant cette alliance – dans cette alliance – entre la nature du monde intérieur et la nature du monde extérieur, balançant doucement. Comme si chaque mouvement de la tête, chaque mouvement respiratoire, traçait un trait d'union, allant d'une présence à l'autre, jusqu'à la communion totale et harmonieuse.

    Qu'advient-il alors? RIEN.

....

    Propos intimes et conventions qui réglementent les rapports entre les choses et les êtres sont de moins en moins convaincants. Les repères sont de plus en plus espacés, nous sommes **en chemin**, ce chemin est personnel, il est solitaire, il est silencieux. Il traverse « un espace sans ciel » et un « temps sans profondeur ». Le sophrologue-accompagnateur se tait alors. Aucune parole n'est souhaitable et n'est souhaitée par aucun des participants, la parole est trop référencée, elle est trop extérieure, trop descriptive et ne correspond pas à ce qui se passe, en ce moment, en chacun.

    Que se passe-t-il alors? RIEN.

....

    Le silence environnant, progressivement, induit le silence intérieur et ce silence fait naître le doute. Tous ces gens, ces choses autour de moi! Pourquoi? Pour qui? Le jugement s'éteint. Les causes et les effets ne trouvent plus d'arguments. Chaque élément semble figé dans un rapport immuable, je respire et tout respire ensemble, je vis et tout vit avec moi, en moi. Vibrations unanimes. De centre à centre. Plus de paramètres, rien ne paraît bouger. Instantané non mesurable. Harmonieuse quiétude. Doute : ces images dans ma tête, comme des braises qui se rallument soudain dans le feu endormi! Pourquoi? Respiration, lente respiration, sereine lenteur. Inquiétude : Rien ne bouge! Suis-je vraiment là? Tout est étrange pour moi et Moi paraît étranger. L'univers entier devient Je.

    Que suis-je alors? RIEN.

....

4. Position debout.

Les mains croisées devant, les épaules en arrière, la tête légèrement inclinée vers le bas. Les yeux toujours entrouverts. **La marche va commencer.** Bien supprimée depuis quelques années, elle garde, à mon sens, toute son importance et sa valeur.

Son rythme est calqué sur celui de la sophro-respiration synchronique. Inspiration-rétention/un pas en avant-expulsion. L'autre jambe vient terminer le mouvement. Repos. Puis, inspiration-rétention/on avance une jambe-expulsion, etc. Le silence est là. Ce fameux silence qui nous prive de repères.

Cette marche, au rythme de la respiration, au rythme de la vie, est fondamentale. Chaque pas est un Tout, une tranche de vie : c'est le rocher que Sisyphe hisse au sommet. L'expiration, la jambe qui vient rejoindre l'autre, le repos qui s'ensuit, ce temps du juste après, c'est encore Sisyphe qui redescend « *vers la tanière des dieux... * **C'est l'heure de la conscience. »... « De la conscience qui contemple cette suite d'actions sans liens qui devient son destin.** » La succession des pas, sans suite logique, sans avant et sans après, sans qu'on nous dise pourquoi, sans qu'on nous indique vers où, cette marche nous enferme... comme *l'oie dans la bouteille.* Alors nos alliés de toujours, notre cerveau et notre corps, viennent à notre rescousse.

C'est ainsi que la corticalité peut envoyer quelques images mentales en référence, histoire de nous rassurer un peu. Cela est normal, efforçons-nous simplement de les laisser sans signification; ignorons-les, elles s'éloigneront d'elles-mêmes.

C'est ainsi, également, que le corps, devant cette nouvelle façon d'être, devant cette manière d'Etre nouveau, peut opter pour un comportement standard (hypothalamique ou thalamique) comme la colère, la fuite pour signifier la révolte qui monte, ou l'ennui, le bâillement, la fatigue et la désynchronisation marche-respiration pour signifier le refus. Cela aussi est normal, mais sachons aller au-delà de ces manifestations; ignorons-les, elles s'estomperont d'elles-mêmes. Et, toujours, souvenons-nous de la phrase du maître zen : « **Continue d'avancer, c'est la devise de la vie** ».

5. La marche se termine.

Chacun retrouve son siège et, les yeux fermés, termine la séance par une attitude contemplative, similaire à celle du deuxième degré afin de reprendre son image et ses références : conscience éclairante qui regarde du dehors.

Dans les groupes que j'accompagne et suivant mon intuition, je dirige le discours de façon à ce que chacun récupère sa corporalité et ses références : conscience éclairée (du premier degré) qui regarde en dedans. Ainsi la totalité de la personnalité est présente, ce qui me paraît primordial après un troisième particulièrement « destructurant ». Comme après tout travail en Sophrologie, la conscience garde une trace de ce qui a été vécu, phénoménologiquement vécu.

6. Deuxième partie du troisième degré (autre séance).

Assis, les mains croisées au niveau de la zone Hara. La relaxation musculaire est maintenant totale, le corps devient de moins en moins « présent » et le sujet est amené à méditer à partir de thèmes généraux : **énergie, vie, nature, cosmos, silence.**

Dans le silence. Le temps, qui a perdu sa mesure, ne compte plus. Le lieu, qui a perdu ses repères, ne limite plus. Chaque participant fait son chemin en solitaire, en toute simplicité, en toute humilité et en toute sérénité.

Il ne faut jamais, avant une séance en méditation, vouloir aller à la recherche de « vécus extraordinaires », il ne faut rien demander à la méditation. L'intention tue l'acte méditatif de conscience. De même, chaque séance ne conduit pas obligatoirement vers une rencontre, vers un contact direct avec la réalité. Rappelons-nous le poème de Tagore :

> « De l'aube au crépuscule, je reste devant ma porte;
> je sais que soudain l'heureux moment viendra
> [où je verrai.
> Cependant je souris et je chante, tout solitaire. »

Et aussi :

> « Mon chant a dépouillé ses parures.
> Je n'y mets plus d'orgueil!
> Les ornements gêneraient notre union. »

Je pense que le lecteur peut maintenant faire de ce poème une bonne lecture et comprendre que :

- « de l'aube au crépuscule » montre que le temps ne se mesure plus;
- « Je reste devant ma porte » est représenté, dans nos exercices, par la mise en relaxation physique et mentale et la mise en réserve de nos structures organisées;
- « soudain » rappelle le Satori, le jaillissement du poème, etc.;
- « dépouillé ses parures... plus d'orgueil... » incite à abandonner le système de représentation car « tout ornement » intellectuel ou émotionnel dénature la nature de l'Union.

Après ce type de séance très méditative, nous devons toujours retrouver la réalité de notre vie et, dans la banalité des gestes et des rapports interindividuels, voir une autre qualité de vie, une autre manière de vivre, avec un regard dépouillé des « ornements » futiles et gênants qui manquaient de sincérité. C'est dans ce but que chacun peut alors, librement se lever, se promener dans la pièce, parler à ses voisins en prenant conscience de l'harmonie entre les personnalités présentes, de l'énergie qui anime et qui réunit. Sincérité et authenticité des pensées et des sentiments, énergie et dynamisme dans le calme et la sérénité, meilleure compréhension de soi et des autres sont les plus grandes qualités qui colorent une conscience enrichie et renforcée par l'expérience sophronique.

Mise en garde et mise au point

Une mise en garde tout simplement pour dire que ce troisième degré ne doit pas être fait à n'importe qui et n'importe quand. Il est la suite et la conclusion des deux premiers degrés. Un certain travail d'évolution échelonné sur plusieurs mois, voire sur plusieurs années, est à mon avis indispensable pour bien intégrer et comprendre cette démarche particulière de la conscience. Il faut aussi, mais cette condition est souvent remplie, que le sophrologue qui dirige les séances soit lui-même rompu à ce genre d'exercice.

Une mise au point pour répondre à la question que le lecteur non averti est en droit de se poser : A quoi cela sert-il ? Quel est le but de cette attitude mentale ou de cet état de conscience ? Il est difficile de donner une traduction concrète, se retrouvant dans la pratique du quotidien, de ce que peut amener le troisième degré de la Relaxation dynamique.

Nous pouvons tout de même signaler un changement d'état d'esprit dans la façon de voir les choses et d'appréhender un problème. Le fait d'avoir su remettre en question certaines de nos certitudes agissantes permet maintenant de pouvoir faire « table rase » et de redéfinir de nouvelles bases de réflexion face à un problème, de savoir reconsidérer l'ensemble des éléments présents et de les réintégrer dans un autre système de références peut-être plus nouveau. En fait, nous pourrions parler d'esprit novateur et dynamique, un esprit qui ne se contente pas de ce qui est admis comme étant immuable mais qui, au contraire, a la possibilité d'envisager une solution de changement ou d'évolution.

Ainsi se termine (ou se terminait) la Relaxation dynamique de Caycedo. Avec ses trois degrés, degrés dont nous allons reprendre succinctement les points essentiels pour mettre en évidence l'évolution qu'ils permettent.

- Premier degré.

Symbole du Carré. Corporalité. Instinctivo-moteur.
Concentration. « JE » est vu « du dedans ». Corporalisation.
Harmonisation. Lever les « barrières » internes.
Volonté. Pulsions.

- Deuxième degré.

Symbole de la Croix. Corporalité. Affectivo-moteur.
Contemplation. « JE » est vu « du dehors ». Décorporalisation.
Harmonisation. Dynamique de **ma** vie.
Volonté. Désir. Sentiment.

- Troisième degré.

Symbole du Cercle. Non-corporalité. Eidéolo-moteur.
Méditation. « JE » devient l'Univers.
Harmonisation. Dynamique de **la** Vie.
Volonté. Libération.

Nous en étions là, il y a quelques mois. Et chaque sophrologue trouvait, selon les circonstances et sa propre sensibilité, une suite à ces trois degrés. Aujourd'hui, le quatrième degré existe « officiellement ».

Il serait inconvenant de parler de ce trop neuf quatrième degré : nous manquons d'expérience et de recul. Cependant, quelques points essentiels, à mes yeux, peuvent déjà être soulignés.

Après cette évolution et cette connaissance extraordinaires que nous apportent les trois premiers degrés, il nous faut maintenant apprendre à intégrer dans notre vie quotidienne les différentes expérimentations vécues. Si le maître zen peut chanter :

> Quelle merveille surnaturelle !
> Et quel miracle que ceci !
> Je tire l'eau, je porte le bois !

pouvons-nous en dire autant ? Pouvons-nous vivre, en plein XXe siècle, en ascètes ? Pouvons-nous nous écrier, tout joyeux :

> Quelle merveille surnaturelle !
> Et quel miracle que ceci !
> *Je prends le métro, je paie des impôts !*

Peut-être que, finalement, nous sommes plus près de Sisyphe et que ce quatrième degré, qui nous voit redescendre « vers la tanière des dieux », nous *surprend* à être heureux !

Depuis le début du chemin, notre regard a changé. Il s'est dépouillé. Nos anciennes références, même si elles n'ont pas toutes disparu, se sont mieux « échelonnées ». Notre conscience a appris à se diriger vers l'essentiel. En suant, peinant, souffrant, pleurant et criant à rouler notre rocher quotidien, sans vraiment rien comprendre à notre supplice, notre conscience sait que *acceptation* ne veut pas dire *soumission*.

L'Homme **debout, entre ciel et terre,** harmonisé dans son Carré, sa Croix et son Cercle, est en marche vers son devenir. Et cette marche sur terre, dans sa vie et malgré les « pierres du chemin », malgré les chagrins, malgré le ciel qui gronde, c'est le quatrième degré de la Relaxation Dynamique de Caycedo.

IL FAUT IMAGINER L'HOMME LIBRE

CINQUIÈME CHAPITRE

LES STRUCTURES MENTALES

**La conscience de base
La suggestion
Le cerveau, siège de la conscience ?**

LA CONSCIENCE DE BASE

Dans l'histoire qui suit, nous allons mettre en place une situation romanesque et mettre en scène des personnages puis les laisser vivre en regardant les différentes attitudes réactionnelles. Nous essaierons ensuite d'analyser les comportements respectifs et de comprendre pourquoi et comment ces individus ont « fonctionné ».

Histoire du château abandonné
ou « Les cauchemars d'un promeneur solitaire! »

Première partie
Il était une fois... sur les hauteurs d'un village du centre de la France, un château abandonné, inhabité depuis fort longtemps, depuis que le dernier occupant, un vieux monsieur un peu fou, y avait trouvé la mort dans des circonstances très mystérieuses. Les gens du village affirmaient que parfois des bruits insolites venaient de là-bas. Surtout certaines nuits de pleine lune. Comme des hurlements, des cris inhumains! Cela durait depuis bientôt vingt ans. Jamais personne n'osait s'aventurer trop près de cet endroit sinistre. Les herbes sauvages envahissaient le parc et quand le vent soufflait, on pouvait entendre de loin les volets grincer... comme s'ils gémissaient. Ces plaintes lugubres duraient ensuite pendant des heures et tout bruit cessait au petit matin. La rumeur prétendait même que ceux qui avaient osé approcher ce château étaient morts dans l'année qui suivait,

victimes du mauvais sort qui protégeait cette ancienne demeure.

Un jour, un homme a entendu cette légende. C'était un promeneur, un étranger, attablé à la terrasse du seul café du village. « Comment de telles histoires peuvent-elles être racontées, au xxe siècle ! » Il a haussé les épaules, a payé et est parti.

Deuxième partie

A quelque temps de là, notre promeneur part en randonnée. Durant des heures il marche, insouciant et admirant la campagne environnante. Son esprit et son corps sont en parfaite harmonie avec la nature. Il se sent bien, alors il marche et marche encore. Mais tous ces chemins creux, qui sentent si bon, se ressemblent tellement ! Ils ont l'air de mener tous au même endroit, de ne mener nulle part ! La nuit arrive vite et notre héros est maintenant quelque peu inquiet. Où se trouve le village ? Et, en plus, ces gros nuages qui arrivent, si menaçants, poussés par un vent fort... « Un vent d'orage » avaient prédit tout à l'heure les paysans !

L'inquiétude est de plus en plus grande. Passer la nuit dehors, sans abri, sous la pluie battante ! La campagne lui semble soudain moins belle, moins accueillante. Un peu hostile même ! Il accélère alors le pas, trébuchant et pestant contre ces cailloux et ces ronces qui l'entravent. Après maints détours, il se retrouve, tout à coup, devant le château ! Il s'en approche lentement, traverse le parc et avant d'entrer, hésite... Toutes ces histoires lugubres racontées l'autre jour ! Il regarde autour de lui et aperçoit au loin, avec un certain soulagement, une silhouette qu'il croit reconnaître. Il court à la rencontre de cet homme, fait de grands gestes pour attirer son attention. « Oh ! s'il vous plaît, attendez-moi ! Où se trouve le village ? » Mais l'autre accélère ses pas et s'éloigne de plus en plus. « Curieux, tout de même, pourquoi part-il aussi vite ? Je suis sûr qu'il m'a vu ! Pourquoi ne s'est-il pas arrêté ? » Notre promeneur se sent bien isolé soudain et le vent qui souffle de plus en plus fort le fait frissonner. Mais il se raisonne. « Des balivernes, des sottises, cet endroit est inhabité depuis longtemps et il n'y a vraiment rien à craindre », pense-t-il tout haut en poussant la porte qui battait sous l'effet du vent d'orage qui redoublait de violence.

Troisième partie
Notre héros, bien malgré lui, se trouve maintenant à l'intérieur de cette vieille demeure. Soulagé de pouvoir s'abriter pendant l'averse mais tout de même quelque peu inquiet, mal à l'aise.

Autour de lui, le silence ! Seulement troublé par les bruits de son cœur qui, décidément, bat de plus en plus fort. Tout son être est tendu. Il est aux aguets, c'est plus fort que lui. Tous ses sens sont mobilisés, tel un animal traqué. Il écarquille les yeux pour tenter de discerner, dans l'obscurité, ce qui l'entoure. Rien. Rien que des vieux meubles poussiéreux et sans valeur et quelques caisses en bois laissées là, il y a bien longtemps. Alors il tend l'oreille pour tenter de discerner, dans le silence pesant, une présence quelconque. Pour essayer d'entendre autre chose que les battements de son cœur dans la poitrine... Rien. Soudain un bruit bizarre le fait sursauter, une sorte de miaulement sinistre ! Surpris, il fait un bond en arrière, tombe sur une vieille caisse en bois, se relève brutalement... Guettant le danger, serrant dans ses mains son bâton de marche comme s'il s'agissait d'une arme... Sa respiration est rapide, saccadée, haletante !

Brusquement il prend une décision : il se dit que finalement le village n'est sûrement pas bien loin. Il se dit qu'en prenant la direction de cet homme qui n'a pas voulu l'attendre, tout à l'heure... qu'en courant vite, très vite... qu'en coupant à travers les champs! Abandonnant son bâton sur place, le voilà courant, dévalant la pente, sautant les buissons, courbant la tête à chaque éclair...

Quatrième partie

Essoufflé, ruisselant, notre pauvre promeneur arrive enfin au village et gagne sa chambre d'hôtel. Là, épuisé, il s'écroule sur son lit pour reprendre un peu son souffle et ses esprits.

Plus tard, bien plus tard dans la nuit, il s'aperçoit que sa jambe droite a saigné. « J'ai dû me blesser avec une branche en courant ou en tombant, tout à l'heure, là-bas... »

En évoquant toutes ces images, il frissonne. Sans trop savoir pourquoi, il se laisse aller à penser à son enfance. Quand sa mère, pour l'endormir, lui racontait des histoires. Puis, bercé par ces souvenirs lointains, notre héros, fatigué, ferme les yeux et s'endort. Mais son sommeil est agité et ses rêves troublés.

Cette petite histoire est terminée. Arrêtons de trembler et analysons ce qui s'est passé dans la tête de notre triste héros.

Dans la première partie :

Cet homme a entendu, par hasard, l'incroyable histoire de ce château abandonné. A son insu, certaines images stockées ont refait surface. On pourrait dire, comme en informatique, que ces images se sont placées en « mémoire vive ».

En effet, dès le plus jeune âge, au moment où ils sont le plus vulnérables, le plus influençables, tous les enfants ont leur imagination nourrie d'histoires analogues. Avec des châteaux hantés, des sorcières méchantes et des fantômes en tout genre, avec, en plus, des frissons d'horreur, des peurs et des angoisses, sans parler des vampires et des cimetières habités. Toutes ces images avec leur cortège de sensations évoquées ont été stockées quelque part dans la mémoire. **Ces images mentales avec leurs émotions associées sont prêtes à resurgir un jour et à placer notre conscience dans un état modifié.** C'est ce qui va se passer chez cet homme. C'est ce qui se passe chez chacun de nous, à tout instant. Nous y reviendrons largement tout au long de ce livre.

D'ores et déjà quelques renseignements concernant l'activité mentale peuvent être notés : le cerveau possède une formidable capacité d'imagination, c'est-à-dire de création d'images; ces images mentales ainsi créées vont être :

1° Stockées dans une mémoire à long terme.

2° Associées à toute la situation, vécue ou suggérée.

3° Associées à toutes les manifestations corporelles présentes.

Dans la deuxième partie :

Le capital confiance, l'insouciance du promeneur se dégradent progressivement. Au début de la randonnée, il était sensible aux suggestions de calme et de paix de l'environnement. Progressivement, les informations seront traitées et analysées différemment. La nature, qui n'a pourtant pas réellement changé, est vue comme hostile, stressante. L'orage qui menace a également une part dans ce début de panique. Arrivé devant le château abandonné, les images mentales anciennes, qui ont été en quelque sorte « mises sous tension », vont resurgir brutalement. Elles vont devenir présentes, plausibles et mettre la conscience du sujet en *état d'alerte*.

Le comportement modifié de ce promeneur nous montre que :

1° Confrontées à une réalité analogue, les images mentales sont actualisées, « mises en mémoire vive ».

2° Il peut suffire qu'un seul élément soit présent (le château) pour qu'aussitôt *toute* l'émotion réapparaisse, dans sa globalité, confuse mais envahissante.

3° Le raisonnement logique est inefficace pour calmer le trouble qui se développe dans le « monde intérieur » fait d'affectivité et non de rationalité.

L'attitude de l'homme qui n'a pas voulu s'arrêter est elle aussi intéressante. Ce personnage, qui visiblement connaît le chemin et qui est donc un habitant du village, obéit à un phénomène bien connu en psychologie qui est une **attitude d'évitement.** Ce mode de fonctionnement consiste à « se voiler la face », ou à pratiquer la « politique de l'autruche » devant une situation difficile à vivre. Evidemment, cette façon d'éviter l'obstacle et non de l'affronter avec courage ne résout en rien les problèmes qui subsistent toujours et qui peuvent réapparaître à tout moment, sous une forme ou une autre !

Dans la troisième partie :

Notre pauvre héros est maintenant complètement dépassé par la situation. Il semble être à côté de la réalité. Son état de conscience est modifié. Il vit pleinement dans l'ambiance des images mentales et son comportement obéit plus à ces images qu'à la situation réelle. Les réponses de l'organisme ne sont que les réactions associées à ces images : le cœur bat plus vite, la respiration est saccadée, haletante...

Tout se passe comme s'il y avait un véritable danger, et ces manifestations corporelles vont très vite devenir la preuve « objective » de la peur vécue maintenant comme réelle. De nouveaux enseignements sont à tirer de cette aventure :

1° Une fois les images mentales installées, il devient de plus en plus difficile de discerner la réalité de la fiction.

2° Le comportement général est tout entier sous la dépendance de cet état de conscience modifié.

3° Les capacités de perception, d'analyse des informations, sont altérées et les sensations sont reçues avec un a priori en conformité avec le seul « vécu mental ».

4° Tout contrôle de la situation échappe et le sujet agit comme « envoûté ».

Dans la quatrième partie :

Nous assistons à la mise en place d'une véritable anesthésie de la jambe droite. Tellement occupée, focalisée dans cette urgence de s'enfuir, la conscience n'a pas enregistré les sensations de la blessure, pourtant bien réelle. La douleur n'a pas été ressentie parce que autre chose était plus important à ce moment-là. Dans d'autres circonstances la douleur aurait été perçue, car la souffrance des tissus organiques a été vraie, l'excitation des terminaisons nerveuses s'est bien produite !

Ceci montre bien la possibilité pour notre cerveau de modifier le contenu d'une sensation, c'est-à-dire d'en modifier la perception :

– le bruit d'un volet qui grince est interprété comme un miaulement ;
– la sensation d'une blessure douloureuse n'est plus perçue !

Pourquoi ne pas penser que cette possibilité peut devenir une capacité contrôlable ?

Avant d'en finir tout à fait avec cette histoire de château abandonné, il faut ajouter un détail, qu'ignore toujours notre homme. Cette même nuit, dans la vieille demeure, un autre promeneur dormait. Il venait d'un autre village et n'avait jamais entendu d'histoires sinistres sur ce château. Egalement surpris par la pluie, il avait tout simplement poussé la porte principale et constaté que l'endroit était inoccupé. Exténué par une belle et grande randonnée à travers la campagne, il s'était endormi tranquillement en laissant passer l'orage.

Cette histoire caricaturale a pour seul but de montrer la manière dont un individu peut réagir lorsqu'il se trouve confronté à un événement. Le cerveau a à sa disposition, pour porter un jugement ou une appréciation, une somme d'expériences emmagasinées dans ses structures. C'est le contenu de cette mémoire qui détermine l'individualité (Carré + Croix + Cercle). Tentons de comprendre comment nous « fonctionnons », nous, êtres humains avec nos souvenirs, nos idées et nos angoisses, avec nos émotions et nos sentiments.

Une des premières affirmations que nous pouvons formuler sans risque d'erreur est que l'homme est en **perpétuelle réaction, en constante adaptation.** Chacun vit « au milieu », il est le centre de son environnement dont il reçoit une multitude d'informations. Que le système soit hostile ou clément, naturel ou social, le bombardement est incessant. A chaque stimulation, la globalité de son être est engagée (Carré, Croix et même parfois le Cercle). Une réponse est alors fournie, réponse plus ou moins violente, plus ou moins consciente mais toujours mémorisée. Cette constatation nous amène à la deuxième affirmation, l'homme est en **constant apprentissage.** Cet apprentissage est influencé par deux types d'expériences.

L'influence des situations vécues

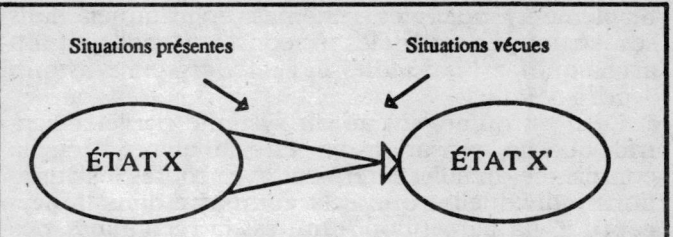

Entre l'état X et l'état X', une certaine modification s'est opérée, due aux traces laissées par la situation vécue. Ces expériences dynamiques tendent vers une spécificité de chaque être vivant et conscient, spécificité d'autant plus grande que la nature même de cette trace va dépendre de l'état X initial. Référence est faite ici à l'importance de la mémoire archaïque et de la mémoire héréditaire (empreintes de la civilisation et de la culture).

Il serait bien hors de propos ici d'entrer dans les détails des théories neurophysiologiques relatives à la transmission de l'influx nerveux. Schématiquement, disons que nous entrons en contact avec les éléments qui nous entourent par l'intermédiaire des récepteurs sensitifs.

Le monde ne nous apparaît que par les sensations qu'il nous procure. Réceptionnée au niveau de la périphérie, la sensation chemine le long des voies nerveuses sollicitées jusqu'à certains centres spécialisés du cerveau. Ce processus afférent (vers les centres) est le reflet d'une activité physicochimique et, bien que cela ne soit que partiellement exact, nous pouvons admettre qu'à ce stade la sensation est neutre. La notion de neutralité de l'information est théorique car dans les faits il faudrait imaginer une stimulation entièrement nouvelle pour l'individu et un individu sans passé, sans histoire personnelle ou sans mémoire! Ce qui ne peut se produire que dans de rares cas pathologiques ou chez le nouveau-né, encore que celui-ci ait déjà une expérience à la naissance de par **sa propre vie in utero** avec en plus, vraisemblablement, quelques schémas engrammés dans ses structures mentales (inconscient collectif ou archaïque) : *l'individu, dès sa naissance est un « fait social »*.

Ce n'est qu'au niveau du système nerveux central que la sensation va être analysée. Ici, la conscience du sujet intervient avec toutes les variations individuelles que cela comporte dans la **perception**. La perception – qui est la reconnaissance secondaire de l'information – donne une note qualitative et quantitative à la sensation. Grâce à ces centres intégrateurs, nous allons pouvoir dire que la sensation de départ est agréable ou pas, bienfaisante ou nocive. Par exemple, si nous donnons à chaque personne d'un groupe une tranche de citron à sucer, certaines vont la savourer avec plaisir, d'autres vont faire des grimaces. La sensation acide du citron est goûtée, analysée grâce au processus de référence. Ces références appartenant au passé individuel, culturel ou collectif, le résultat de l'analyse, donc le comportement, sera lui aussi individualisé.

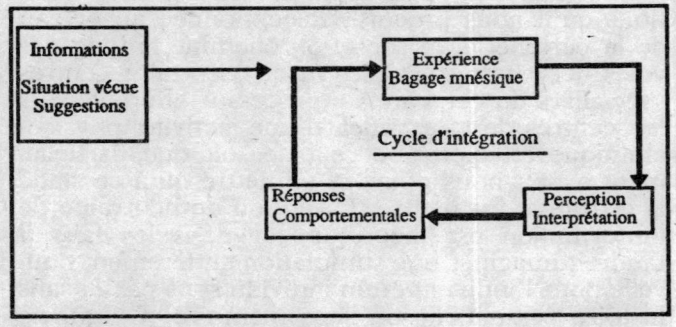

Dans nos expériences quotidiennes, ces deux étapes – sensation, perception – sont confondues en un seul et même temps d'appréciation et la stimulation reçue est immédiatement perçue (analysée) sans perte de temps notable et acquiert d'emblée une valeur. L'analyse de la sensation, très subtile, très fine (c'est un modèle du genre!), porte essentiellement sur les modifications organiques occasionnées par la stimulation qui, elles-mêmes, sont souvent en étroite relation avec l'état mental initial.

Les structures mentales ont une extraordinaire capacité de mémorisation dont il faut bien comprendre toutes les conséquences. Quand une situation se présente, elle est formée d'un événement principal et de plusieurs éléments secondaires dont la présence peut échapper sur le moment à notre perception consciente... mais ils sont tout de même pris en mémoire. Ceux-ci, et surtout s'ils ont suscité une émotion forte (positive ou négative), pourront être rattachés à certains autres éléments précédant l'événement; considérés comme « facteur déclenchant », ils interviendront à ce titre dans l'expérience globale. Nous pouvons ainsi résumer ces notions par cette équation :

$S = (a + b + c + d) + E + (f + g + h + ...$ etc.$) + R$

S représente la situation globale mémorisée.
$(a + b + c + d)$ l'ensemble des éléments précurseurs.
E représente l'élément principal.
$(f + g + h + ...)$ l'ensemble des éléments secondaires.
R représente la réponse fournie (réaction comportementale).

Prenons un exemple concret : le cas d'une personne hospitalisée à la suite d'un accident de ski.
L'événement principal E est l'hospitalisation et

prendra donc, dans la mémoire, une place privilégiée. Le vécu au niveau du corps (douleur, inconfort, immobilité provisoire, etc.) comme le vécu au niveau psychologique (angoisse, douleur, perte de temps, projets immédiats contrariés...) seront directement associés à l'élément principal (E + R). Dans l'avenir, toute situation ayant un rapport avec un hôpital sera analysée en référence à ce souvenir précis avec la probabilité de voir le retour des réactions R. La relation de cause à effet, dans ce cas, est évidente.

Mais ce qui l'est moins, c'est qu'ont été associés également des éléments comme, par exemple, l'endroit où s'est passé l'accident, le temps qu'il faisait ce jour-là ou peut-être même la tenue de ski ou la morphologie du skieur responsable! Cette multitude de petits souvenirs, pas toujours formulés, peuvent à eux seuls faire renaître, un jour, au hasard d'une similitude de faits, une sorte de malaise non expliqué. Nous connaissons tous, dans notre entourage, des gens qui ne veulent plus retourner à tel ou tel endroit parce qu'un jour...! En fait, ils ont peur d'être en situation de revivre, par images mentales interposées, de mauvais souvenirs.

Par cette mécanique mentale pourraient être vraisemblablement expliquées certaines attirances ou certaines répulsions (sympathie – antipathie) pour des personnages, sans raison apparente. Tout se passerait un peu comme si l'ensemble psychomorphologique du protagoniste était référencé, à notre insu, au niveau des couches profondes de la conscience, à quelque chose, déjà en mémoire, que nous avons vécu comme positif ou négatif.

Egalement, à cet ensemble E + R ont été reliées d'autres sensations présentes au moment de l'événement principal. Ces différents éléments concomitants, même s'ils n'ont pas été pris en compte consciemment, participent à l'élaboration de l'image mentale globale et, à ce titre, seront individuellement associés aux réactions. Ceci est d'autant plus important que cette relation échappe elle aussi à la compréhension consciente, au filtre de la logique, mettant directement en réaction l'image d'un objet et sa signification subjective avec le corps végétatif. (La « vision » globale d'une image ou d'une situation est la particularité fonctionnelle du « cerveau droit » qui en donne un jugement intuitif.)

C'est ainsi que, dans l'exemple choisi, l'expérience de l'hospitalisation s'étendra et englobera « les blouses blanches », les longs couloirs où « résonnent les pas rapides des soignants », le bruit métallique des instruments, la vue d'une seringue, l'odeur des produits désinfectants, etc. La liste est évidemment très longue et le chemin qui conduit à la mémorisation inconsciente de tel ou tel souvenir et surtout au rappel de certains d'entre eux qui paraissent pourtant moins importants que d'autres (à des regards extérieurs) est mystérieux car il relève du même processus général de choix selon des critères individuels. En effet, le pseudo-choix de retenir un élément particulier dans un ensemble donné est, bien entendu, conditionné par les expériences antérieures.

Quoi qu'il en soit, la situation vécue au travers des images mentales préexistantes, et objectivée par les réactions organiques ressenties, va se traduire dans les structures mentales et dans le souvenir par de nouvelles images, une nouvelle mise en scène de notre entité psycho-physique (comportement). Cette image de soi en réaction se loge dans nos schémas intrinsèques pour les modifier ou les renforcer. Il peut suffire parfois qu'un seul de ces éléments évocateurs (même accessoire) réapparaisse pour que tout le cortège des sensations refasse surface. Toutes les combinaisons sont possibles et certaines peuvent aboutir à des « associations d'idées » souvent déroutantes.

L'attitude affichée est dite déraisonnable, c'est-à-dire qu'elle échappe à la raison, qu'elle est hermétique au raisonnement. Avec son intelligence, le sujet sait parfaitement que, par exemple, la piqûre est tout à fait supportable. Il sait que son médecin va tout faire – et bien faire – pour éviter la douleur, il sait que c'est pour son bien et pour le soulager que cet acte est réalisé, mais... mais... « c'est plus fort que moi, je ne peux me contrôler... ». Les thérapeutes connaissent bien ces phrases pour les avoir souvent entendues dans leur cabinet. Il est vraiment tout à fait singulier de voir à quel point le contrôle de la situation échappe à certains patients : ils en sont bien conscients mais avouent qu'ils ne peuvent rien faire ! Oui, leurs images mentales sont, à ce moment, plus fortes que leur volonté !

Le stockage des informations analysées constitue le bagage mnésique, une véritable banque de données, servant de référence aux jugements à porter sur une nouvelle situation. Ces connaissances semblent se fixer dans les structures nerveuses du cerveau sous forme de **graphes** ou **assemblées neuronales** ayant chacun des fonctions spécifiques. Nous verrons plus loin que Jean-Pierre Changeux explique que ces graphes peuvent s'organiser en images mentales par l'évocation autogène ou hétérogène.

Comme une glande peut fabriquer et sécréter une substance chimique, les structures mentales fabriquent et « sécrètent » des images mentales. Cette sécrétion déclenche un état de conscience modifié qui engendre à son tour une réponse objectivée par l'attitude comportementale adaptée non pas à la situation réelle mais à l'idée que l'on s'en fait, c'est-à-dire aux images mentales qui s'imposent. A un moment de la vie, nous avons tous été en présence de ces images mentales quelque peu envahissantes et incontrôlées. Nous avons vécu ce phénomène profond, comme si quelque chose soudain échappait à notre contrôle (« indépendant de notre volonté ») et semblait s'imposer à nous, souvent contre toute attente ou contre toute logique. Comme le promeneur solitaire à l'entrée du château abandonné, nous perdons la vision objective et raisonnée de la situation. Impressions sourdes et idées confuses... toute tentative de rationalisation est vouée à l'échec car les mots n'appartiennent pas au même monde ! Expression de notre subconscient, réveillées et stimulées par l'événement à vivre, ces images mentales dépassent et défient l'entendement.

Les exemples choisis ont trop montré le côté négatif de ce mode de fonctionnement. Il me faut rétablir un certain équilibre et préciser qu'il est également responsable de notre capacité d'adaptation au milieu naturel et culturel. Grâce à cette particularité, nous sommes capables de comprendre, d'agir et de réagir par des actions.

En donnant à l'individu la possibilité de rêver puis de créer selon son imagination, les images mentales sont incontestablement le carburant du moteur psychique.

Et si parfois elles font naître la peur ou l'angoisse, elles sont aussi à l'origine de l'envie et du désir qui poussent vers demain. Elles sont des repères placés sur la route déjà faite et des formes de projets sur le chemin à faire. Elles dessinent le parcours à vivre et montrent les buts à atteindre dans le devenir.

Dans l'interprétation d'une situation, plusieurs paramètres rentrent en jeu. L'un de ceux-ci est le **système sensoriel préférentiel.** C'est-à-dire par quel sens prioritaire l'événement va-t-il être appréhendé ? Certains sujets sont plutôt des visuels, d'autres des auditifs, d'autres des intuitifs (privilégiant le senti intérieur), etc. Ils prendront ainsi des éléments de la situation qui entrent en interaction avec leur système sensoriel et rejetteront ceux qu'ils ont plus de mal à intégrer.

Le processus de représentation qui préside à la libération d'images mentales spécifiques influence

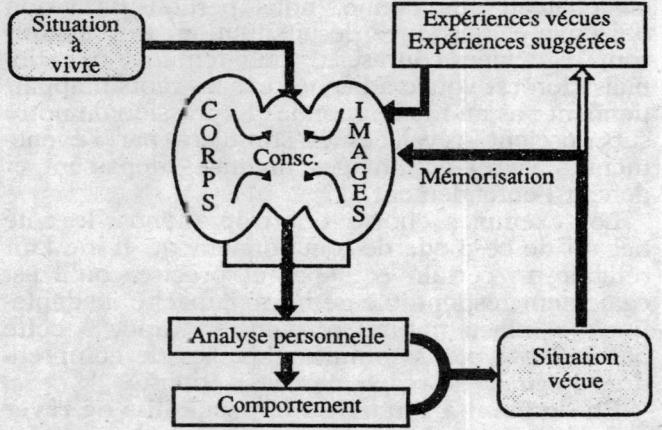

Mécanisme interne de la perception transformant par analyse (consciente ou non) une "situation à vivre" en "situation vécue".

inévitablement l'analyse de la situation (par le choix des stimuli) et donc le comportement global qui en résulte.

Un autre paramètre est celui de la **tendance motrice.** Nous savons maintenant que l'être humain est un ensemble de trois plans, le Carré (instinctivo-moteur), la Croix (affectivo-moteur) et le Cercle (eidéolo-moteur). Au moins deux de ces trois composantes (Carré et Croix) participent et réagissent à l'événement. Mais souvent, l'une d'entre elles est prédominante et sa réaction prend le pas et s'impose. Les sensations corporelles engendrées orientent également le vécu. Si la situation est génératrice de douleur ou de peur ou d'angoisse, l'instinctivo-moteur dictera le comportement, le jugement porté et la mémorisation qui suit n'auront pas la même valeur que si le chagrin, le désespoir ou la joie prédomine.

Chaque individu a une tendance motrice qui conditionne son regard. Par exemple, au moment d'un examen ou d'un concours. Certains engageront dans cette épreuve tout leur instinctivo-moteur; ils parleront alors de « lutte sans pitié pour s'en sortir » et par cette vision des choses ils donneront une dimension de survie (dans la jungle sociale), renieront « père et mère », amis et camarades. D'autres seront plus sensibles à la résonance affective, anxieux pour leur avenir, auront tout de même « à cœur » de réussir, voire d'offrir leur réussite à ceux qui les ont aidés. Il apparaît clairement que l'événement examen prendra une connotation fondamentalement différente pour ces deux types d'individus et que l'approche qu'ils en ont influencera l'analyse personnelle et l'attitude réactionnelle.

Un autre facteur intervient dans la perception, c'est la **prédominance hémisphérique.** Nous verrons en détail dans un chapitre ultérieur que le cerveau comprend deux hémisphères, un droit et un gauche. Chacun a une particularité fonctionnelle. Leurs actions réciproques ne sont pas toujours en synergie et nous aurons alors un côté dominant. D'une façon générale, il est admis que le « cerveau gauche » comprend de la situation l'aspect logique, analytique et verbalisé alors que le « cerveau droit » donne la priorité à la globalité, l'irrationnel et l'intuitif. Le type cerveau gauche sera, par exemple, moins sensible à l'ambiance d'un événement et consacrera plus d'intérêt à ce qui est dit ou fait. En revanche, un cerveau droit va accorder plus d'importance à ce qu'il ressent et laissera au second plan les éléments plus pratiques ou plus méthodiques. Bien sûr, le vécu d'une même situation de départ sera, *finalement*, très différent.

Analyse personnelle + comportement de réponse forment un ensemble indissociable qui sera mémorisé avec deux conséquences :

> Un renforcement des idées *préconçues*.
> Elaboration d'un système de référence *prédéterminant*.

D'où l'importance de l'état d'esprit avec lequel nous abordons un problème. De cet état de départ dépend en grande partie la suite des événements. Entre la situation extérieurement présente et celle qui est vécue existe tout un monde... « le monde du dedans ». De très nombreuses techniques sophrologiques reposent sur ce mécanisme intime de perception. Certaines d'entre elles sont décrites en annexe à la fin de ce livre. En particulier :

> La sophro-acceptation progressive.
> La technique conditionnée.
> La sophro-correction sérielle.
> La sophro-substitution sensorielle.
> Les techniques de sophropédagogie dans
> – la préparation à l'accouchement;
> – la préparation aux examens;
> – la préparation à la compétition sportive.

LA SUGGESTION

L'influence des situations suggérées

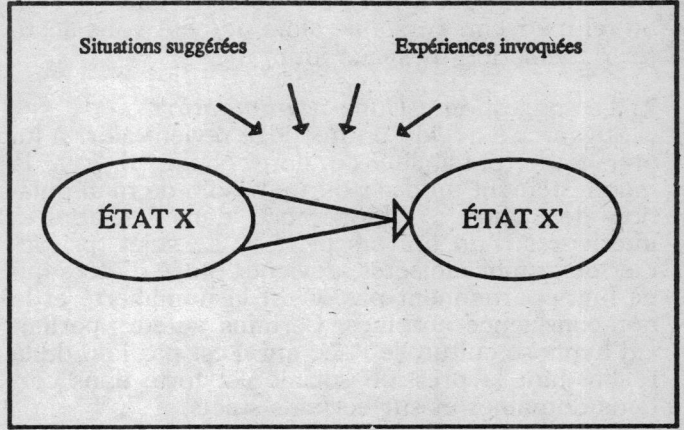

Etymologiquement, « suggérer » vient du latin *gerere* qui signifie transporter et *sub* (dessous). *Subgerere* traduit l'idée de transporter quelque chose sous une autre. La suggestion consiste donc à placer, à transporter (on pourrait dire à transplanter) une idée chez quelqu'un d'autre et ceci à son insu – c'est-à-dire sans la prise de conscience nécessaire à l'analyse. Dans le vocabulaire usuel, le mot suggestion a pris deux sens différents et même contradictoires.

1. La suggestion est une *proposition*.

Suggérer à quelqu'un une idée, une solution, revient à lui laisser, en toute finalité, l'entière liberté de choix. Rien n'est imposé et aucune sanction (ou pénalité) n'est envisagée en cas de faute par défaut ou manquement. Suggestion est alors synonyme de conseil et l'individu se déterminera en fonction de critères personnels, dans le strict respect de sa liberté. Par exemple si quelqu'un vous fait part de ses ennuis de santé, vous pouvez tout à fait lui *suggérer* d'aller voir tel ou tel médecin. Personne alors ne peut vous accuser de violation d'espace intime !

2. La suggestion est une *manipulation*.

Suggérer à quelqu'un une idée revient alors à lui ôter toute possibilité de libre choix. Il y a là manifestement un désir ou un besoin de manipulation de l'autre, « d'ingérence dans les affaires intérieures d'un univers privé ». Le sujet, prisonnier de graphes injectés, devient l'otage d'idées qui ne lui appartiennent pas. C'est la non-liberté et la non-conscience absolues. Certains auteurs parlent « d'hypnose culturelle », ce qui n'est pas loin de la réalité tant la pression sociale est forte dans certains domaines et sur certains sujets.

Nous verrons que, dans les relations interindividuelles, la suggestion peut être positive et libératoire ou négative et aliénante selon la personnalité et la motivation de « l'émetteur », la puissance, la répétition et le moment de la suggestion et enfin de l'état de conscience du « receveur ».

Si la suggestion est inévitable (chacun de nous y est confronté tous les jours !), elle n'a cependant pas de valeur absolue mais son influence va dépendre en grande partie de notre état de réceptivité c'est-à-dire de notre prédisposition. Reportez-vous au schéma de la page 195.

En fait, l'homme est en perpétuel échange biologique, émotionnel et intellectuel avec son environnement. Dans cet environnement (ou écosystème) à la fois naturel, artificiel, social et culturel, le « commerce » constant avec l'extérieur a pour langage les symboles. Il est tout à fait certain que, qu'elle soit proposition envisagée en toute conscience ou qu'elle soit transplantation insidieuse dans des couches plus profondes, la suggestion n'est réelle que si elle se traduit dans les structures mentales du sujet par l'élaboration de graphes.

L'homme est le centre d'une série de cercles concentriques. Un cycle d'actions-réactions réciproques s'établit entre lui et ces différentes sphères.

Du cercle le plus large à la sphère la plus intime

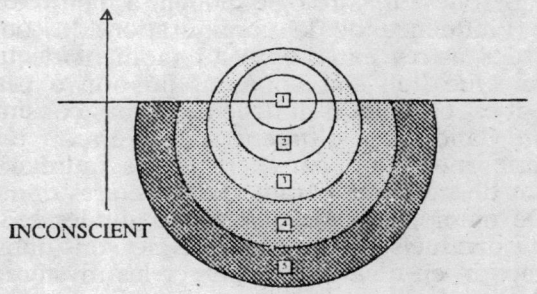

1 - Sphère privée. Monde intérieur strict.
2 - Cercle familial. Monde intérieur élargi.
3 - Sphère culturelle et sociale.
4 - Cercle des influences héréditaires. Déterminisme d'espèce.
5 - Sphère des influences cosmiques. Conscience universelle.

de son espace secret, l'homme est en constante communication, en éternel dialogue. Il est réceptif aux influences venant de tous ces éléments et, à son tour, les influence dans une mesure variable. A tous les niveaux il y a **suggestion**.

Sphères 5 et 4

Dans lesquelles nous verrons se développer les influences cosmiques qui alimentent la conscience universelle. Dans lesquelles nous sentirons la présence des influences héréditaires qui induisent les couches les plus profondes de l'inconscient collectif.

Les rapports qui lient l'homme à ces deux sphères lointaines sont mystérieux. Les influences cosmiques émanant de cet infiniment grand où règne l'idée de Dieu et où s'accrochent les rêves d'éternité conditionnent vraisemblablement une grande part du comportement général de chaque individu.

Les recherches en astrologie tendent à mettre en évidence l'influence de la configuration du ciel (rapport des astres entre eux) au moment de la naissance. Que l'on soit adhérent ou non à ces théories, il est cependant difficile de ne pas constater qu'un Cancer est différent d'un Verseau ou d'un Capricorne et que, par exemple, les Taureaux présentent de nombreux traits de caractères communs! De même, les études réalisées sur les biorythmes individuels ou en numérologie vont dans cette direction en essayant de percer les mystères de la relation de l'homme au cosmos. Egalement certains points d'acupuncture ont pour but « d'ouvrir » à l'organisme les portes donnant accès à l'énergie cosmique. Ces différentes approches ne peuvent être qu'**intuitives** et la démarche **empirique**, mais elles sont tout de même troublantes et la relation semble réelle même si elle échappe à la compréhension rationnelle.

En revanche, est plus concret, pour peu que l'on

veuille bien en prendre conscience, le dialogue très puissant qui unit l'homme à la Nature. La Nature nous parle.

Les sentiments vécus devant l'immensité et la puissance de l'océan sont d'évidence différents de ceux suggérés par un sous-bois ombragé ou par un saule pleureur au bord d'une rivière tranquille. L'influence des saisons sur le psychisme et sur l'organisme est maintenant admise par la « Faculté » comme facteur déclenchant de nombreuses maladies. Le caractère lénifiant de l'automne ou de certains paysages (sur les rives du lac Léman, on parle de la « molle du lac ») contraste avec la sensation d'énergie et le besoin de renouveau du printemps et de l'été. La pluie, la neige, le soleil et le grand vent, le crépuscule, la nuit, la lune et les étoiles ont inspiré à nos poètes tant de si beaux vers !

Ces poètes, qui ne sont peut-être pas plus réceptifs ou sensibles que d'autres aux influences de la Nature mais qui savent mieux que quiconque traduire ce qu'ils ressentent par des chants aux accents de vérité, donnent la main aux peintres qui devant leur chevalet et leur toile blanche vont bientôt signer, au nom de tous les hommes, l'œuvre que leur inspire la Nature vécue en toute sincérité.

> Oh ! contemplez le ciel ! et dès qu'a fui le jour,
> En tout temps, en tout lieu, d'un ineffable amour,
> Regardez à travers ses voiles ;
> Un mystère est au fond de leur grave beauté...
> Victor Hugo, *Soleils couchants*

Les éléments naturels perceptifs servent souvent de liaison entre la conscience de l'homme et l'univers, le cosmos et Dieu. C'est par l'intermédiaire de la Nature que certains croyants peuvent avoir accès au vécu intérieur de l'idée d'un Dieu créateur.

L'un des principaux moyens d'échange avec cet environnement est la respiration et c'est la raison pour laquelle cette fonction vitale a revêtu depuis toujours et dans toutes les cultures une connotation mystique et c'est pour la même raison que toutes les méthodes de relaxation (1), de méditation et de thérapie naturelle accordent à la respiration une place primordiale. « Es atmet mich », disait Schultz dans son Training autogène, ce qui peut se traduire par : « Ça me respire » ou encore par : « Quelque chose respire en moi » et ce quelque chose c'est le monde ! Tout le monde respire et tout respire dans le monde. Par ma respiration, je participe à la Vie universelle, je prends et je donne, je m'échange et donc je suis dans le monde.

> Air que je respire à fond
> Tant de soleils l'ont fait dense
> Je respire, je respire
> Si à fond que je me vois
> Jouissant du paradis... (2)

La communication qui s'établit entre l'homme et le cosmos représenté par la Nature est l'exemple le plus pertinent de la relation suggestive. En effet, les sensations évoquées et ressenties s'insinuent sournoisement dans la conscience, font naître certaines images mentales qui déforment – et parfois même transforment – notre vision du monde et la perception de nous-même.

Le dialogue est discret mais d'une réalité profonde et profitable. De nombreux individus ont fermé leur cœur et leur corps à ce dialogue. Trop accaparés, trop préoccupés dans des tâches immédiates et urgentes, ils se sont perdus. Si vous en rencontrez sur votre chemin, dites-leur d'ouvrir

---

(1) Nous avons vu dans la Relaxation Dynamique de Caycedo l'importance de la respiration.
(2) Jean Supervielle, « Le Corps tragique ». Extrait de *La Poétique de la rêverie*, G. Bachelard.

enfin les portes et d'abaisser le pont-levis de leur château fort dans lequel ils vivent prisonniers! Dites-leur qu'il faut savoir écouter la musique du vent et le chant des oiseaux, sentir la force du soleil et la douceur de la nuit... Qu'il faut savoir laisser son cœur et son âme percer le mystère de la Vie, se libérer du temps et de l'espace pour revenir, chargé de calme et d'énergie, nous aider à vivre notre vie de tous les jours. Et ceci malgré les tâches immédiates et urgentes qui jalonnent le parcours quotidien. Et si vous leur parliez de ces « mouvements de conscience » que nous abordons dans les deuxième et troisième degrés de la Relaxation dynamique de Caycedo?

Ne vous est-il jamais arrivé d'être attiré par le Grand Espace, assis à une table de travail avec devant vous la fenêtre ouverte sur un paysage de campagne? Mais tout absorbé à résoudre un problème ou à remplir votre feuille d'impôts, vous n'avez pas encore remarqué ce bel oiseau blanc qui passe et qui repasse devant vous! Puis, soudain votre regard est attiré. Le ciel, les quelques nuages, l'arbre, l'oiseau vous parlent et vous leur répondez par la pensée. Un véritable dialogue s'instaure entre votre conscience et la Nature. A cet instant précis, vous devenez poète, et les problèmes et les soucis s'éloignent le temps d'une rêverie. La suggestion de calme, de sérénité et de force agit lentement sur vous. Certaines images mentales apparaissent alors devant vos yeux, vous êtes en train de vivre « Oiseau » symbole qui sait faire vibrer les puissants archétypes d'Eternité et d'Immensité. Comment comprendre cette communion, cet échange, ce dialogue? Nous retrouvons ici le schéma classique de la subjectivation d'une situation.

Depuis le début de l'histoire de l'humanité, l'homme est confronté, par une relation directe et concrète, à son environnement naturel. Mille et mille fois, ces situations de confrontation ont été vécues, interprétées, idéalisées et somatisées. A chaque événement correspond une expérimentation psycho-physique et une mémorisation sous forme d'engrammes. La répétitivité et la très forte charge émotionnelle qui accompagnaient ces différentes expériences ont donné à ces graphes élaborés une grande densité. La somme du savoir et de la connaissance de la Nature s'est progressivement organisée dans les structures mentales des premiers hommes pour finalement former de véritables circuits primordiaux ineffaçables.

Nous en sommes les héritiers et aujourd'hui encore la Nature est capable de réveiller ces schèmes affectivo-moteurs et eidéolo-moteurs, c'est-à-dire que la Nature est heureusement encore susceptible de stimuler nos réactions affectives, émotionnelles et de nous faire vivre sur le plan de l'imaginal et de l'imaginaire. Ces **archétypes** (Jung) participent à notre inconscient et sont partagés par l'ensemble des hommes. Ce sont des modèles préformés et préexistant à toute forme de pensée de telle sorte qu'ils constituent une trame, une matrice douée d'une dynamique inductrice quasi universelle. Les archétypes, dans ce sens, abolissent certaines différences superficielles et réunissent les êtres humains dans un même **inconscient collectif.** Et un jour, au « hasard » (?) d'un regard quelque peu différent, ces circuits de mémoire archaïque sont réveillés, réanimés, réactivés. L'ensemble du psychisme se trouve alors mobilisé dans un vécu privé et indicible et rentre en résonance avec le symbole. De ce fait la réalité perd sa valeur évidente par une sorte d'alchimie ressentie et perçue dans la transformation vers un autre réel.

Voici sûrement ce que traduit le remarquable poème de Jacques Prévert, « Page d'écriture » :

> ... Et les murs de la classe
> S'écroulent tranquillement.
> Et les vitres redeviennent sable
> L'encre redevient eau
> Les pupitres redeviennent arbres
> La craie redevient falaise
> Le porte-plume redevient oiseau.

Sous le regard rêveur de l'écolier, les vitres, l'encre, les pupitres, la craie et le porte-plume abandonnent leur parure triste de la réalité concrète pour revêtir des habits de lumière. Le regard intérieur vit sans plus aucune retenue maintenant les images symboles du sable, de l'eau, de l'arbre et de la falaise pour terminer dans une sorte d'apothéose par le symbole vivant de l'oiseau. Et quand on tient dans sa main l'oiseau, comment résister à son appel, comment résister à l'envol ? Les menaces de réprimandes ou de punition devant la rêverie perdent toute signification puisqu'elles appartiennent au monde devenu absent des pupitres et de l'encre.

Dans le dialogue privé avec la nature, le langage est silence !

Sphères 3 et 2

Plus les sphères se rapprochent du centre, plus les influences sont fortes et les situations suggestives déterminantes. Parmi les différents éléments qui interfèrent sur le comportement, nous rencontrerons ceux appartenant à l'environnement matérialiste et artificiel liés au contexte social et culturel puis ceux composant l'entourage direct et immédiat.

1. La relation aux objets

L'Arc de triomphe, la tour Eiffel, la Muraille de Chine, les pyramides d'Egypte comme l'Empire

State Building (arrêtons là une liste qui serait trop longue!) sont autant de marques de puissance et de prestige laissées dans l'histoire des nations en symbole de leur gloire. De tout temps, l'homme a voulu se construire un décor *à son image*. Ce monde de la représentation a une fonction bien précise de suggestion et se retrouve à l'échelle individuelle avec une dimension supplémentaire : l'environnement sera fait *pour son image*. Les marques ainsi créées par un individu représentent l'être qu'il est et ce symbole, une fois en place, va entretenir l'image du Moi et déterminer alors l'être qu'il devient. Il y a dans cette action une véritable autosuggestion, en forme de miroir, par objet interposé. Par exemple :

– L'homme d'affaires aura besoin d'un bureau à la dimension de sa réussite pour être le reflet de son épanouissement professionnel. Ce symbole de confort et de prestige agira sous une forme suggestive sur toute personne franchissant le pas de la porte mais aussi, et d'une façon plus intéressante, sur le propriétaire de ce local qui, chaque fois qu'il rentrera dans la pièce, recevra, en retour, les suggestions de réussite dont il a besoin.

– L'écrivain se réfugiant dans une pièce « bien à lui », décorée par ses soins avec **sa** table de travail, **ses** livres, **ses** tableaux, se met volontairement dans un bain de suggestions propices à l'inspiration. Il est en confiance, cet environnement est fait pour lui.

– Tel homme dont l'attitude est totalement différente selon qu'il se trouve en maillot de bain sur la plage ou en survêtement dans son jardin ou dans son contexte habituel professionnel en tenue de travail. La tenue vestimentaire a un déterminisme psychologique primordial. D'où l'importance de certains rites vestimentaires : la robe de l'avocat, la blouse blanche du médecin, les perruques (apparemment) ridicules des magistrats anglo-saxons, et même les cravates club de nombreux collèges ou associations. Les exemples illustrant ce type de réactions sont illimités. Un grand nombre d'expressions en témoignent : « Se mettre dans la peau du personnage », personnage que l'on joue dans le grand théâtre de la vie. « Se mettre dans l'ambiance du travail »; chaque fois que l'ambiance est favorable à une activité quelconque, nous en recueillerons les influences positives et dynamisantes et les résultats en seront, sans aucun doute, meilleurs.

2. La relation aux groupes

L'éducation religieuse, politique ou civique fait appel à la suggestion pour *faire passer* son message dans la conscience du sujet, même si cette transplantation doit se faire à son insu. Il faut bien comprendre le « but de la manœuvre » : faire en sorte que le message soit admis au niveau des structures mentales – sans doute ni critique possible – et qu'il y soit gravé, engrammé, sous forme d'objets mentaux dont les graphes, sans cesse activés, vont orienter le percept; et la suggestion est considérée comme réussie quand les images injectées servent de références lors de l'analyse d'une situation ou lors d'un choix à faire. Ce processus d'imprégnation sert de base à la démarche publicitaire, au sens large du terme, c'est-à-dire à toute communication. L'infiltration inconsciente est facilitée par le caractère répétitif de l'information, sa force percutante (« le poids des mots, le choc des photos »), et la fragilité (relative au message en question) de la conscience du sujet. Nous pouvons dès lors comprendre l'aspect très ambigu de la suggestion et les dangers que ceux qui en font un mauvais usage peuvent faire courir à l'humanité. Malheureusement, de bien dramatiques exemples jalonnent l'histoire des peuples dont certains ne sont pas si loin de nous! Noyé dans la foule, l'homme abandonne alors son identité, son individualité Il devient « homme collectif », anonyme, perméable et vulnérable.

Le dialogue est mort. Il n'y a plus de Personne.

L'homme soumis, démissionnaire de sa propre identité, court derrière une image imposée, une idée « toute faite » par un groupe dominant, un modèle à suivre.

L'influence de l'environnement social s'exerce dès l'adolescence, au moment où le jeune être sort timidement du cocon familial et où il fait ses premiers pas seul dans la société. L'apprentissage à vivre avec les autres passe par le processus bien connu d'*imitation*. Si l'adhésion se fait à un groupe culturel majoritaire et dans la lignée sociale, on parle d'*intégration* et dans le cas contraire, on parle de marginalisation. Mais il faut bien comprendre que le processus est identique car cette prétendue indépendance vis-à-vis du groupe socioculturel numériquement plus fort correspond à une soumission, souvent plus aliénante, à un autre groupe (les groupes minoritaires ayant besoin de règles et de diktats intransigeants pour survivre).

Ce besoin impérieux explique et excuserait le comportement de la jeunesse. C'est une étape nécessaire vers l'âge adulte. Malheureusement, trop souvent, cette attitude, somme toute très « pratique », persiste bien après... l'âge de raison ! La puissance des médias (journaux, radio, télévision) et leur place dans la vie moderne entretiennent la soumission aux « idées reçues » en véhiculant à longueur de temps des images modèles. A cet égard, nous pouvons penser que l'homme vivant au milieu de ses champs et de ses animaux, et donc plus à l'abri de la « contagion », aura plus de contact avec lui-même que celui qui vit au milieu du tintamarre incessant qui se fait au nom de la communication, de l'information et de la libre circulation des idées. Mais accuser une fois de plus les médias (ils ont décidément bon dos!) serait injuste et relèverait de la même attitude d'abandon de ses propres responsabilités envers soi-même, le « don-quichottisme » a fait long feu : le monde est ce qu'il est! A nous de faire en sorte de résister à ses multiples agressions et à ses suggestions constantes en élargissant notre champ de conscience (pour qu'aucune « goutte ne fasse déborder le vase »), en structurant notre entité psycho-physique, en renforçant et en respectant notre personnalité pour une plus grande liberté. C'est très exactement le but poursuivi, dans l'évolution sophrologique, par les méthodes de sophroprophylaxie.

3. La relation à la sphère immédiate

Là, plus qu'ailleurs, la suggestion est présente et puissante. C'est avec son Cercle, sa Croix et son Carré que l'individu participe à la relation qu'il entretient avec l'espace proxémique rapproché. Espace qu'il va tenter d'intégrer aussi bien avec son intellectualité qu'avec son intuition. Parents, enfants, conjoints, collègues et voisins, habitant cette sphère, exercent une action directe sur le sujet. Leur présence, leurs idées, leur amour et même leur absence, leur silence et leur indifférence, tout ce qui peut venir de ces proches aura un retentissement certain sur le centre du cercle, le Moi. Mais ce Moi, dans cette relation étroite, aura également une forte influence de retour sur l'environnement. Le dialogue qui s'instaure est fait d'échanges quotidiens subtils, non formulés, et conduit à un véritable modelage des uns par rapport aux autres. Cette interrelation très intime est facilitée par l'appartenance préalable à un système partagé et qui a été élaboré justement par les influences suggestives émanant de la sphère socio-culturelle.

Nous profiterons de ce chapitre pour aborder la suggestion dans les rapports de sujet à sujet. Plusieurs paramètres entrent en considération dans ce que nous pourrions appeler la **communication transindividuelle.**

- D'une part, « l'émetteur » avec :
- Ce qu'il a à dire (l'information).
- Pourquoi il veut le dire (motivation ou intention).
- Comment il va le dire (formulation).

- D'autre part le « récepteur » avec :
- Ce qu'il va entendre (perception).
- Ce qu'il va comprendre (interprétation).
- Ce qu'il va en déduire (intégration).

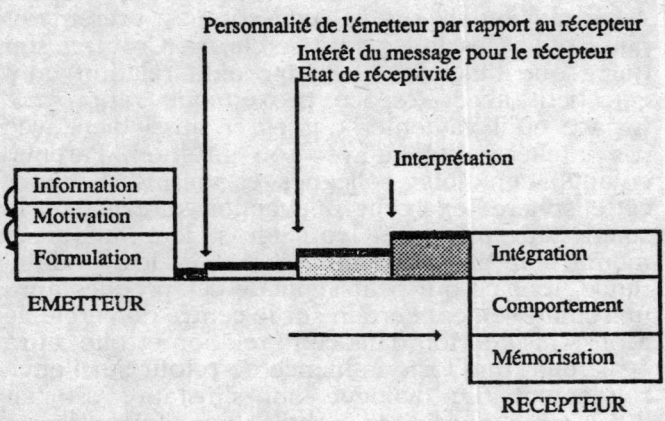

Emetteur, point de départ de la tentative de communication

Le point de départ du message est l'émetteur qui, en dehors de quelques cas rares de création, a lui-même joué le rôle de récepteur de cette information qu'il a dû intégrer. C'est donc le résultat *subjectif* de l'interprétation qui va maintenant être émis. Le message est ainsi fonction de la personnalité du sujet dans la mesure où celle-ci préside à la motivation et à la formulation du message.

Dans le domaine de l'apprentissage des langues, des études très poussées faites à l'Institut de suggestopédie de Sofia (Bulgarie) ont montré l'importance de la formulation de l'information. Il en ressort que, d'une façon générale, le message « passe mieux » s'il présente un caractère attractif ou captivant. Si l'attention de l'auditeur peut « s'endormir » devant un discours morne et fade, elle peut être littéralement captivée lors de variations pendant le récit. Variations dans le rythme et dans le ton mais aussi variations dans la présentation de l'orateur (gestes, mimiques et parfois même déguisement!), tous ces éléments permettent une répétition de l'information sans susciter d'ennui et nous savons que la répétition, en favorisant la mémorisation, est à la base de l'enseignement.

La personnalité de l'émetteur intervient aussi dans la mise en condition favorable de l'interlocuteur. Toute personne jouissant d'un certain prestige, d'une notoriété reconnue (et d'ailleurs pas nécessairement dans le domaine du message) donnera à l'information plus de poids, plus de vérité.

L'information, vecteur de la communication

La relation interindividuelle se situe simultanément sur deux plans, avec une information à « deux étages ».

Le premier est le plan conscient susceptible de saisir l'étage superficiel du message et son contenu émis en langage clair... et même le plus clair possible! Ce niveau de communication mobilise les possibilités de compréhension du receveur, c'est-à-dire son cerveau gauche essentiellement. Ici les différentes informations émises doivent passer les barrières antisuggestives, qui protègent le receveur, pour être admises par lui.

Le deuxième plan est celui de « l'insu » où, avec l'information analysable et critiquable, sont véhiculées diverses sensations non conscientisées qui contribuent à l'impression générale. Elles s'infiltrent dans les structures mentales, non pas par la porte d'entrée surveillée par la critique mais par une porte dérobée, échappant ainsi à l'attention. Elles jouent alors dans le « commerce » interindividuel un rôle primordial en favorisant le jugement intuitif et en donnant à la situation globale une connotation plus subtile. Ces données informatives alimentent l'inévitable communication non verbale représentée, entre autres, par les mimiques faciales, la gestuelle et les attitudes ainsi que par les symboles.

A cet égard, le symbole a, dans la relation à l'autre, une fonction sociale et culturelle. Il met le sujet en relation avec son milieu et en faisant naître et vivre le sentiment confus de connaissance et de *re*-connaissance, il apporte sécurité, confiance et amour. Il témoigne de la convergence d'idées et d'affectivité et devient un élément intégrateur en favorisant la transformation du témoin en acteur. A l'origine, le symbole est un objet coupé en deux. Chaque personne en garde une partie en témoignage du lien qui l'unit à l'autre. La réunion, par concordance parfaite des deux moitiés, permettait de prouver l'appartenance ou la filiation à la dette envers quelqu'un, etc. Il y a donc dans le symbole les deux sens de séparation et de réunion, de divorce et de mariage.

Logée dans les profondeurs de la conscience, se trouve une moitié de « *quelque chose* », image mentale privée de support (graphe qui sommeille), et « *quelque part* » dans l'univers, dans la société ou dans un autre inconscient, se cache la deuxième moitié. Un jour, l'alliance se réalise, le courant passe, les deux moitiés se rejoignent et concordent. Le symbole est vécu, les images stagnantes sont vivifiées et le corps réagit. On pourrait peut-être trouver dans l'expression populaire, à la mode chez les jeunes, « ça me branche », la traduction de cette reconnaissance et de cette appartenance à un système, révélées par le symbole culturel vécu instantanément, intuitivement et globalement. Nous verrons plus loin que les dernières recherches sur le cerveau tendraient à prouver que l'hémisphère droit, responsable de la fonction globalisatrice et intuitive, pourrait être le siège de cette rencontre symbolique.

C'est ainsi que, croyant être *seulement* deux, dans un dialogue en tête à tête, nous tenons une conférence... à quatre !

Quatre personnes qui se réunissent de la façon suivante.

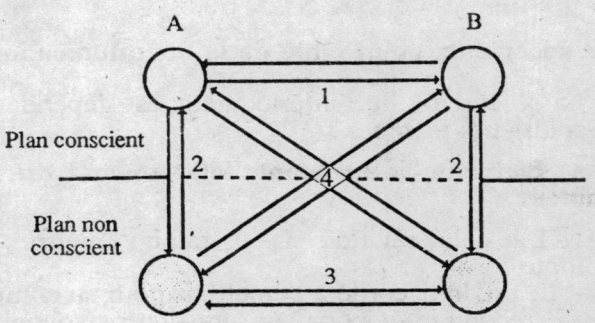

1. *Rapports interindividuels conscients, objectifs et rationnels*.

Messages émis en « clair » et reçus en priorité. Parfois éclairants (souvent aveuglants !), ils sont soumis à la critique intelligente.

2. Rapports intra-individuels conscience/inconscience.

Sondage individuel avec interrogation et mise en jeu d'images-mémoire interactives relatives à des expériences antérieures, à la force des symboles et de la suggestion.

3. Rapports inter-individuels inconscients et irrationnels.

Echanges d'informations « codées » intervenant dans le jugement définitif sous forme « d'impressions ». Niveau de perception des « choses non dites » et d'interprétation intuitive. Zone réactive aux symboles.

4. Rapports interindividuels affectifs et émotionnels.

Certains messages codés sont décryptés et traduits par le langage et le comportement personnel : l'analyse intègre la sensation. La décision est prise « tout compte fait » ! La satisfaction de l'un est évidente quand il s'aperçoit que l'autre « s'est trahi » et qu'il a pu « percer ses intentions » !

Le récepteur, point cible de la communication

La réceptivité de l'interlocuteur est dépendante de plusieurs facteurs.

a) Eléments influençant l'état mental du récepteur

1. Dans la relation 1, il faudra mettre en compte :
– Le crédit accordé à l'émetteur pour sa compétence reconnue et pour son prestige personnel et qui amène le récepteur dans un état de réceptivité optimale et volontaire. C'est la relation qui existe entre l'élève et son maître, l'auditeur et le conférencier de renom, le malade et son médecin.
– L'intérêt, pour B, de l'information reçue et ses

capacités de compréhension rationnelle donc son niveau de connaissances, son intelligence et ses facultés de curiosité intellectuelle. Un bon enseignant est celui qui sait adapter son cours aux possibilités d'intégration de ses élèves.

Dans ce type de relation, le message se heurte à la *barrière antisuggestive de la logique*. Barrière, bien sûr, éminemment variable d'un sujet à l'autre, mais toujours présente. Il est très difficile de « faire croire » à quelqu'un qu'un arbre parle en anglais ou que des feuilles puissent pousser sur les bois d'un cerf! Sur ce mode de communication, je peux à tout moment opposer mon veto quand je sens que l'autre veut « faire passer des vessies pour des lanternes »!

2. Dans la relation 2, interviendront :

– L'état de la conscience du récepteur, c'est-à-dire sa disponibilité au moment de l'émission du message. Dans un esprit « pré-occupé », les nouvelles informations ne trouvent pas de place! En revanche, le plaisir et l'émotion prédisposent favorablement et ouvrent les portes de la communication. Savoir se mettre en état de recevoir et d'apprendre est un travail abordé dans certaines séances de sophrologie.

– L'état de son inconscient, c'est-à-dire ce qu'il peut ou ne peut pas accepter. Se mettent en place ici les barrières antisuggestives présentes en tout individu et qui le protègent des agressions portant sur « l'essentiel ». L'essentiel vital correspond à l'instinct de conservation qu'aucune suggestion ne peut altérer. La *barrière antisuggestive intuitive et affective* interdit l'accès aux suggestions portant atteinte aux sentiments de sécurité ou de confiance. Tout thérapeute, pédagogue et même les dresseurs d'animaux savent qu'il faut d'abord mettre l'autre en confiance! La *barrière antisuggestive éthique* varie selon les civilisations, les cultures, les époques et l'éducation de chaque individu mais quelle que soit sa place, elle se dresse toujours à un moment donné, comme un rempart infranchissable protégeant la sphère privée de l'homme.

3. Dans la relation 4, seront à considérer :
– L'état de réceptivité vis-à-vis des influences indirectes et la capacité de les prendre en conscience éclairée. Le processus d'intégration de toutes les informations inhérentes au dialogue est fondamental dans les rapports entre individus car il permet de donner un jugement plus complet sur la situation vécue. Percer les intentions de l'interlocuteur, comprendre ses motivations profondes, en bref, deviner et percevoir l'autre à travers son comportement inconscient permet de s'ouvrir (ou de se fermer) à son influence.
– La possibilité de « s'extraire de l'événement », pour voir l'autre en train d'émettre et se voir soi-même en train de recevoir, diminue la relation de soumission et autorise une plus grande maîtrise de soi. Ceci correspond en fait à « prendre du recul » par rapport à la situation mais ce recul ne se fait pas dans le temps (en différant la décision) mais « in situ », en prenant une « certaine hauteur ». Cette aptitude réflexive s'acquiert et se développe, entre autres, dans le deuxième degré de la Relaxation Dynamique et à ce titre rend de très grands services dans, par exemple, les techniques de vente.

b) Eléments influençant le niveau de conscience

– L'hyperéveil, ou l'hypervigilance, mobilise les facultés de concentration mais cette focalisation de l'attention réalisée en conscience ordinaire aura aussi pour conséquence de favoriser l'admission d'informations secondaires, à la « dérobée ». Rappelons-nous l'expérience du promeneur solitaire qui, focalisé sur la nécessité de fuir, n'a pas perçu les sensations de coupure à la jambe. De même quand nous sommes absorbés (et le terme est en lui-même révélateur !) dans la lecture d'un livre intéressant, nous ne percevons pas les bruits alentour qui pourtant existent : en focalisant notre « su », il se « rétrécit » pendant que notre « insu » s'élargit.

— Il s'agit de savoir manœuvrer entre une trop grande distraction qui diminue l'efficacité de l'information principale et une trop grande focalisation qui diminue la prise en conscience des informations secondaires.

— L'hypovigilance (ou relaxation mentale) modifie également la réceptivité du sujet à l'égard des informations de type rationnel et de la suggestion directe : suggesto-pédagogie, suggesto-thérapie et sophrologie. La détente physique et mentale favorise l'apprentissage et la mémorisation et bien sûr la suggestion sophronique. Ces différentes notions sont développées dans le chapitre sur la mémoire et la concentration de mon livre : *Se préparer aux examens et concours par la Sophrologie*.

Sphère 1

Nous sommes au centre de la problématique humaine. Le Centre du centre d'intérêt, le Milieu du milieu dans lequel l'individu évolue. Ici convergent les influences venant de toutes parts, d'ici partent, par les chemins du désir, les élans de vie. Cet espace privé, aux multiples facettes, s'est progressivement élaboré au fil des jours, à la somme d'expériences, au gré de la mémorisation : nous entrons ici dans le *jardin secret* qui fait de chaque homme un être unique. Deux grandes forces servent de moteur à nos actions et orientent les grands axes de la vie : l'**inconscient** et le **cons-**

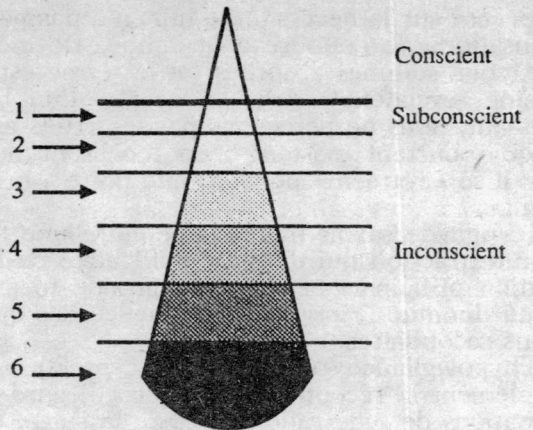

Inspiré du schéma extrait de
Sophrologie et Sport de R. Abrezol.

1. Subconscient.
2. Inconscient personnel.
3. Inconscient familial.
4. Inconscient ethnique.
5. Inconscient collectif.
6. Inconscient biologique.

cient, avec, entre les deux, une couche tampon faite de conscience profonde, peu accessible, et d'inconscient « superficiel », pas vraiment inaccessible, le **subconscient**.

Image en « iceberg » (la partie immergée, plus importante, représente les couches profondes de l'être humain) qui symbolise l'organisation en strates du complexe conscient-inconscient.

Notons avec intérêt la similitude entre ce schéma classique et celui des différentes sphères d'environnement contribuant à modeler la conscience.

• **A la couche n° 6**, représentant la zone la plus profonde de l'inconscient, correspondrait la sphère n° 5 des influences cosmiques dont la présence au niveau de la mémoire globale retrace l'histoire de la Vie, depuis son apparition sur terre. Les innombrables étapes, souvent dramatiques, jalonnant l'Evolution de la forme la plus primitive de la Vie jusqu'à l'homme, se trouvent gravées dans cette mémoire cellulaire ou « inconscient biologique », et participent, à ce titre, à la définition de l'être vivant.

• **A la couche n° 5** est née la sphère n° 4 du déterminisme d'espèce et des influences héréditaires. Le passé lointain de l'humanité est toujours agissant et se manifeste sous la forme de schèmes susceptibles d'être « réveillés » par la rencontre des grands symboles universels. Ici, dans l'inconscient collectif, au plus intime des structures mentales, s'élaborent les images premières et s'organisent les modes de pensées conduisant au comportement instinctivo-moteur.

• **A la couche n° 4** de « l'inconscient ethnique » pourrait s'associer la sphère n° 3 regroupant les influences culturelles et sociales larges, c'est-à-dire l'histoire de la race à laquelle « *appartient* » l'individu et dont les différentes péripéties vont le « *marquer* »! Les très nombreux symboles culturels qui marquent le parcours historique ne manqueront pas de lui rappeler son appartenance à une lignée héréditaire. Ces liens ancestraux se manifestent par un attachement parfois excessif à un peuple et se concrétisent dans les mythes du martyr et du héros au nom desquels d'autres martyrs se fabriquent... afin que jamais ne s'éteigne le Souvenir.

• **A la couche n° 3**, de « l'inconscient familial », et à la **couche n° 2**, de « l'inconscient personnel », s'apparente la sphère incluant le cercle familial. Dans ces zones de l'inconscient se retrouvent stockées les connaissances apportées par l'ascendance directe. La tradition familiale est ainsi souvent entretenue par la survivance de symboles qui se transmettent « de génération en génération ». Le processus de filiation peut dépasser le cadre du patrimoine héréditaire et génétique pour s'étendre à la famille culturelle, philosophique, politique ou idéologique. Ici aussi, de multiples signes de reconnaissance et de témoignage d'appartenance à... sont nécessaires pour stimuler l'affectivo-moteur et replonger l'individu dans son « *milieu* ». Cette zone inconsciente de l'individu délivre son contenu et ses messages par tout un système de communication non verbale dont il faut posséder la « clef » pour pouvoir le décoder et le comprendre.

● **A la couche n° 1** représentant le subconscient de l'individu se mêlent les éléments composant la sphère n° 1 du monde intérieur strictement privé. Cette zone particulière de la conscience globale, parfois accessible par les techniques d'analyse, renferme l'histoire personnelle de la vie de chaque être et est peuplée d'images mentales très vivaces et déterminantes quant aux motivations secrètes de tout acte de vie.

● Puis vient la ligne fatidique de « démarcation » entre l'énorme masse de l'inconscient et la petite et fragile partie du conscient. Si cette frontière est infranchissable et se constitue en un véritable couvercle hermétique, la communication entre les deux mondes est impossible. Il en résulte un bouillonnement intense qui finit par faire « sauter le couvercle » et par faire irruption dans le conscient : c'est la maladie sous toutes ses formes et l' « état ordinaire » de la conscience se transforme en « état pathologique ». En revanche, la censure entre ces deux mondes peut être partiellement levée par un travail sophronique, ce qui permet d'avoir accès à des structures plus profondes. N'oublions pas que c'est précisément dans ces régions que se logent certaines images mentales responsables de bon nombre de nos faits et gestes quotidiens et s'il devient souhaitable, pour quelque raison d'ordre thérapeutique ou pédagogique, de modifier un comportement ou une attitude, on comprend l'intérêt de cette communication rétablie.

Ceci explique le mode d'intervention de la sophrothérapie, en particulier, par les techniques découvrantes (sophro-analyse, sophro-mnésie, sophro-onirie, etc.) qui permettent de faire affleurer à la conscience des événements inconscients en établissant certaines « passerelles » allant de « **l'insu** » au « **su** ».

La sophropédagogie et la sophroprophylaxie, qui ont des visées à plus long terme, tendent à un abaissement de cette fameuse ligne. Examinons, à un fort grossissement, la région frontière séparant les deux mondes.

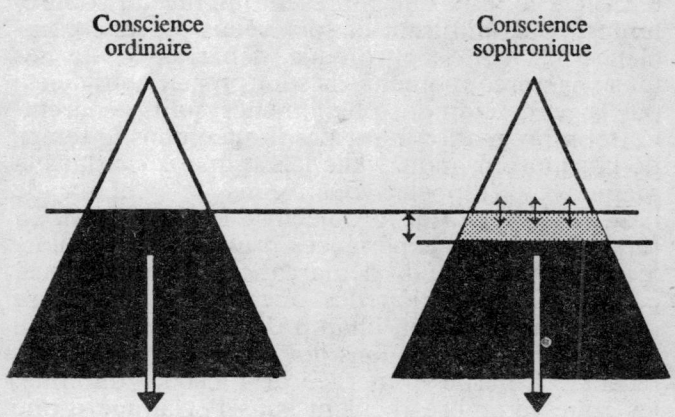

Vers les " grandes profondeurs " de l'inconscient, au cœur des schèmes.

Attention ! Que le lecteur veuille bien relever quelques instants son niveau de vigilance : les phrases qui suivent vont – peut-être – l'éclairer sur le fondement de la philosophie sophrologique. Le docteur A. Caycedo (fondateur, je le rappelle, de la Sophrologie) a défini ce mouvement scientifique comme étant une approche phénoménologique de la conscience ou, plus exactement, de la part de la conscience. Il faut entendre par là que la conscience doit s'ouvrir aux phénomènes perceptibles. *Prendre conscience* d'un nombre de plus en plus important de phénomènes qui définissent son Être revient à dire prendre *en* conscience, *dans* la conscience, des « choses » qui, à l'état ordinaire, se situent **en dehors** de celle-ci.

L'entraînement sophronique conduit donc à apprendre à ouvrir progressivement quelques « postes frontières » pour avoir accès à ces « choses » du subconscient qui nous déterminent. Lors de la sophronisation, ces éléments de base infusent à travers le filtre que représente le niveau sophroliminal, puis diffusent et sont vécus par une conscience en état sophronique débarrassée de ses tensions : à ce moment, ils sont pris en conscience par la perception des phénomènes qu'ils génèrent. Cette imprégnation n'est pas limitée dans le temps de la sophronisation... elle laisse une trace dans la mémoire... (rappelez-vous, dans le schéma de base, les points A et A' objectivant un progrès). La répétition de ces expériences privées conduit alors à abaisser la ligne de démarcation. La conscience, par l'expérimentation des phénomènes vécus, se trouve élargie et son champ d'action va s'étendre maintenant à des régions qui, jusque-là, lui échappaient. La partie immergée de l'iceberg diminue, les zones d'ombre reculent sous l'éclairage d'une conscience renforcée par une plus grande connaissance des phénomènes.

Bien sûr, en le lisant, ceci peut paraître théorique mais (et c'est ce qu'il y a d'intéressant en « sophro ») nous nous apercevons très vite que les grandes phrases se traduisent par des mots simples et que ces mots conduisent à des vécus authentiques et enrichissants. Personnellement, je fais débuter toutes les séances de sophronisation par une « invitation » à prendre conscience des phénomènes si simples et si naturels liés à l'activité respiratoire. Cette prise de conscience passe par la perception des sensations présentes qui elles-mêmes conduisent à l'expérimentation de l'idée que « quelque chose respire en moi ». Alors, après ce passage du livre un peu ardu, je ne peux résister au plaisir d'inviter le lecteur à baisser son niveau de vigilance et à vivre un court instant son corps « en train » de respirer. (Première séance extraite de la méthode globale de préparation aux examens.)

Un petit pas vers soi !...

Gardez la même position, mettez-vous simplement un peu plus à l'aise. Relâchez les tensions existantes au niveau des pieds et des jambes. Détendez les épaules... les muscles du visage. Lisez d'abord le texte très court pour savoir comment vous mettre en contact avec votre respiration, ensuite vous fermerez vos yeux afin de mieux « écouter ».

« Ne modifiez en rien le rythme naturel de votre corps... depuis un grand moment, il respire de façon automatique et réflexe... continuez... laissez-le faire. Et tandis que le corps respire seul, nous ouvrons notre conscience... calmement » (encore une fois, sans rien modifier aux phénomènes naturels). La respiration se présente à vous comme une situation globale : « *Quelque chose respire en moi* ».

Très bien. Maintenant, nous allons prendre conscience des sensations qui accompagnent cette activité instinctive. Quelles régions de mon corps participent le plus activement à cette activité ?

Au niveau de la peau du thorax, du ventre... peut-être, légères sensations de frottement des vêtements... sensations d'étirement des muscles de la cage thoracique, de l'abdomen, mais aussi de muscles plus lointains dans les épaules, le dos, etc.

« Je vis ma respiration par le mouvement qu'elle donne à mon corps... sans mouvements, même discrets, il n'y a plus de respiration donc plus de vie! Ses mouvements sont visibles par ma conscience grâce à la perception que j'en retire.

« Je sens que je respire, je sais que je respire... »

« Ma respiration est-elle rapide? lente? saccadée? souple? Le temps réservé à l'inspiration est-il égal au temps expiratoire? Y a-t-il un temps d'arrêt (apnée)?

« Ne changez en rien la cadence naturelle. Prenez en conscience, tout simplement, les phénomènes qui se déroulent. »

Il ne faut pas oublier la composante indispensable à toute respiration : l'air. *L'odeur et la température* de l'air inspiré... de l'air expiré... Est-il pur? Suffisamment oxygéné? Cet élément à la fois extérieur et intérieur fait partie de la situation globale qui se présente à ma conscience.

Maintenant fermez les yeux et consacrez cinq petites minutes de votre vie à l'écoute de votre corps..
....
....

Vous venez d'expérimenter les phénomènes liés à la respiration et, soyez-en certain, votre conscience s'est enrichie de cette expérience. La ligne de démarcation s'est très légèrement abaissée, des zones d'ombre ont été éclairées, le champ de la conscience s'est un peu élargi et elle s'est renforcée par une nouvelle connaissance... Et c'est très bien ainsi. Remarquez comment, pendant cette écoute, les bruits extérieurs et les images-pensées ont cessé d'être gênants. Vous avez tout simplement, sans effort, réalisé une parfaite concentration. Il suffit maintenant de déplacer cette concentration sur vous vers votre livre pour maintenir éloigné le monde du dehors, toujours sans effort.

Poursuivons notre exposé sur cette **sphère n° 1** où s'épanouit le centre du centre, le Moi intégré dans le monde et intégrateur de ce même monde.

La mémoire est à la base de toute conscience. Sans mémoire, pas de conscience! Mais il faut donner à ce terme un sens le plus large possible car il s'étend de la mémoire biologique et cellulaire (qui défie et dépasse le temps mesuré de la vie d'un individu) à la pauvre mémoire à « très » court terme (qui définit et limite la vie de l'homme à quelques petits pas dans son passé). Il est d'usage de localiser les capacités de mémorisation dans les structures supérieures du système nerveux : le cerveau, mais il faut bien savoir que, en fait, une première mémoire active se situe dans le système nerveux périphérique au niveau des synapses (zones de transmission des influx nerveux entre deux ou plusieurs neurones).

La stimulation, après ce premier « examen de passage » périphérique où elle prend déjà une certaine coloration, chemine le long des voies nerveuses spécialisées jusqu'au système nerveux central. Là, elle va subir, au niveau des différents centres corticaux et sous-corticaux, toute une série d'analyses : elle va être référencée (mémoire), elle va arriver, « les ailes chargées d'avis divers », dans les régions corticales (le cortex, centre intégrateur) où va se faire un ultime point de la situation en fonction de tous les éléments perçus et où va se décider la réponse (comportement) à fournir pour faire face à la stimulation. Cette réponse est elle-même analysée et le dossier complet (de la cause à l'effet) est ficelé, photocopié et des exemplaires (dont certains sont d'ailleurs incomplets) sont envoyés dans les différents centres de première instance.

Existe-t-il, dans un endroit « top secret », le dossier complet comportant toutes les analyses faites, le jugement porté et les réponses fournies ? Sûrement, mais où ?

LE CERVEAU, SIÈGE DE LA CONSCIENCE?

Les structures mentales

Il est hors de propos ici de rentrer dans les détails de la neurophysiologie d'autant qu'il existe sur le sujet d'excellents ouvrages. (Voir bibliographie.) Je voudrais simplement souligner quelques points qui paraissent importants et mettre en évidence, en matière de conclusion sur le chapitre, une certaine coïncidence troublante et... amusante!

Le cerveau humain se « compose » de trois cerveaux, apparus à différentes étapes de l'évolution des espèces et marquant chez l'homme trois niveaux d'adaptation à l'environnement. Ces trois formations contiennent chacune plusieurs centres fonctionnels spécifiques qui sont, bien évidemment, en étroite relation entre eux grâce à la présence d'interconnexions organisées en réseaux très denses (substance réticulée et système limbique, en particulier), l'ensemble formant ce qu'il est convenu d'appeler, en terme générique, le cerveau.

« Premier cerveau » ou cerveau végétatif

Présent chez les espèces animales dès le bas de l'échelle de l'évolution, il assure une fonction végétative et instinctive. Le centre le plus significatif est l'hypothalamus. Ici sont prises les décisions ayant pour objet les fonctions essentielles de la vie organique. Les motivations sont des motivations de vie et de survie et les réponses en relation avec des programmes génétiques inscrits dans la mémoire cellulaire et archaïque.

Le centre hypothalamique règle les grands équilibres thermique, hydrique, pondéral et sexuel. Il est à ce titre considéré comme le centre régulateur de la faim, de la soif et de la sexualité, équilibre homéostatique; les réponses comportementales instinctives qu'il induit sont de nécessité vitale : quête de nourriture, réflexes de survie individuelle (fuite, attaque ou camouflage) et pulsions sexuelles (reproduction = survie de l'espèce).

Pour assumer cette fonction de régulateur et de chef d'orchestre de la symphonie de la vie, le thalamus dirige et oriente l'action des deux principaux systèmes de relations internes : le système endocrinien (sécrétions hormonales) et le système nerveux parasympathique et orthosympathique. Chaque fois que l'organisme est soumis à une stimulation, il est là pour analyser, en toute priorité, l'importance de l'information sur le plan vital afin de fournir le plus tôt possible une réponse appropriée. La résolution des problèmes fondamentaux avec comme corollaire la récompense du retour à l'équilibre homéostatique ou, dans le cas contraire, le châtiment de l'atteinte à l'intégrité corporelle a fait du centre hypothalamique le siège de l'émotion et de l'apprentissage des gestes automatiques par la nécessaire rapidité de ces actions.

A ce niveau d'intégration, l'émotion se définit comme l'ensemble des modifications internes (organiques) associées aux changements de conduites (comportement) en réponse à une situation définie. L'hypothalamus n'a pas pour rôle d'interpréter mais de réagir... et vite! On pourrait dire de lui qu'il « agit avant de réfléchir » mais ses réactions se réfléchissent *ensuite* sur les régions corticales d'intégration plus élaborées mettant ainsi l'individu devant le « fait accompli » ou plus justement devant le fait que le corps est en train de réagir. Les manifestations conduites par l'hypothalamus sont très standardisées à tel point que l'observateur extérieur (et même parfois l'acteur!) peut se « tromper » sur l'interprétation de la réaction. Les larmes de joie et de peine, les cris de douleur ou de bonheur, les battements du cœur de la peur ou de l'amour, etc. Il n'est d'ailleurs pas rare de voir, chez des personnes sujettes à des crises d'angoisse, une émotion, positive à l'origine, se transformer en une crise de larmes.

D'une façon générale, l'hypothalamus est responsable des modifications notables sur :
- Le rythme cardiaque, en plus et en moins.
- Le rythme respiratoire, en plus et en moins.
- La motricité intestinale et la motricité vésicale en général.
- Le système pileux (horripilation visible, par exemple, chez le chat).
- La sécrétion d'adrénaline (réaction au stress).

Le centre hypothalamique, le relais nécessaire de la somatisation, est en relation avec les « hautes sphères corticales » où règne, dans un monde d'images mentales, l'activité psychique et intellectuelle. En relation, ou plus justement, en interrelation, car des inférences partent des régions nobles vers les noyaux sous-corticaux. On comprend dès lors mieux comment l'imagination peut, par thalamus interposé, se somatiser et devenir réalité vécue au niveau du corps – par « décret venant des autorités supérieures » pourra être ordonné un **état d'alerte** fictif, sans réalité extérieure concrète – et comment l'organisme va s'épuiser à trouver des réponses jamais satisfaisantes puisque « l'attaque » est imaginaire! Il s'agit d'une formidable tromperie de la part de la corticalité, réputée intelligente, envers notre corporalité, trop obéissante. C'est le cas de ce pauvre promeneur solitaire dans le sinistre château abandonné, il vivait l'aventure en plein leurre, « victime de son imagination », et l'hypothalamus (pouvoir exécutif), soumis aux images mentales (pouvoir législatif), gérait les ordres par des réactions qui échappaient au jugement (pouvoir judiciaire du thalamus).

Avec sa principale structure hypothalamique, cette région cervicale est responsable de la gestion de l'organisme et prend en charge l'activité neurovégétative et endocrinienne (instinctivo-moteur). L'émotion est vécue au niveau du corps. Les motifs et les types de réactions sont génétiquement inscrits dans une mémoire héréditaire et les réponses, qu'elles soient innées ou acquises par apprentissage, sont standardisées et non contrôlables.

« Deuxième cerveau » ou cerveau perceptif

Apparu plus tard dans l'évolution des espèces, il participe, avec ses deux principales structures (le thalamus et le système limbique), à la vie émotionnelle évoluée, c'est-à-dire à **l'expression des sentiments et à l'analyse des sensations.**

Le thalamus représente, chez les animaux non pourvus de néocortex, le niveau le plus élevé de conscience et conservera chez l'homme une certaine fonction de « pré-conscience ». Ce centre de conscience élémentaire est un très important carrefour par lequel passent obligatoirement TOUTES les stimulations sensitives et sensorielles (à l'exception des stimulations olfactives qui passent d'abord par les centres supérieurs). Les différents noyaux thalamiques concourent à donner un premier avis sur la stimulation. **C'est ici que commence la sensation.**

L'analyse ébauchée n'est pas encore très précise ni très différenciée. Mais si le jugement porté est flou et indéfini, il n'en est pas moins fondamental car, à partir de cette première approche, vont être présélectionnées certaines zones corticales qui auront la mission du verdict définitif. (Nous verrons dans les paragraphes suivants que les neurones de cette région participent à la formation dynamique du graphe des objets mentaux.) Avec cette première ébauche s'esquisse déjà une expression corporelle du sentiment, expression qui, venant en renfort ou en « preuve » du sentiment, oriente plus fortement le vécu au niveau des aires corticales d'intégration. Se « sentir rougir » fait peur au timide, car cette légère vasodilatation *objective* et renforce sa timidité jusqu'à ce qu'il devienne vraiment écarlate !

Si le thalamus envoie au cortex supérieur le résultat de ses impressions et de ses premières réactions, il reçoit également de lui des influences significatives et se comporte alors comme un véritable filtre de la sensibilité. Ce processus explique la technique de Sophro-substitution-sensorielle décrite dans le chapitre suivant.

L'action corticale peut également jouer dans le sens de l'apaisement général si, par évocation ou suggestion, des images mentales associées aux sensations de relaxation envahissent progressivement la conscience. La Relaxation largement développée au début de ce livre utilise cette capacité corticale à influencer l'activité thalamique. L'image mentale libérée dès la première séance de sophronisation devient par la suite inductrice du calme par action inhibitrice référente sur le thalamus (vécu du stress) qui lui-même est en interconnexion avec l'hypothalamus (réactions au stress). L'induction en spirale suit son cours et conduit la conscience vers « le bord du sommeil », niveau de confiance et de sécurité où toute mise sous tension devient inutile. Ces « dialogues » dans cet espace cervical passent par des structures spécifiques ayant pour rôle de réunir les différents centres régulateurs dans les deux sens : ascendant, le cerveau associatif, et descendant, la substance réticulée et le système limbique.

Le **système réticulaire** s'étend de la moelle épinière au thalamus. Il est chargé de l'activation et de l'inhibition des centres qu'il traverse (l'hypothalamus, en particulier). Il intervient dans la régulation des niveaux de vigilance, des états de calme et de tension, en bref de la **relaxation** et, par voie de conséquence, du sommeil.

Reprenons le schéma d'induction en spirale de la sophronisation. Plusieurs éléments peuvent « rassurer » l'hypothalamus : la baisse des stimulations extérieures et le début du relâchement musculaire (en particulier, les muscles de la face). La substance réticulée véhicule alors des messages de calme en direction des organes internes et vers le thalamus. Celui-ci recevant ainsi des invitations de paix entre le monde intérieur et le monde extérieur, va donc baisser son affectivité et envoyer, en retour, à l'hypothalamus une incitation à la paix « sociale », à une détente plus grande et plus profonde et encourage l'attitude du « lâcher prise »... jusqu'au niveau sophroliminal où, par une sorte de consensus général de tranquillité, la conscience peut alors s'ouvrir sur... elle-même !

Le **système limbique** quant à lui est le grand coordinateur de la pensée. Il est le traducteur de l'activité psychique et abstraite des centres corticaux supérieurs. Si « là-bas en haut », dans les zones cognitives et associatives, réside le Moi à l'état latent sous forme d'images assoupies, le système limbique, par sa capacité d'intégration des sensations, confère à ce MOI une **dynamique de vie** et le transforme en Moi vécu. Par ces structures s'établit la relation entre l'être et le non-être, entre l'être et le paraître et entre la conscience et « *la conscience consciente* ». Il réunit le haut et le bas, la pensée la plus abstraite au corps le plus organique, le Cercle au Carré.

Dans une dialectique ésotérique et alchimiste, on pourrait dire que ce système de réunification et de transformation de la pensée en matière et du silence en parole est le symbole de la Croix. Amusons-nous à mettre en parallèle le « petit bonhomme chinois » et l'organisation du cerveau humain.

Le **Carré**, symbolisant le concret, le terrestre et l'organicité, se retrouve au premier niveau de la structure du cerveau avec son action très directe sur les organes par le contrôle des systèmes nerveux et endocrinien. Ici se trouvent symbolisées notre vie instinctive et nos réponses réflexes, nos luttes pour vivre et survivre, nos motivations profondes, innées et inconscientes. C'est la base (le fondement) de notre être dont la priorité se manifeste par le maintien des grands équilibres homéostatiques et par le souci constant de préservation de l'intégrité corporelle.

La **Croix**, symbolisant la réunion et la synthèse

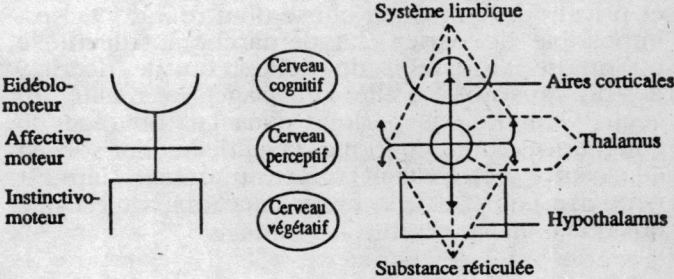

entre la terre et le ciel, en même temps qu'elle représente la relation affective avec le monde environnant par les sensations imprécises qu'il nous suggère, est tout entière dans le thalamus. La similitude sera complète quand on aura ajouté les structures de liaisons (les systèmes limbique et réticulaire) qui plongent dans l'organique et s'élèvent dans le psychisme. C'est à partir du vécu sensitif et sensoriel que s'élabore notre conscience d'être au monde et c'est par lui qu'elle se transforme et se renforce. Les principaux échanges qui s'opèrent à ce niveau répondent à une dialectique symbolique, que les symboles soient universels, culturels et archétypiques.

Le **Cercle**, symbolisant le dépassement de l'immédiat par la pensée abstraite et l'image projective, est présent dans l'activité mentale de l'homme. Au niveau des « sphères corticales » se situent le stade terminal de l'élaboration de la pensée et le stade primal de la réponse. Pour ces raisons, nous pouvons admettre que le cerveau abrite la conscience, au sens figuré. C'est-à-dire une conscience qui a un visage, un passé, un maintenant et un avenir. Une conscience d'homme. Mais la conscience transcendée, celle qui s'évade et qui dépasse les limites du temps et de l'espace... Où se situe-t-elle ? Peut-on la situer ? Nous avons affaire à un état particulier et transitoire qui apporte des expérimentations spécifiques et privées de « quelque chose d'autre » dont il est impossible de parler. La démarche intellectuelle qu'impose l'intention de définir ou de décrire, détruit, aussitôt qu'elle l'envisage, la réalité du vécu. Quand nous parlons dans cet ouvrage de conscience, nous parlons essentiellement de la conscience d'être-vivant, d'être au monde. Ce n'est peut-être pas TOUTE la conscience, mais c'est elle qui nous fait vivre !

« Troisième cerveau » ou cerveau cognitif

Le paragraphe qui suit est incontestablement l'un des plus difficiles à écrire depuis le début de ce livre. L'état des connaissances sur le fonctionnement du cerveau est encore loin d'être complet. La science ne peut qu'apporter quelques hypothèses élaborées avec prudence à partir de faits, d'expériences et d'observations et commence à peine à explorer les mystères de cette « boîte noire » qui semble présider à la vie de l'*Homo sapiens*. Tout ici s'enchevêtre et s'entremêle, s'inhibe et s'active tour à tour, par des voies nerveuses et chimiques, si bien que la notion de « début », comme dans le dessin d'un cercle, semble bien fragile et impossible à déterminer.

Cependant, puisqu'il faut bien commencer, commençons par une vue d'ensemble de ce fameux cerveau humain.

Le cerveau humain est formé de dizaines de milliards de cellules nerveuses : les neurones. Ces neurones se regroupent en des zones anatomiques et des zones fonctionnelles réparties sur l'ensemble du territoire cérébral. Chaque neurone est relié à un certain nombre d'autres et ces interconnexions (synapses) constituent un gigantesque réseau synaptique. A la naissance, le réseau synaptique est peu dense alors que le nombre des cellules cérébrales est maximal (il ne fera que diminuer par la suite, les neurones ne se régénérant pas). Le volume et le poids du cerveau se multipliant par cinq jusqu'à l'âge adulte, cette augmentation est donc due à la multiplication des interconnexions. Soulignons cette particularité, elle a son importance et nous y ferons référence par la suite.

A l'origine, le cerveau possède son contingent de neurones reliés par un relativement faible réseau de synapses. L'augmentation rapide et

considérable de cette trame se réalise aux moments des différents apprentissages par contact avec le milieu naturel et social.

En effet, l'homme doit apprendre son environnement. Par l'intermédiaire de ses cinq sens, il aura une perception de plus en plus affinée de ce monde qui l'entoure et avec lequel il entretient des relations étroites.

Capté au niveau des récepteurs périphériques, le stimulus, véhiculé par les fibres nerveuses intéressées, arrive dans les régions du cerveau concernées par le traitement de l'information. Par exemple, dans la stimulation visuelle, le trajet est le suivant : œil → aire primaire 17 → aire secondaire 20 puis 21. Cette propagation de l'influx et la mobilisation de zones particulières sont assurées par le réseau synaptique. Mais, en même temps que celle-ci, une autre voie se crée. Les fibres du nerf optique, comme toutes les autres (à l'exception des voies olfactives), passent par le thalamus avant d'entrer dans le cortex. Nous savons le rôle joué par ce noyau sous-cortical dans la coloration affective de la sensation. Il y a ainsi mobilisation simultanée d'un ensemble de neurones différents quant à leur localisation et à leur activité. Jean-Pierre Changeux, dans son livre *l'Homme neuronal*, nous dit que cette assemblée peut être décrite « mathématiquement par un graphe, elle est discrète, close mais non homogène ». La matérialité de ces graphes, c'est-à-dire l'état physique créé par la mobilisation « corollée et transitoire » des neurones les composant, correspond à *l'objet mental*. **L'objet mental peut, à ce titre, être considéré comme l'élément mémoire de base.**

Au moment de la constitution du graphe d'un objet mental, un neurone va prêter son particularisme, apportant ainsi sa contribution à l'élaboration de la représentation mentale. Cette participation transitoire ne l'empêche nullement d'entrer dans la formation d'autres graphes, d'autres objets mentaux. Ceci expliquerait le processus d'association d'idées : la mise sous tension d'un graphe réveille un neurone (ou sous-ensemble de neurones) qui, participant à la composition d'un autre graphe, libère la représentation de l'objet mental correspondant. L'esprit, laissé libre de tout contrôle, vagabonde de pensée en pensée... nous avons parlé de ce degré de l'attention dans l'état de rêverie et de distraction.

De même, reliés par un neurone commun, deux objets mentaux peuvent s'unir et former un nouvel objet mental : la création serait alors la reconstruction d'un nouveau graphe à partir de ceux préexistant à la création. Quel est le devenir de cet objet mental, de cette mémoire ? Potentialité structurelle, il a trois destinées.

1° Si le graphe est mis en activité par interaction avec le monde extérieur, l'objet mental se définit comme un *percept* (perception d'un objet concret). Comme le lapin blanc qui soudain sort du chapeau noir du prestidigitateur : l'objet mental « lapin » rallume son graphe, avec tous les neurones qui y participent (dont ceux du thalamus → connotation affective qui peut faire s'écrier « le pauvre lapin ! »), certains d'entre eux pourront ramener en mémoire (même insue) quelques souvenirs de jeunesse ou de vacances. **Les neurones et leurs liaisons synaptiques mis en activité se localisent dans les grandes régions corticales où se projettent les organes des sens et préexistent à l'interaction avec le monde extérieur.**

2° Si le graphe est mis en éveil par évocation autogène ou suggestion hétérogène, sans prise directe avec l'extérieur, l'objet mental ainsi formé est une *image mentale*. Sa mobilisation sera facilitée si des neurones thalamiques, avec leur part affective, entrent dans sa composition. En revanche, l'objet mental dont le graphe est éveillé seulement par évocation se trouve privé des neurones résidant dans les régions de projection des organes des sens (puisque ceux-ci ne sont pas stimulés comme dans le percept) et l'image mentale aura de ce fait un caractère plus global avec moins de détails. Il faut bien entendu que le graphe qui préside à sa formation préexiste à l'évocation. C'est ainsi que nous ne pouvons imaginer que ce qui réside déjà dans nos structures ou tout au moins nous ne pouvons le faire qu'à partir des éléments en notre possession, la création, comme nous l'avons dit, n'étant qu'une façon originale de ré-assembler ces éléments.

3° Enfin, l'objet mental, élément mémoire de base, peut se révéler en concept. Le concept est, comme l'image, sans contact avec une réalité extérieure, mais il se trouve en plus privé d'une grande partie des neurones véhiculant l'affectivité. Sans objet extérieur, sans affectivité, le concept sera encore plus global, plus générique.

Voici un exemple concret en illustration de ces différentes données. Un sujet est placé dans une pièce, assis à un bureau ne comportant qu'un seul tiroir. Devant une feuille de papier blanc. Une voix lui dit : « Vous allez noter ce que vous entendez ! Prenez dans le tiroir de quoi écrire. » Le sujet ouvre ce tiroir et cherche en référence la notion générale, le *concept* « de quoi écrire », et ce concept englobe, sans les définir, stylo, crayon, porte-plume, feutre, stylo à bille, etc. Dans sa quête seront éliminés tous les objets hors concept (trombones, règle, gomme). Aucun objet, dans le bric-à-brac du tiroir, ne correspondant au concept, la voix dit encore : « Avec quoi voulez-vous écrire ? Nous vous l'apporterons. » Pour répondre avec précision, le sujet stimule par évocation personnelle le graphe (d'un stylo à plume) qui prend alors la forme d'une *image mentale*. Dans le choix par préférence interviennent des neurones de l'affectivité chargés de mémoire positive et cela même à l'insu de l'intéressé. Au moment où l'objet cité apparaît dans le champ visuel, se forme alors le graphe du *percept primaire* qui permet de reconnaître que l'objet est conforme : c'est l'épreuve de la réalité.

Dans la même direction de pensée, mais avec un vocabulaire plus conforme à la terminologie psychologique et psychanalytique, ne pourrait-on pas dire que certains de ces graphes prennent une force agissante en tant que symbole, archétype et schème ? Il y a dans cette classification une hiérarchie allant du particulier et du composite au général et unitaire.

Le symbole correspondrait à un percept primaire dont l'objet mental (A) préexistant se compose d'un graphe aux multiples charges et aux multiples connexions. Par un enchaînement dynamique de mise en activité des neurones où un autre objet mental serait associé, une image mentale (B) déjà signifiante peut apparaître. Le symbole retrouve ainsi sa définition première de rencontre, après déchirure, des deux éléments, l'un extérieur et l'autre intérieur : le percept et l'image mentale.

L'archétype pourrait être le lieu de cette rencontre. Ou plus justement, la structure dynamique préalable qui permet la réunion percept-image. Des auteurs ont donné à l'archétype le rôle de prototype, d'engramme ou d'image primordiale suivant ainsi le psychanalyste Jung quand il dit que l'archétype est « le stade préliminaire, la zone matricielle de l'idée ». G. Durand, dans son livre *Les Structures anthropologiques de l'imaginaire*, souligne « l'importance essentielle des archétypes qui constituent le point de jonction entre l'imaginaire et les processus rationnels » et cite Jung : « L'image primordiale doit incontestablement être en rapport avec certains *processus perceptibles de la nature* qui se reproduisent sans cesse et sont toujours actifs, mais d'autre part il est également indubitable qu'elle se rapporte aussi à *certaines conditions intérieures de l'esprit* et de la vie en général. »

Le schème serait une de ces conditions intérieures de l'esprit. Une sorte d'organisation de base donnant une potentialité ou une prédilection à certains neurones de se relier. Possibilité innée de combinaisons, le schème est « théorique »... une pensée en attente, une connaissance encore insue et non formulée. Les schèmes forment le squelette dynamique, le canevas fonctionnel, sur lequel vont venir s'organiser les archétypes, puis les symboles, puis les percepts, les images et les concepts. Devant cette préorganisation qui détermine avec autant de force toute forme de pensée, nous sommes en droit de nous poser la question de son origine. Vraisemblablement les schèmes ont deux sources principales d'inspiration : la nature d'une part, et la gestuelle corporelle réflexologique d'autre part, auxquelles nous pouvons ajouter l'organisation sociale et culturelle.

La nature, source inépuisable de renseignements et d'enseignement. Dans un vécu par intégration dans l'environnement naturel, l'homme est amené à prendre dans sa conscience certaines constantes universelles qui présideront ensuite à toute imagination du monde.

Ces constantes peuvent se regrouper en plusieurs catégories : la notion de cycle et donc de rythme, celle de bipolarité reliée à la dualité et aussi l'appréciation des rapports et des distances avec comme corollaire l'idée d'isolement et de multitude.

L'aspect cyclique de la nature, donnée essentielle car vécue, installe les schèmes de vie et de mort, de reproduction et de sexualité, de lumière et de ténèbres, de fin qui coïncide avec un début, etc. Tout ceci peut se résumer en un schème principal d'Eternel Recommencement ou d'Eternité qui trouve sa traduction archétypale dans la roue et sa représentation symbolique essentielle par le cercle. Il est à noter que toutes les grandes découvertes en physique comme en biologie qui témoignent du processus de transformation et de recyclage n'ont été permises que grâce à ces schèmes préexistant dans les structures mentales de l'homme.

La nature enseigne aussi la loi universelle de la bipolarité. Les objets naturels qui présentent un haut et un dehors (schème *ascensionnel*, archétype du sommet, de la lumière, du savoir et avec pour symbole principal la branche montante de la croix mais aussi l'arbre, l'oiseau, la flèche...) et un bas et un dedans (schème de la *descente*, archétype du creux, de l'intimité, de la nuit, du secret ou de l'inconnu dont les représentations symboliques sont le vase, la grotte ou caverne et, au niveau du corps, le ventre digestif et le ventre sexuel, etc.). Comment ne pas remarquer que le jour « se lève » toujours alors que la nuit et le soir sont condamnés à toujours « descendre »!

Les quatre éléments fondamentaux qui se complètent et s'opposent, l'Air et le Feu, la Terre et l'Eau, viennent renforcer ces schèmes et les rendre ambivalents. Par exemple, le feu qui brûle la surface de la peau mais, quand il réchauffe, se retrouve à l'intérieur : il éclaire la nuit et le secret du dedans et par sa symbolique flamme verticale montre, depuis le bas, le *chemin vers le haut*. L'eau également intègre deux schèmes différents, l'eau noire et profonde, peuplée de monstres inconnus, dans laquelle on ne peut que *descendre* et l'eau de surface, claire et limpide, purificatrice et vitalisante qui n'aspire qu'à *l'ascension* vers les cieux par évaporation.

Le schème de polarité fait vivre chaque chose et son contraire, ainsi nous pouvons concevoir qu'à la dualité correspond un principe d'unicité. Comme le vide peut être conçu à partir du plein, la réalité de l'*Un et Indivisible* peut être vécue à partir de la réalité perçue du multiple et du divisible.

A ces schèmes d'**imprégnation naturelle** s'associent les schèmes sensori-moteurs engendrés par le geste et la posture. A la position debout correspond le schème d'*ascension* avec son cortège d'archétypes et de symboles, à la position couchée ainsi qu'au réflexe de déglutition s'intègrent les schèmes de *descente*, de nuit, etc. N'est-ce pas la nuit que surgit l'inconscient « profond » dont le langage codé vient peupler les rêves !

N'est-ce pas dans le ventre maternel (symbole de la Terre nourricière) que se conçoit le mystère de la vie, et dans le ventre digestif (symbole du corps profond et animal) que se somatisent les angoisses devant les choses et les événements inconnus ! Les exemples pourraient se multiplier mais ce n'est pas l'objet de ce livre de rentrer dans les détails.

Avant de terminer, soulignons encore une fois l'aspect hiérarchique et l'organigramme des structures mentales :

Le schème, structure primordiale, préorganisatrice mais sans réalité vécue.

L'archétype, schème matérialisé, universel, globalisant et inducteur.

Le symbole, archétype révélé et vécu, généralisant mais aussi spécifique et individuel.

Par ces graphes prédominant et résidant au niveau de zones inconscientes, sous forme d'objets mentaux, l'homme accède à une certaine intégration du monde par trois modes de compréhension :

Le percept primaire. Eveil d'un objet mental en « prise directe » avec un objet extérieur par stimulation périphérique des récepteurs sensoriels.

L'image mentale. Mise en activité d'une assemblée neuronale par évocation sans support extérieur et faisant intervenir la mémoire sensorielle et affective.

Le concept. Objet mental organisé, sans contact avec un objet extérieur, pauvre en participation sensorielle, et généralisateur.

Dans sa configuration générale, le cerveau présente deux hémisphères, un à gauche et un à droite, reliés par plusieurs structures dont la plus importante est le corps calleux. Cette région du corps calleux peut se représenter comme un pont ou une immense avenue parcourue par plusieurs millions de fibres nerveuses assurant une communication efficace entre les deux hémisphères. Nous allons, dans un but didactique de clarté, envisager les particularités de chaque hémisphère séparément mais, bien entendu, il faut savoir qu'ils travaillent en totale synergie, que l'un a besoin de l'autre et que, pour un meilleur rendement, il est indispensable qu'ils s'accordent – au sens politique et au sens musical – c'est-à-dire qu'ils soient en parfaite harmonie. Dans le cerveau de l'homme, la droite et la gauche cohabitent et mettent leurs différences au service du bien commun!

Pendant de nombreuses années « on » a cru que seul le « cerveau gauche » était important. En effet, c'est à ce niveau que se situent les centres de l'écriture et du langage parlé, « on » l'a donc appelé cerveau intelligent, dominant... masculin. Le « cerveau droit », en comparaison, paraissait terne, dominé et sans grande activité, « on » l'a nommé cerveau... féminin! C'était au début du siècle. Il fallut attendre le début des années 50 pour que s'ébauche une clarification du rôle respectif des deux hémisphères mais c'est surtout en 1976 que furent publiés d'importants travaux mettant en évidence les fonctions très précises de chaque hémisphère. Il est maintenant admis que ces deux « cerveaux » ont des fonctions différentes.

L'hémisphère gauche. L'accès au savoir.

C'est la pathologie qui, par défaut, a permis de mettre en évidence les qualités fonctionnelles de cette partie gauche du cerveau. Lors de processus lésionnels situés dans cette région du cerveau, les malades présentent une symptomatologie bien précise. En particulier, ils parlent avec d'énormes difficultés en employant des phrases sans conjugaison, sans grammaire et sans syntaxe. Leur allocution est pénible, lente, et leurs propos sont dénués de sens logique. Le ton est monotone, un peu à la manière d'un robot, sans variation et sans vie. En outre, ils sont incapables de nommer les objets dont pourtant ils connaissent la forme (grâce à l'hémisphère droit), incapables de mettre des noms sur les visages familiers. La psychologie expérimentale a mis en évidence certaines caractéristiques de cet hémisphère.

Responsable du langage oral, il a dû apprendre un vocabulaire riche, varié et nuancé, parlé et écrit, dont il se sert pour rendre concrètes et communicables les idées abstraites. Par la syntaxe, la grammaire et autres règles de convention, il est devenu un **cerveau logique, capable de raisonnement et de concrétisation.** Tout naturellement, il a aussi appris les chiffres et il sait donc compter. Aidé par son bagage mnésique, il sait passer de la conceptualisation à la réalisation et il est alors directement impliqué dans la communication conventionnelle. Le sujet « cerveau gauche » est réputé comme quelqu'un de brillant et d'intelligent. C'est le cerveau scientifique par excellence qui calcule, cherche et trouve les solutions aux problèmes sur un mode logique et rationnel.

Peu sensible à l'émotion, il classe, trie, compare et structure avec « sang-froid » les données nouvelles. Stimulé par la nouveauté, il est le cerveau de l'**apprentissage** et de l'**application**. Il sert aussi bien au mathématicien et au philosophe qui tentent, par des mots et des signes, une traduction des concepts abstraits qu'au technicien au moment où il doit comprendre, pour mieux apprendre, certains gestes précis et rationnels. Brillant, intelligent, ouvert au dialogue et apte à apprendre, cet hémisphère gauche a intéressé le système éducatif tel qu'il est en vigueur dans nos civilisations. Orienté vers les sciences et les techniques, l'orthographe et la syntaxe des langues écrites et parlées, il sait compter et calculer, parler et écrire, concevoir et réaliser, il a le « savoir-faire » et le « faire savoir ». Mais, en revers de médaille :

- Il peut quelquefois confondre la forme et le fond... de notre pensée et nous mettre dans l'impossibilité d'exprimer certains états d'être (drame que connaissent bien les poètes !) par des mots classiques.
- Il est, paradoxalement, à la fois imprégné de certitude dans la fatuité de croire qu'il détient la vérité et qu'il peut tout changer et modifier et, à la fois en prise avec le doute dans l'attente du jugement et de la preuve « par quatre » ! Notons que ce chiffre nous ramène, d'une façon « magique », au Carré, symbole fondamental présent dans le « bonhomme chinois » et signifiant le « rendu concret et compréhensible ».
- D'apprentissages en apprentissages, de récompenses en punitions, le cerveau gauche a inscrit dans ses graphes directeurs la satisfaction de la réussite mais aussi la possibilité de l'ECHEC ! L'enfant développe son cerveau gauche au moment de la scolarité et le jeu subtil des « bons points » et des « mauvaises notes » qui régit le système éducatif introduit une connotation émotionnelle qui peut s'avérer préjudiciable pour l'épanouissement de son « intelligence ». La flatterie du « prix d'excellence » et l'humiliation du « bonnet d'âne » ne

constituent peut-être pas les moteurs les plus appropriés au développement des qualités de ce cerveau gauche et risquent même de mettre en péril son bon fonctionnement.

Laissons maintenant ce cerveau gauche à ses calculs et à son travail pour nous tourner vers l'autre hémisphère : le cerveau droit.

L'hémisphère droit.
Accès à la connaissance.

Ne possédant pas, par ses structures essentielles, la manière de paraître... intelligent, ce cerveau droit fut longtemps victime d'une véritable discrimination. Muet, il apparaissait comme terne, secondaire. C'était le cerveau dominé à qui on n'accordait aucune participation effective dans l'activité cérébrale volontaire et consciente. Ce n'est qu'à partir des années 60 que certains auteurs ont commencé à mettre en évidence la spécificité de ses fonctions. La psychologie expérimentale entreprit l'étude de malades (certains cas d'épilepsie grave) dont le traitement avait conduit à une séparation chirurgicale des deux hémisphères par section du corps calleux. Ces sujets, dont l'activité des deux cerveaux avait été rendue indépendante, ont été soumis à des tests tout à fait révélateurs.

C'est ainsi que le rôle important du cerveau droit a pu être mis en lumière. Il semblerait que l'une des principales caractéristiques de la spécificité du cerveau droit réside dans la gestion de la vie quotidienne grâce à la capacité de **mémorisation des éléments coutumiers.** En effet, dans cet hémisphère seraient stockés, dans une sorte de mémoire à long terme et sous forme d'images globales, les parcours topographiques habituels, les visages familiers et les objets usuels. Les situations se présentant seraient alors comparées aux « tableaux » typiques mémorisés induisant une attitude de réponse conventionnelle et conforme. Mais si une anomalie est relevée, une mise en alerte se produit avec intervention du cerveau gauche, plus apte à résoudre les problèmes nouveaux. Cette prise en charge du quotidien est rendue possible par certaines capacités fonctionnelles maintenant reconnues. L'une de ces fonctions est la **perception spatiale** par **l'appréciation des distances et des formes.** Le cerveau droit, globalisateur, ne s'attarde pas sur les détails. Il réalise une vision immédiate de la situation dont il appréhende « grosso modo » les formes, les couleurs, l'harmonie, les sensations d'ensemble.

Il fait la synthèse de ce qu'il ressent, sans en faire l'analyse précise. Par ce fait il participe au jugement intuitif et à la perception non consciente des sensations présentes dans une situation. De cette activité primordiale découle une « impression générale » ou un « sentiment vague » et s'enchaîne un comportement « non réfléchi ». Car, si le cerveau gauche a, pour s'exprimer, la parole et l'écriture, le cerveau droit a tout le reste. Tout ce qui est regroupé sous la dénomination de « communication non verbale » : les arts (musique, peinture et, dans une certaine mesure, la poésie) et surtout les gestes et mimiques. La communication gestuelle est du ressort du cerveau droit qui sait traduire (ou trahir!) par l'attitude corporelle les différents et très secrets « états d'âme ». Nous sommes en présence du monde des images mentales, pauvres en détails mais riches en sensations par lesquelles se révèlent la sensibilité, l'affectivité et l'émotion.

La façon d'énoncer, sous forme de chapitres distincts, les spécificités fonctionnelles de chaque hémisphère, ne doit pas nous faire oublier qu'ils « travaillent » en étroite collaboration et que chacun d'eux apporte son concours pour la compréhension, l'intégration et la mémorisation des éléments qui composent une vie. Et si l'un permet le « savoir » et l'autre amène la « connaissance », tous deux contribuent à l'élaboration de la personnalité de l'individu et participent à l'adaptation à son environnement naturel et culturel.

Cerveau droit – cerveau gauche...
Un seul et même cerveau !

Cependant, devant telle ou telle circonstance de la vie nous pouvons être amené à mobiliser ou à privilégier une fonction hémisphérique plutôt qu'une autre. De même, les différentes confrontations à des situations particulières au cours du temps (métier, loisirs, etc.) aboutissent à un développement fonctionnel plus important de la partie droite ou gauche du cerveau. Ceci nous permet de

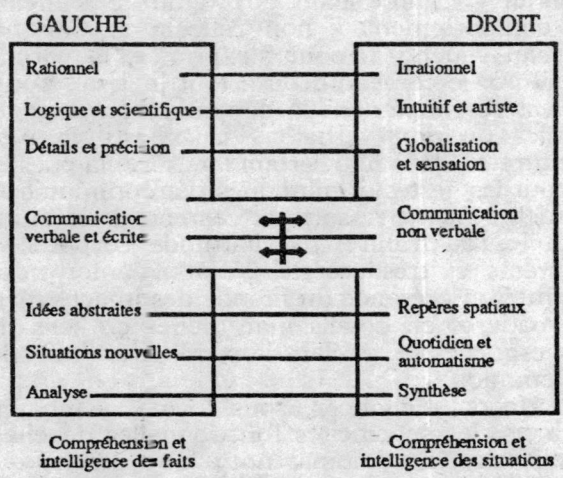

relever des tendances ou des orientations chez les individus et de les classer comme sujet « cerveau droit », sujet « cerveau gauche » ou, chez un même individu, de déceler un comportement « droit » ou « gauche ». Bien sûr, il est absolument faux de vouloir localiser topographiquement une attitude dans une partie précise du cerveau, comme d'ailleurs il est absurde de localiser la générosité ou l'amour dans l'organe cœur et le courage ou le « culot » dans l'estomac ! Il n'en reste pas moins vrai que tout le monde comprend le comportement d'un homme qui a « le cœur sur la main ! » et l'attitude de celui qui a « de l'estomac ». Il faudra entendre « cerveau droit » et « cerveau gauche », en tant que symboles (culturels) exemplaires d'une tendance, d'une approche, d'une façon d'être et de voir les choses.

C'est ainsi que le sens de l'orientation du « vieux marin » met en valeur les qualités du cerveau droit tandis que le jeune navigateur aura plus volontiers recours aux instruments de navigation (utilisés par son cerveau gauche) pour se repérer. De même que la sympathie (ou l'antipathie !), la camaraderie et l'amitié seraient vécues au niveau du cerveau droit alors que les accords sur le plan des idées ou des affaires se feraient sur la base d'une estime réciproque entre... deux cerveaux gauches.

Pour essayer de rendre signifiants ces nouveaux symboles, suivons ensemble monsieur Pierre X... dans les différents moments de sa journée. Nous noterons en italique les endroits où la fonction du *cerveau gauche* sera en éveil, en caractères gras quand le **cerveau droit** entrera en activité et en italique gras les passages où les ***deux cerveaux***, mettant leurs capacités en commun, ont une activité synergique.

Pierre est un homme d'une quarantaine d'années, marié, père de deux enfants. Depuis cinq ans, il est installé à son compte et exerce le passionnant métier d'architecte. Afin de pouvoir surveiller les différents chantiers qu'il conduit, il a pris l'habitude de se lever tous les matins vers 6 h 30. Toute sa famille dort encore et la maison est calme. Pierre aime bien cette heure de la journée. A cette époque de l'année, le jour éclaire d'une douce lumière le jardin qui entoure la villa. **En buvant machinalement son café** à petites gorgées, il prend un plaisir certain à laisser **aller son regard sur ce paysage**. Ce jardin, c'est lui qui l'a **imaginé**, *agencé, planté en choisissant soigneusement chaque fleur et chaque arbre*. Ce spectacle fait partie du **rituel** du matin et lui procure un réveil en douceur. Les problèmes du travail sont pour tout à l'heure. Maintenant, il savoure cet état de quiétude, encore un peu « au radar », à mi-chemin de l'éveil et du sommeil.

En sortant de chez lui, il retrouve avec plaisir l'ambiance de fraîcheur. La rue est déserte, abandonnée aux oiseaux qui traversent sans hâte la chaussée, à peine troublés par les quelques habitués des heures matinales. De la main, il **adresse un amical bonjour à sa voisine**, monte dans sa voiture, et, en mettant le contact, *réalise qu'elle a changé de coiffure*. « Les cheveux courts lui vont bien. Elle semble rajeunie! » Le trajet jusqu'à son bureau dure environ vingt minutes, ce qui lui permet de se « remettre dans le bain ». **Tout en conduisant**, il *repense à la conversation* qu'il a eue hier avec un jeune couple qui désire construire une maison. Après une longue discussion, il commence à entrevoir ce qu'ils veulent, le volume et la forme, l'agencement des pièces, en bref l'**allure générale** de leur « nid ». Mais il est interrompu dans sa « **construction mentale** » par des travaux sur la route qui l'obligent à prendre une longue déviation... et à rentrer dans un embouteillage monstre. *Réfléchissant* rapidement, il *tourne dans une petite rue* pour éviter la zone bloquée, *récu-*

père le bon chemin et arrive avec seulement quelques minutes de retard à son étude.

Pierre trouve, comme chaque matin, rangée sur son bureau la pile de lettres qu'il a *dictées* la veille à sa secrétaire. Il y **jette un rapide coup d'œil** et les signe. Maintenant la journée peut commencer. Journée bien remplie avec, au milieu de la matinée, visite d'un chantier pour des *problèmes de fenêtres non conformes au plan*, à midi, repas en présence d'entrepreneurs *pour discuter d'un gros projet*, etc., jusqu'au soir. Comme tous les hommes très occupés, Pierre tient à respecter le planning et à être toujours à l'heure à ses rendez-vous. « *Il faut de l'ordre, de la méthode et de la rigueur* », aime-t-il à répéter sans cesse à ses collaborateurs.

Confortablement installé dans son fauteuil, le regard au bord d'un quelconque horizon, Pierre **revivait en pensée** l'entrevue avec ce couple. Par expérience il sait qu'il existe un monde entre ce que les gens **désirent** et *ce qu'ils disent vouloir* et c'est pourquoi, presque par jeu, il s'exerce à **percevoir**, *au-delà de leurs mots*, la véritable envie de ses interlocuteurs. Surtout pour la construction d'une maison, il sait que souvent le côté *raisonnable* (problèmes financiers, configuration du terrain, etc.) prime et étouffe le **désir** profond. Chacun **rêve** de pouvoir un jour construire sa maison et ce rêve est compromis par la dure réalité des choses. Il estime que cela fait partie de son métier que de savoir ***déchiffrer les messages non formulés*** et d'aller chercher les **images** secrètes qui animent les rêves de ses clients. Il appelle cela « les **motivations structurelles émotionnelles** » qui s'opposent aux « *impératifs structurels conjoncturels* » !

L'alliance de ces deux facteurs constitue une périlleuse **gymnastique cérébrale** stimulante. Chaque cas est particulier, ce qui l'oblige à *envisager les réponses sous des angles différents*. Faire siens les fantasmes de celui qui est en face et, grâce à ses connaissances et par la technique, les rendre concrets relèvent selon lui du *travail d'artiste*. Sur sa table à dessin, le rêve devient réalité et l'*image floue* trouve des *contours précis*.

Pierre, comme tout homme sur terre, poursuivra ainsi sa journée de travail utilisant les qualités et les capacités fonctionnelles de ses « deux cerveaux », alternativement ou conjointement, dans une parfaite harmonisation.

Dans un ouvrage général où plusieurs thèmes sont abordés, il est toujours difficile de naviguer entre le désir d'expliquer et de donner un maximum d'informations sur chaque sujet et la nécessité de ne pas trop alourdir le texte et de ne pas noyer le lecteur dans un flot de données. Je sais que ce chapitre sur la conscience ordinaire ou conscience de base est incomplet et mériterait sans doute un plus grand développement, mais j'espère qu'il aura permis tout de même d'entrevoir ce que nous sommes nous, êtres humains, et comment nous « fonctionnons ».

Ce pauvre petit « bonhomme chinois » semble bien fragile, coincé entre « la manne céleste » aléatoire et impitoyable qui signe son destin et la masse profonde et insondable de l'inconscient qui motive ses actes en privilégiant trop souvent « l'insu ». Bouchon de liège ballotté au gré des vents et secoué par la tempête, au milieu de l'océan des désirs, qu'en est-il de ce Moi et de ce Soi que je trimbale en moi ? Ne suis-je en fait que l'objet du désir des océans qui s'agitent à leur fantaisie et mon existence n'est-elle qu'un lieu de bataille où s'affrontent, en se jouant de moi, des vents contraires ?

Comment accepter sans se mettre à genoux et comment rester debout sans risquer de tomber ?... Jean de La Fontaine nous a montré ce qu'il advenait du chêne et de son arrogante fatuité à vouloir défier la tempête alors que le roseau, lui, modeste dans son apparence, pouvait plier sous l'orage, sans se rompre! Mais comment, quand on est homme, plier sans courber l'échine?

Doit-on, pour se protéger (mais contre quoi et contre qui?) vivre avec une cuirasse dans un château fort aux minuscules ouvertures et au pont-levis toujours relevé? (Tout en sachant que même les plus forts, les plus imprenables des châteaux sont un jour « tombés » sous les coups du sort.) Il semble cependant que le village de notre héros national, Astérix, soit plus attrayant. Les habitants sont protégés par une palissade qui les met à l'abri des problèmes mineurs, leur permettant ainsi de vivre le quotidien en toute tranquillité, sans agressivité et sans inquiétude majeures, laissant aller leurs émotions et petites querelles internes. Nous les retrouverons toujours unis dans les moments graves avec cette fameuse potion magique qui les rend invulnérables.

Bien sûr, les sophrologues ne sont pas des druides et la sophrologie n'est pas une potion magique qu'il suffit d'avaler pour être fort. Mais la connaissance qu'elle apporte permet de renforcer et d'harmoniser le « monde intérieur » afin de pouvoir faire « sauter les cuirasses », de baisser le pont-levis et de s'ouvrir au « monde extérieur » sans agressivité ni crainte excessives mais avec une vigilance mesurée par la conscience éclairée des événements de la vie.

Alors l'Homme devient roseau,
mais un roseau conscient
qui se tient debout,
entre ciel et terre comme un chêne!

SIXIÈME CHAPITRE

APPLICATIONS PRATIQUES

Faisons confiance à notre mémoire
Le lâcher prise
Le sport
Méthode globale : SooSport

FAISONS CONFIANCE
A NOTRE MÉMOIRE

Henri a une formidable mémoire, il se souvient de tout !

Jean serait capable de réciter des poèmes de Baudelaire, mais oublie les dates de naissance de ses parents et de sa femme.

Yvette, qui n'a pas de mémoire, oublie le prix d'achat de son manteau mais se souvient, des années après, des moindres phrases d'une conversation.

Henri a une formidable mémoire : trente ans plus tard, il peut citer la liste de ses anciens camarades de classe.

Jean-Marie connaît, sans se tromper, les performances des athlètes olympiques mais, en lisant « L'Equipe », oublie un rendez-vous avec un ami.

Martine a une mémoire très précise du concret et des « petits détails » mais ne retient pas facilement le nom des ministres du gouvernement.

Henri, qui a une formidable mémoire, a cependant oublié de prendre son carnet de chèques avant de partir, a aussi oublié de téléphoner au réparateur de télé... heureusement, Yvette, qui n'a pourtant pas de mémoire, le lui a rappelé à temps !

Tous ces personnages existent dans votre entourage et vous-même êtes sûrement l'un d'eux. Si les uns n'ont que de très vagues souvenirs de leur passé, les autres retiennent sans difficulté une date d'histoire ou les paroles d'une chanson. Si certains n'oublient jamais un nom, d'autres sont physionomistes à l'entrée des salles de jeu. Qui a de la mémoire, qui n'en a pas?

Si avoir ou ne pas avoir de la mémoire est la question, s'agit-il de juger la quantité ou la qualité de la mémoire?

Chaque homme a, vis-à-vis de cette capacité essentielle et indispensable de la conscience, des prix d'excellence et des zones de déficience.

Avant d'entrer dans les détails, j'aimerais m'adresser tout particulièrement à ceux qui pensent souffrir d'un « manque de mémoire » et leur demander de bien vouloir prendre un stylo et une feuille blanche et de noter le contenu de leurs connaissances. Par exemple en commençant par leurs nom, prénom, date et lieu de naissance, puis de leurs parents ou conjoint, les noms de leurs amis, de leurs collègues ou voisins, des marques de voitures, de lessives, des termes professionnels, des noms de chanteurs, d'acteurs, des titres de films, de livres... etc. Bien sûr, la liste est pratiquement illimitée.

Prétendez-vous après cet exercice, manquer de mémoire! Votre cerveau est plein de choses sues sur lesquelles vous pouvez compter. Alors, je vous en prie, cessez toute critique injuste et remerciez plutôt ce riche cerveau d'avoir des structures aussi accueillantes et rétentives.

Votre mémoire fonctionne bien, faites-lui confiance.
Qu'est-ce que la mémoire?

Ne tentons pas de la définir, toute tentative de définition serait vouée à l'échec. Nous pouvons en décrire quelques caractéristiques, énumérer certains critères qui l'influencent dans un sens ou dans un autre... mais nous ne pourrons donner une définition recouvrante qui soit suffisante pour prendre en compte les différentes natures de mémoire.

De nombreux ouvrages existent sur ce sujet avec des classifications et des subdivisions de plus en plus subtiles. Ainsi nous savons qu'il existe une mémoire héréditaire et une mémoire acquise, une mémoire à court terme, d'autres à moyen et à long termes, une mémoire visuelle, une auditive, une sensitive, une mémoire émotionnelle, une autre logique et enfin une mémoire du « par cœur » qui n'est ni logique ni émotionnelle, malgré son nom ! Certains auteurs parlent de mémoire cellulaire, de mémoire archaïque résidant dans l'inconscient. Si vous n'êtes ni un neurophysiologiste ni un psychologue spécialisé dans la question, il paraît inutile d'entrer dans ce dédale compliqué !

Je crois plus clair de partir du processus de base qui peut se schématiser ainsi :

1° PERCEPT EXTÉRIEUR → 2° INTÉGRATION DANS LES STRUCTURES MENTALES → 3° RESTITUTION FORTUITE OU VOLONTAIRE

Nous pourrons ainsi faire état de trois phases :
L'entrée avec les problèmes de perception et de sélection de l'information.
Le séjour avec les notions de durée, d'interférences et de stabilisation du fait acquis.
La restitution avec les paramètres de fiabilité et de rapidité d'exécution.

Dans la « pratique courante », ces trois phases sont interdépendantes et forment un tout et nous ne prendrons conscience d'un défaut de fonctionnement de ce processus global qu'à la phase 3. Mais ce n'est pas toujours l'activité de restitution qui est en cause, le problème pouvant se situer en amont, soit au niveau de la perception, soit dans la rétention de l'information.

Une analyse de l'historique de chaque élément

retenu dans les structures mentales nous permettrait de distinguer :

Deux types de perception (percepts primaires) :
- **Les percepts de l'affect.** Ils s'accompagnent d'une mobilisation émotionnelle plus ou moins importante.
- **Les percepts de l'intellect.** Ils sont potentialisés par les états de concentration et de focalisation de l'attention.

Deux modes de mémorisation :
- **La mémorisation passive.** Certains faits mémorisés se sont gravés sans effort.
- **La mémorisation active.** L'entrée et le séjour relèvent d'une démarche volontaire d'apprentissage.

Deux modes de restitution :
- **Le rappel fortuit** qui libère des souvenirs souvent liés à une émotion sensitive.
- **Le rappel volontaire**, véritable outil d'accès aux connaissances intégrées. Ce rappel volontaire est régi par deux mécanismes, l'un automatique et l'autre dit de « recherche ».

Ce rappel à la nomenclature classique de la mémoire étant fait, j'aimerais aborder ce sujet sous un angle quelque peu différent. (Nous retrouverons bien sûr ces notions expliquées tout au long de ce chapitre.) En effet la pratique des problèmes de mémoire montre qu'il est possible de diviser les « demandeurs » en deux catégories :

– Ceux qui ont besoin de plus de mémoire générale relative à leur vie quotidienne ou à leur vie professionnelle. Ils vont devoir développer la **mémoire de situation.**

Mémoire d'anticipation.
Mémoire de participation.
+ Mémoire passive.
+ Mémoire active.

– Ceux qui ont besoin de plus de mémoire spécifique relative aux études. Ils devront travailler la **mémoire d'apprentissage**.

La mémoire de situation

1° Mémoire d'anticipation

Certains ont une affligeante facilité à oublier ce qu'ils avaient prévu de faire : acheter le journal le matin, téléphoner à un ami, date d'anniversaire, heure de rendez-vous, etc. Je crois savoir que ces gens-là sont légion ! Nous pourrions appeler cela la *mémoire d'anticipation*. En fait, ce n'est pas vraiment un problème de mémoire, puisque la situation n'a pas encore été vécue. Il s'agit d'un projet à court terme non réalisé. Observons que généralement les projets qui « tiennent à cœur » ne sont que très rarement oubliés comme d'ailleurs ceux dont la réalisation nous rend mal à l'aise. Si vous avez rendez-vous mercredi prochain avec l'inspecteur des impôts, il est fort probable que vous ne l'oublierez pas ! En revanche, les projets qui sont plus anodins ou banalisés auront tendance à « sortir de l'esprit ».

Un projet est une prévision de ce qui est à faire. Il se forme et réside dans les structures mentales une image mentale prévisionnelle qui va, quand tout marche bien, s'allumer au moment opportun, se rappelant ainsi à votre bon souvenir. Si elle ne s'allume pas, on parle d'oubli.

Les deux principaux facteurs d'oubli sont :
– Le temps écoulé entre la décision (fabrication de l'image mentale) et son éventuelle réalisation.
– Une surcharge d'activités qui préoccupent et envahissent l'espace mental ne laissant aucune place aux pensées considérées comme accessoires.

Les solutions à cette mémoire projective déficiente sont :

– Eviter un délai trop long, surtout si le fait en question ne mobilise pas l'affect.

– Ancrer profondément l'image projective, surtout si vous êtes préoccupé et surchargé de travail. Il faut que l'image d'anticipation ait une certaine force de présence. Pour cela, il est possible d'associer le projet à un geste automatique (pour que ce geste, obligatoirement réalisé, devienne un élément déclenchant la mémoire) et de le colorer d'une émotion positive. Expliquons-nous.

Voilà plusieurs jours que vous oubliez d'acheter des piles pour le poste de votre fils. Pour vous en souvenir demain, voici comment vous pourriez procéder :

1. Ancrage de l'image prévisionnelle : Trouvez dans votre journée deux points de repère et vivez en pensée chacun de ces deux moments. Imaginez-vous, par exemple, sortant de votre lieu de travail, faisant comme d'habitude quelques pas avec un de vos collègues, mettant la main dans la poche de la veste pour prendre les clés de la voiture (geste automatique)... C'est à ce moment-là que se fera le déclic : acheter les piles. Anticipez la suite de l'histoire, le magasin, la tête du buraliste, peut-être même pourriez-vous acheter un journal, etc. Puis un deuxième repère imaginé de la même façon. Sous forme de bande dessinée, le personnage verrait, au moment où il met sa main dans la poche, sa bulle s'éclairer d'une lumineuse ampoule avec pour légende : Acheter les piles !

2. Mobilisation de l'affect : Le plaisir fait à votre fils (qui attend depuis plusieurs jours ce petit achat) et peut-être votre propre plaisir à lui rendre ce service.

Cette technique, car c'est une véritable technique, dépasse le cadre strict de la mémoire et conduit progressivement à renforcer et à élargir la conscience. Pour qu'elle donne toute son efficacité, il est indispensable que chacun l'adapte à son plan personnel, à ses habitudes et à sa forme de pensée en respectant toutefois cette idée maîtresse : ancrage de l'image projective et son association à un geste ou à un moment de la journée.

2° Mémoire de participation

Le contenu de cette mémoire est formé des traces qui subsistent, après un temps plus ou moins long, d'une situation vécue. Généralement, la fixation des souvenirs se fait d'une manière involontaire et aléatoire. Analysons cette mémoire passive et nous verrons ensuite comment l'améliorer volontairement.

a) La mémorisation passive

Il me souvient de...

Il me souvient d'un petit restaurant en Tunisie, il y a quinze ans... de la tête du vieux doyen de la faculté de médecine, il y a vingt ans... Je revois la villa où nous allions avec mes parents, il y a vingt-cinq ans... Je me souviens de tout cela et de bien d'autres choses encore ! Tous ces souvenirs sont très présents et très précis et pourtant je n'ai jamais fait le moindre effort pour les retenir. J'ai vécu ces événements, je n'ai fait que les vivre et ils sont restés !

Nous avons tous, en mémoire, une foule de souvenirs que nous avons vécus. Vécu est bien le mot magique pour ce genre de mémoire (qui participe de la mémoire globale). Nous avons été engagés – corps et âme – dans l'événement, c'est-à-dire qu'il y a eu participation de l'affect au moment de la perception. Affect et perception, deux paramètres interdépendants et essentiels. En termes plus généraux, nous parlerons de subjectivité de la perception. Le bagage mnésique (accumulation des expériences passées), la participation affective et la charge émotionnelle de l'information, son importance pour nous, ce à quoi nous sommes sensibles, notre propre attente ou recherche, tous ces faits fortement personnels et subjectifs conditionnent la perception de la situation extérieure et de son séjour dans les structures mentales. C'est une évidence que chacun a pu vérifier au cours de sa vie. Certaines choses, vécues une fois et il y a longtemps, ne s'oublieront jamais.

La subjectivité et la participation de l'émotionnel peuvent cependant devenir négatives.

– Un excès de subjectivité conduit à une interprétation erronée de l'information initiale, à une déformation durant le séjour et donc à une restitution ultérieure faussée (une mauvaise mémoire des faits tels qu'ils se sont déroulés).

Une trop forte émotion (ainsi que le stress) peut entraîner une non-perception ou une perception très incomplète de la situation vécue avec pour conséquence une amnésie partielle ou totale comme après une frayeur, une douleur ou une peine, une agression... etc.

b) La mémorisation active

Les données du problème sont bien claires : comment améliorer la mémoire d'une situation vécue, par exemple, une entrevue avec un client, une conférence, le nom ou le visage d'une personne dans une réunion, etc.

Essayons de comprendre ce qui se passe en de tels moments. Nous sommes placés dans une situation pendant laquelle nous recevons un très grand nombre de stimulations. Comme chaque fois en de pareilles circonstances, nous allons faire un tri pour ne sélectionner que quelques-unes d'entre elles. Ceci rejoint ce que nous venons de voir dans le précédent paragraphe avec toujours cette même participation de l'affect au moment de la perception. Ces informations ainsi triées vont séjourner quelque temps en mémoire, certaines disparaîtront à leur tour... si bien que, les jours passant, ne seront retenus que des souvenirs vagues et non fiables. Pour éviter ce processus d'oubli, deux conditions paraissent primordiales : augmenter la perception et favoriser la répétition.

La perception : Voies d'accès à la mémoire.

La perception est assurée par les organes des sens. Dans les situations qui nous intéressent ici, nous parlerons des perceptions visuelles, auditives et sensitives (kinesthésiques). Chaque individu va privilégier, pour comprendre un événement, une voie d'accès. Etes-vous plutôt un visuel (mémoire des couleurs, des formes, des visages), plutôt un auditif (mémoire des sons, de la musique, des conversations) ou enfin un sensitif (mémoire des impressions, des odeurs, des ambiances, etc.)? Pour le savoir, et c'est intéressant de savoir comment nous « fonctionnons », faites le test de laisser venir, par une mémoire spontanée, un de vos bons souvenirs et notez les sensations qui arrivent en premier. Il est un fait remarquable que nous développerons plus loin : les voies de rappel et les voies d'accès sont semblables. Une autre façon d'établir un « diagnostic » est d'observer la fréquence, dans le langage courant, de certains mots et verbes révélateurs. Voici, pour nous amuser, quelques exemples :

Mots ou expressions utilisés
de préférence par un « visuel »

Image, point de vue, voir, dépeindre, imaginer, tour d'horizon, perspective, voyez-vous (pour comprenez-vous), voyons voir, soyons clairs, etc. Tout cela donne de curieuses phrases dans le genre « J'ai vu Untel au téléphone et il m'a dit que... » ou « Tu as vu la dernière chanson de Machin, quelle merveille ! »

Mots ou expressions utilisés par un « auditif »

Mettre l'accent sur, entendre, entendu (pour compris), se mettre d'accord, harmoniser, grincer (pour irriter), son de cloche, cela a fait du bruit, etc. Et nous aurons des « J'entends bien aller le voir demain », « J'en suis capable, c'est dans mes cordes ».

Mots ou expressions utilisés volontiers par un « sensitif »

Faire impression, choc, contact, toucher du doigt, tâtonner, casser, briser, porter, tomber, impact, porter sur les nerfs, être sur les dents, etc. Ces gens diront : « Ce cadeau m'a beaucoup touché ! » ou « Dès les premiers instants, sa mauvaise humeur m'a frappé ! »

Ainsi, engagés dans une situation, nous privilégions une (ou deux) voies d'accès aux informations. Cette phrase pourrait être écrite au négatif : engagés dans une situation, nous laissons passer un très grand nombre d'informations qui ne nous « correspondent » pas pour n'en retenir finalement qu'une infime partie, environ un pour cent. C'est peu, c'est très peu de matériaux pour construire une bonne mémoire. Nous risquons d'avoir retenu des paroles sans visage (qui bientôt s'envoleront), des personnages muets (qui s'effaceront vite), des situations figées et impersonnelles par lesquelles nous ne nous sentons pas concernés.

Le rappel du fait mémorisé consiste en un assemblage de divers éléments fixés çà et là dans les structures mentales, comme les pièces d'un puzzle. Plus il y a d'éléments, plus le puzzle reconstitué sera cohérent et fidèle à la réalité. <u>Mobiliser l'ensemble de notre système de perception</u> est le moyen le plus efficace pour forger une excellente mémoire ultérieure de la situation globale.

En d'autres termes, pour augmenter la mémoire, il faut apprendre à **devenir conscients...** de ce que nous vivons. Il est souvent dit que la conscience est la perception intégrée. Il est indispensable d'apprendre à percevoir, dans un processus conscient, le maximum d'informations. C'est un apprentissage comme un autre qui doit commencer par des choses simples pour aller vers des choses plus complexes, c'est-à-dire qu'il faut commencer avec des situations sans grande importance.

Apprenez, dès à présent, à être présent!

Voici quelques exercices faciles à réaliser.

- Réservez 2 ou 3 minutes par jour (surtout pas plus) pendant lesquelles vous exercerez votre conscience à percevoir le maximum d'informations constituant le moment présent. Par exemple, vous êtes assis à votre bureau (attitude quotidienne et banale) et posez-vous la question : « Que se passe-t-il en ce moment? » ou bien : « Quels sont les éléments présents et qui définissent cet instant? » Ecoutez, regardez, ressentez tout... ou presque tout (car au début vous ne percevrez qu'une faible partie des composants). Mais répétez cet exercice, si possible à la même heure et au même endroit, pendant une semaine et vous serez surpris de découvrir chaque jour des choses nouvelles.

- Profitez d'un moment de disponibilité mentale pour compléter cet exercice d'un mouvement de conscience plus large. Par exemple lors d'une promenade à la campagne, d'une balade en ville... Amusez-vous à prendre mieux conscience de ce qui se passe autour de vous. Ne marchez plus avec dans la tête des idées ou des images mentales étrangères à la situation vécue. Regardez mieux, écoutez mieux, ressentez plus précisément. Non point pour retenir tout mais simplement pour apprendre à être tout à fait présent à ce que vous faites et plus conscient de ce que vous êtes au moment où vous le faites, plus conscient de vous-même et des multiples sensations qui représentent une incroyable richesse.

Ainsi, exercé à cette gymnastique lors de moments de moindre importance, l'esprit saura intégrer et donc retenir des situations plus spécifiques.

**C'est en écoutant qu'on apprend à entendre...
C'est en regardant qu'on apprend à voir...**

En revanche, si vous ne « voyez pas plus loin que le bout de votre nez », si vous « n'entendez qu'un son de cloche » et si vous vous laissez piéger par cet « arbre qui cache la forêt », vous n'aurez de la situation vécue qu'une perception incomplète, donc, plus tard, une mémoire qualitativement et quantitativement imparfaite.

Les informations ainsi perçues vont séjourner dans le cerveau un certain temps. C'est ici qu'interviennent les notions classiques de durée : très court et court termes, moyen et long termes. Certains auteurs affirment que rien de ce qui a été vécu ne peut s'oublier (la mémoire hypnotique, certaines techniques de sophrologie, les rêves nocturnes révèlent parfois certains faits très anciens apparemment oubliés). Nous n'entrerons pas dans ce débat qui s'adresse surtout aux théoriciens car dans la pratique, et en état de conscience « ordinaire », si un fait réside en un endroit d'où il ne sortira que grâce à des états de conscience particuliers, il peut être considéré comme perdu... puisque non utilisable. Or ce qui nous intéresse, c'est bien que cette réserve de mémoire soit disponible à tout instant, selon notre gré et notre besoin.

Pour rendre un fait mémoire rapidement accessible, une chose est importante : la répétition. Tout le monde le sait, chacun le vit. Vous vous rappelez sans aucune difficulté des numéros de téléphone souvent utilisés alors que souvent votre numéro personnel est plus délicat à retenir !

Comment faire pour rafraîchir la mémoire d'un événement vécu ? **Par la technique du bilan.** Technique que vous pouvez faire le soir, avant de vous endormir, ou à tout autre moment. Elle doit être accompagnée d'un état de relaxation et de calme et ressemble aux révisions des étudiants. Dans cette vision a posteriori, il est facile de faire le tri de ce qui doit être retenu et en favoriser l'ancrage dans les structures mentales libérées par le repos.

Prenons le cas d'un vendeur qui sort de chez un client après une entrevue très importante. Dans les minutes qui suivent, il re-visionne son entretien, avec tous les éléments perçus : la décoration de la pièce, la tenue vestimentaire de l'interlocuteur (ces détails donneront des renseignements utiles quant à la psychologie générale du client), ce qui a été dit (le timbre de la voix, le débit des paroles), les mots employés (ce personnage est-il un visuel, un auditif, un sensitif ?), les arguments développés, sans oublier les impressions ressenties pendant l'entrevue. Puis le soir, revoir en pensée les différentes phases de la journée, les réveiller pour mieux les inscrire et les graver. Cette attitude, que l'on pourrait traduire par l'idée toute simple de « penser à son travail », décuple les possibilités de la mémoire sans effort. Un de mes amis doté de ce type de mémoire, ce qui fait l'admiration de ses collègues, pousse le perfectionnement de la technique en réservant, en fin de journée, une demi-heure à la rédaction par écrit des faits importants de la journée. Sur son journal de bord, avec un style bien à lui, on peut lire ce genre de compte rendu :

« Lundi 12-01-88. Visite chez Paul R. Gros, moustache, convivial, visuel, sensitif, tableaux couleurs vives, tenue sport marron, lui téléphoner début 03 (après R.D.V. chez dentiste = ancrage et association). » Suivent alors des renseignements plus techniques concernant la vente d'un ordinateur. Cet ami prétend – et je le crois à juste titre – que ces fiches sont le secret de sa mémoire... et de ses performances professionnelles.

Il ne sert à rien de se plaindre de sa mémoire, il suffit tout simplement de faire en sorte de l'améliorer... et de lui faire un peu plus confiance !

Résumé en quelques points essentiels et sous forme de conseils pour accroître la mémoire active de situation.

– Faire taire toute activité mentale « hors sujet », se rendre disponible au moment où se déroule la situation afin de devenir de plus en plus (de mieux en mieux) conscient de ce qui se passe.

– Alimenter la mémoire de références diverses : privilégier son système de perception préférentiel mais savoir ouvrir son esprit aux autres perceptions.

– Profiter d'intervalles de calme dans la journée pour des petits bilans ou réflexions afin de permettre, par la répétition, un ancrage puissant dans les structures mentales des éléments à retenir.

La mémoire d'apprentissage

C'est, bien sûr, le type même de mémoire utile aux étudiants.

Mémoire avec les trois phases classiques : perception, fixation et utilisation de l'information. Les mêmes paramètres entrent en jeu : mise en disponibilité de l'esprit et mobilisation de l'affect, les modes de perception préférentiels et la répétition. A ces facteurs agissant sur l'efficacité de la mémoire, nous pouvons ajouter les états de l'attention (concentration et focalisation).

Pour comprendre le processus dynamique de cette mémoire volontaire, essayons d'entrer dans ces fameuses structures mentales et de saisir leur fonctionnement.

LE CERVEAU

Reprenons rapidement certaines données du chapitre sur les structures mentales décrites page 223 et suivantes. Vous le savez, le cerveau est formé de plusieurs milliards de cellules nerveuses (les neurones) reliées les unes aux autres par un réseau très dense de fibres (les synapses). Sur un plan fonctionnel, le cerveau est divisé en régions d'activité spécifique (aire visuelle, aire auditive, etc.).

Certaines régions ont un rôle associatif, d'autres sont spécialisées dans le traitement de l'affectivité et de l'émotion. Les subdivisions sont très nombreuses et encore loin d'être toutes connues. En plus, l'étude macroscopique d'un cerveau nous montre la présence d'un hémisphère droit et d'un hémisphère gauche dont nous avons déjà étudié les fonctions particulières.

Quand une information quelconque est captée au niveau des organes des sens, elle chemine de la périphérie pour arriver dans ce complexe cervical. Là, un certain nombre de neurones, appartenant aux régions spécialisées dans la « gestion » de ce type de stimulation, vont entrer en activité... conjointement.

Cette assemblée de neurones, mise en éveil pour traiter tel type de stimulation, s'organise en un graphe et correspond à un objet mental. Quand la stimulation extérieure cesse, ce graphe reste « allumé » encore un certain temps (une trentaine de secondes), c'est la *mémoire à très court terme*. Puis il s'éteint... mais son trajet est gravé ! **Il reste toujours une trace de ce que nous avons vécu** et cette trace sera d'autant plus vivace qu'un nombre important de neurones auront été sollicités (surtout les cellules nerveuses appartenant aux zones de l'affectivité).

Cet élément de base de la mémoire (connaissance) est appelé un **objet mental.**

Qu'advient-il de cet objet mental ?

Une fois formé, l'objet mental contenu dans un graphe réside dans les structures du cerveau. C'est un élément mémoire de base qui sommeille. Mais il est toujours susceptible d'être réveillé à la première occasion.

Il existe comme une potentialité destinée à être actualisée. La destinée d'un objet mental est triple, il peut devenir :

Percept primaire. C'est la perception simple, par un de nos organes des sens, d'un « objet » extérieur.

Image mentale. Sans rapport direct avec un « objet » extérieur. Le graphe se reforme et l'objet mental est présent par activité cérébrale autogène d'évocation. Les graphes ainsi réactualisés sont ceux qui ont mobilisé, au moment de leur formation, un nombre important de neurones issus des régions sensorielles. Cette activation correspond à l'« imagination de restitution » (1) des objet mentaux présents en mémoire.

Concept. Sans aucune relation avec un objet extérieur, le graphe qui se reconstitue mobilise peu de souvenirs sensoriels mais surtout recrute au niveau des aires frontales associatives. C'est une imagination de création.

---

(1) *Se préparer aux examens par la sophrologie*, J.Y. Pecollo, Retz.

                    Présence de l'objet extérieur
                         ... PERCEPT PRIMAIRE
                    ↗
OBJET MENTAL → Évocation de souvenirs sensoriels
graphe mémorisé ↘   **... IMAGE MENTALE**

                    Idée pauvre en souvenirs sensoriels
                                    ... CONCEPT

APPLICATIONS CONCRÈTES

A la lumière de ce qui vient d'être dit, nous comprenons qu'aucun travail sur le plan de la mémorisation ne peut être efficace si nous n'avons pas l'esprit libre de toute activité.

Prenons comme exemple le cas d'un lycéen en terminale. Au cours de sa journée il a vécu : 1 heure de math, 2 heures de philo, une leçon d'anglais, un exposé de géographie, etc., des discussions avec ses amis, une pensée affective pour sa « petite copine », ses dernières et ses prochaines vacances... autant de graphes tour à tour allumés, autant d'images mentales créées ! Quand arrive le moment de se mettre au travail, il a la « tête ailleurs » !

Ceci se traduit par une autre expression classique : « Je suis pré-occupé », c'est-à-dire que mon espace mental est déjà occupé à gérer d'autres percepts, d'autres images.

Voici notre étudiant distrait par le chant des sirènes intérieures avec son livre de math ouvert devant lui. Les informations « math » (percept) arrivent dans son cerveau et ne rencontrent que des graphes d'images mentales étrangères et hors sujet ! Si bien que, ne trouvant aucune structure d'accueil adéquate, elles s'envolent tranquillement. (« Ça rentre par une oreille et ça sort par l'autre. »)

N'insistons pas sur cet état de dispersion et de

non-disponibilité, nous l'avons tous plus ou moins vécu et nous avons tous lutté contre cette tendance si douce à la rêverie. Il est évident que cette dualité entre le percept imposé (le problème de math) et les évocations autogènes de l'imagerie mentale fait une victime la mémorisation. Pour remédier à ce <u>défaut de concentration</u>, c'est simple : « Il faut é-li-mi-ner ».. les <u>images</u> mentales parasites. Pour cela quelques secondes de **relaxation concentrative** suffisent. (La technique est précisément décrite dans mon livre *Comment se préparer aux examens*, Ed. Retz.)

Ce court instant de concentration sur la respiration, ou certaines sensations corporelles, fait gagner un temps appréciable. C'est une technique qui permet de régler tous les problèmes de mémoire dus à un manque de concentration (c'est le cas le plus fréquent).

Les informations soumises à l'apprentissage (perception, fixation, utilisation) peuvent être de nature différente.

1° Les informations totalement nouvelles

Elles ne « correspondent à rien » de déjà su. Le cerveau va alors devoir créer de nouveaux graphes d'objets mentaux. Pour que ces graphes offrent toutes les garanties nécessaires de fiabilité dans le temps, il faudra :

a) Que l'espace mental soit libéré de toute autre activité.

– Relaxation concentrative.

b) Mobiliser un grand nombre de neurones par une perception <u>multimodale</u> visuelle, auditive, etc.;

– une compréhension de type « cerveau gauche »;

– une approche de type « cerveau droit »...

c) Si possible, intégration des nouvelles données par les processus d'_analogie_, de comparaison ou tout autre moyen mnémotechnique.

Durant cette période du premier apprentissage, il faut savoir qu'un certain temps est nécessaire à l'élaboration de nouvelles structures mentales. Après une première vision, on peut estimer qu'il reste 10 ou 20 % du nombre global des données à apprendre. Cette mémoire quasi spontanée a bénéficié d'une perception préférentielle (ou d'un processus analogique intéressant). Cela permet de créer une structure d'accueil suffisante pour les prochaines révisions.

2° Les informations entrent dans le cadre du « déjà-vu »

C'est-à-dire qu'il existe déjà dans les structures mentales une organisation adéquate. Il s'agit alors d'intégrer une information complémentaire qui viendra enrichir les connaissances en la matière. Pour que les neurones mobilisés dans le traitement puissent coopérer efficacement et que l'assemblée neuronale ainsi formée puisse se rattacher aux graphes du « déjà-vu », il semble important de :
  a) « Eteindre » tous les graphes indésirables.
     Relaxation concentrative.
  b) « Allumer » ceux correspondant à la matière en question.
     Mode « cerveau droit ».
  c) Faire rapidement un « état de sa mémoire » sur le sujet.
  d) Sans se « creuser la cervelle ».
  e) Maintenant seulement ouvrir livre, cours ou cahier.
     Tout est prêt pour accueillir et retenir les informations.

Ce protocole est très rapide (5 à 10 minutes) et

augmente considérablement la concentration et la mémoire.

D'autres paramètres entrent en jeu dans le processus de la mémoire. En particulier la spécificité de chacun des deux hémisphères cérébraux dont nous avons parfois évoqué les rôles.

Pour conclure, nous pourrions énoncer en quelques points les principes de base d'une bonne mémoire.

– **Participation de l'affect et de l'émotion.**

Facilite surtout les « mémoires de situation » tant au niveau de la perception et de la fixation qu'au niveau du rappel du souvenir. Dans la mémoire d'apprentissage l'affect intervient également, par exemple, dans le système de punition-récompense ou dans la joie de trouver par la recherche.

– **La fréquence des contacts.**

Facilite toutes les sortes de mémoire. C'est la mise en éveil répétée des graphes concernés par le souvenir, soit par évocation volontaire soit par des révisions, dans le cas des études.

– **La qualité et la quantité des assemblées neuronales** mises en jeu.

C'est-à-dire une perception sensorielle optimale et variée, toutes ces sensations servant de références pour la fixation et le rappel de l'objet mémoire.

– **La préexistence de graphes.**

Ils peuvent jouer un rôle de support à une nouvelle organisation neuronale qui se « branchera » secondairement : similitude de situation, changements ou ajouts d'éléments sur un objet mental engrammé et branchement sur le mode logique et déductif. D'où l'intérêt de posséder les bases nécessaires pour progresser.

– **La mise en disponibilité de l'activité mentale.**

Facilite surtout la mémoire d'apprentissage en libérant le cerveau de toute activité parasite étrangère à l'objet de l'apprentissage et en favorisant les états de l'attention favorables à la mémorisation (concentration et focalisation).

– **La confiance en sa mémoire et le « lâcher prise ».**

Deux conditions qui influencent surtout la restitution des connaissances. Nous avons tous été soumis à cette véritable torture du « trou de mémoire » soudain au moment de dire un nom ou une date : plus nous nous obstinons à vouloir trouver, plus nous creusons le trou... et quelques heures plus tard, alors que le sujet n'est plus d'actualité, émerge des profondeurs de la mémoire ce qui faisait défaut tout à l'heure !

LE LÂCHER PRISE

**Comment *lâcher prise* alors que
je suis *en prise* avec autant de problèmes!**

Comment comprendre cette notion fondamentale de « lâcher prise » alors que notre éducation nous enseigne l'attitude inverse? Ne nous a-t-on pas toujours dit que « dans la vie il faut se battre pour arriver »... « qu'il ne faut pas se laisser marcher sur les pieds »... « qu'il faut s'imposer pour gagner et rendre coup pour coup si on veut se faire respecter », etc.?

Bien sûr, le lâcher prise n'est en aucune façon synonyme de « je-m'en-foutisme », de « baisser les bras » ou de laxisme. C'est par une plus grande conscience des paramètres qui définissent l'« ici et maintenant » à vivre que le lâcher prise prend toute sa valeur et son efficacité.

Et comment moi, sophrologue, écrivant ces quelques lignes, je peux vous dire que c'est précisément dans cette attitude que se résolvent nos ennuis... que c'est peut-être là le *secret pour réellement supprimer les effets négatifs du stress* et vivre sa vie dans une plus grande tranquillité, avec une plus grande sérénité.

Pour parler de cette notion de lâcher prise applicable à chacune de nos activités, je ne vais pas vous donner une méthode ou des exercices à faire. Dans le but de vous inciter, je l'espère, à réfléchir sur votre propre attitude et à trouver par vous-même la meilleure façon de pratiquer le lâcher prise, nous allons opter pour une forme plus « légère » : histoire, anecdote ou « nouvelle ».

Le lâcher prise dans le travail

Johnny et Billy, trappeurs

Depuis plusieurs semaines, le loup rôdait. Un loup particulièrement rusé et vorace. Il s'attaquait à tous les animaux domestiques et même, par deux fois, à des jeunes gens qui s'étaient trop éloignés des abords de la ville. Le loup inquiétait les habitants de cette petite ville du nord du Canada. Les différentes battues organisées pour le capturer avaient échoué. Si bien qu'il fut décidé de faire appel à deux trappeurs pour dresser des pièges : **Johnny et Billy.**

Johnny et Billy se connaissaient depuis longtemps mais une certaine rivalité, datant de leur plus jeune âge, les séparait. Et quand le sort les désigna pour attraper le loup... Billy décida d'être le plus fort et se jura de capturer le fauve le premier.

Comme dans toutes ces petites villes où les festivités sont rares, le moindre événement prend l'allure d'une fête. Le dimanche matin, à la sortie de l'office religieux, hommes, femmes et enfants étaient réunis sur la place principale pour définir les règles de cette compétition et assister au départ des deux trappeurs. Chacun avait le droit d'emporter une ration de survie pour trois jours, une boussole, une carabine de chasse et cinq pièges à loup. Bénis par le prêtre afin que Dieu les inspire et les protège, les deux hommes attendaient que le plus vieux du village donne, avec une voix dont la solennité prêterait à sourire, le départ vers l'aventure... « Que le meilleur gagne ! »

Johnny partit vers le nord, Billy vers le sud. Tous deux sont des trappeurs émérites et leur tableau de chasse témoigne de leur grande expérience. Ils ont chacun la ferme intention de capturer ce loup, mais ils ont des caractères différents... très différents! Suivons-les dans leur chasse pour nous en rendre compte.

Johnny n'avait qu'une idée très vague de l'endroit où il poserait ses pièges et comme c'était encore un peu trop tôt pour y penser, il profita tout simplement du paysage grandiose que ses yeux connaissaient parfaitement mais que son regard découvrait chaque fois. En trappeur expérimenté, il se souvenait qu'il y a bien longtemps des loups de la forêt empruntaient un chemin particulier pour venir rôder autour du village. Mais ce loup aujourd'hui paraissait bien plus rusé, il agissait en solitaire comme s'il ne connaissait pas le chemin classique. Il décida de se fier à son instinct ou à son intuition pour choisir l'endroit où il pourrait traquer la bête dangereuse.

Est-ce par ce que l'on appelle le hasard, est-ce par une odeur particulière ou par quelques feuilles mortes déplacées mais soudain Johnny sut qu'il fallait piéger le loup ici. Il disposa donc le premier piège puis le second. La façon d'armer ces mâchoires d'acier et le choix des appâts utilisés sont des secrets, aussi je ne vous les dévoilerai pas. Toujours est-il qu'il ne se servit que de deux pièges, gardant les autres en réserve : il avait affaire à un loup rusé et, comme chaque fois que l'on a affaire à quelqu'un de très malin, il vaut mieux ne pas dévoiler tous ses atouts tout de suite. Johnny accomplit son travail avec beaucoup de sérieux, de minutie et de compétence. Il prend plusieurs fois du recul pour voir si tout se passe bien et même monte en haut d'un arbre pour avoir une vue d'ensemble... tout est parfait. Ne rien faire d'autre, ne rien faire en plus, ne rien faire en trop!

Le soleil se couchant très tôt en cette période de l'année, il est maintenant l'heure de chercher un endroit tranquille pour dormir. Johnny qui, comme tous ces grands solitaires, a un vocabulaire assez pauvre se dit ce qui se dit en de pareilles circonstances : « Demain il fera jour ! » Dès son réveil, il alla voir si ses pièges avaient fonctionné : rien. Examinant avec attention les alentours immédiats, il sut que le loup n'était pas passé par là, donc pas besoin de changer son dispositif, simplement il se mit en quête d'autres passages possibles pour installer les pièges qu'il avait en réserve. Si le fauve était bien dans le coin, il ne pourrait lui échapper... mais bien sûr si le loup était parti vers le sud... c'est Billy qui aurait la chance de le prendre.

Car Billy, lui, était parti vers le sud. C'est un homme courageux, robuste et décidé. Ah ça, pour être décidé, il est bien décidé à capturer cette fameuse bestiole qui fait trembler toute la ville ! Avec la prime offerte pour sa capture, il compte s'acheter une belle veste en fourrure dont il a tant besoin. Emballé par cette idée et motivé par cette conviction d'être le meilleur trappeur, son allure s'accélère... il court presque. Il sait d'ailleurs où il va car les loups, dans cette région du Sud, viennent souvent boire à l'endroit où la rivière fait un coude et rend l'eau plus calme. Sitôt arrivé, il installe tous ses pièges : cinq mâchoires toutes neuves disposées en demi-cercle et formant un terrible traquenard. Billy est fou de joie : il a choisi la bonne direction et le bon endroit, c'est sûr, il va gagner.

Billy se dit perfectionniste. Il fignole son travail. Il met quelques feuilles mortes de plus pour être sûr que ses pièges sont invisibles; il va même jusqu'à amasser troncs d'arbres et branches cassées pour fabriquer une sorte de mur et obliger ainsi le loup à passer juste sur un des pièges. Son ouvrage terminé, il se retire pour dormir. Plusieurs fois dans la nuit il se lève pour vérifier si tout est bien en ordre. Il est perfectionniste. Le matin, les pièges sont vides. Enfin presque puisque l'un d'entre eux a capturé un renard! Il va falloir retirer ce piège car l'odeur du renard mort risque d'alerter le loup.

Plus que quatre pièges en place. Il aurait dû en garder un ou deux en réserve! Billy est furieux, il veut absolument avoir la peau de ce loup et puisqu'il ne vient pas tout seul, il décide de battre la campagne aux alentours pour rabattre ce gibier vers la rivière. Le voilà donc parti! Il fait un maximum de bruit, tape avec un gros bâton dans les fourrés, tire plusieurs coups de fusil en l'air. Il est courageux et solide, l'effort ne lui fait pas peur; toute la journée il fait ce qu'il juge bon de faire pour gagner la partie. La seconde nuit arrive et comme il est consciencieux et perfectionniste, il met vraiment toutes les chances de son côté et se lève encore de nombreuses fois pour vérifier que tout est bien en place. Le matin, rien. Les pièges sont toujours vides.

Côté nord, Johnny, après avoir placé les deux autres pièges, s'est éloigné afin que sa présence trop évidente ne mette pas le loup en alerte. Il profita de sa journée libre pour cueillir quelques plantes rares dont il faisait commerce. La grosse prime du loup, c'est bien beau mais il faut assurer le quotidien et les plantes séchées, ça rapporte quand même un peu d'argent. Sa deuxième nuit se passa sans problème et le lendemain, il sauta de joie en découvrant le loup pris au piège.

La capture ne devait pas remonter à bien longtemps car la fourrure de la pauvre bête était encore toute mouillée de transpiration comme si le loup avait couru toute la nuit, comme s'il venait de l'autre côté... côté sud!

Billy et Johnny sont tous les deux de bons trappeurs mais si Johnny fait juste ce qu'il faut,

Billy en fait parfois un peu trop. L'un gagne, l'autre perd.

Et dans le nord du Canada où l'on donne facilement des surnoms aux héros, tous les habitants de la ville parlent de Johnny avec fierté en le nommant :

« JOHNNY LE LÂCHER PRISE »

Alors, vous qui êtes engagé à fond dans votre vie, dans vos affaires et dans votre travail, faites-vous comme Billy ou comme Johnny ?

Avez-vous déjà pensé à laisser sur place votre lot de soucis professionnels avant de rentrer chez vous ?

Savez-vous profiter pleinement des moindres instants de détente ?

Pouvez-vous au cinéma regarder un film, au théâtre apprécier le jeu des acteurs, au concert écouter l'œuvre musicale... alors que le résultat d'une importante négociation n'est pas encore connu ?

Pouvez-vous vivre chaque « ici et maintenant » dans l'exclusivité de ce que cet instant vous apporte sans parasitage de pensées appartenant à hier ou à demain ?

Si oui, vous pratiquez le lâcher prise et c'est parfait.

Si non, souvenez-vous de nos deux braves trappeurs et rapprochez-vous de Johnny. Il nous donne l'exemple à suivre.

***Faire toujours juste ce qu'il faut,
au moment où il le faut,
sans jamais trop.***

Le lâcher prise et le stress

Le jardin de Gaspard

Juché sur une grosse pierre, Gaspard contenait mal sa fierté en contemplant le terrain qu'il venait de s'acheter à quelques kilomètres de la ville. Des années de labeur acharné et d'économies pour réaliser son rêve : avoir une maison de campagne avec un jardin.

« La vieille ferme aux murs décrépis sera facile à restaurer », expliqua-t-il à sa femme puis, parcourant à grands pas l'espace que désormais il possédait, il cria enfin sa joie : « Ici je planterai des arbres fruitiers, ici une étendue de pelouse, là un bosquet de fleurs... » Jouant à l'équilibriste sur une vieille planche il franchit la petite rivière qui partageait le terrain en deux et poursuivit : « Au fond du jardin nous ferons un potager avec des tomates, quelques salades... »

Quelques mois plus tard, le jardin de Gaspard commence à prendre une certaine allure. Les herbes sauvages arrachées et remplacées par un gazon bien vert, et l'imagination peut rendre beaux et grands les maigres bouts de bois qui deviendront des arbres fruitiers. Tout est parfait... ou presque ! Car il y a quelque chose qui gâche un peu la satisfaction de Gaspard : la rivière qui coupe le jardin en deux. Rivière est d'ailleurs un bien grand mot, c'est plutôt un ruisseau qui oblige Gaspard à laisser en permanence des planches de bois pour accéder aux plantations de légumes. « Pas de problème, se dit le propriétaire, je vais construire un petit barrage à l'entrée du terrain et le tour sera joué ! » Aussitôt dit, aussitôt fait. Le barrage est érigé avec de grosses pierres et quelques branches.

Mais l'eau du ruisseau ne se laisse pas impressionner par ce petit obstacle et très vite organise de chaque côté un chemin pour suivre son cours. *Gaspard fait un barrage plus large.*

En amont, l'eau du ruisseau réunit ses forces et passe par-dessus les pierres. *Gaspard fait un barrage plus haut.*

L'eau du ruisseau trouve la parade et creuse un passage souterrain pour ressortir quelques mètres plus loin... en plein milieu du jardin. *Gaspard fait un barrage plus profond.*

Plus large, plus haut, plus profond, l'obstacle devient sérieux ! Si bien que, devant ce monticule inesthétique, les gouttes d'eau tiennent conseil et demandent le renfort de gouttes venant d'en haut : elles ont l'habitude de franchir des obstacles. Il y a foule et devant le gros tas de pierres se forme, sous la haute vigilance de Gaspard, un véritable lac ! « Nous sommes nombreuses, s'écrient les gouttes d'eau, attendons l'arrivée de nos amies venant du ciel et ensemble nous ferons éclater tout cela et nous retrouverons notre liberté et notre territoire... » Et par une nuit d'orage, unissant leurs forces, elles franchissent l'obstacle roulant les pierres et les répandant dans tout le jardin. *Gaspard fait un barrage plus solide.*

Un mur en béton, bien solide, bien haut, bien profond, bien large. Et l'eau passe encore. Gaspard n'en dort plus, son jardin lui fait horreur. Lui qui rêvait de calme et de tranquillité, le voilà stressé, nerveux, obsédé par ce défi et bien décidé à ne pas se laisser faire. Et son mur est de plus en plus haut et large. Le jardin est maintenant entouré d'un grand mur en béton et l'accès à la maison devient problématique les jours de pluie car le ruisseau ceinture la propriété !

Mon vieux Gaspard, et si tu lâchais prise !

« Je ne peux plus, c'est trop tard ! Si je démolis le mur, l'eau va envahir mon jardin et inonder mes plantations.. C'est foutu, je ne peux plus reculer ! »

« Essaie seulement de faire une petite ouverture là où devrait passer le ruisseau. »

Quelque peu étonnée mais toute joyeuse, l'eau du ruisseau reprit progressivement ses habitudes. Et en regardant l'eau couler dans son jardin, Gaspard eut un petit sourire. « Que d'énergie gaspillée ! » Les jours suivants, le mur fut totalement démoli et tout reprit son cours normal. Bien sûr, Gaspard regrette toujours la présence de ce cours d'eau qui divise son jardin en deux mais il a appris à utiliser l'eau pour irriguer son champ et il se console en s'endormant bercé par le son si joli de l'eau qui saute par-dessus les pierres du ruisseau.

Combien de fois avons-nous grossi démesurément un fait pourtant minime au départ !

Combien de fois avons-nous fait « une montagne » d'un petit détail !

Combien de fois, nous croyant menacé ou agressé, nous nous sommes entêté à lutter contre des choses qui n'existaient que dans notre imagination ! Combien de fois nous sommes-nous stressé, vexé, fâché sans raison vraiment valable !

Chaque fois que dans notre vie un événement prend une trop grande importance, posons-nous la question de savoir si nous n'avons pas eu tendance à surdimensionner la situation et s'il n'y a pas un moyen plus simple de résoudre le problème. Souvenons-nous, souvenons-nous que...

Pour vivre dans la tranquillité,
heureux et non stressé,
il n'est jamais trop tard,
comme dans le jardin de Gaspard...

LE SPORT

La démarche sophronique, tout au long de ce livre, a été conduite à travers la méthode essentielle et globale de la Relaxation Dynamique de Caycedo. Cependant, la Sophrologie offre un très large éventail de techniques permettant de répondre à de nombreux problèmes posés par la vie d'un homme.

Il serait possible de dresser une nomenclature de ces différentes techniques selon, par exemple, un ordre alphabétique... mais cette présentation me semble monotone et sans saveur. C'est la raison pour laquelle j'ai choisi de montrer les possibilités sophrologiques dans une méthode globale adaptée à un exemple concret : le sport.

Ainsi, même non directement intéressé par l'activité sportive, le lecteur doit comprendre que les techniques et les exercices proposés peuvent s'étendre et s'adapter à d'autres domaines relevant eux aussi de la sophropédagogie, comme la préparation à la naissance ou aux examens, mais également de la sophrothérapie.

Cette sophrologie appliquée que nous proposons maintenant a pour objectif essentiel l'efficacité, et donc son orientation doit être ciblée sur des problèmes précis qui peuvent surgir à des moments précis. C'est dire que le « Cercle », son contenu et son langage méditatif seront laissés de côté alors que, au contraire, le « Carré », avec son cortège de sensations vécues, son attitude de concentration et son expression de volonté, sera mis en évidence en même temps que sera abordée la participation inévitable de la « Croix » avec tout ce qu'elle contient d'affectivo-moteur.

La Sophrologie est présente dans le sport depuis de nombreuses années et ceci grâce, en tout premier lieu, à l'action dévouée et toujours renouvelée du docteur Raymond Abrezol, responsable du Collège Suisse de Sophrologie. De nombreux sophrologues et sportifs de haut niveau lui doivent beaucoup.

Qu'il veuille bien me permettre de lui rendre hommage en lui dédiant ces quelques réflexions sur la sophropédagogie sportive. En toute simplicité. En toute amitié.

> Décidez de marcher et le corps avance...
> Décidez de courir et le corps accélère son allure...
> Décidez de sauter et, encore une fois, le corps obéit et s'élève...

L'esprit se plaît à commander son corps puis à vivre en retour les sensations du mouvement. Quel plaisir de pouvoir synchroniser l'activité de ses muscles pour qu'aussitôt l'intention se réalise...

L'activité physique en général et le sport en particulier objectivent les rapports que nous pouvons entretenir avec le corps. Plus exactement avec la dynamique du corps.

En effet, le corps est articulé et autour de ces nombreux points d'articulation, grâce notamment aux systèmes musculaire et nerveux, il peut bouger. Cette capacité se traduit par des **mouvements**, des **gestes** et des **actions**. Notons dans ces différents termes une certaine gradation témoignant d'une relation de plus en plus étroite avec l'esprit (ou le mental) du sujet.

Sans vouloir entrer dans une bataille de mots mais simplement pour tenter de définir quelques notions de base, nous dirons que :

Le mouvement est l'expression dynamique du corps la plus élémentaire. Le mouvement, en relation avec l'instinctivo-moteur, est archaïque. Il est sous la dépendance de centres nerveux médullaires ou sous-corticaux qui gèrent tout le processus de réflexes innés. Par exemple, les mouvements instinctifs de la marche, ceux qui permettent de jeter au loin quelque chose de nuisible ou encore les mouvements liés aux comportements instinctifs de la peur ou de l'attaque (mouvement de recul ou d'esquive, etc.).

Mû par des pulsions primaires, le corps s'active et cette activité donne d'ailleurs parfois des résultats étonnants. Ne dit-on pas que « la peur donne des ailes » ou ne parle-t-on pas d'une « force démentielle » et de *force-né*.

Le geste est un ensemble de mouvements appris et dont l'ordonnancement des mécanismes neuro-musculaires nécessaires à sa réalisation tend à devenir automatique.

L'acquisition du geste (du « bon » geste !) est à la base de tout entraînement sportif. C'est-à-dire que l'un des buts de l'entraînement est de créer, à partir d'un ou plusieurs mouvements innés, un geste précis. Ce geste technique devra être alors gravé dans certaines structures sous-corticales et devenir un réflexe acquis. Acquis progressivement par l'apprentissage et la répétition, ce geste, secondairement qualifié de naturel, ne réclamera pas, pour être exécuté, de participation volontaire, réfléchie et consciente. C'est ce processus qui provoque l'admiration des spectateurs pour les champions de haut niveau tant leurs gestes semblent naturels... voire « faciles » ! Admiration équivalente (car travail équivalent) devant les gestes précis, apparemment simples et dépouillés, d'un grand technicien professionnel.

Le geste appris, rendu automatique et réflexe, échappe, pendant son exécution, à l'analyse immédiate rationnelle et affective et présente alors deux avantages et un inconvénient. Les deux avantages sont :

1° Augmentation de la rapidité globale. « Réagir au quart de tour ! »

2° Suppression du doute et de la peur présents au départ de l'action.

L'inconvénient qui en découle est qu'il sera beaucoup plus difficile d'apporter une éventuelle correction à un geste devenu automatique puisqu'il est passé, dans sa genèse et son traitement, au niveau de l'insu. Nous verrons comment, grâce à certaines techniques sophroniques, il est possible de pallier cet inconvénient.

L'action est placée sous la responsabilité directe de l'acteur qui participe, en pleine conscience, à sa réalisation. Toute action est dirigée, elle se place sur un axe et admet donc une origine, un déroulement et une conclusion.

- **Point de départ de l'action.** Nous parlerons de buts à atteindre, de motivations (désir, envie ou besoin), de projection (capacité d'anticipation) et de préparation. En d'autres termes nous prendrons conscience du *pourquoi* de notre vouloir et du *comment* le satisfaire.

- **Le déroulement de l'action** renvoie au(x) geste(s) et donc à l'apprentissage préalable, lors de l'entraînement, d'un certain automatisme. La mise en jeu d'un certain automatisme pendant l'exécution du geste permet de libérer « l'esprit » du sportif. Ceci a également quelques conséquences qu'il convient de souligner.

Positives : Meilleure mobilisation de l'attention vers l'action à entreprendre.
« Regard plus lucide. »
Réconfortante sécurisation dans l'action.
« Valeur sûre ! »

Négatives : Découragement devant une difficile adaptation à une situation évolutive. (Durant le déroulement d'un match, par exemple.)

Lassitude engendrée par la répétition d'un défaut dans un geste technique qui freine tout progrès.

● **La conclusion ou le bilan.** Etape importante dans la réalisation d'une action car elle conduit à une analyse du résultat obtenu, « ce que j'ai *effectivement* fait », par rapport à ce qui avait été prévu, « ce que je voulais faire ». Cette attitude de bilan que le sportif apprend à faire seul (qui donc pourrait le faire à sa place !) est fondamentale car elle permet :

– de corriger d'éventuelles erreurs ;
– de renforcer et de stabiliser le bon résultat ;
– de prendre conscience, c'est-à-dire de faire passer dans le « su » la globalité de l'action qui, sans ce bilan, aurait pu rester dans « l'insu » et donc ne pas servir d'expérience.

L'activité physique libre

Si le cœur a ses raisons, le corps a ses besoins. Besoins de bouger, de courir, de sauter et, pour employer un mot à la mode, de s'exprimer. Avant la modernisation de la société, l'activité physique faisait partie du quotidien. Le corps était *utile*. Hommes et femmes faisaient parfois des kilomètres à pied ou à vélo pour aller travailler et, pour abattre un arbre ou creuser un trou, il n'y avait que des pioches, des haches et... les bras. Souvenons-nous de ces images (qui appartiennent maintenant au passé) montrant nos « braves » gendarmes ou nos « gentils » facteurs parcourant la campagne sur de vieilles et lourdes bicyclettes ! Aujourd'hui tout cela a pratiquement disparu et le fait d'appuyer sur la pédale de frein ou de changer de vitesse en conduisant n'est guère exaltant pour le corps. Le dialogue entre le corps et l'esprit s'est peu à peu éteint, alors parfois, par cris ou chuchotements, le corps reprend la parole. Il parle de ses envies, de ses désirs, de ses besoins. Certains savent l'écouter et faire de leur corps... un allié, un compagnon à part entière, un ami. Sans autre souci que le plaisir de passer quelques instants en tête à tête avec lui dans une activité physique libre.

Souvenez-vous de cette impression de bien-être après une journée en plein air, longue marche, sortie en mer ou partie de tennis. Souvenez-vous de ce qu'il est admis de nommer une « saine fatigue », celle qui survient après avoir donné libre cours à son corps, corps qui nous est rendu « fatigué mais heureux » !

Depuis quelques années, et fort heureusement, l'activité physique est à la mode. De plus en plus de citadins envisagent des vacances actives et les « joggeurs » du dimanche sont nombreux dans les bois des villes. Pourquoi ? Tout simplement pour contrebalancer les effets négatifs de la surcharge stressante du quotidien. L'esprit (ou le mental) semble dépassé par le trop-plein de stimulations de tous ordres et n'arrive plus à s'autoréguler, c'est-à-dire ne parvient plus à se calmer par ses propres moyens. Alors il demande de l'aide. De l'aide extérieure, de la médication la plus aliénante aux forfaits vacances les plus lénifiants. Mais aussi de l'aide à son plus fidèle compagnon : **le corps**. « Après une semaine de boulot, quand je suis crevé, je sens que j'ai besoin de me remuer, de faire un peu d'exercice... Ça me fait du bien de transpirer... etc. »

Assailli par les soucis, les ennuis ou les chagrins, nous n'arrivons plus à calmer la tempête mentale (intellectuelle ou affective) qui gronde et nous avons besoin de chercher secours dans l'effort physique. Les stimulations neuromusculaires chassent, par leur présence envahissante, toutes les autres idées ou images mentales parasites. Nous nous laissons saisir par cet afflux de sensations corporelles « sans penser à rien ». Puis, après l'effort physique, la fatigue arrive et le corps doit se reposer... Repos et détente qui se transforment en calme dans la tête... La tempête s'apaise et tout notre être profite de ce bien-être.

Ce processus va bien dans le sens ascendant dans

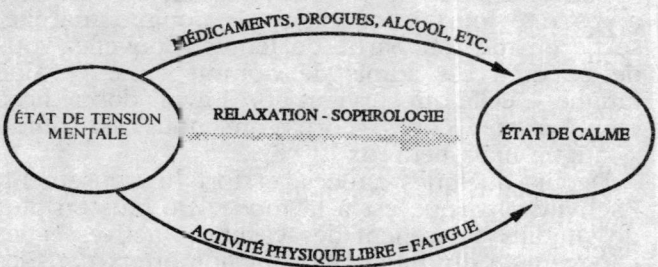

la mesure où nous laissons au corps, par une libre expression autorisée, le rôle de grand régulateur de la tension intérieure.

Il faut comprendre que dans ce cas l'attitude est volontairement libérée de toutes contraintes : pas de performances, pas de compétitions, pas de vrais matches, pas de gestes techniques... surtout pas !

Libre, l'activité physique se doit d'être libre pour être libératoire.

La motivation essentielle de ce type d'activité est de faire naître des sensations physiques. Ainsi certaines personnes, ayant perdu tout contact avec leur corps depuis longtemps, vont avoir besoin, pour ressentir sa présence, de sensations fortes et donc risquent d'abuser et de dépasser leurs capacités physiques. C'est un piège dans lequel il faut évidemment éviter de tomber en prenant garde de ne pas aller jusqu'à l'épuisement sous prétexte de faire « un peu d'exercice ». Les « retrouvailles » avec son corps ne peuvent se faire que progressivement et de même qu'on ne doit pas « forcer la porte » d'un ami avant d'être vraiment sûr de lui, il est dangereux de forcer son corps avant de le connaître.

L'activité sportive

Dans la pratique d'un sport, la démarche est toute différente et, sous certains aspects, contraire à ce que nous venons de voir. Le sport doit être considéré comme une *activité physique contrôlée*. Je pense que le tout premier point dont le sportif doit prendre conscience est que le sport, et ce, quelle que soit la discipline, exige un contrôle mental du corps.

Ici, le dialogue est centrifuge, c'est-à-dire que « l'ordre » part d'en haut et que le corps doit obéir. Se trouvent ainsi réunis dans une seule et même personne, le commandant et l'exécutant. Il faut donc que le sportif ait, d'une part un esprit capable de commander et de se faire obéir et d'autre part, un corps capable de comprendre puis d'exécuter l'ordre reçu. Cette alchimie ne pourra se réaliser et se concrétiser dans les faits que s'il y a une véritable alliance, voire complicité, entre le corps et l'esprit. Nous verrons que tout ceci n'est absolument pas une élucubration intellectuelle mais représente une réalité authentiquement vécue lors du travail sophronique.

L'alliance entre le mental et le physique s'élabore progressivement par des « rencontres » (il faudrait inventer le mot « d'autorencontre ») successives. C'est un véritable **apprentissage** favorisé

par l'entraînement, hors compétition. Cet entraînement devrait être, à mon sens, un entraînement à mieux se connaître, pour « mieux se commander et mieux s'obéir ».
- Apprendre à **définir** le but à atteindre.
- Apprendre à **vouloir** atteindre ce but défini.
- Apprendre à **calmer** ses doutes et ses craintes.
- Apprendre à **connaître** son corps, à reconnaître ses **droits**.
 (Schéma corporel – Vécu des sensations – Relaxation.)
- Apprendre à **respecter** son corps, à satisfaire ses **besoins**.
 (Hygiène de vie – Diététique – Musculation.)
- Apprendre à **maîtriser** son état psychologique.
 (Dynamisation-Détente.)
- Apprendre à **contrôler** son état physique.
 (Tonicité – Relâchement.)

Cet apprentissage, conjuguant le travail de l'entraîneur technique et le travail de « l'entraîneur sophronique », contribue à l'éclosion de la personnalité de l'athlète et à l'élaboration d'un véritable esprit sportif.

Esprit sportif qui, par le désir conscient et exprimé, stimule le vouloir et admet le devoir.

Activité de compétition

Quand le sport devient compétition et s'organise en concours, un autre monde apparaît. Toutes les références antérieures, tous les repères qui ont jalonné la route du jeune athlète changent complètement. Jusqu'à présent, il fut confronté aux

« moins mauvais » et le voilà en compétition contre les « meilleurs » ! Et quelquefois il doit se battre contre des sportifs renommés qui lui servaient de référence : *Il faut tuer l'idole* et ce n'est pas une chose évidente ! Le virage psychologique est, à ce moment, difficile à négocier car l'Autre (à qui on peut mettre un grand A !) conserve encore un certain ascendant, une certaine « aura », et ce fait peut être très inhibant.

Au début de son « parcours », le jeune sportif agissait pour son propre compte et selon son seul plaisir. Maintenant les données du problème sont fondamentalement différentes : il se doit de partir à la recherche d'une performance imposée par d'autres. Les motivations changent et n'est-il pas compréhensible qu'à certains moments « l'esprit » se demande si « la barre n'est pas placée trop haut » ? Le doute apparaît alors, doute essentiel qui jaillit et se développe à partir de l'instant où le but à atteindre ne correspond plus à ce que « je veux et peux faire » mais à ce que « je dois faire » pour être le meilleur. Or c'est, je pense, l'intime conviction de nos capacités qui détermine les limites de nos possibilités. Aller au-delà de ces limites, intuitivement fixées, c'est aller au-devant d'un échec.

En d'autres termes, nous trouverons toujours la motivation et la pulsion nécessaires à atteindre le but que nous nous sommes fixé à et pour nous-même, en revanche, devant un objectif pré-établi et non « assimilé », les efforts paraîtront plus importants. Il faudra alors trouver d'autres motivations, d'autres raisons (que le seul plaisir) pour continuer le difficile chemin vers la victoire. Les raisons évoquées ne sont souvent que des « **valeurs ajoutées** » car elles appartiennent au monde social : fortune, prestige, voyages... etc. Elles sont extérieures et parfois même étrangères au sportif. Si dans certains pays ces raisons peuvent être très

« motivantes », en Europe et particulièrement en France, elles ne sont pas toujours suffisantes. Et on comprend alors que, au moment d'un « passage à vide » ou d'une contre-performance, l'athlète, déçu et découragé, rejette tout son engagement et remette en cause les raisons mêmes de cet engagement.

« On me demande de me *dépasser... surpasser... défoncer... m'éclater*! Alors que j'ai envie de me retrouver, de retrouver un peu de mon identité et de mon premier plaisir, ce plaisir qui faisait de mon sport un jeu! » Progressivement l'esprit sportif, qui représente l'harmonie et l'équilibre entre le « vouloir-faire » et le « pouvoir-faire », se trouve dissous sous l'emprise de l'esprit de compétition qui oblige et souvent objective le divorce entre le « vouloir-pouvoir » et le « devoir-pouvoir ».

Il en est de même pour toutes les activités, sportives ou autres : le chemin qui mène au but semble très long et astreignant si le but n'est pas clairement connu ou n'est pas totalement accepté en tant qu'objectif. Les obligations vécues comme des contraintes ne résistent jamais au doute qui peut surgir à tout instant ni au temps qui érode les convictions les plus grandes. Nous assistons alors à une sorte de glissement général : la motivation première se dénature et devient raison... raisonnable. Le désir initial cède la place aux « valeurs ajoutées » pour jouer le rôle de moteur... pendant un certain temps. Jusqu'au moment où celles-ci perdent leur valeur(!) et laissent le sportif *sans envie*.

A ces difficultés d'ordre général s'en ajoutent d'autres : celles relatives à la vie privée de l'individu et celles liées aux problèmes conjoncturels de la compétition elle-même.

La démarche sophronique doit consister en une approche globale de la personnalité du sportif et tenter de résoudre (ou d'aider à résoudre) les difficultés à tous les niveaux. C'est la raison pour laquelle il convient d'offrir à l'athlète, en même temps qu'un entraînement technique, un entraînement à une méthode sophronique de prise en charge de soi sur le plan psychologique.

MÉTHODE GLOBALE :
SOOSPORT

Pour comprendre le pourquoi des différentes techniques sophroniques choisies et développées qui composent cette méthode globale, revenons à l'essentiel, essentiel que nous pouvons symboliser par la « **règle des trois grands trois** ».

I. Philosophie générale selon trois principes

1. Le sport : activité physique sous « contrôle » du mental.

C'est un parfait *exercice du vouloir* dont le résultat est concret, objectivable. Pour que ce vouloir puisse s'exercer dans sa totalité, il faut acquérir :

A) Un « état d'esprit » disponible, clair et reposé, pour une bonne aptitude à commander. (Techniques de détente mentale et de concentration. Prise de conscience du vouloir et du devoir.)

B) Un « état physique » disponible, sain et libéré, pour une bonne aptitude à obéir. (Techniques de libération et de dynamisation corporelles.)

C) Une parfaite alliance « corps-esprit », harmonisation nécessaire, sinon suffisante, pour que se réalise pleinement le vouloir. (Techniques pour affiner la perception du schéma corporel par la réception des sensations corporelles dans la relaxation contrôlée et par le mouvement maîtrisé.)

2. Le haut niveau : véritable carrière.

La pratique d'un sport exige de nos jours, et surtout pour le haut niveau, l'acceptation pleine et entière de nombreuses « obligations ». Ces nécessités, sous peine d'être vécues comme aliénantes, ne doivent pas occulter l'objectif à long terme : la réalisation du désir, le but essentiel, le vrai moteur du vouloir étant le plaisir de pratiquer un sport de haut niveau. – On pourrait être tenté de dire, **même** à un haut niveau ! En dénudant à l'extrême la réflexion, il n'y a en fin de compte que deux grandes motivations qui poussent à agir et entretiennent l'effort :

– Le besoin, presque vital, de réussir : « Tout faire pour s'en sortir ! » Stimulation par l'instinctivo-moteur du « Carré ».

– Le désir, presque « idéalisé », de SE réussir : « Tout faire pour et par le plaisir ! » Stimulation par l'affectivo-moteur de la « Croix ».

(Techniques stimulant la volonté – quels que soient les motifs qui l'animent – afin d'intégrer l'ensemble du parcours de sportif et les efforts nécessaires.)

3. La compétition : moment de la carrière.

Moment par lequel le sportif va pouvoir (ou devoir !) se mesurer aux autres... et les autres se comparer à lui ! Cette confrontation est le type même du stress, pris dans le sens premier : situation hors routine déclenchant une réaction d'adaptation. De cette obligation d'adaptation découle toute une série de problèmes bien connus des sportifs et de leurs entraîneurs :

Trac avant et pendant l'épreuve.

Manque de confiance en soi, doute et inhibition dus à :
- L'importance de l'épreuve.
- La personnalité du ou des adversaires.
- L'environnement (foule, pays étranger).
- Une défaite récente.

Manque de combativité dû à :
- Une fatigue physique.
- Une fatigue morale (lassitude).

II. Organisation pratique selon trois plans

1. Ensemble des sportifs, quels que soient niveau et discipline.

Relaxation rapide et contrôlée.
- Mise en place du « geste conditionné ».
- Mise en place des techniques d'autorelaxation spécifique et volontaire.

Prise de conscience du schéma corporel.
- Mise en place de la « commande corticale ».
- Mise en place de « l'exécution corporelle ».

Dynamisation mentale.
- Définition et objectivation du désir.
- Exercice du vouloir.
- Mise en place de la technique de « l'autobilan ».

2. Athlètes d'une même discipline (ou de disciplines similaires).

Ici pourront être envisagés les problèmes plus spécifiques au sport pratiqué, en mettant l'accent sur l'un des thèmes suivants :

Rapidité et puissance.

Endurance et cadence.

Tension – relâchement de muscles précis.

Découpage séquentiel de l'action en gestes, et réintégration des gestes dans l'action globale.

Réflexions sur ces séquences et mise en place de techniques sélectives de :
- Concentration de l'attention avant, pendant ou entre les épreuves.
- « Défatigabilité » musculaire sélective.

Esprit d'équipe.
- Consolidation des rapports entre les joueurs.
- Définition des rôles respectifs.

Mise en place d'une approche de la compétition.
- Lutte contre le trac et libération mentale.
- Augmentation de la combativité.

3. Individu : personnalité du sportif.

Ce chapitre se rapporte aux problèmes propres à chaque athlète en fonction de la façon dont il aborde son activité sportive et sa vie en général.

- Approche personnelle du sport pratiqué :

Le travail sophronique, étant, pour une part, un travail sur le corps lors de gestes très précis, doit se faire en étroite relation avec l'entraîneur qui surveille et conseille sur le plan technique, le médecin qui surveille et conseille sur le plan physiologique, le sportif qui exécute, vit et ressent l'action, et le sophrologue qui contribue à la prise de conscience des sensations vécues et qui aide, lors de séances ultérieures, à leur mémorisation. Cette approche, qui s'effectue et s'objective sur le terrain, pendant l'action, est un travail d'équipe dans lequel chacun apporte un regard spécifique selon sa spécialité. Le dialogue qui en résulte crée un mouvement dynamique tout à fait constructif, dialogue auquel le principal intéressé prend une part de plus en plus importante.

- Approche psychologique :

Dans un deuxième temps, les techniques déjà vues en groupe sont reprises en séances individuelles et leur « contenu » retrace les préoccupations personnelles. Avec en particulier un vécu sophronique des progrès réalisés lors de l'entraînement physique, ceci ayant pour but de stabiliser la performance et les gestes corrigés – considérés alors comme une valeur sûre – et de renforcer la confiance en soi.

Dans certains cas, par exemple lors d'un blocage manifestement psychologique, il peut être nécessaire de tenter une recherche, par des techniques appartenant à la sophrothérapie, des causes profondes de ce blocage. Je pense cependant qu'il faut être très prudent dans ce genre de démarche afin de ne pas transformer l'aide sophronique en psychothérapie. Ce genre d'investigation qui touche forcément à la vie privée et intime du sujet ne doit être entrepris qu'en total accord avec le sportif et dans un but bien précisément défini.

III. Les techniques choisies selon les trois moments

Nous ne verrons pas en détail les différentes techniques employées. Ici encore moins que dans les précédents chapitres, car le contenu des séances étant essentiellement pratique, il ne peut se traduire, sous peine d'être dénaturé, en mots écrits. Exception sera faite pour quelques-unes d'entre elles, bien connues des sophrologues, qui n'ont pas été encore abordées dans ce livre, et dont nous allons essayer d'expliquer le **pourquoi** de leur très grande efficacité et de les intégrer dans la préparation à l'activité de compétition.

1. Avant les compétitions

a) Technique n° 1
Relaxation rapide et contrôlée

Explications théoriques
La relaxation a été largement développée au début de ce livre et nous ne reviendrons pas sur les détails de la théorie. Précisons cependant que pour

le sport, plus que dans d'autres domaines, le contrôle devra s'exercer aussi bien sur les niveaux ou degrés de relaxation que sur les zones corporelles à détendre.

La Sophrorelaxation est un *acte*, un acte volontaire. Il n'est pas question de se faire relaxer comme on se fait masser, mais bien d'effacer, par soi-même, toutes tensions inutiles, que celles-ci soient mentales, affectives ou physiques. En ce sens, la relaxation prend toute sa valeur sophronique. Nous avons déjà imaginé cette démarche comme étant un chemin que le sujet fait lui-même... Une route qui conduit à la détente. Comme tout chemin, il se fait d'autant plus facilement, rapidement et sûrement, que l'on connaît :

1º L'endroit où l'on va : le but à atteindre.

2º L'itinéraire à prendre : les repères ou les étapes.

3º Un moyen d'accélérer le mouvement : les respirations spécifiques.

Description sommaire de la méthode

Au début, le rôle du sophrologue est d'amener, par tous moyens connus, le sujet en relaxation. Tous moyens connus : musique appropriée, suggestions générales de calme, etc., mais sans utiliser les suggestions de sensations précises (pesanteur, chaleur ou autre). Quand, par l'action du sophrologue, le sujet est détendu, il doit alors prendre conscience de cette relaxation grâce aux sensations présentes et perçues. Quelles que soient celles-ci ! C'est pour cela qu'il est important de ne pas « injecter », pendant l'induction, des sensations étrangères au vécu perceptif de l'individu.

« ... Nous sommes maintenant arrivés au terme de notre projet de relaxation et votre corps est parfaitement détendu.

« Parce que vous l'avez voulu, nous avons fait ce chemin à deux et c'est normal au début. Mais j'aimerais que vous regardiez maintenant votre corps, que vous preniez conscience de son état de tranquillité.

« Remarquez les sensations présentes... Le sentiment de bien-être... Et gardez bien en mémoire cette globalité de repos agréable... cette harmonie d'ensemble... Dans le dialogue privé entre le corps et l'esprit, les phrases et les mots sont absents.

« **Le langage du corps est sensation,**
« **le langage de l'esprit est image mentale...**

« Vivez et ressentez les sensations libérées en même temps que se dessine, dans votre tête et peut-être devant vos yeux, une image mentale de calme. »

La séance peut alors, après la reprise qui suit, s'arrêter là. Elle constitue ainsi une version simplifiée de la classique sophronisation de base. Dans une deuxième séance, nous expliquons que nous pourrons retourner dans la relaxation un peu plus rapidement, puisque nous savons déjà où nous allons mais qu'il est important de prendre maintenant quelques repères de façon à jalonner la route. Repères au nombre de trois que nous considérerons comme des étapes sur le chemin de la détente. Chacune de ces trois étapes devra être reconnue par les sensations présentes puis franchie pour continuer la route. Elles recevront un nom : la première, *l'étape calme*, la deuxième, *l'étape relax* et la troisième, le *bien-être intérieur*.

Après l'induction d'une sophronisation de base classique, le *terpnos logos* se poursuit ainsi :

... « Vous êtes de nouveau dans la relaxation... reconnaissez-la...

Retrouvez vos sensations globales de bien-être... Vous allez maintenant jalonner votre route et mettre en place certains repères...
- **La première étape est le visage**... Prenez conscience des présentes sensations, ici et maintenant, afin de mémoriser cette détente

réelle. Appelons cette étape, l'étape du calme.
- Puis dirigez-vous vers le **deuxième repère** : la relaxation des bras, des jambes, du dos... Sensations vécues, précises, réelles, concrètes. Etape **relax !**
- Allons maintenant vers **la troisième étape : le ventre**... Vivez sans retenue cette impression de plénitude, de tranquillité... le ventre respire calme et serein... dernière étape avant le bord du sommeil, l'étape du bien-être intérieur.
- A partir de maintenant, vous ferez seul cette route qui mène à la détente, vous retrouverez chaque fois ces étapes, ces repères, de plus en plus nettement et sûrement, et vous les appellerez toujours par leur nom. »

Le sportif peut ainsi *expérimenter* sa propre capacité à la relaxation. L'expérimentation d'un phénomène (ici, les sensations liées au relâchement musculaire) est la base même de l'attitude sophronique et sert à renforcer la conscience par l'expérience vécue.

Au niveau pratique, on comprend que le sportif, après avoir « engrammé », mémorisé sa relaxation (grâce aux images mentales et aux noms donnés), pourra, à volonté et tout seul, en reproduire les sensations et les effets. Ce genre d'exercice constitue le premier contact réel avec la volonté (de se détendre) et la réalisation du vouloir (présence des sensations). Le fameux rêve de contrôle et de maîtrise de soi commence ici à se concrétiser et il est important de s'apercevoir que cette capacité passe avant tout par le calme et la détente. Après les séances nécessaires à la mise en place de la technique de Relaxation rapide et contrôlée, un grand pas vient d'être franchi, le sujet entraîné est maintenant prêt à aller plus avant dans la conquête de soi.

b) Technique n° 2
Technique conditionnée (T.C.)

Explications théoriques

A l'origine, cette technique utilisée dans une optique thérapeutique est individuelle. Elle vise à créer un conditionnement de type pavlovien en substituant un geste à un symptôme. Le conditionnement se fait pendant les séances de sophronisation. (Plusieurs séances sont souvent nécessaires.) La méthode est relativement simple mais doit s'appliquer à des sujets déjà entraînés à la relaxation. En état sophronique, le patient vit une situation déclenchant les symptômes dont il signale l'apparition par un signe convenu. (Par exemple en levant l'index.) A ce moment, les effets négatifs de la manifestation pathologique sont dissipés par suggestion et laissent place à une sensation de calme. Cette sensation de calme est elle-même associée à un geste prévu. Ainsi, placé en situation réelle de stress, le patient pourra lui-même substituer le geste appris au symptôme dès son apparition. C'est, bien entendu, une sorte de traitement d'urgence, un palliatif, avant de trouver la cause profonde de ce malaise mais avec l'avantage de ne pas déplacer le symptôme vers une autre manifestation puisque celui-ci continue d'être présent même si son développement est stoppé.

La mise en place de ce geste peut rendre de réels services en sophropédagogie et, en particulier, en sophrologie sportive. Avant la séance et en total accord avec le sujet, ce geste choisi est :

- Soit extrait de la gestuelle comportementale habituelle (protocole classique du sportif : mettre son bandeau ou son poignet au tennis, remonter les chaussettes, etc.). Ces gestes rituels – qui ont l'avantage d'être discrets et instinctifs – servent à induire un état global de calme et peuvent s'inscrire dans la technique de *sophro-substitution sensorielle* que nous décrirons plus loin.

● Soit, au contraire, un geste inhabituel qui deviendra une sorte « d'arme secrète » à utiliser à certains moments difficiles. Le geste inhabituel pourra être réservé à la résolution d'un problème particulier qui survient à un moment précis, avant ou pendant l'épreuve.

Il est d'ailleurs possible de travailler sur les deux types de gestes, chacun ayant une « fonction » différente. Prenons, pour illustration de cette technique, le cas d'un athlète vivant un état de panique en entrant sur un stade « plein à craquer » de spectateurs bruyants.

Description sommaire de la technique

Lors de discussions préalables, le problème doit être précisément défini aussi bien dans ses modalités d'apparition que dans ses conséquences corporalisées : énervement, agitation, modification des rythmes respiratoire ou cardiaque, etc. De même, le sophrologue et le « sophronisé » se mettent d'accord sur un signe conventionnel de dialogue pendant la séance, par exemple lever l'index de la main droite pour dire « oui ».

Le sujet conduit son corps et son mental dans une profonde relaxation (grâce aux techniques de relaxation rapide et contrôlée), la respiration est calme et régulière. Il lui est alors demandé de se mettre, mentalement, en position de vivre le début de la situation stressante. Grâce à l'anamnèse préalable, le sophrologue peut aider à faire venir, par l'évocation de certains éléments, cet événement afin que celui-ci soit vécu, ici et maintenant, dans toute sa dimension psycho-physique. Au moment où les manifestations apparaissent, le sujet lève l'index pour les signaler (bien que celles-ci soient généralement visibles par un observateur attentif!).

« Très bien ! Vous êtes dans l'événement que vous revivez, ici et maintenant, dans votre tête et dans votre corps, avec toutes les manifestations de ce stress. Sans restrictions, en toute lucidité, en toute conscience...

« Vous voulez ne plus être troublé par cette foule... Eloignez-la de vous. Imaginez que ces gens deviennent petits... Les clameurs se taisent.

« Reprenez le contrôle de votre respiration... Très bien... Je fais respirer mon ventre. Mon cœur bat, calme et tranquille... Je dirige volontairement toute mon attention sur ma respiration que je laisse libre maintenant...

« Concentrez-vous, comme vous savez le faire, sur une sensation quelconque, corporelle, bien présente... Une valeur sûre...

« Je retrouve tout mon calme, toutes mes capacités de contrôle et de maîtrise. Je retrouve également la totalité de mes moyens physiques et ma force mentale... Je rends insignifiant (sans signification pour moi) cet environnement... C'est très bien.

« Vous venez de réussir et prenez conscience de ce sentiment de sérénité et de sécurité qui vous habite. La prochaine fois que vous serez en présence effective de ce genre de situation, vous retrouverez ce calme et cette force.

« Et pour vous aider dans ce contrôle volontaire et conscient, vous pourrez faire un certain geste... Ce geste que vous avez choisi tout à l'heure et que vous allez faire maintenant... Prendre la décision et faire ce geste, c'est décider de se mettre, par le calme retrouvé, en position de gagner... de réussir et de se réussir dans l'action qui suit...

« C'est aussi se dire que « rien d'autre ne compte pour moi que cette formidable envie, ce vrai désir de me libérer totalement... de retrouver intact mon authentique vouloir et mon pouvoir de l'exprimer... »

« La foule de spectateurs et le bruit ne vous dérangent plus. Au contraire. C'est vous qui regardez maintenant les autres et votre regard a changé !

« Vous puisez dans cet environnement une très grande énergie positive.

« Ce geste qui n'appartient qu'à vous, votre geste, est un allié, une arme secrète et vous la garderez secrète. Vous pourrez l'utiliser chaque fois que vous en aurez besoin **et chaque fois vous retrouverez immédiatement le calme intérieur en alliance avec l'énergie.** »

Il est, je pense, important d'insister sur le fait que cette démarche est volontaire. C'est le sportif lui-même qui s'autoconditionne pour résoudre ce type de problème que l'on pourrait assimiler à une phobie légère. Pour rendre la technique conditionnée efficace, il faut la renforcer par la répétition. Elle est donc enregistrée sur une cassette que le sujet garde afin de la refaire chez lui quand il le souhaite et, en particulier, quelque temps avant une compétition.

Ce geste peut être associé à une image mentale comme il peut être renforcé par la présence d'un objet personnel. Mais alors il est absolument nécessaire de bien expliquer la portée et la signification de cet objet qui n'est rien d'autre qu'un moyen d'autogestion de l'émotion afin d'éviter de développer une attitude fétichiste envers tel ou tel gadget « porte-bonheur ». En revanche, l'expérience montre que le geste de manipulation d'un objet appartenant au matériel sportif est particulièrement efficace. Par exemple, pour un joueur de tennis, faire rebondir la balle ou la presser dans la main. Ce peut être également boire une gorgée d'eau, se lacer la chaussure, sautiller sur place ou même un geste technique simplifié comme un revers, un coup de pied... Ces gestes ne peuvent bien entendu être faits pendant la séance mais leur exécution mentale est souvent tout aussi efficace.

c) Technique n° 3
Sophro-Projection positive (S.P.P.)

Explications théoriques

Technique originale qui permet d'intégrer, dans un vécu sophronique, l'épreuve à venir avec ses différentes séquences. Nous profitons de cette séance pour revoir et renforcer les techniques d'autocontrôle mises en place ultérieurement. Un peu à la manière d'un étudiant qui révise avant un examen, la S.P.P., par son approche à la fois globalisante et séquentielle, est sécurisante pour le sportif qui peut ainsi se « préparer » à la compétition toute proche.

Avant la séance nous établissons, d'une façon très précise, les différentes étapes de la journée (ou des journées) de compétition, depuis la veille jusqu'à la fin de l'épreuve. Pour chaque étape, nous définissons ensemble les points essentiels à surveiller. Tous les détails ne peuvent et, à mon avis, *ne doivent pas* être envisagés. Il faut insister sur le fait qu'il y a toujours, et dans toute situation, l'important et le secondaire. L'important est de rester, quoi qu'il arrive, en parfait contrôle de soi pour « la part qui m'incombe, pour ce que j'ai à faire », le reste n'étant que détail. (Il n'existe d'ailleurs dans les rencontres d'une certaine importance que peu d'imprévus, d'ordre matériel, qui doivent être réglés par le sportif lui-même.) Cette récapitulation faite en toute conscience et en toute logique est déjà une façon positive de démystifier l'événement en faisant passer toutes les incidences dans le « su ». C'est une manière de « savoir comment ça se passe ». Reste maintenant à ressentir « comment ça se vit ».

C'est exactement ce que nous nous proposons de faire, en une ou plusieurs séances. L'athlète va, *volontairement*, se placer dans la situation et vivre ici et maintenant, par projection mentale, l'événement, étape par étape. A chaque séquence, le moment important est souligné et l'attitude de contrôle à adopter est renforcée. Le sujet sophronisé dirige lui-même ses pas à son propre rythme et c'est toujours lui qui décide si une étape peut être franchie. L'intérêt de ce genre de séance réside dans la démarche volontaire du sportif qui prend l'initiative et le contrôle de son vécu. Il est incontestablement responsable de ce qu'il advient, responsable d'utiliser ou non les techniques sophroniques qu'il connaît au moment opportun et donc, en dernière analyse, responsable de la façon dont il peut assumer non seulement le stress de la compétition mais aussi sa propre vie.

Placer quelqu'un devant ses responsabilités peut parfois être inhibant quand surviennent le doute puis la crainte de ne pouvoir y faire face. C'est pourquoi il faut également permettre au sportif de tester ses facultés de contrôle et de renforcer ainsi la confiance en soi. Dans cette optique, je pense qu'il est intéressant de faire des séances de S.P.P. en phase intermédiaire et en se référant à des situations d'entraînement ou à des compétitions de moindre importance. Après chacune d'entre elles, il faudra analyser le comportement adopté, les techniques sophroniques utilisées et leur efficacité. Ces expérimentations successives des capacités d'autogestion de « l'état d'être » en situation réelle doivent être considérées comme autant de tests, des « travaux pratiques » objectivés par des résultats concrets.

Nous passons ainsi de la théorie à la pratique,

démarche qui convient parfaitement à l'esprit sportif.

d) Technique n° 4
Sophro-Programmation Dynamique (S.P.D.)

Explications théoriques

« Comme à la parade ! » Le rêve de tout sportif, quel que soit son niveau, est d'avoir, au moment de la compétition, l'aisance et le naturel de l'entraînement. C'est pour tenter de retrouver cette liberté du geste et les qualités de l'esprit sportif que j'ai été amené à mettre au point cette « petite » séance, enregistrée sur cassette (8 à 10 mn), à écouter juste avant d'entrer en action. Cette technique est une application directe de la théorie des graphes s'organisant en images mentales, théorie que nous avons exposée dans le chapitre précédent.

Elle est toute simple : il s'agit de réactiver certaines références positives et dynamisantes, références relatives à des situations sportives de « top niveau » *déjà* vécues par le sujet. En d'autres termes, nous allons ramener en mémoire vive des souvenirs satisfaisants et essayer de revivre, en cet instant critique qui précède la compétition, toutes les sensations enregistrées alors. Par exemple, les sensations de souplesse, de coordination et de libération d'énergie ressenties dans le geste du service au tennis. Retrouver dans son passé tennistique les matches gagnants « où tout réussit, tout passe, où on avait la forme olympique ! » Par exemple encore, le geste délié, parfaitement synchronisé et libéré d'un bon « swing » du golfeur, à l'entraînement, sur le practice... etc.

En vue de cette séance, il est d'ailleurs demandé au sportif de mémoriser, pendant son entraînement et par les sensations qu'il déclenche, un geste technique (ou une action sportive globale) lorsqu'il estime l'avoir parfaitement réalisé. Il crée ainsi, en améliorant l'écoute du corps, ses propres références, son modèle à retrouver. A partir de cette idée de base, tout un travail sophronique peut être élaboré visant à s'adresser aux centres nerveux sous-corticaux régulant les automatismes acquis par la répétition et être ensuite inclus dans une activation intrasophronique de la très classique et très connue technique de **sophro-acceptation progressive.** Pour renforcer l'effet positif de cet « état de grâce » et favoriser, pendant l'épreuve, sa réapparition, il convient de lui donner un nom.

Sous des aspects quelque peu anodins, cette S.P.D. présente de nombreux avantages avant une compétition :

> Retrouver confiance et dynamisme à un moment où le doute et la crainte peuvent surgir.
> Installer une programmation mentale de réussite par un état d'esprit de gagnant.
> Réviser ses automatismes acquis et se référer aux « valeurs sûres ».
> Se concentrer et se calmer, ce qui permet de ne plus « gamberger » avant de commencer.
> Se mettre en présence de soi-même, de ses capacités et de sa responsabilité personnelle dans l'action.

e) Technique n° 5
La Sophro-Acceptation progressive (S.A.P.)

Explications théoriques

Elle est vraisemblablement la technique la plus connue et la plus utilisée en Sophrologie. Dans son *Dictionnaire abrégé*, Caycedo décrit la S.A.P. de la façon suivante : Après une sophronisation de base, le sujet se place, *in anima* et *in corpore*, dans une situation à vivre dans un proche avenir. Dans ces images mentales, le sophronisé se voit lui-même étant un élément participant de cette situation. Par son discours (terpnos logos) le sophrologue contribue à l'acceptation du schéma corporel et à l'acceptation du schéma existentiel du sujet-acteur de la scène pré-vue. En termes plus simples, par cette activation intrasophronique, le patient réalise, dans la mise en scène imaginaire d'un moment de vie, l'harmonisation dans les rapports de soi à soi et dans les rapports de soi avec les éléments qui composent son environnement (les personnes présentes, le cadre général de vie, etc.).

En sophropédagogie, la S.A.P. a un avantage tout à fait particulier, celui de faire prendre conscience que, après l'événement qui se prépare, la vie continue. Trop souvent, l'importance de l'épreuve devient un obstacle à la perception du devenir à long terme. « On s'en fait une montagne! » Cette idée est renforcée par la structure de l'organigramme social : les éliminatoires, les premiers et deuxièmes tours des tournois, le baccalauréat (seule porte valable à la poursuite d'une carrière...). Le problème est surdimensionné et prend l'allure d'une nécessité vitale qui parfois stimule mais qui souvent inhibe et décourage à la moindre difficulté. Il faut, pour éviter ce problème, donner à l'obstacle à franchir une valeur relative et l'inclure dans un processus dynamique de devenir. Il prend alors un sens nouveau : une étape dont on sortira inévitablement (vainqueur si possible). Il est bien plus rassurant de considérer cette étape a retro car on acquiert alors la certitude vécue qu'elle va être dépassée.

Plusieurs séances sont nécessaires pour mener à bien une Sophro-Acceptation progressive. La première se situe dans un espace temps de un à deux mois après l'épreuve, puis les suivantes raccourcissent la projection et nous rapprochent à quelques heures après la compétition ou l'examen (ou l'accouchement dans la préparation à la naissance). Dans une S.A.P., le jour « J » est regardé a posteriori mais jamais a priori, comme dans la Sophro-Projection positive.

Un certain nombre d'autres techniques peuvent être envisagées pour la préparation du sportif. En particulier, bien sûr, toutes celles issues des premier et deuxième degrés de la Relaxation Dynamique de Caycedo. Elles ont été décrites plus haut sous une vue générale et leur adaptation pour le sport est extrêmement importante. Mais il existe déjà des ouvrages spécialisés les décrivant, j'invite le lecteur intéressé à s'y reporter et à lire tout particulièrement celui du docteur Raymond Abrezol, *Sophrologie et Sport* (1), livre très riche en expériences concrètes.

A ces techniques de préparation psychologique avant la compétition, s'ajoutent celles à utiliser **pendant** l'épreuve. Après entraînement préalable, elles seront donc applicables par l'athlète lui-même, sans aide extérieure, par ses propres capacité et volonté.

2. Pendant la compétition

a) Technique n° 1
Sophro-Substitution sensorielle (S.S.S.)

Cette technique, décrite dès 1972 dans le *Dictionnaire abrégé* de Caycedo, a pour but essentiel de substituer une sensation choisie à une sensation désagréable, comme la douleur. La **sophro-analgésie** est fréquemment employée (et avec succès!) dans de nombreux domaines en médecine (soins dentaires, accouchements... etc.). Cependant, dans le domaine sportif, même si l'analgésie sophronique peut quelquefois rendre service, elle ne peut être utilisée en pratique courante. Nous n'en parlerons donc pas ici. Mais nous pouvons nous servir

(1) Ed. du Signal, 1985.

de cette capacité à remplacer une sensation indésirable par une autre pour lutter contre la **fatigue musculaire** et dans une certaine mesure pour gommer la **lassitude mentale**, les deux étant d'ailleurs liées. Si la sensation de lourdeur est synonyme de fatigue, celle de légèreté représente la libération, l'aisance ou la facilité. Ces substitutions de sensations sont faciles à vivre pendant les séances de sophrologie et, avec un entraînement approprié, peuvent être parfaitement contrôlées et induites par le sujet lui-même pendant l'exercice de son activité sportive. Cette possibilité de modification des sensations pour une « défatigabilité » musculaire peut être renforcée et accélérée par le geste conditionné et s'appliquer d'une façon très sélective (sur une seule partie du corps). L'expérience montre que, par effet de généralisation souvent constaté en sophrologie, la sensation de légèreté se transforme en impression globale de liberté ou de libération et fait vivre le sentiment d'avoir retrouvé toute sa « forme olympique » !

J'insiste, pour ma part, sur l'importance de l'apprentissage de cette technique de substitution sensorielle car elle présente de nombreux avantages. Au début de l'entraînement sophronique, elle permet à l'intéressé de prendre concrètement conscience du pouvoir de son mental sur le corps. Pouvoir modifier à volonté une sensation, la supprimer, la remplacer par une autre, aller même jusqu'à l'analgésie(!) est une expérience dynamisante et encourageante. Nous verrons plus loin comment cette technique peut apporter une aide précieuse dans l'amélioration de la concentration. Et surtout, l'athlète réalise que très souvent la fatigue qu'il ressent n'est qu'une pseudo-fatigue, une fausse excuse à sa lassitude ou à de mauvais résultats. (Par exemple, la perte successive de plusieurs sets au tennis.) Le fait qu'il puisse maintenant, par sa propre volonté, réagir et combattre cette impression de fatigue et redonner à son corps toute sa force et sa puissance, est un élément très sécurisant.

b) Technique n° 2
Sophro-Concentration

Le but de l'entraînement en Sophrologie est d'acquérir un contrôle et une maîtrise de soi. Contrôle de l'activité corporelle, et le sportif est bien placé pour cela, et aussi maîtrise de l'activité mentale. C'est l'objet de toutes les techniques de concentration.

Le travail consiste à diriger son attention vers une idée, pensée, image mentale ou sensation, et à laisser « l'objet » de concentration prendre place, une place exclusive dans les structures corticales. Ce mouvement de conscience vers... permet de refuser ou de chasser toute pensée ou sensation indésirable et négative. Une fois obtenu cet état de concentration (c'est-à-dire de non-distraction), nous pourrons admettre la situation sportive à vivre. N'oublions pas (cf. le chapitre sur le premier degré de la Relaxation dynamique) que l'attitude de concentration est large et ouverte afin de favoriser la prise en conscience de *tous les éléments* de la situation. A partir de cette position mentale concentrative, l'esprit peut facilement se focaliser sur un de ces éléments présents et le traiter en « connaissance de cause » et compte tenu du contexte puis, une fois le travail temporaire terminé, revenir en concentration large.

Pour objectiver ces mouvements de la conscience (qui sont d'ailleurs vécus et expérimentés dans des séances « sophro » spéciales), mouvements d'éventail allant de la distraction à la focalisation, regardons les dessins que nous avons adaptés à, par exemple, un joueur de tennis.

La zone la plus étendue, A-A', correspond à un état de distraction totale pouvant admettre des éléments de toute sorte et d'une façon aléatoire. Ainsi se retrouveront pêle-mêle, et sans priorité, les soucis et les problèmes personnels, l'adversaire et les caractéristiques de son jeu, le bruit, les spectateurs, hier et demain, etc.

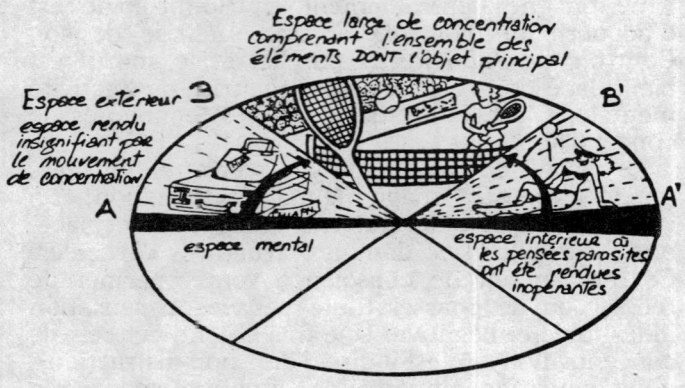

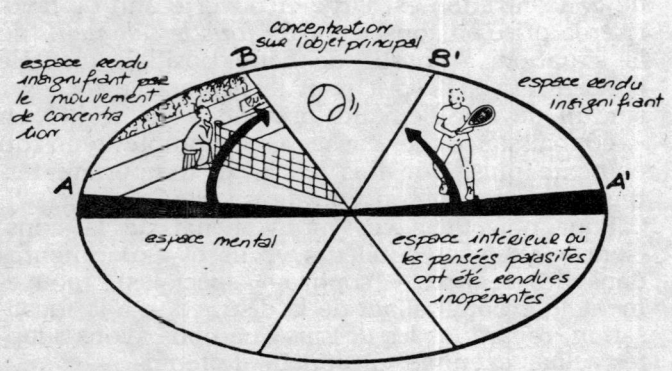

Le chemin A-B et A'-B' conduit à un état de **concentration**, état qui est le *résultat de la non-dispersion de l'attention.* C'est dire que, quel que soit le moyen pour y parvenir et quel que soit l'objet de la concentration, le résultat est le même : idées, pensées ou sensations indésirables (par exemple, hier et demain, la vie personnelle, les individus de la foule, le bruit... etc.) résident en un lieu de « l'insu » et ne viennent plus parasiter et encombrer le vécu de la situation. Dans cette position, nous pouvons parler « d'esprit clair, disponible et ouvert ».

La zone B-B' est considérée comme le champ de concentration, champ relativement large, qui permet de prendre en compte tous les éléments appartenant à la situation envisagée. A chacun de ces éléments correspond un « vécu mental », sorte de « traitement » de l'information que le travail sophronique peut rendre très efficace. Un joueur de tennis concentré (on dit qu'il est rentré *dans* la partie) peut ainsi prendre en considération tous les éléments informatifs liés à la situation : le sens du vent ou la position du soleil, les caractéristiques de l'adversaire (la faiblesse ou l'efficacité de certains de ses coups, son énervement ou sa fatigue... etc.). La prise de conscience de ces différents éléments, dans un état d'esprit concentré, permet une très bonne adaptation du comportement. On parle alors de « sens du jeu », de « bonne vision du jeu » qui sont les caractéristiques des joueurs habitués aux compétitions et qui savent garder une certaine hauteur par rapport à l'action qui se déroule.

Cet état transitoire de l'attention est le résultat d'une **sélection.** Sélectionner un élément appartenant à la situation globale et le traiter en toute exclusivité et en toute urgence est une capacité normale de la conscience. Ce mouvement de direction vers... peut (et doit) faire l'objet d'un entraînement particulier. Sorte de gymnastique mentale qui confère à l'esprit une grande souplesse et une grande adaptabilité. Cette qualité essentielle de l'esprit sportif engagé dans l'action doit être « travaillée » et devenir une activité réflexe au moment critique du « passage à l'acte ».

Il est impossible de décrire, surtout par écrit, le détail des séances permettant de développer les capacités de concentration et de focalisation de l'attention. Disons tout simplement que le sportif peut, par sa propre volonté, obtenir l'état de concentration en dirigeant son « regard » vers sa respiration dont il sait contrôler rythme et amplitude ou vers une partie du corps (la main, par exemple) dont il extrait une sensation particulière. Cette attitude de maîtrise permet de chasser toute pensée indésirable, de faire taire le doute inhibant et, par le dialogue avec le corps qui s'instaure, de retrouver la confiance en soi.

Le Training autogène modifié, le T.R.A.M., est une méthode complète mise au point par Abrezol qui donne accès à une prise de conscience du schéma corporel et qui favorise la concentration au moment de l'épreuve par quelques exercices très simples. Les exercices décrits maintenant, bien qu'ayant été adaptés, sont extraits du protocole proposé dans le T.R.A.M. Ils ont deux objectifs : libérer certaines zones corporelles (la région diaphragmatique et celle de la nuque et du cou) et stimuler la concentration et la focalisation de l'attention sur les sensations produites afin de chasser toutes les autres idées ou pensées négatives. Ils sont exécutés debout, en total relâchement musculaire.

Les différents exercices respiratoires sont toujours réalisés en complète relaxation et surtout dans une grande concentration sur soi. Dans un état d'esprit particulier qui n'admet dans le champ de conscience que « la chose à faire, ici et maintenant : respirer », à l'exclusion de toute autre préoccupation. Progressivement, la zone diaphragmatique se libère de certaines contractures que peuvent engendrer la peur ou l'angoisse.

Les trois exercices suivants permettent de décontracter la région de la nuque et du cou ainsi que les muscles de la mâchoire inférieure. Ils sont à réaliser dans la concentration sur les sensations du mouvement et en synchronisation avec la respiration. Chacun des exercices est fait au moins une fois.

Exercice n° 1 : Mouvements de la tête de droite à gauche et de gauche à droite.

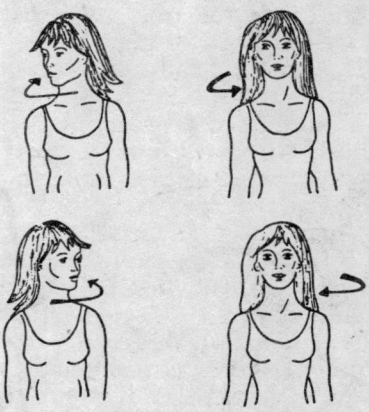

Exercice n° 2 : Mouvements de la tête de haut en bas et de bas en haut.

Exercice n° 3 : Mouvements circulaires de la tête.

Toujours en synchronisation avec la respiration. En soufflant, nous laissons tomber la tête vers la poitrine, la rotation commence alors : en inspirant, la tête se porte en arrière et en haut puis, en expirant, le cercle se termine pour retrouver la tête penchée sur la poitrine.

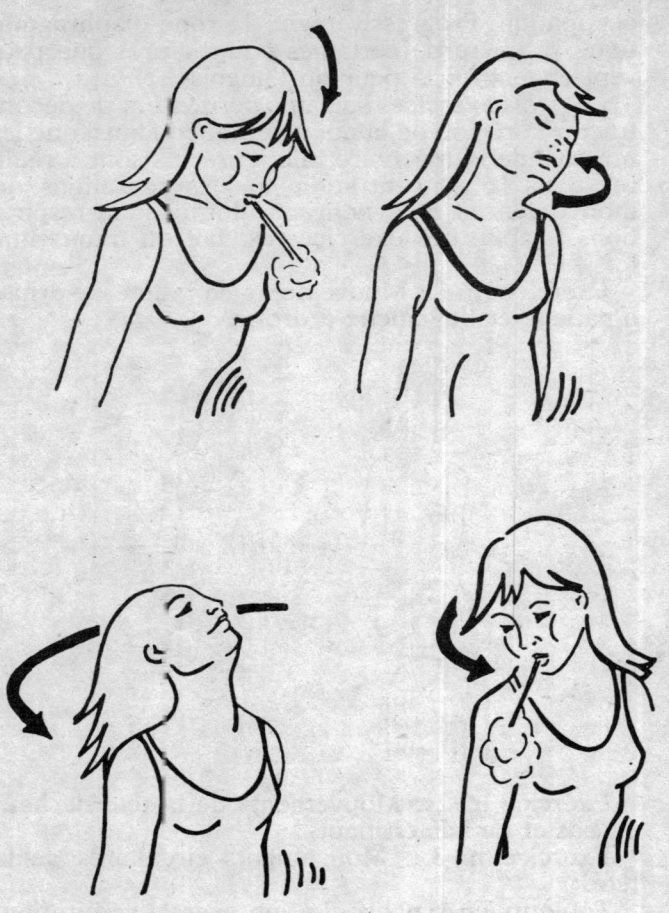

3. Après la compétition

Technique du bilan rétrospectif et projectif

Indispensable, cet autobilan doit être, à mon avis, systématique et intervenir dans les heures qui suivent la compétition. Il faut que l'événement sportif qui vient d'être vécu, avec toutes ses composantes, réside dans la conscience du sujet, c'est-à-dire dans le « su ». Le regard sophronique rétrospectif autorise cette prise de conscience et le regard projectif intègre le bilan dans une situation d'avenir : nous parlons alors, et alors seulement, **d'expérience.** Le moment de l'épreuve sportive qui vient d'avoir lieu doit pouvoir s'inscrire dans la suite logique suivante :

Projet → **Action** → (Bilan → Projet)
   → **Action** → (Bilan → Projet)... etc.

Ce n'est donc qu'après en avoir fait l'analyse que l'on peut estimer l'action terminée. Le **regard rétrospectif** commence par une discussion avec l'entraîneur ou le conseiller sportif qui apporte un avis « objectif » (ou tout au moins extérieur) sur certains points qui auraient pu passer inaperçus. Ensuite le sujet est invité à revivre, à repenser l'action en essayant de faire taire ses émotions (regard lucide) et à en tirer les enseignements utiles. Il ne faut ni se culpabiliser inutilement ni se congratuler béatement. La démarche n'est pas aisée car il est souvent très difficile de se regarder en train d'être sans porter sur soi un jugement d'ordre affectif. Ici il s'agirait plutôt de tri : d'un côté les attitudes inadaptées (mauvais points) et de l'autre le comportement positif (bons points). Nous garderons les « bons points » comme références et nous envisagerons dans le calme sophronique les moyens de se débarrasser des « mauvais points ». Réalisons l'aspect constructif de ce bilan qui permet de :

1° Prendre conscience d'une erreur faite et de pouvoir prévoir les moyens d'y remédier (promesse faite à soi-même).

2° Prendre conscience d'une réussite et d'en comprendre le pourquoi afin de pouvoir prévoir les moyens de la reproduire (promesse faite à soi-même).

Le regard projectif fait maintenant apparaître la notion de durée et de carrière sportive. La compétition qui vient de se terminer n'est qu'une étape, un tremplin pour la poursuite des événements. Le repos bien mérité qui va suivre n'est pas une démobilisation mais une préparation pour demain.

Cet autobilan objective également la responsabilité que l'athlète engage vis-à-vis de lui-même, de son avenir sportif et de son propre devenir. Ceci ne peut être que bénéfique à un moment de la vie où l'incertitude du lendemain peut entraver le désir de se réussir car il ne faut pas oublier que pour l'individu, généralement très jeune, la réussite sportive n'est qu'une facette de sa vie et qu'il doit en même temps assumer son présent affectif et émotionnel et pouvoir projeter une image positive de son « moi » dans un avenir qui commence à prendre forme.

Bien qu'ayant évité volontairement tout au long de ce livre d'écrire des textes de séances de « sophro », je sens ne pas pouvoir résister à la tentation de donner de larges extraits de cette technique d'autobilan, tant elle me semble importante. Supposons que vous soyez confortablement installé, assis ou allongé, les yeux naturellement fermés, en parfaite relaxation, « au bord même du sommeil »...

> « ... C'est l'heure du bilan ! Et quel que soit le résultat, ce que vous venez de faire et de vivre vous servira d'expérience.
>
> « Toute expérience est positive, encore une fois, quel que soit le résultat.
>
> « Remémorez-vous le schéma de base de la sophrologie que nous avons expliqué : toute situation laisse une trace dans la mémoire, un

circuit gravé dans la conscience sous forme de graphe.

« Ce vécu devient maintenant une référence pour d'autres situations qui sont semblables.

« Pour que la situation actuelle devienne une expérience positive, il est nécessaire de faire le bilan de vos gestes, de vos actes, de vos émotions, de comprendre le pourquoi et le comment.

« Il faut se garder d'isoler le résultat et de l'attribuer à la chance ou à la malchance. **Il faut le regarder comme une conséquence puis comme un point de départ vers de nouvelles expériences.**

« Nous allons remonter le fil conducteur de ce cycle de préparation en partant du résultat final.

« Si vous avez réussi une bonne performance, ce n'est pas par hasard, retrouvez l'ensemble des conditions qui ont permis la réussite.

« L'entraînement régulier, le moral, la motivation, les petits et grands sacrifices que vous avez dû faire.

« Dans le sport, comme dans la vie, **tout comportement a une conséquence, toute conséquence a une suite.**

« Laissez-vous aller à la légitime fierté d'avoir mérité votre réussite et envisagez la suite de votre carrière.

« **Continuez votre chemin...**

« **... trouvez de nouveaux projets, de futures étapes !**

« Si le résultat n'a pas été aussi bon que prévu, nous allons essayer de voir pourquoi.

« Quelles ont été les erreurs commises ? Ne les regardez pas avec regret mais avec lucidité.

« **Tout acte est conséquent, toute conséquence a une suite...**

« Chacun a le droit, dans sa vie, à un moment de moindre efficacité... mais chacun a le **devoir d'en faire une analyse lucide.**

« En prenant conscience de la relation directe qui unit l'acte à son résultat, et je suis certain que vous pouvez le faire, alors cette situation n'est pas un échec.

« Vous aurez acquis une **expérience par expérimentation** directe et personnelle de la réalité.

« A partir d'ici et maintenant, la conscience, votre conscience, se renforce et c'est tout à fait bien.

« Le cycle qui se termine n'a pas été inutile, il inaugure une autre période plus riche.

« **Continuez votre chemin de vie, trouvez de nouveaux projets, de futures étapes!** »

Affirmons avec conviction que chaque situation de vie doit être considérée comme une étape. C'est-à-dire un endroit que l'on traverse, que l'on visite, que l'on vit avec la profonde et intuitive sensation que **le chemin continue...** Aucune situation ne doit être vue comme un but final, un terminus. La dynamique d'une vie se meurt dans l'immobilisme et se nourrit du mouvement. Cette idée très positive ne signifie en aucun cas instabilité et errance car le mouvement peut se produire à l'intérieur même de la situation.

Qu'il soit question d'une compétition sportive, d'un examen, de la naissance d'un enfant, d'un accident de santé ou de tout autre chose, il faut savoir que la vie continue sa route et la conscience d'un homme qui possède la fabuleuse capacité de s'adapter et d'évoluer ne doit pas s'arrêter « au bord du chemin » mais savoir aller de l'avant : nous sommes responsables de ce qu'il advient de notre vie, même si ce qui survient dans notre vie échappe souvent à notre contrôle. Pour s'en convaincre, regardons ceux que le sort a frappés : au-delà de leur handicap brille une si belle flamme que leur regard sait toujours chanter l'amour et l'espoir.

CONCLUSION

Conclure un livre sur la Sophrologie me paraît être une tâche difficile : la Sophrologie, en constante évolution, n'admet aucun point final à son discours et aucune pause à son devenir. Aussi je préfère consacrer ces dernières pages à un résumé et tenter d'ouvrir la voie vers une réflexion autre qui, même si elle dépasse le cadre strict de la Sophrologie, n'a pu être introduite que grâce à elle.

Nous pourrions nous poser la question de savoir où et quand commence la démarche sophrologique! Répondre à cette question reviendrait à déterminer des limites à l'action sophronique avec un « avant », un « pendant », une fin et un « après ». Ce serait aussi rendre le sophrologue seul juge de l'évolution de l'autre et ceci est en contradiction flagrante avec l'esprit « sophro » qui apprend à ne point juger mais simplement à répondre à la demande de celui qui désire. Il faut bien comprendre que celui qui entame un processus de connaissance avait en lui, en sa conscience, déjà en germe le chemin à parcourir et que le sophrologue, avec sa technique et sa présence, ne fait qu'aider à découvrir ce chemin dans un pas à pas progressif qui laisse, à tout moment, l'explorateur libre de s'arrêter.

Tout au long de ce livre, je me suis efforcé d'expliquer le processus par lequel la Sophrologie peut conduire à une plus grande et plus harmonieuse relation de soi à soi et de soi au monde qui nous entoure. J'ai fait cela en prenant garde de ne point trop mettre en avant une conception personnelle afin de préserver la liberté de chacun. En effet, vouloir montrer une voie d'épanouissement est une chose, édicter des règles, établir des dogmes et obliger par des diktats et des sentences, en est une autre qui relève plus du complexe de Pygmalion que de l'attitude d'un sophrologue responsable.

Arrivé au terme du livre, je me prends à imaginer que le lecteur a déjà sa propre idée, sa propre opinion sur la Sophrologie, c'est pourquoi je pense pouvoir me permettre d'introduire, dans cette conclusion, une vision personnelle de la destinée humaine, liée au destin de chaque individu. Comme toute réflexion personnelle, la mienne prend source dans de nombreuses lectures (en particulier, les poètes), et s'inspire du très riche enseignement de mes maîtres puis (mais comment pourrait-il en être autrement pour un « Cancer » ascendant Cancer!) passe par le filtre privé d'un vécu libéré, lors de méditations à l'abri de toute fatuité et de toute vanité.

Depuis quelques années, la découverte de la théorie holistique (et la réalisation de l'hologramme) a permis à certains scientifiques occidentaux de redécouvrir ce que les mystiques savaient depuis des millénaires d'une façon intuitive : l'ensemble (ou le Tout) est formé non pas de la juxtaposition d'éléments indépendants mais par la relation étroite de ces éléments et chaque élément de l'ensemble contient le Tout. Connaissez-vous la théorie de l'hologramme? Elle fut découverte en 1947 par Dennis Gabor (il eut le prix Nobel pour cette découverte) mais elle ne fut mise en application qu'au moment de l'invention du laser. L'hologramme est l'une des inventions les plus troublantes de la physique moderne : elle permet de « fabriquer » une image dans les trois dimensions, image fantomatique, suspendue dans l'espace, possédant une particularité remarquable.

L'ensemble des informations relatives à l'image formée est contenu dans chacune des parties constituantes. C'est-à-dire que si l'on détourne ou que l'on agrandit une partie de l'objet projeté, on obtiendra non pas cette partie en plus grand mais bien la totalité de l'image initiale. Cette expérience de physique pure, « cartésienne », met en évidence et en application l'idée jusque-là abstraite que chaque élément participe au Tout et le contient, et donc, c'est par l'unité de base que nous pouvons accéder à l'Unicité, rejoignant ainsi toutes les pensées religieuses qui soutiennent que « Bouddha est dans la nature de toute chose » ou que « Dieu est en chacun de nous ».

Nous comprenons bien toutes les implications que cette évidence peut avoir. En regardant, par une belle nuit d'été, l'immensité et la profondeur du ciel, qui n'a pas été mis devant l'infiniment petit de son être face à l'infiniment grand de ce qui l'entoure ? Qui n'a pas eu, au moins une fois dans sa vie, l'impression d'être un minuscule grain de sable dans l'océan cosmique ? Grain de sable faisant partie intégrante de l'Univers ! Or, nous le savons, rien ne peut être conçu sans préexister en nous... L'univers tout entier, à la façon d'un hologramme, est contenu dans chaque « grain de sable ». Mais, si à regarder en haut nous attrapons parfois le vertige, à regarder en nous, nous retrouvons le vestige de la Création qui, dans un immense éclatement holistique a rendu multiple le « Un » tout en laissant subsister le « Un » dans chaque partie. Comment comprendre cette part universelle qui réside au plus profond de chaque être vivant ? Le schéma qui suit a, comme tout schéma, l'ambition de donner forme à une pensée mais aussi l'inconvénient de la dénaturer quelque peu. Regardons tout de même la représentation de ce que j'aimerais appeler le **Principe unitaire humain.**

1. Le principe décisionnel

Empruntant à la terminologie de Jung, Bachelard le désigne, aussi bien chez l'homme que chez la femme, comme « l'animus », d'autres auteurs l'ont nommé le « sur-moi », nous pourrions aussi l'assimiler à la conscience ordinaire. Située à la périphérie de l'entité humaine, un peu comme la surface arable de la terre, c'est une partie vulnérable et plastique. Exposée aux tempêtes du dehors, en constante adaptation aux variations ambiantes (et tout particulièrement aux stimulations sociales), cette zone vivante se trouve dans l'obligation de prendre des décisions souvent très rapides, court-circuitant alors les « avis intérieurs ».

Ce principe décisionnel s'alimente de nos engagements, se motive par nos ambitions et nos pro-

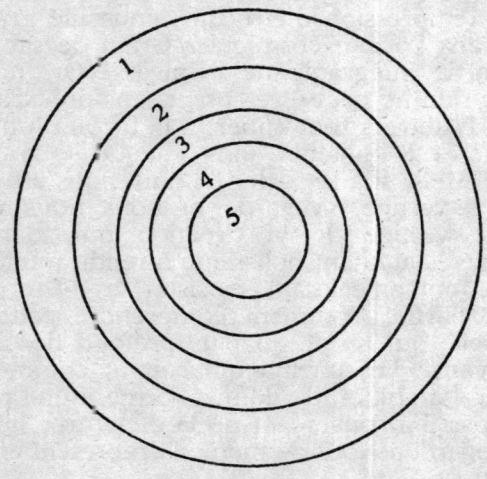

jets et, sensible au langage (mots, signes et emblèmes grâce auxquels la communication est rendue possible), il préside à la formation de la *personnalité* du sujet.

Au départ de la vie, c'est un espace vierge, peu dense qui doit et qui va apprendre à vivre, au milieu du monde, au gré des expériences qui se présentent. Progressivement, il s'enrichit et s'organise en un système de plus en plus autonome dont les références mémorisées s'élaborent à partir de motivations induites.

2. Le principe intentionnel

Le « Moi » qui confère à la personnalité une dimension supplémentaire : l'Individualité. Toujours selon la terminologie jungienne, Bachelard le désigne sous le terme de « anima » et en fait un principe de calme et de bien-être. C'est une réalité intérieure qui se renforce ou se blesse, se réjouit ou se lamente des différentes attitudes du « Je » périphérique... du « jeu du Je » dont il distribue certaines cartes.

Le Moi donne à l'être une part de vérité, son langage est intuitif et symbolique. Il communique avec le principe décisionnel par des manifestations intéroceptives. Je pense que ce principe intentionnel réside dans la corporalité, qu'il répond aux archétypes grâce à sa mémoire héritée. C'est par lui que l'Etre profond prend corps humain, prend « cœur » humain, prend vie humaine.

3. Le « Être-Moi »

Au-delà de l'image vécue du moi existe quelque chose d'essentiel et de secret où se vivent, dans une complémentarité binaire, « l'animal-fait-homme » et le « Dieu-fait-homme ». Par ce voyage par-delà le moi X. ou Y., Pierre, Paul ou Jacques, nous abordons un principe de base indéfinissable. Structuré en schèmes primaires, j'aimerais nommer ce « Ça », ce « Das Ein », cette étrangeté et ce mystère, le... « Etre-Moi ».

En adoptant l'idée philosophico-religieuse de la réincarnation (ou de la transmigration), nous pourrions dire que c'est la zone où l'Etre perdurant s'incarne, c'est-à-dire intègre les principes personnels et individuels et où la quintessence des expériences de la vie de l'individu s'inscrit dans une mémoire immortelle.

4. L'Être karmique

Plus loin, plus profond, se trouve « L'Être-qui-vit-en-moi ». Cet Etre qui a choisi Moi, le temps d'une vie, l'espace d'un corps, pour tenter l'expérience terrestre... pour s'enrichir de la condition humaine dont il a (sans doute) besoin pour sa propre évolution. A la manière d'un futur directeur qui se doit de passer par tous les postes clés de son entreprise avant d'arriver au sommet.

Il serait trop long de développer ici le thème de la réincarnation, mais le lecteur intéressé a à sa disposition un grand nombre d'ouvrages fort passionnants. (Voir bibliographie.) Cette conception rejoint bien entendu la croyance bouddhique qui se fonde sur l'espoir que la vie de « l'ici et maintenant » est un instant, un jalon, une épreuve sur une route qui se poursuit après la disparition du « Je » et du « Moi », dans la destinée du Karma.

5. Dieu

Encore plus profond, encore plus haut, au centre du centre de ce principe humain se trouve condensé et résumé le principe divin. Le Tout ou le Un contenu en chacun comme l'image holistique dont chaque photon contient et restitue l'ensemble. Ce noyau de Vie universelle peut révéler sa présence en chacun de nous et chacun de nous lui donnera le nom qu'il veut. La Sophrologie n'est pas une philosophie déiste et, affirmons-le encore une fois, elle laisse à chaque individu le soin de résoudre sa propre problématique selon lui-même.

Peut-être pourrions-nous imaginer que ce principe universel, passant au-delà des différences, unit tous les êtres vivants et les rend solidaires.

Peut-être pourrions-nous également appeler ce lien passant au-dessus des amours courtisanes, Amour absolu.

Peut-être pourrions-nous, passant loin des références partisanes, appeler cet Amour tout simplement Dieu.

L'Etre-Moi, l'Etre karmique et la part divine sont des composantes essentielles et immuables du principe humain. Mais qu'advient-il de la composante décisionnelle et de la composante intentionnelle quand celles-ci sont soumises à l'impérative obligation de vivre ? Comment préserver l'harmonie entre elles ?

A la naissance, et pendant les premières années, le « Je » n'est pas encore formé et la zone de Moi affleure à la périphérie de l'être. Déjà les tendances majeures de l'enfant apparaissent, les actes sont des gestes d'amour qui témoignent de l'influence des composantes essentielles de l'Etre karmique et de la part divine. (Voir le « voyage vers l'enfance, page 114). Il serait aussi tout à fait probable que la mémoire de l'Etre karmique soit encore agissante et émerge au niveau du comportement du jeune enfant.

Les premières expériences surviennent vite, la personnalité se structure, le « Je » fait entendre sa voix. Par son langage spécifique, sa mémoire propre, ses motivations induites, le principe décisionnel « prend du poids » et de l'autonomie. Parfois, sa manière de vivre déplaît au Moi intentionnel qui, par quelques manifestations intimes, exprime son désaccord... et peut, après plusieurs tentatives de réconciliation, dresser entre lui et la partie périphérique une barrière, une cuirasse de protection. Le principe décisionnel décide alors de vivre indépendant et s'éloigne progressivement du principe intentionnel. La dysharmonie préside et les rapports entre le « Je » et le « Moi » sont de plus en plus tendus, le dialogue s'éteint.

En laissant évoluer la situation, nous arriverons au stade terminal de totale incompréhension, de divorce entre des partenaires faits pourtant pour s'entendre mais qui deviennent des étrangers. Les actions de l'un sont en contradiction avec les réactions de l'autre. Jusqu'au moment où « on ne se sent pas bien dans sa peau... on ne se comprend plus » et alors « on ne se reconnaît plus », « ce n'est pas possible, ce n'est pas Moi qui ai fait cela, etc. ». Il est, à ce stade, urgent de rétablir la communication, de restaurer le dialogue et d'harmoniser la décision et l'intention.

Lentement les cuirasses érigées, les barrières et les frontières s'abaissent... un peu comme si nous retrouvions un ami perdu de vue. Les premiers contacts ne peuvent se faire que dans le calme et dans la confiance : c'est le rôle des exercices de relaxation sophronique.

Le Moi se libère de ses tensions enfermées et le « Je » apprend à faire du désir réel une noble motivation dans l'expression du vouloir : **c'est le rôle des exercices du premier degré de la Relaxation dynamique.**

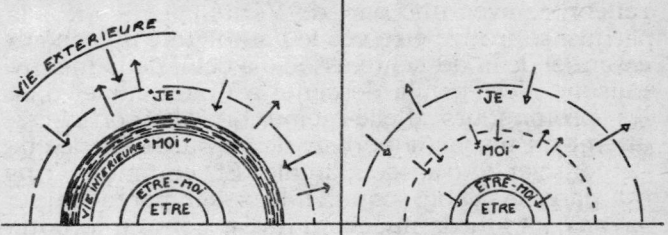

La vie se situe à la "périphérie" de l'individu. Des cuirasses intérieures cloisonnent le "monde privé" : le Principe Unitaire Humain se fractionne en plusieurs parties qui ne se (re)connaissent plus. Il y a DYSHARMONIE FONCTIONNELLE par absence de dialogue.

Echanges et harmonie entre les différentes composantes de l'individu : le Principe Unitaire Humain intègre la notion dynamique du Devenir dans le respect des valeurs profondes propres à chaque individualité.

Le Moi apprend les nécessités et les obligations du « Je » et le regarde vivre au milieu du monde alors que le principe décisionnel apprend à se débarrasser de toutes les notions surajoutées qui encombrent et dénaturent son regard : **c'est le rôle des exercices du second degré de la Relaxation dynamique.**

Ces deux composantes se mettant en harmonie, l'Etre-Moi diffuse sa mémoire que la conscience peut maintenant écouter : **c'est le troisième degré de la Relaxation dynamique.** Alors le Principe Unitaire Humain retrouve son unité par l'intégration de toutes ses composantes, sans en exclure l'une et sans en privilégier une autre : **c'est le quatrième degré de la Relaxation dynamique.**

Cette vision du Principe Unitaire Humain, intégrant *toutes* les composantes symbolisées par le Carré, la Croix et le Cercle, induit un premier rêve d'un Dieu vivant en chaque être et un autre rêve qui fait que chaque pas réalisé dans *ce voyage au-delà de l'image de soi* nous conduit vers la rencontre avec une part de Vérité.

Ainsi se trouve être vécue l'ambiguïté du schème essentiel de la descente associé à celui de la montée puisque c'est par la descente à l'intérieur et dans les profondeurs d'elle-même que la conscience atteint un niveau supérieur de supraconscience ou de conscience transcendantale. Et, comme le Ying est dans le Yang, comme le soleil perce de ses rayons les lourds nuages d'hiver, comme le bourgeon encore invisible préexiste à lui-même sur la branche automnale, comme l'œil du cyclone est un espace préservé, l'infiniment petit parvient à contenir l'infiniment grand et l'Amour divin colore le cœur de l'Homme d'une lueur d'espoir.

Etre intéressé et passionné par ce que l'on fait est-il suffisant pour communiquer cette passion ? Rien n'est, hélas, moins sûr !

Ce livre aura-t-il répondu à mes espoirs et rempli ses objectifs ? Objectifs multiples :

– Privilégier la réflexion sur la Sophrologie en évitant le piège de longues séances écrites qui seraient restées sans valeur réelle.

– Eveiller en chacun le désir de partir à la recherche et à la rencontre du meilleur de lui-même, dans l'épanouissement de son individualité et de sa liberté.

– Retrouver et stimuler cette force, présente en tout être humain, qui fait toujours aller devant, vers son devenir, dans une marche sereine animée par le vouloir authentique.

– Et enfin, pouvoir dire, avec toute la conviction de ma propre expérience vécue :

Il faut avoir le courage de s'avouer fragile.
De cette fragilité prise en conscience
naissent le désir et la volonté de se renforcer.

*Laissez, maintenant que vous l'avez lu,
Ce livre de côté...
Plus tard, vous le retrouverez.
Allez.
Chaque pas que vous ferez
Vous rapprochera, en toute sérénité,
de vous-même... Et peut-être au-delà.
En toute liberté.
Dans une authentique volonté retrouvée.
      ... Bonne route!*

BIBLIOGRAPHIE

ABREZOL Raymond :
Sophrologie dans notre civilisation, Ed. du Signal, Lausanne, 1972.
L'Anti-Mouton humain, L'âge d'Homme, 1976.
Naître et Bien-Être, L'âge d'Homme, 1980.
Sophrologie et Sport, Ed. du Signal, 1985.
Traité de sophrologie, Tome II, Le Courrier du Livre, 1985.

ALEXANDER Gerda :
Le Corps retrouvé par l'eutonie, Tchou, 1981.

BACH Richard :
Jonathan Livingston le Goéland, Flammarion, 1975.
Le Messie récalcitrant, Flammarion, 1978.

BACHELARD Gaston :
La Poétique de l'espace, P.U.F., 1957.
La Flamme d'une chandelle, P.U.F., 1961.
La Poétique de la rêverie, P.U.F., 1968.
Le Droit de rêver, P.U.F., 1970.
L'Eau et les Rêves, José Corti.

BARUK Henri :
L'Hypnose, P.U.F., 1972.

BERTRAND Paul :
La Sophro-Relaxation obstétricale, Actualités odonto-stomatologiques, déc. 1983, n° 144.

BOHM David :
L'Imagination et l'ordre impliqué. Science et conscience, Stock, 1980.

BOON H. - DAVROU Y - MACQUET J.C. :
La Sophrologie, Retz, 1976.

BOSCO Henri :
Le Jardin d'Hyacinthe, Gallimard, Coll. Folio, n° 1434.

BROWN Barbara :
Le Pouvoir de votre cerveau, Le Jour, 1980.

Camus Albert :
　Le Mythe de Sisyphe, Gallimard, Coll. Folio Essais, n° 11.

Caycedo Alfonso :
　Progrès en sophrologie, Scienta, Barcelone, 1969.
　Dictionnaire abrégé de sophrologie, Emégé, Barcelone, 1971.

Caycedo A. et Davrou Y. :
　L'Aventure de la sophrologie, Ed. du Moustier.

Changeux Jean-Pierre :
　L'Homme neuronal, Fayard, 1983.

Chauchard Paul :
　Hypnose et Suggestion, P.U.F., 1970.
　Volonté et contrôle cérébral, Science et Conscience, Stock, 1980.

Cherchève et Beranger :
　Hypno-Sophrologie en art dentaire, Privat, 1970.

Chertok L. :
　Les Méthodes psychosomatiques de l'accouchement sans douleur, Ed. L'Expansion, 1958.
　L'Hypnose, Payot, 1965.

Chevalier Jean et Gheerbrant Alain :
　Dictionnaire des symboles, Robert Laffont, 1982.

Corraze Jacques :
　Les Communications non verbales, P.U.F., 1980.

Dardart E. et Jost J. :
　Lumière, couleur et relaxation musicale.
　Actualités odonto-stomatologiques, déc. 1983, n° 144.

Davrou Yves :
　Le Nouveau Guide pratique de la sophrologie, Retz.
　La Sophrothérapie, Retz.
　Les Etonnantes Possibilités de la mémoire, Retz.
　Comment relaxer vos enfants, Retz.

Denis Michel :
　Les Images mentales, P.U.F., 1979.

Donnars Jacques :
　La Transe. Techniques d'épanouissement, Sand, 1985.

Durand Gilbert :
　L'Imagination poétique, P.U.F., 1964.
　Les Structures anthropologiques de l'imaginaire, Dunod, 1969.

Feijoo Jean et Renner Jean-Paul :
　Traité de sophrologie, tome III, Le Courrier du Livre, 1986.

FELINE André :
Mémoire, Attention et Vigilance, Editions médicales Inava.

FERGUSSON Marylin :
La Révolution du cerveau, Calmann-Lévy, 1974.

FERNANDEZ Luis :
La Préparation psychologique de l'athlète, Amphora, 1986.

GABAI et JOST :
Détente psycho-musicale en odonto-stomatologie, Maloine, 1972.

GALLWEY Timothy :
Gagner le match, Le Jour, 1976.

GUIRAO Miguel :
Anatomie de la conscience, Maloine, 1979.

GUYONNAUD :
Le Karaté sophronique, Maloine.

HALL Edward :
Au-delà de la culture, Points, 1979.
La Dimension cachée, Seuil, 1979.

HUBERT Jean-Pierre :
La Relaxation dynamique, Centre de Sophrologie de Paris, 1980.
Traité de sophrologie. Tome I. Le courrier du Livre, 1985.
Lexique de sophrologie et de termes usuels. Ed. de la Norière.

HUBERT José et ZANELLA Chantal :
Notre expérience pour vivre votre expérience, Ed. Médicales, Charleroi.

IKEMI Yujiro :
Les Etats modifiés de conscience, Science et Conscience, Stock, 1980.

JEZIC Hervé :
La Sophrologie, le corps et l'âme, Buchet-Chastel.

JUNG C.G. :
Psychologie de l'inconscient, Buchet-Chastel, 1963.
Ma vie, Gallimard, 1967.
Les Racines de l'inconscient, Buchet-Chastel, 1971.

KOLHER Marianne :
La Relaxation, art et science du corps, Robert Laffont, 1970.

LACOUE-LABARTHE Philippe :
La Poésie comme expérience, Christian Bourgois, 1986.

LAGROST-BERRANGER Michèle :
  Sophrologie et circulation périphérique, thèse de Doctorat en Médecine.

LEREDE Jean :
  La Suggestopédie, P.U.F., 1983.

LOWEN Alexandra :
  La Bio-Energie, Tchou, 1975.

MERLEAU-PONTY Maurice :
  La Structure du comportement, P.U.F., 1967.
  Le Psychisme et le corporel, Aubier.

MILLER David :
  Le Chat de Schrödinger et l'imaginaire, Science et Conscience, Stock.

MUSASHI Miyamoto :
  Le Traité des cinq roues, Albin Michel, 1977.

OSTRANDER Sheila et SHROEDER :
  Les Fantastiques Facultés du cerveau, Robert Laffont, 1980.

PECOLLO Jean-Yves :
  Contribution à l'étude de la sophrologie en pratique courante.
  Thèse de Doctorat en Chirurgie Dentaire, 1974.
  Se préparer aux examens et concours par la sophrologie, Retz, 1987.
  Endormissement et Réveil (cassettes), Retz, 1988.
  Se préparer à un examen et à un entretien (cassettes), Retz, 1988.
  Mémoire et Concentration (cassettes), Retz, 1989.

PEGAND Georges :
  Christianisme à cœur ouvert, Le Courrier du Livre, 1966.

PERNOUD Laurence :
  J'attends un enfant, Pierre Horay, 1986.

PIAGET Jean et CHOMSKY Noam :
  Théories du Langage. Théories de l'apprentissage, Seuil, 1979.

PIBRAM Karl :
  Esprit, cerveau et conscience, Science et Conscience, Stock, 1980.

POMPIDOU Georges :
  Anthologie de la poésie française, Hachette.

RAGER :
  Hypnose, Sophrologie et Médecine, Fayard, 1973.

REIFLER Sam :
  Yi King, Albin Michel, 1974.

RENNER Jean-Paul :
    Neuro-psycho-physiologie de la sensibilité et de l'affectivité, Actualités odonto-stomatologiques, déc. 1983, n° 144.

RENYNGHE de VOXVRIE Guy :
    Tout savoir sur son cerveau, Favre, 1985.

RICHARD Jean-François :
    L'Attention, P.U.F., 1980.

SARTRE Jean-Paul :
    L'Imaginaire, Gallimard, 1940.

SCHAETTEL Marcel :
    Bachelard critique, L'Hermès, 1977.

SCHULTZ :
    Le Training autogène, P.U.F., 1958.

SIVANANDA Sjri Swâmi :
    Yoga de la Kundalini, Epi, 1980.

DE SMEDT Marc :
    Cinquante techniques de méditation, Retz, 1985.

DE SOUZENELLE Annick :
    Le Symbolisme du corps humain, Dangles, 1984.

SUZUKI D.T. :
    Essai sur le bouddhisme zen, Albin Michel, 1972.

VINCENT Jean Didier :
    Biologie des passions, Seuil, 1986.

VIVEKANANDA Swâmi :
    Jnâna Yoga, Albin Michel, 1972.

WATTS Alan :
    L'Esprit du Zen, Dangles, 1976.

WATZLAWICK Paul :
    Le Langage du changement, Seuil, 1980.

TABLE

Introduction 5

PREMIER CHAPITRE
APPROCHE GÉNÉRALE 23

Définitions essentielles 25

La Relaxation rapide et contrôlée .. 31

    Définir le but 38
    Mise en place des repères 40
    Les types de respiration 43

Les images mentales 47

Le schéma corporel 53

DEUXIÈME CHAPITRE
LE CARRÉ 61

Le contenu symbolique 63

Premier degré de la Relaxation dynamique 67

Les états de l'attention 76

    La rêverie 76
    La distraction 77
    La concentration 78
    La focalisation 79

Expression du Désir et exercice du Vouloir 83

TROISIÈME CHAPITRE
LA CROIX 99

Le contenu symbolique 101

Deuxième degré de la Relaxation dynamique 105

La perception du monde 120

   L'ouïe et la vue 121
   Le toucher 126
   Le goût 128
   L'odorat 130

L'intuition 132

QUATRIÈME CHAPITRE
LE CERCLE 143

Le contenu symbolique 145

Réflexions sur la méditation 148

   Approche du Zen 149
   Approche occidentale philosophique .. 153
   Approche occidentale religieuse 156
   Approche universelle poétique 158

Troisième degré de la Relaxation dynamique 163

CINQUIÈME CHAPITRE
LES STRUCTURES MENTALES 173

La conscience de base 175

   Histoire du château abandonné 175

La suggestion 193

Le cerveau, siège de la conscience ? 223

SIXIÈME CHAPITRE
APPLICATIONS PRATIQUES 251

Faisons confiance à notre mémoire . 253

Mémoire de situation 257
Mémoire de participation 259
Mémoire d'apprentissage 266

Le lâcher prise 274

Le lâcher prise dans le travail . . . 275
Le lâcher prise et le stress 280

Le sport 283

Méthode globale : SooSport 296

Conclusion 327
Bibliographie 339

Aventure Mystérieuse

BELLINE Marcel	Un voyant à la recherche du temps futur 2502/4
BERLITZ Charles	Le Triangle des Bermudes 2018/3
DERLICH Didier	Intuitions 3334/4
FLAMMARION Camille	Les maisons hantées 1985/3
GASSIOT-TALABOT Gérald	Yaguel Didier ou La mémoire du futur 3076/7
MAHIEU Jacques de	Les Templiers en Amérique 2137/3
MARTINO Bernard	Les chants de l'invisible 3228/8
MURPHY Joseph Dr	Comment utiliser les pouvoirs du subconscient 2879/4
PRIEUR Jean	La prémonition et notre destin 2923/4
	L'âme des animaux 3039/4
	Hitler et la guerre luciférienne 3161/4 Inédit
RAQUIN Bernard	Retrouvez vous-même vos vies antérieures 3275/3
ROUCH Dominique	Dieu seul le sait 3266/3 Inédit
SADOUL Jacques	Le trésor des alchimistes 2986/4
VALLEE Jacques	Autres dimensions 3060/5

RAMPA T. Lobsang

Histoire de Rampa 1827/3
La caverne des Anciens 1828/3
Le troisième œil 1829/3
Les secrets de l'aura 1830/3
Les clés du nirvâna 1831/3
Crépuscule 1851/2
La robe de sagesse 1922/3
Je crois 1923/2

C'était ainsi 1976/2
Les trois vies 1982/2
Lama médecin 2017/3
L'ermite 2538/3
La treizième chandelle 2593/3
Pour entretenir la flamme 2669/3
Les lumières de l'Astral 2739/3
Les univers secrets 2991/4
Le dictionnaire de Rampa 3053/4

Les Nouvelles Clés du Mieux-être

ASHLEY Nancy	Construisez vous-même votre bonheur 3146/3 Inédit
BONDI Julia A.	Amour, sexe et clarté 2817/3 Inédit
BOWMAN Catherine	Cristaux et prise de conscience 2920/3 Inédit
BRO H. H.	Voir à Cayce
CAMPBELL Joseph	Puissance du mythe 3095/5 Inédit
CAYCE Edgar	...et la réincarnation (par Noel Langley) 2672/4
(Voir aussi à Koechlin)	Les rêves et la réalité (par H. H. Bro) 2783/4
	L'homme du mystère (par Joseph Millard) 2802/3
DAMEON-KNIGHT Guy	Karma, destinée et Yi King 2763/3 Inédit
DENNING M. & PHILLIPS O.	La visualisation créatrice 2676/3 Inédit
DOORE Gary	La voie des chamans 2674/3 Inédit
GIMBELS Theo	Les pouvoirs de la couleur 3054/4
HAYES Peter	L'aventure suprême 2849/3 Inédit
JAFFE Dennis T.	La guérison est en soi 3354/5
KOECHLIN de BIZEMONT Dorothée	L'univers d'Edgar Cayce 2786/5
	L'univers d'Edgar Cayce - 2 3246/5
	L'astrologie karmique 2878/5
	Les prophéties d'Edgar Cayce 2978/6
LANGLEY Noel	Voir à Cayce
LEVINE Frédérick G.	Pouvoirs psychiques 3162/4 Inédit
MAcLAINE Shirley	L'amour foudre 2396/5
	Danser dans la lumière 2462/5
	Le voyage intérieur 3077/3
	Miroir secret 3188/5
MILLARD Joseph	Voir à Cayce
MONTGOMERY Ruth	Au-delà de notre monde 2895/3 Inédit
MOODY Raymond Dr	La vie après la vie 1984/2
	Lumières nouvelles... 2784/2
	La lumière de l'au-delà 2954/2
PEARCE Joseph Chilton	La fêlure dans l'œuf cosmique 3022/4 Inédit
PECK Scott	Le chemin le moins fréquenté 2839/5
	Les gens du mensonge 3207/5 Inédit
PECOLLO Jean-Yves	La sophrologie 3314/5
ROBERTS Jane	Le Livre de Seth 2801/5 Inédit
	L'enseignement de Seth 3038/7 Inédit
RYERSON et HAROLDE	La communication avec les esprits 3113/4 Inédit
SIEGEL Bernie	L'amour, la médecine et les miracles 2908/4
SMITH Michael G.	Le pouvoir des cristaux 2673/3 Inédit
STEVENS Jose & Lena	Secrets du chamanisme 3265/6 Inédit
TALBOT Michael	L'univers : Dieu ou hasard 2677/3 Inédit
WAGNER McLAIN Florence	Guide pratique du voyage dans les vies antérieures 3061/2
WAMBACH Helen	Revivre le passé 3293/4
WATSON Lyall	Supernature 2740/4
	Histoire naturelle du surnaturel 2842/4
WEISS Brian L. Dr	De nombreuses vies, de nombreux maîtres 3007/3 Inédit

Littérature

extrait du catalogue

Cette collection est d'abord marquée par sa diversité : classiques, grands romans contemporains ou même des livres d'auteurs réputés plus difficiles, comme Borges, Soupault. En fait, c'est tout le roman qui est proposé ici, Henri Troyat, Bernard Clavel, Guy des Cars, Frison-Roche, Djian mais aussi des écrivains étrangers tels que Colleen McCullough ou Konsalik.

Les classiques tels que Stendhal, Maupassant, Flaubert, Zola, Balzac, etc. sont publiés en texte intégral au prix le plus bas de toute l'édition. Chaque volume est complété par un cahier illustré sur la vie et l'œuvre de l'auteur.

ADLER Philippe	Bonjour la galère 1868/2
	Graine de tendresse 2911/3
	Qu'est-ce qu'elles me trouvent ? 3117/3
AGACINSKI Sophie	La tête en l'air 3046/5
AMADOU Jean	La belle anglaise 2684/4
AMADOU - COLLARO - ROUCAS	Le Bébête show 2824/5 & 2825/5 Illustrés
AMIEL Joseph	Le promoteur 3215/9
ANDERSEN Christopher	Citizen Jane 3338/7
ANDERSON Peggy	Hôpital des enfants 3081/7
ANDREWS Virginia C.	Fleurs captives :
	- Fleurs captives 1165/4
	- Pétales au vent 1237/4
	- Bouquet d'épines 1350/4
	- Les racines du passé 1818/4
	- Le jardin des ombres 2526/4
	La saga de Heaven :
	- Les enfants des collines 2727/5
	- L'ange de la nuit 2870/5
	- Cœurs maudits 2971/5
	- Un visage du paradis 3119/5
	- Le labyrinthe des songes 3234/6
APOLLINAIRE Guillaume	Les onze mille verges 704/1
	Les exploits d'un jeune don Juan 875/1
ARCHER Jeffrey	Le pouvoir et la gloire (Kane et Abel) 2109/7
	Faut-il le dire à la Présidente ? 2376/4
ARSAN, Emmanuelle	Les débuts dans la vie 2867/3
ATTANÉ Chantal	Le propre du bouc 3337/2
ATWOOD Margaret	La servante écarlate 2781/4
	Œil-de-chat 3063/8
AVRIL Nicole	Monsieur de Lyon 1049/3
	La disgrâce 1344/3
	Jeanne 1879/3
	L'été de la Saint-Valentin 2038/2
	La première alliance 2168/3
	Sur la peau du Diable 2707/4
	Dans les jardins de mon père 3000/3
BACH Richard	Jonathan Livingston le goéland 1562/1 Illustré
	Illusions/Le Messie récalcitrant 2111/2
	Un pont sur l'infini 2270/4
	Un cadeau du ciel 3079/3

Littérature

BAILLY Othilie	L'enfant dans le placard 3029/**2**
BALZAC Honoré de	Le père Goriot 1988/**2**
BARBELIVIEN Didier	Rouge cabriolet 3299/**2**
BARRIE James M.	Peter Pan 3174/**2**
BATS Joël	Gardien de ma vie 2238/**3** Illustré
BAUDELAIRE Charles	Les Fleurs du mal 1939/**2**
BÉARN Myriam et Gaston de	Gaston Phébus :
	1 - Le lion des Pyrénées 2772/**6**
	2 - Les créneaux de feu 2773/**6**
	3 - Landry des Bandouliers 2774/**5**
BEART Guy	L'espérance folle 2695/**5**
BELLEMARE Pierre	Les dossiers d'Interpol 2844/**4** & 2845/**4**
BELLEMARE P. et ANTOINE J.	Les dossiers extraordinaires 2820/**4** & 2821/**4**
BELLETTO René	Le revenant 2841/**5**
	Sur la terre comme au ciel 2943/**5**
	La machine 3080/**6**
	L'enfer 3150/**5**
BELLONCI Maria	Renaissance privée 2637/**6** Inédit
BENZONI Juliette	Un aussi long chemin 1872/**4**
	Le Gerfaut des Brumes :
	- Le Gerfaut 2206/**6**
BERBEROVA Nina	Le laquais et la putain 2850/**2**
	Astachev à Paris 2941/**2**
	La résurrection de Mozart 3064/**1**
	C'est moi qui souligne 3190/**8**
BERG Jean de	L'image 1686/**1**
BERGER Thomas	Little Big Man 3281/**8**
BERTRAND Jacques A.	Tristesse de la Balance... 2711/**1**
BEYALA Calixthe	C'est le soleil qui m'a brûlée 2512/**2**
BISIAUX M. et JAJOLET C.	Chat plume (60 écrivains...) 2545/**5**
	Chat huppé (60 personnalités...) 2646/**6**
BLAKE Michael	Danse avec les loups 2958/**4**
BLIER Bertrand	Les valseuses 543/**5**
BOGGIO Philippe	Coluche 3268/**7**
BORGEN Johan	Lillelord 3082/**7**
BORY Jean-Louis	Mon village à l'heure allemande 81/**4**
BOULET Marc	Dans la peau d'un Chinois 2789/**7** Illustré
BRAVO Christine	Avenida B. 3044/**3**
	Les petites bêtes 3104/**2**
BROOKS Terry	Hook 3298/**4**
BRUNELIN André	Gabin 2680/**5** & 2681/**5** Illustré
BURON Nicole de	Les saintes chéries 248/**3**
	Vas-y maman 1031/**2**
	Dix-jours-de-rêve 1481/**3**
	Qui c'est, ce garçon ? 2043/**3**
	C'est quoi, ce petit boulot ? 3297/**4**
	Où sont mes lunettes ? 3297/**4**
CARDELLA Lara	Je voulais des pantalons 2968/**2**

Achevé d'imprimer en Europe (France)
par Brodard et Taupin à la Flèche (Sarthe)
le 14 décembre 1992. 1631G-5
Dépôt légal déc. 1992. ISBN 2-277-23314-5

Éditions J'ai lu
27, rue Cassette, 75006 Paris
Diffusion France et étranger : Flammarion